Orello Cone

Paul: the man, the missionary, and the teacher

Orello Cone

Paul: the man, the missionary, and the teacher

ISBN/EAN: 9783741158384

Manufactured in Europe, USA, Canada, Australia, Japa

Cover: Foto ©Andreas Hilbeck / pixelio.de

Manufactured and distributed by brebook publishing software (www.brebook.com)

Orello Cone

Paul: the man, the missionary, and the teacher

PAUL
THE MAN, THE MISSIONARY, AND THE TEACHER

PAUL

THE MAN, THE MISSIONARY, AND THE TEACHER

BY

ORELLO CONE, D.D.

AUTHOR OF "GOSPEL-CRITICISM AND HISTORICAL CHRISTIANITY," "THE GOSPEL AND ITS EARLIEST INTERPRETATIONS," ETC.

New York
THE MACMILLAN COMPANY
LONDON: MACMILLAN & CO., Ltd.
1898

All rights reserved

To

Otto Pfleiderer, D.D.

PROFESSOR OF THEOLOGY AT THE UNIVERSITY OF BERLIN

IN GRATEFUL APPRECIATION OF AN IMPULSE TO AND HELP IN THE
STUDY OF PAUL RECEIVED FROM HIS WRITINGS
AND OF PERSONAL KINDNESS AND FRIENDSHIP EXPERIENCED
FROM HIM DURING A RECENT WINTER'S
RESIDENCE IN BERLIN

This Book is Affectionately Dedicated

BY THE AUTHOR

PREFACE

SINCE the beginning of serious biblical study a profound interest has been felt in the personality, life, and teachings of the great apostle to the gentiles. This interest is not confined to Bible-students, but has extended to the large number of persons who are attracted by the history of civilisation and of liberty and by the study of the causes which have effected the enfranchisement and progress of human thought. Its highest degree and its widest extent are amply justified both by the wonderful character and genius of the man and by the epoch-making force of his thinking and his religious insight. It is not to be put to his credit that he emancipated Christianity from Judaism. To have separated it from what is best in the Jewish religion and ethics would have been to render it a great disservice. That he liberated it from bondage to externalities and formalism, and gave it to mankind not only as a doctrine, but also as a power of the Spirit and as an ethical life, is his indefeasible merit.

One of the most remarkable phenomena of the history of mankind is presented in the personality and character of this man who suddenly appeared "as one born out of due time" with incalculable force and resistless enthusiasm upon the field of primitive-Christian activities. Though he be called a man of God, a providential man, in the eminent sense of the words, he must remain inexplicable until he is interpreted with due regard to his natural antecedents and his intellectual and religious environment. From these he could not free himself. By the highest flights of his genius he could not escape from the atmosphere in which his spirit drew the breath of life. It is in the hope of contributing somewhat to such an interpretation of the life and teaching of the greatest of the apostles of Jesus that this book has been written. Aware of the difficulty of the task and conscious of his own limitations the author craves the considerate judgment and the helpful criticism of his readers.

It is not in accordance with the purpose of this book, which it is hoped will meet the wants of the general reader interested in its subject, as well as satisfy the requirements of the biblical student, to enter upon an elaborate criticism of the Pauline Epistles. The discussion of the apostle's teachings has, however, been based upon those writings of his which are accepted as genuine by all except a small minority of scholars. These six Epistles, Romans, 1 and 2 Corinthians, Galatians, 1 Thessalonians, and Philippians, not only contain all that is important in his teaching, but also present his views in the most succinct and self-consistent form.

The consideration of the apostle's missionary work has been conducted not from the external point of view of Acts, but from the inward aspect presented in the Epistles, which reveal the internal condition of the churches, as well as the personality of the great teacher and his demeanour in the midst of the trials and conflicts incident to his work, while they disclose the forces which were operating in primitive Christianity.

The frequent reference to certain doctrines of the apostle in the course of the book will not incur the criticism of repetition from any one who considers how intimately his fundamental teachings are related not only to one another, but also to numerous subsidiary matters treated of in the Epistles.

A few of these chapters have been previously published in *The New World* and *The American Journal of Theology*, but they have all received revision and additions.

O. C.

CONTENTS

PART I.—THE MAN

CHAPTER I

FORMATIVE INFLUENCES 3

CHAPTER II

PERSONAL TRAITS 22

CHAPTER III

THE CONVERSION 53

PART II.—THE MISSIONARY

CHAPTER IV

THE FIRST YEARS—GALATIA AND THE GALATIAN EPISTLES . 69

CHAPTER V

PHILIPPI, THESSALONICA, CORINTH 95

CHAPTER VI

EPHESUS—ROME 128

CHAPTER VII

THE PAUL OF THE ACTS AND THE PAUL OF THE EPISTLES . 146

PART III.—THE TEACHER

CHAPTER VIII

THE LAW 179

CHAPTER IX
THE PAULINE TERMS, "DEATH," "LIFE," AND "SALVATION" . . . 199

CHAPTER X
THE DOCTRINE OF SIN 218

CHAPTER XI
SALVATION — ATONEMENT 251

CHAPTER XII
THE PERSON OF CHRIST 280

CHAPTER XIII
SUPERNATURALISM — THE SPIRIT . . 311

CHAPTER XIV
FAITH AND JUSTIFICATION 342

CHAPTER XV
ETHICS 370

CHAPTER XVI
PREDESTINATION 398

CHAPTER XVII
THE CHURCH AND THE SACRAMENTS . . 412

CHAPTER XVIII
ESCHATOLOGY 423

INDEX OF SUBJECTS AND NAMES 459

INDEX OF PASSAGES 466

PART I
THE MAN

PAUL, THE MAN, THE MISSIONARY, AND THE TEACHER

CHAPTER I

FORMATIVE INFLUENCES

OF the early years of the great apostle to the gentiles we have unhappily only meagre information. As to his education in boyhood and youth and the influences and associations amid which he grew up, we have no definite knowledge, and must resort to conjectures drawn from what we know of his situation and surroundings and of the customs of the time. His birthplace, Tarsus, in Cilicia, the southwest province of Asia Minor, was a city of some commercial importance, one of the chief occupations of whose inhabitants was the manufacture of sail-cloth from the hair of goats. This handicraft the young Saul doubtless acquired here, and we may assume that his early years were occupied with its pursuit. That he was of humble parentage and under the necessity of supporting himself by his own labour is as evident as it is that he did not think self-support discreditable. Rather he was inclined to boast of the renunciation of his right to be nurtured by his churches and of living by the work of his own hands (1 Cor. ix. 5-15; 1 Thess. ii. 6, 9). The fact that it was the custom for Jewish boys to learn a trade does not render the poverty of Saul's family improbable. It is evident from his own declarations that he was not a man of fortune or even of a competency, and that his missionary travels and work were performed under the conditions attendant upon extreme indigence. Here in Tarsus the youthful Saul was surrounded by the unadulterated cult of the rankest heathenism. But the seclusion of the Jewish quarter, his education at home, and the natural antipathy of a Jew to polytheistic rites, must have preserved him from close contact with the corrupting influences of idolatrous worship. On the other hand, it is not improbable that the impression made upon his young mind by the moral degradation of heathen Tarsus was reproduced in the dark picture of gentile vice and shame drawn in Rom. i. 21–32, just as the inscription upon the pedestal of the statue of Sardanapalus in a neighbouring city : " Eat, drink, enjoy thyself ; the rest is nothing," may have suggested the pessimistic words : " Let us eat and drink, for to-morrow we die " (1 Cor. xv. 32).

The schools of the sophists, the rhetoricians, and the grammarians in Tarsus appear to have excited disgust rather than interest in the mind of the young man, who later in life could speak only with contempt of the "disputes" and "the wisdom of this world" (1 Cor. i. 20). It is probable accordingly that he was less influenced by Greek culture than some have supposed, a strong repugnance to which as degrading and corrupting was a settled feeling in Jewish houses. An education in the Greek language would have rendered him more skilful in writing it than he was according to his own confession (Gal. vi. 11), and would have made it unnecessary for him to dictate his letters to amanuenses. His Greek style denotes that his knowledge of the language was not acquired in the schools of the rhetoricians, but was rather such as a Jew of the Dispersion, a Hellenist, might gain from living in a community in which it was spoken and from the reading of the Greek translation of the Old Testament and the apocrypha. As to Greek literature in general, there is no indication in his writings of an acquaintance with it. He does not write like a man who has formed his style upon Greek models, and he certainly does not reason after the manner of a student of the Grecian philosophers. His citation of current adages from Greek poets should not be adduced as an evidence of his familiarity with their writings. The quotation from Menander, "Evil communications corrupt good manners" (1 Cor. xv. 33), was probably in everybody's mouth, and attention has been called to the circumstance that in writing it the apostle "missed the metre," and thus showed that he was not familiar with the Greek prosody. Whatever culture he had was that of a Hebrew who had diligently studied the literature of his own people. He thought in Hebrew, expressed himself in the Hebrew idiom, and his writings betray throughout the absence of the breadth and refinement of a cosmopolitan literary training. His own boast was that he was "of the stock of Israel, of the tribe of Benjamin, a Hebrew of the Hebrews; as touching the law, a Pharisee" (Phil. iii. 5), and his entire performance as a writer makes good the boast.

Whether Saul could ever have become Paul the apostle to the gentiles or not, if he had been reared in a Palestinian village instead of in the commercial centre Tarsus, is a question that we need not discuss. If, however, we take account at all of natural causes in his development, we may well believe that a youth passed in Tarsus could not be without important consequences in the production of such a capacity for dealing with men as the apostle displayed. Natural qualifications must of course have their rights; but these do not come to their fruitage without dependence upon early influences and associations. The impressions and impulses received in youth may contribute to form breadth of view and great policies in manhood, just as they show themselves in the writer, while he cannot tell how it happens that his style is such as it is. The contrast has been pointed out between the illustrations employed by Jesus and those with which Paul embellished his teachings, the former drawn from the fields and gardens of Palestine, the latter from the Jewish household, the city, and the arena. The difference, however, is not altogether due to education and environment in youth. To Paul was wanting the poetic soul of Jesus. Tarsus was surrounded by magnificent natural scenery, and in his journeys the apostle passed where the most delightful views of mountain and plain must have been before him. But he does not appear to have been impressed by the grandeur and beauty of nature, and of close observation of the outer world he could have had none, or he would not have assumed that a wild olive slip was grafted upon a fruitful tree (Rom. xi. 17). Who will say that his disposition toward the gentiles, which made his mission as their apostle possible, did not have its roots in the same early associations and culture that led him to introduce as a matter of course into an Epistle to one of his churches an illustration from the Grecian games, which were an abomination to the average Jew?

As "a Hebrew of the Hebrews" the youthful Saul must have had in his father's house the education and training of the Jewish boy of pious parentage. An outline of this preëminently religious education has been gathered from Jewish sources, and is in general to the following purport: "With the fifth year began in the house of the Pharisee the reading of the Scriptures, and not much later the visiting of the synagogue on the three hours of prayer, which to the Jews of the Dispersion signified the three daily sacrifices in the temple in Jerusalem. On Mondays, Thursdays, and Saturdays, the reading of the law was listened to. The scholar gradually grew into the school and into the office of a teacher. He read the law, undertook its interpretation, and shared in the controversies. Attendance upon the catechetical and disputatorial exercises and zeal in copying the sacred Scriptures completed the scribe." This was essentially a biblical training, by means of which the boy became familiar with the text of the Old Testament, lived in the history of his race, that wonderful history of miracles and providential guidance, and held converse with the great lawgiver and with prophets and psalmists. One cannot read a page of Paul's writings without finding the traces of such an education. So penetrated was he with the ideas of the Old Testament that he could not write on a doctrinal or religious theme without reference to them. Hence it has been said that he "judaised," and that "his thinking was a thinking in quotations." It cannot, however, but appear to us with our regard for exact interpretation of the text as an inconsistency in the apostle that, holding the Old Testament to be the word of the Spirit, he should have been so indifferent to the actual meaning of passages in it as to employ the incorrect Septuagint version whenever it gave a sense better suited to his purpose than that of the Hebrew.

In order, however, that the Old Testament should be one of the formative influences in the education of the young man, it must be interpreted, and its interpretation is itself an influence which has innumerable hazards. The interpretation dominates the book, and subjects it to its point of view and purpose. Accordingly, it should not surprise us to find that the Old Testament pure and simple, that is, interpreted by a strict grammatical and historical method, influenced Paul less than did the method of treating it in which he was reared, or, in other words, than the Jewish theology in the light of which it was expounded to him. In the first place, it was a fundamental principle in this theology that the sacred writings were the immediate expression of the divine thought and will, and as such were to be regarded as an infallible authority. Secondly, there was wanting to its conception and treatment of the Scriptures a definite view of the relation of its parts to one another, or, in other words, an historical apprehension of the whole, so that separate passages instead of being interpreted in their proper connection were arbitrarily torn from it, and applied according to the exigencies of the particular case or occasion. The Jewish theologians also adopted the allegorical method of interpreting the Scriptures. Proceeding from their premises of inspiration, they believed that every passage must contain a profound and important sense, and when the grammatical rendering did not give such a sense, they made the passage mean something else, or allegorised it.*

This allegorical method of interpretation, conspicuously represented by the Alexandrian school, was adopted by Paul in conformity with the ideas of the time, and he makes frequent use of it apparently without a consciousness and certainly without a purpose of distorting the Scriptures in order to make them subserve his ends. Wishing to maintain by a biblical passage the doctrine that the preachers of the gospel were entitled to support from the churches, he refers to the direction in Deut. xxv. 4, that the ox which threshes the corn should not be muzzled, and declares that it was not written on account of the oxen, since God does not care for them, but with reference

* From ἄλλα and ἀγορεύω, "to say other things," *i.e.* other things than the literal or obvious sense conveys.

to the missionaries, "for our sakes" (1 Cor. ix. 9, 10). A sense directly opposed to that conveyed by the word in the original Hebrew is imposed upon "seed" in Gal. iii. 16, where reference is made to the promise to Abraham that in his seed should all nations be blessed. In order to make an application of the passage to Christ he says that the singular form of the word, which evidently means the entire posterity of Abraham, is used, and that the writer did not mean, "and to seeds as of many, but as of one, and to thy seed, which is Christ." In Gal. iv. 22–27 the history of the two sons of Abraham, Isaac and Ishmael, is allegorised in the sense that they represent the two covenants, although in the original there is not the slightest hint that such a meaning was in the thought of the writer. "Hagar," he remarks, "is Mount Sinai in Arabia, and answereth to Jerusalem which now is, and is in bondage with her children." In this laboured allegorising he overlooks the fact that the legislation of Sinai was given to the descendants of Isaac, and that it was they who were "in bondage" to the law. Sarah, nevertheless, represents the "Jerusalem which is above," the free Jerusalem, "which is the mother of us all;" and in proof of this he quotes from Isaiah words addressed by the prophet to the new Jerusalem that was to be built, as if they had application to Sarah and her descendants. In like manner he reads into the account of Abraham's faith, which was reckoned to him for righteousness, the quite foreign sense that this was not written for his sake alone, but for us also, "if we believe on Him who raised up our Lord Jesus from the dead" (Rom. iv. 23 f.).

In this connection an argument is constructed to prove that the promise to Abraham was not to "his seed through the law," that is, to his Jewish descendants, but to "his seed through the righteousness of faith." This turn is given to the passage in order to bring the gentiles under the promise, and the proof is found in the words from the Old Testament, "I have made thee a father of many nations." This citation is made with the utmost *naïveté*, as if the writer quoted were thinking of the same application which Paul makes of the passage, while it is evident that such a sense was as remote as possible from the intention of the former. This imposing upon a passage of a meaning remote from its original sense cannot be regarded as furnishing a proof from Scripture even on the presumption of its authority by any one who holds to established principles of interpretation, and it is not surprising that Luther thought this kind of scriptural argument "too weak to hold." But Paul's preoccupation with a dogmatic purpose led him to see in the Jewish Scriptures the ideas which filled his own mind, and his education in the current theology of his time had not taught him to read his Bible with a view to ascertaining its historical sense. In this respect he was as truly a child of his age as was Philo, and his exegesis must be judged as we judge that of the latter.

To one who does not regard the matter in this light, it is surprising to find the apostle proceeding naïvely to condemn the Old Testament doctrine of legal righteousness out of that collection itself by bringing different parts of it into conflict with one another. In order to prove, for example, his great proposition that righteousness is not by the works of the law, he quotes Deut. xxvii. 26, "Cursed is every one that continueth not in all things which are written in the book of the law to do them" — a passage which evidently implies that every one ought to keep the law, and can keep it if he will, and so avoid the curse. Then in order to show that this very thing is impossible, and that "no man is justified by the law," he quotes from Habak. ii. 4, "The just shall live by faith," as if the writer of Habakkuk had in mind precisely the Pauline doctrine of justification by faith. Immediately he adds, "And the law is not of faith," and again quotes: "The man that doeth them shall live in them," that is, the man who keeps the commandments of the law shall live in them, the very thing of which he is arguing the impossibility (Gal. iii. 10–12). His preoccupation with justification by faith leads him to another even more arbitrary treatment of an Old Testament passage (Deut. xxx. 11-15) in which the writer represents the law as so near to every man that he is inexcusable who does not observe its requirements. It is not in heaven, that it should be brought down by a messenger sent up for it, and it is not beyond the sea, that some one should go and fetch it, but "it is very nigh unto thee in thy mouth and in thy heart, that thou shouldst keep it." The doctrine of righteousness by works, which Paul vehemently repudiated, could not be more explicitly declared than it is here. Yet he interprets the passage to a directly opposite intent, by putting the words of Deuteronomy into the mouth of Righteousness by faith personified and referring them to Christ instead of to the law: "But the Righteousness which is by faith speaketh in this wise, Say not in thine heart, who shall ascend into heaven (that is, to bring Christ down from above), or who shall descend into the deep (that is, to bring Christ up from the dead). But what saith it? The word is nigh thee, even in thy mouth and in thy heart." This "word," however, is not the word of the law, as in Deuteronomy, but with a most astonishing simplicity the apostle adds, "that is, the word of faith which we preach" (Rom. xi. 6–8).

Paul also learned from his Jewish teachers the interpretation known as the typological, the principle of which is that events and persons of a past time may be regarded as prefiguring occurrences and individuals of a later age. It is evident that if this method of interpretation has any validity at all, it must be because the earlier historian or biographer was conscious of the relation of the historical incidents and personages of his record to the future, and definitely indicated that relation. This alone could furnish a check upon the arbitrary reference of any event or personality in the past to any subsequent occurrences under the relation of type and antitype. The fact, however, is that the typological interpretation, as it was practised by the ancients, was entirely without such a restraint, and was accordingly fanciful and wholly unsound, unless one is willing to adopt the presumption that the writers who employed it were infallibly inspired, and thus qualified to discern in the history of the past relations and profound meanings which the authors of that history give no intimation of having intended to convey. But there is no need to resort to a supernatural explanation of typology, since an historical account of its origin is at hand. It was doubtless an adaptation by the Hellenistic Jews, that is, the Jews whose thought was influenced by Greek ideas, from the Platonic doctrine of idea and type, and was extensively employed by Philo, the Alexandrian Hellenist, to whom the entire Old Testament history was full of types whose antitypes he had no difficulty in finding. The writer of Hebrews, in whom the Hellenistic influence is more conspicuous than in Paul, finds in Melchisedec a type of Christ and in the Jewish sacrifices the "shadow of heavenly things." For to him "Christ did not enter into the holy places made with hands, which are a figure of the true, but into heaven itself, now to appear in the presence of God for us."* In like manner Paul interprets the his-

* Heb. v. 6, vi. 20, viii. 5, ix. 24.

tory of the Israelites in the wilderness. They were all baptized unto Moses in the cloud and in the sea, ate the spiritual food, drank the spiritual drink of the spiritual Rock that followed them, that is, Christ, displeased God, became some of them idolaters, and committed fornication. All these things happened to them for ensamples or types, and are written for our admonition upon whom the ends of the world are come (1 Cor. x. 1-11). Jewish rabbinical and Hellenistic influences are manifest in this interpretation. In the rabbinical tradition the rock is represented as having rolled through the desert after the Israelitish host, and the Hellenistic book, the Wisdom of Solomon, finds in the overshadowing cloud the person of the divine Wisdom, while Philo takes the rock for Wisdom and the Logos.

Such coincidences are most naturally explained by the supposition that the education of Paul was influenced by the current ideas of the time, and that he derived from his teachers the method of interpretation which they employed. Various contacts in his writings with ideas and expressions contained in the book of the Wisdom of Solomon already mentioned indicate that Hellenistic ideas as well as the Hellenistic method of interpretation were among the influences that formed the apostle's thinking. "This book, written by an Alexandrian Jew in the first century before Christ, contains a polemic against heathen materialism and idolatry and an apology for the Jewish belief in God as the true Wisdom which secures the blessedness of man in this life and in that which is to come." The author was familiar not only with the Old Testament, but also with the philosophy of the Greeks, of which he makes use in his argument, particularly of the Platonic doctrine of the immortality of the soul. It is probable that Paul was acquainted with this book, though he so far surpasses its point of view that its influence upon him cannot be regarded as of great importance. If Hellenism gave him his ideas of the outward and inward man, the "mind" (νοῦς), the "soul" (ψυχή), "conscience," and the "flesh," the use which he makes of them shows how far he passed beyond his teachers, and how the religious genius can transform to divine ends materials which in other hands serve only trivial purposes. The Book of Wisdom says that the body weighs down the soul, and oppresses the mind, and in this fact the writer finds an explanation of the defects of the human understanding and of spiritual incapacity. But all that he says bears no comparison with Paul's arraignment of the flesh as the seat of sin and his graphic and powerful delineation of the fruitless struggle of the inward man with the outward, of the mind which serves the law of God with the fatal law in the members (Rom. vii. 15–25). Paul was himself a Hellenist, and owed not a little to Greece, but the ideas which he received from his Hellenistic teachers were subordinated to his gospel of the cross, and came out of his Christian consciousness transformed.

Whether the education of the youthful Saul was completed in the synagogue at Tarsus, or in Jerusalem "at the feet of Gamaliel," as the writer of Acts represents, is a question which we must leave without discussion.* We have no declaration on the subject in the letters of the apostle, which also contain no intimation of his presence in Jerusalem at the time of the trial and crucifixion of Jesus.† His own assertion that he was a Pharisee of the

---

* Acts xxii. 3. The speeches ascribed to Paul in Acts must in the nature of the case be regarded as composed by the writer of that book.

† The fact that Paul gives no intimation in his Epistles of a knowledge of the preaching of the Baptist and of a personal acquaintance with Jesus does not indeed exclude his prior residence for a few years in Jerusalem. The know-

strictest sort is borne out by his teachings and his attitude in general toward the questions with which the Jewish teachers were occupied. Although the doctrine of the resurrection of the dead underwent important modifications at his hands, and was stripped of its materialistic features, its source is evident. His gospel of the cross is Christian rather than Jewish; but only a man imbued with the Jewish doctrine of satisfaction, of atonement for sin, could have conceived it. His doctrine of righteousness had its roots in Judaism, but it was a bold and radical modification of all that he had learned on the subject from his Jewish teachers. His transformation of the national doctrine of the Messiah furnished him with a solution of the problem, how the mass of men in whom the evil impulse predominated could attain the righteousness requisite for the Messianic kingdom, which his teachers were unable to resolve. To them the Messiah was to be a national deliverer, and they had no idea of his religious office as an atonement for sin. Paul solved the problem by the original conception of the Messiah as the second Adam, the representative of the human race, in which capacity his death on the cross satisfied the demands of the law for all, and made accessible to them a new righteousness by faith. In this teaching, however, he

ing of Christ "according to the flesh" (κατὰ σάρκα), to which he confesses in 2 Cor. v. 16, does not imply a personal acquaintance with him, but rather denotes a knowledge of him prior to his conversion the opposite of that spiritual apprehension of his person and mission which he afterwards entertained. The interpretation of the passage given by Jowett (*The Epistles of St. Paul to the Thessalonians, Galatians, and Romans*, Vol. I., pp. 8 ff.) to the effect that the knowledge "according to the flesh" was "in a more Jewish and less Christian manner," that it was subsequent to the conversion, and that the apostle later attained a more spiritual point of view, is not supported in the Epistles. The fact that the profounder apprehension of Christ does not appear in 1 Thessalonians is explained by the point of view of that letter and the matters with which he had to deal in writing it.

held fast to the Pharisaic doctrines, that there is no forgiveness of sin without a satisfaction which accords to the law its indefeasible rights, that death is the divinely ordained penalty for sin, and that atonement for the transgressions of men who have not themselves rendered satisfaction may be representatively made by another. In connection with his Messianic doctrine the Pharisaic teaching as to the coming end of the age, eschatology, the establishment of the Messiah's kingdom, appears to have made a most indelible impression upon him.

This hope of his race did not, however, escape the transformation which the apostle's religious genius effected in everything that it appropriated. Yet in its fundamental features it remained an important factor in his thinking. With eager and intense expectation he looked for "the day of the Lord," which would "come as a thief in the night" (1 Thess. v. 2) to the joy of the believers and to the "sudden destruction" of the unbelievers, who "say peace and safety." His doctrine of salvation was constructed with reference to this impending consummation, and to be "saved" was for him to be received in the kingdom which Christ would establish at his coming (Parousia*). His solicitude for his converts was that they might be "unblamable in holiness before God at the coming of our Lord Jesus Christ with all his saints" (1 Thess. iii. 13). The Jewish doctrine of the resurrection of the righteous at the coming of the Messiah to introduce "the age to come" he held under the modifications that the righteous were the believers in Christ, that these would be raised with spiritual bodies, and the living Christians would be "changed," the mortal putting on incorruption. His intense preoccupation

---

* This word, which to the primitive church denoted the expected presence (παρουσία) of the absent Jesus, is frequently employed in this volume to designate his second coming.

with this idea reacted upon his ethics, and affected his views of marriage, of slavery, and of the relation of the citizen to the state. For "the time is short," he writes to the Corinthians, "it remaineth that both they that have wives be as though they had none, and they that weep as though they wept not, and they that buy as though they possessed not, and they that use this world as not abusing it; for the fashion of this world passeth away" (1 Cor. vii. 29-31).

From his Pharisaic teachers Paul also adopted the idea of a supersensible world of spiritual existences, good and bad, whose interference in earthly matters affects the course of affairs and individual fortunes. He formulates no specific doctrine of good and evil spirits, but his incidental mention of them shows how his beliefs were to a degree determined by his environment. The angels, principalities, and powers of Rom. viii. 38 denote ranks or hierarchies of spiritual existences supposed to inhabit the upper regions of the atmosphere. So far as they were conceived as evil, their chief was designated "the prince of the power of the air, the spirit that now worketh in the children of disobedience" (Eph. ii. 2). Accordingly, the wrestling of the Christians was not against flesh and blood, but against principalities, powers, the rulers of the darkness of the world, spiritual wickedness in the high (heavenly, upper-air) places (Eph. vi. 12). In like manner, "the rulers of this world" (age) are conceived as interfering in human affairs and being instrumental in putting Christ to death (1 Cor. ii. 8). Angels are conceived as looking down upon the apostles, who become to them a "spectacle" (1 Cor. iv. 9). In his hymn to love the apostle says that though he "speak with the tongues of angels, and have not love, he is become as sounding brass and a tinkling cymbal (1 Cor. xiii. 1), and in Gal. 1. 8, that if he or an angel from heaven preach any other doctrine than his gospel of the cross, let him be accursed. The Galatians are commended in that despite their temptation in the flesh they received him as an angel of God or as Christ Jesus (iv. 14). There is nothing inconsistent with his doctrine of angels in the passage in 1 Cor. xi. 10 to the effect that a woman ought to have her head covered when she prayed or prophesied in the worshipping assemblies, "because of the angels." It cannot be rejected on grounds of textual criticism, and has been regarded by some expositors as a gloss only because it is grammatically inappropriate. According to Gen. vi. 2 and its rabbinic interpretations, with which Paul may have been acquainted, although they were not in his time committed to writing, angels were seduced by the beauty of earthly women, and the passage in question was evidently written with reference to this tradition. Chrysostom's proposed interpretation retains the angelology, but gives the passage a more agreeable aspect: "Because good angels present at Christian worship rejoice to see all things done decently and in order." But this does not explain why it should be regarded as decent and orderly for women to be veiled.

Paul has little to say of demons, but that he shared the current view of his Jewish environment with regard to them is evident from his directions to the Corinthians respecting their eating of the flesh offered to idols in the gentile sacrifices. He declares that "the things which the gentiles sacrifice they sacrifice to devils [demons] and not to God; and I would not that ye should have fellowship with devils" (1 Cor. x. 20). Though "there be gods many and lords many" (1 Cor. viii. 5), the idols are not anything; but behind them lies the realm of evil spirits, who make use of the idolatrous worship for their unholy purposes. The evil spirit by preëminence, the great adversary, who is called "diabolus" and "the evil one," in Eph. iv. 21; vi. 11, 16, Paul designates "the god of this world," who has blinded the minds of his Jewish opponents (2 Cor. iv. 4). In his indignation at the fornication among the Corinthians he declares himself determined to deliver the guilty man to Satan "for the destruction of his flesh" — an expression in which is doubtless implied a miraculous punishment, a long and painful affliction of the flesh, through which the offender had sinned, until it should be destroyed, in order that his "spirit might be saved in the day of the Lord," the Parousia (1 Cor. v. 5). Since this punishment was to be inflicted by Satan, he must have been conceived as subject to the control of a higher power, so as to be constrained to serve the purpose of the salvation of a sinner, just as in the book of Job the adversary is sent by Yahweh under orders which he is not to exceed. Accordingly, when Paul says that there "was given" to him "a thorn in the flesh, the messenger of Satan to buffet" him, he doubtless conceived the affliction as of divine appointment and as effected by Satan, as whose messenger or "angel" the disease was regarded. Or he may have thought that Christ dealt with him through the adversary, since he says he besought him thrice that it might depart from him (2 Cor. xii. 7 f.).

That Paul's education in the Jewish schools included instruction in the Hagadah or the rabbinical traditional lore has already been made apparent. He was at home in this "maze of flowery walks" as well as in the Scriptures themselves, and it is especially noteworthy that, with all his reverence for the Old Testament as the word of the Spirit, he quotes from the Hagadah as if it were equally valid with the latter, just as ideas of the Wisdom of Solomon flow readily from his pen. All the literature with which he was acquainted was good for him, if it only served to support his argument. The declaration that "Satan is transformed into an angel of light" (2 Cor. xi. 14) was doubtless derived from the tradition that an angel of Satan disguised wrestled with Jacob. The persecution of Isaac by Ishmael (Gal. iv. 29) is unknown to the Old Testament, but is recorded in the book of Jubilees, where is also found the tradition that Abraham before his call was an uncircumcised idolater, and that he received the promise that he should be "the heir of the world" (Rom. iv. 10, 13), all of which is foreign to the Old Testament record. The current Jewish idea of orders of heavens is adopted in 2 Cor. xii. 2, 4, as if there were actually such a succession of abodes of the blessed (cf. Rev. ii. 7). Further illustrations are not needed to show to how great an extent the Hagadah constituted the background of the apostle's thought, and to serve as a commentary on his own declaration that he had profited in the Jews' religion above many of his equals in his own nation, being more exceedingly zealous of the traditions of his fathers (Gal. i. 14).

These considerations show, what indeed is *a priori* manifest without them, that Paul, like every other man, could not escape from his environment, or resist its influence upon his thought, and that he was a son of his race and age intellectually as well as by physical descent a Hebrew. Only by a miracle could he have been otherwise developed. The treasure of his apostleship was, as he himself says, in an "earthen vessel," and in the troubled earthly atmosphere he saw "through a glass darkly." A knowledge of these limitations is necessary as a guide to the interpretation of his thought and as a check upon the too prevalent error of regarding him as a divine oracle where he is only speaking the language of his time. With the choice before him between expounding the Pauline Epistles in accordance with these facts or of resorting to exegetical artifices, violence to the rules of grammatical and historical interpretation, and even to the apostle's own allegorical method, the conscientious exegete cannot hesitate as to which course he ought to pursue. The apostle is fairly treated, and his greatness made apparent, not by the attempt to show that he did not act like a man, and think like a Pharisee, and interpret the Bible like a rabbi or an Alexandrian Jew, and put the Hagadah and the current literature under contribution like his contemporaries; but much rather by such a sympathetic interpretation of his thought along with an acknowledgment of his limitations as will make it manifest that in the penetration of his spiritual insight, in the flight of his religious genius, in his original comprehension of the gospel, in lofty courage and heroic sacrifice, in devotion to his Master, and in love for mankind, he rose above the pettiness and formalism and legal bondage of his race, above Pharisaism, the Hagadah, and Alexandrian speculation, and became by the strength and soundness of his intellectual and moral character one of the great religious forces of the world.

CHAPTER II

PERSONAL TRAITS

THE materials for forming an idea of the personality of Paul are extremely meagre, and we are obliged to put up with intimations scattered through his writings and with traditions not altogether trustworthy in the attempt to construct a picture of the man as he lived and worked. In the Acts of Paul and Thecla written in the third century, he is represented as "short, bald, bow-legged, with meeting eyebrows, hooked nose, full of grace." John of Antioch, writing in the sixth century, has preserved the tradition that he "was in person, round-shouldered, with a sprinkling of gray on his head and beard, with an aquiline nose, grayish eyes, meeting eyebrows, with a mixture of pale and red in his complexion, and an ample beard. With a genial expression of countenance, he was sensible, earnest, easily accessible, sweet, and inspired with the Holy Spirit." The pseudo-Lucian's contemptuous reference to him, in the fourth century, is to a similar effect, and there are hints in his writings which confirm the general impression that tradition has preserved. In 2 Cor. x. 10 ff. he quotes what his Jewish opponents said of him to the effect that "his letters are weighty and powerful, but his bodily presence is weak, and his speech contemptible." We may fairly assume that this was not an altogether groundless statement, although it came from men who were hostile to him, yet who could hardly so speak of him in one of his churches without a basis of fact. It is accordingly probable that he was not a man of

ersonal appearance calculated to make a pow-
ession as an orator. The reference to the
essel" in which he bore the treasure of his
have sprung from a sense of the frailty of
rd man" which he speaks of as perishing day
or. iv. 7, 16).

ition preserved in the Acts that in Lystra the people took Barnabas for Jupiter and Paul for Hermes of inferior stature goes to confirm the inference that may fairly be drawn from his own reference to his weak personal presence (Acts xiv. 12). To the Corinthians he writes: "I was with you in weakness and in fear and much trembling," and to the Galatians: "Ye know that through [on account of] infirmity of the flesh I preached the gospel to you at the first" (1 Cor. ii. 3; Gal. iv. 13). He who always "bore about in his body the dying of the Lord Jesus" writes to the Corinthians: "For we who are in this tabernacle do groan, being burdened, not that we would be unclothed, but clothed upon, that mortality might be swallowed up of life" (2 Cor. iv. 10, v. 4). This must at least be regarded as the expression of a man who had had a sad experience of the burden of a troubled physical existence, if it was not written with an immediate reference to bodily ills. When we think of his long and wearisome journeys and the hard labour with his hands for his own support, we may well wonder that no more complaints flowed from his pen. When he "might have been burdensome," he says to the Thessalonians: "For ye remember, brethren, our labour and travail; for labouring night and day because we would not be chargeable unto any of you, we preached unto you the gospel of God" (1 Thess. ii. 9). He gloried in this renunciation, and would rather die than that any man should make his glorying void, willing to suffer all things lest he should hinder the gospel of Christ (1 Cor. ix. 12, 15). To the Corinthians he writes: "Behold the third time I am ready to come to you, and I will not be burdensome to you; . . . and I will very gladly spend and be spent for you, though the more abundantly I love you, the less I be loved" (2 Cor. xii. 14).

In two passages (2 Cor. xii. 7 and Gal. iv. 13, 14) Paul makes specific reference to an affliction in the flesh which doubtless had important relations to his inward experiences and to personal peculiarities. In the former passages he calls it "a thorn in the flesh," given him that he may not be too much exalted by reason of the revelations that he received. As if he conceived a diabolical influence to have been employed to inflict the calamity, he calls it "a messenger of Satan to buffet him." His prayer, thrice offered to Christ that it might depart from him, was answered only by the assurance that his grace was sufficient. "Most gladly, therefore," he says, "will I rather glory in my infirmities, that the power of Christ may rest upon me." In the second passage he writes: "Ye know that on account of infirmity of the flesh I preached unto you the first time, and your temptation in my flesh ye despised not nor rejected [loathed], but received me as an angel of God, as Christ Jesus." These are certainly extremely vague intimations from which to derive a conclusion as to the nature of the affliction in question. That it was some sort of physical infirmity is now generally maintained in opposition to the theory of spiritual attacks of Satan, solicitations of unholy thoughts, or conflicts with sensual impulses. The "thorn in the flesh" and the buffeting or smiting as with the fists indicate severe bodily suffering, and it appears from verse 9 that he could not get rid of it even by an appeal to Christ, but was still undergoing the affliction. Light is thrown upon the nature of the malady only when it is brought into connection with the foregoing account of his "visions and revelations of the Lord" (verses 1-6). Such a connection is obvious from the remark that the "thorn in the flesh" was given him lest he be too much exalted on account of these visions and revelations. The natural meaning is, that as a sequence of the high nervous tension and excitement attendant upon the visions there was a physical suffering which he describes as a buffeting or beating by a demonic agency.

The phenomena of epilepsy which have been gathered from numerous examples in ancient and modern times fit the case better than any other explanation that has been proposed. The ancient physicians are said to report that affections of the eyes accompany the attacks of this disease (Gal. iv. 15), and they prescribed a three-days' fast and a shearing of the head (Acts ix. 9, xviii. 18). If not too frequent, the epileptic attacks would not seriously interfere with the prosecution of such a work as Paul's. It appears from the passage in Gal. iv. 13 f. that he was detained in Galatia by an "infirmity of the flesh," and he commends the Galatians because they did not despise that in his flesh which was a "temptation" to them ("your temptation" is the proper reading), a circumstance from which the inference is natural that the affliction was one which, like epilepsy, was calculated to excite disgust on account of the distressing phenomena which accompany it.*

That Paul was not married at the time when he wrote the first Epistle to the Corinthians is manifest. The

---

* Reference has been made in this connection to Mahomet, whom on the occasions of his "visions and revelations" an angel was supposed to torment, so that "he foamed at the mouth, and struck wildly about him, until a fast, death-like sleep restored him" to his normal condition. Many other similar examples are adduced by Krenkel, *Beiträge sur Aufhellung der Geschichte und der Briefe des Paulus*, 1890, pp. 117-125.

question addressed to this church: "Have we not power [the right] to lead about a sister, a wife, as well as other apostles and as the brethren of the Lord and Cephas?" (ix. 5), contains at least an implication that he was not a married man. Decisive of the question, however, is another passage in the same Epistle (vii. 7), in which he expresses the wish that all men were even as himself, in connection with remarks depreciative of the marriage relation. Whether he had formerly been married, and was at this time a widower, is a question on which interpreters differ. The passage in the eighth verse of the chapter in question has accordingly received different explanations: "I say therefore to the unmarried and widows it is good for them to abide even as I." It is maintained by some expositors that the word "unmarried" (ἀγάμοις) here means "widowers," and that Paul intended simply to enjoin upon them and upon widows that they should follow his example as a widower by not remarrying. The word itself, however, does not mean exclusively widowers, but all the unmarried, and no good reason has been assigned for giving it here the limited signification. The fact that the unmarried in general are the subject of consideration in the earlier verses does not exclude them from consideration in this general declaration. There is no ground for supposing that his own widowerhood was prominent in his thought, and that in verse 7 he expresses the wish that all men were as he was in that respect. The dominant idea is that the unmarried state is preferable for all, and he would have all men remain, as he has remained, unmarried. The keynote of the section is in the first verse: "It is good for a man not to touch a woman," and the succeeding verses cannot be properly interpreted without reference to this.

Luther's opinion that the directions to married people

contained in verses 3-5 indicate the apostle's experience in the marriage relation is not well taken, although Dr. Farrar thinks it shows "a deep and fine insight." They are simply such rules as a man might lay down who regarded marriage as permissible only in order that "fornication" might be prevented (verse 2), and who would have that relation when entered upon furnish no occasion for temptation to unlawful sexual intercourse (verse 5). To draw, as Hausrath does, from such expressions as, "We were gentle among you even as a nurse cherisheth her children" (1 Thess. ii. 7); "My little children, of whom I travail in birth again until Christ be formed in you" (Gal. iv. 19); and "Sudden destruction shall come upon them, as travail upon a woman with child" (1 Thess. v. 3); the conclusion that they show "so deep a feeling for family life and such rich experience in it" as to strengthen the supposition that he had been married, only betrays the weakness of a position which requires such support. It is questionable, too, whether the same scholar's remark is confirmed by the experience of conspicuously successful unmarried men, that "only in a man of experience [in which marriage is implied] are all ages and sexes accustomed to have the confidence which greeted the apostle everywhere in his churches." On the whole, the presumption is against the supposition that a man was ever married who held the views of the relation of husband and wife which Paul expresses in 1 Cor. vii. 1 and 9. Rather the implication is that he wished to have it understood that he possessed the "gift" of continence, (verse 7), and meant to assign this according to verses 2 and 9 as a reason for his celibacy. One who believed, as he did, that a father who does not allow his virgin daughter to marry "does better" than the one who gives her in marriage, could hardly with a good conscience have taken a maiden as his wife.

The apostle's confession of his ante-Christian relation to the religion in which he was reared, to the effect that he was, above his equals in his own nation, "exceedingly zealous of the traditions of his fathers" (Gal. i. 14), discloses an interesting aspect of his personality. His nature was of that eager, tempestuous sort in which intensity of conviction and resoluteness of purpose are leading characteristics. He could do nothing by halves. His aim, once clearly set before him, became the dominant power of his life, and pushed him to its realisation without fear of consequences and without self-regard. As a Jew, he believed that the Christian sect was an enemy of his religion, an offence to God, and a menace to the institutions of his race, and he threw himself into the cause of an unsparing extermination of them. On the other hand, "when it pleased God . . . to reveal his Son in me," he writes, "immediately I conferred not with flesh and blood, neither went I up to Jerusalem to them who were apostles before me." This consciousness that he had a revelation, a divine commission, induced "immediately" a resolution to act independently of all human counsel, and to preach his own gospel in his own way,— a resolution to which he adhered with all the intensity and energy of his determined nature throughout his life. Opposition, persecution, the attempt to alienate the confidence of his churches, could not turn him from his great purpose to preach the gospel to the gentiles, or shake his conviction that without submission to Jewish rites, those of them who believed in Christ were entitled to an equal rank with Jews in the coming kingdom.

Such a man could take the uncircumcised Titus with him into the stronghold of the circumcision, and at Antioch could withstand Peter to the face, and charge him with dissembling (Gal. ii. 3, 11, 13). The quality of the zealot which he manifested as a Jew remained, transfigured by Christian love, his prominent characteristic as a missionary of the new religion, so that "more" than his judaising opponents he was "a minister of Christ"—"in labours more abundant, in stripes above measure, in prisons more frequent, in deaths oft." He was undaunted by long and laborious journeys through wild and perilous regions. He was not turned aside from the pursuit of his great mission by the "forty stripes save one" five times inflicted by the Jews; by being "thrice beaten with rods," "once stoned," "thrice shipwrecked"; by "a night and a day upon the deep"; by perils of waters, of robbers, from his own countrymen, from the heathen, in the city, in the wilderness, among false brethren; "in weariness and painfulness, in watchings often, in hunger and thirst, in fastings often, in cold and nakedness." Rather, he exclaims, "I take pleasure in infirmities, in reproaches, in necessities, in persecution, in distresses for Christ's sake; for when I am weak, then I am strong" (2 Cor. xi. 24-27, xii. 10). Besides all this, with unbending resolution he carried out his purpose of self-support, "working day and night."

The zealot Saul, who was a vehement persecutor of the Christians, naturally became the zealot Paul in his advocacy and defence of his peculiar interpretation of Christianity. His Christian experience did not radically change his nature. If he was indefatigable, self-sacrificing, and fearless in the prosecution of his mission to the gentiles, he was impatient of the opposition which those who did not share his apprehension of the gospel felt called upon to put in his way. There was a vein of intolerance in his nature which rendered him severe and unsparing in his judgment of those who represented a point of view opposed to his. He could not put up with a course of conduct which he regarded as trimming. But whether Peter's change of attitude at Antioch under the influence of the emissaries from James, with whose point of view he probably sympathised, deserved so hard a name as "dissembling," may be questioned. One cannot but think that Peter and his associates must have looked upon the charge as not a little harsh and savouring of assumption from a man who in support of his authority could only appeal to "revelations" which he claimed to have had, that the original apostles of Jesus did not "walk uprightly according to the truth of the gospel," because they did not believe with him that uncircumcised gentiles were entitled to equal privileges with Jewish Christians in the kingdom of Christ, and that a man is justified by faith and not by the works of the law, in opposition to all that they had learned from Moses and the prophets (Gal. ii. 11–17). It does not concern us here which of the two views was right, and which was destined to prevail in accordance with the tendency of human thought. There was right on both sides. The gentile mission prevailed, and became one of the great forces in human history; but justification by faith, as Paul apprehended it, has not enjoyed such a fortune, and is a doctrine of doubtful ethical worth.

We are concerned only to point out that Paul's charges and his withstanding to the face indicate a trait of his personality that did not render him a calm and unpassionate judge of the attitude and the grounds of his opponents. In the same Epistle (i. 7 f.) he charges the judaising Christians with an intention to "pervert the gospel of Christ," and calls down a curse on any one who preaches a gospel different from that which he had preached to the Galatians, and to make the anathema doubly strong he repeats it. In the excess of his irritability and the intensity of his indignation against the men who sought to impose "another gospel" upon the Galatians, he expresses with terrible irony the wish that these advocates of Jewish rites might intensify and make more thorough their own circumcision (Gal. v. 12)!* In 2 Cor. ii. 14-17 the apostle characterises his opponents as "those that perish" in contrast with "those that are saved," thus, according to his doctrine of the last things, dooming them to the death from which there is no resurrection. He then proceeds to charge them with corrupting the word of God, that is, making it a source of gain (καπηλεύω), and in xi. 13-15 he arraigns them as "false apostles, deceitful workers, transforming themselves into apostles of Christ." "No marvel," he goes on to say, "for Satan himself is transformed into an angel of light. Therefore it is no great thing if his ministers also be transformed as the ministers of righteousness, whose end shall be according to their works." This is the climax of an *odium theologicum* which is not softened by a touch of sympathy or consideration for an opponent's point of view.

The apostle's relations to his churches often placed him in difficult and delicate situations which called for great tact and skill in the management of men and affairs. These circumstances bring into view important traits of his character. The situation in the Galatian churches was especially trying. The judaising opponents had endeavoured to convince the simple-minded believers here that Paul had misled them with his gospel of the uncircumcision, that he was really no apostle of Christ, and that in order to become real members of the Christian fold and participants in the blessedness of the coming kingdom they must submit to the Jewish rites. The Epistle to the Galatians was intended to counteract this influence, and though it

* ὄφελον ἀποκόψονται, make themselves eunuchs.

was evidently written in a white heat of indignation and under great excitement, it is a masterpiece of apologetic-polemic writing in its adaptation to the circumstances. Even in the salutation, in which he invokes "grace and peace from God the Father and from our Lord Jesus Christ" upon the churches, he cannot refrain from touching upon the subject of his apostleship which lay so near his heart, and accordingly begins: "Paul, an apostle, (not of men, neither by man, but by Jesus Christ, and God the Father, who raised him from the dead)." Then he throws himself immediately into his theme: "I marvel that ye are so soon removed from him that called you into the grace of Christ unto another gospel, which is not another," that is, is no real gospel at all, for, he adds, those who preach it "pervert the gospel of Christ." Then follows the harsh anathema already referred to.

Immediately Paul proceeds to the defence of his apostleship, which was vital to the discussion, with a rapid sketch of his call, of the revelation of the Son of God in him, and of his subsequent contest with and victory over the original apostles in Jerusalem. "I certify to you, brethren," he exclaims, "that the gospel which was preached of me is not after man" (Gal. i. 11). In his indignation and irritability he bluntly calls the Galatians "foolish," and repeats the epithet (iii. 1, 3). He declares that they have been "bewitched," and as if he knew by report or by his knowledge of the method of his opponents that they had appealed to the promise to Abraham, he enters upon an exposition of that matter from his own point of view (iii. 16–19, iv. 22–28). He draws from the armory of the judaisers the weapons with which he overcomes them, and shows from the Scriptures themselves that the promise to Abraham had no validity through the law, which brought only a curse, but that its entire significance rested upon the atonement of Christ, whereby was provided the sole true righteousness, that by faith (iii. 13, 14, 22-26, v. 5, 6, 18). But though he could rebuke unsparingly, and denounce with impassioned zeal, he knew how to mingle tenderness for his converts with reproach of them and invective against those who would alienate them from him. After charging them with returning to "the weak and beggarly elements whereunto they desire again to be in bondage," after expressing the apprehension lest the labour he had bestowed upon them had been in vain, and after the implication that they regarded him, their best friend, as an enemy, because he had told them the truth, he gives expression to the love and yearning in his heart for his spiritual children, whom he had taught in the midst of suffering from the infirmity of his flesh, in the pathetic outcry: "My little children, of whom I travail in birth again until Christ be formed in you, I desire to be present with you now, and to change my voice" (iv. 9, 11, 13, 19, 20). "For," he says, "I am in doubt of you." He is not clear in his mind whether the tone of severity and reproof which he had assumed in the Epistle was the one best adapted to the end he had in view, and evidently felt that if he could see and talk with them face to face, he could better adapt himself to the emergency. There is a note of kindliness and consideration in these words which reveals the gentleness and the greatness of his heart.

The situation in the Corinthian church prior to the writing of the two Epistles addressed to it was extremely complicated, and these letters may be regarded as furnishing the best example that the apostle has left of his ability to deal with divisions and strife and to adjust delicate affairs. The believers here who were mostly of the common sort of people, "not many wise men after the flesh, not many mighty, not many noble" (1 Cor. i. 26), had evidently for their self-sufficiency and pride, for glorying in what they had as if it had not been given them, and for assuming to act the part of rulers and judges! "Now ye are full, now ye are rich, ye have reigned as kings without us; and I would to God ye did reign, that we also might reign with you." This irony is heightened by the picture immediately following, of the humiliation and self-denial of the apostle himself: "For I think that God hath set forth us the apostles last, as it were appointed unto death; for we are made a spectacle unto the world and to angels and to men. We are fools for Christ's sake, but ye are wise; we are weak, but ye are strong; ye are honourable, but we are despised." Then the masterpiece of invective is completed by a pathetic delineation of the hunger and thirst and nakedness and buffeting and homelessness and labour with his own hands which had been his wretched lot (1 Cor. iv. 7–14). Immediately, however, his heart asserts itself, and as if he repented of his severity he says: "I write not these things to shame you, but as my beloved sons I warn you. For though ye have ten thousand instructors in Christ, yet have ye not many fathers; for in Christ Jesus I have begotten you in the gospel." Then again the mood changes, and he remembers the salutary uses of fear: "Now some are puffed up, as though I would not come to you. But I will come to you shortly, if the Lord will, and will know, not the speech of them who are puffed up, but the power. What will ye? shall I come to you with a rod, or in love?"

With reference to the judgment pronounced upon the fornicator or incestuous man (1 Cor. v. 5), to which reference has been made in the foregoing chapter, one cannot but admire the moral earnestness of the apostle and his zeal for the purity of the church, while one is compelled to admit that the proceeding indicates the impetuosity of his character and a haste and passionateness which, as Rückert remarks, can never do any good. One cannot but ask how he could be certain of the issue with respect to the ethical results of the terrible ordeal to which he determined to subject the man. Was it certain that in the power of Satan for "the destruction of the flesh" the man's "spirit" would be "saved in the day of the Lord"? Could he have considered whether the satanic agency was trustworthy in the matter of saving a soul through a disciplinary penalty? The idea proposed by Heinrici that he had excommunication in mind, the casting out of the man into the non-Christian world, of which Satan was the ruler according to 2 Cor. iv. 4, and that Satan by giving his passions full sway would finally destroy his flesh, neither removes the difficulty involved in the delivery of the man to demonic powers, nor explains how unrestricted indulgence of the flesh could save his spirit. In either case the judgment was harsh and the proceeding hasty, and we may as well frankly acknowledge this fact, and say with Schmiedel, "But an apostle also remains after all a man, and does not sit in the council of God." With regard to the contention that "all things are lawful," Paul concedes it with an important qualification. It was probably urged by those who favoured the eating of things offered to idols, on the ground that what concerned the flesh was of no importance. But while maintaining that he cannot permit himself to be brought under the power of anything, he says that all things are not expedient, and every one must consider in his conduct the welfare of the weaker (1 Cor. vi. 12, viii. 9).

The principle of personal liberty, which the apostle expresses in the declaration that he cannot permit himself to be brought under the power of anything, denotes in its application by him a prominent characteristic. He would not have his "liberty judged of another man's conscience" (1 Cor. x. 29). The injunction to the Christians, however, not to use their liberty as an occasion to the flesh, indicates his sane and sober view of freedom, and shows that he regarded it as the worst kind of bondage, if it were not subject to reason and employed in subordination to right ethical principles. He conceived himself to be a freeman only in the sense that he was Christ's freeman. In his sense of independence we see a natural characteristic which was not only intensified by his Christian experience of liberation from the restrictions of the Jewish law, but also subdued and chastened by "the love of God shed abroad" in his heart, and by the sentiment of brotherhood and self-sacrifice, which could not but prevail in him as one having his life "in Christ." Accordingly, though "free from all men," he made himself "the servant of all," that he "might gain the more," becoming to the Jews as a Jew, to them that were without law as without law, to the weak as weak, and all things to all men; that he "might by all means save some" (1 Cor. ix. 19–22). The qualification which he inserts in connection with the declaration that he was "without law," "under the law to Christ" ($\H{\epsilon}\nu\nu o\mu o\varsigma\ \chi\rho\iota\sigma\tau\hat{\varphi}$), is significant of the salutary subordination of his liberty and of his sense that in being free in Christ he was dependent upon him, and recognised in his indwelling presence the source of his ability to serve and save. How his independence asserted itself without any mitigation we have already seen in his dealing with those who opposed his mission and "perverted" the gospel among his churches. His attitude toward the original apostles in Jerusalem was similar to that which he assumed toward the "false brethren" who "came in privily to spy out our liberty which we have in Christ Jesus, that they might bring us into bondage" (Gal. ii. 4).

He speaks of them with an undisguised consciousness of his own equality with, if not of superiority to, them. He asserts the right as an apostle to claim as they did the hospitality of the churches for a wife, were he so disposed (1 Cor. ix. 5).* These men who "seemed to be somewhat," "added nothing" to him. He recognised in them no authority to control his conscience. Men, whatever their standing and antecedents, were nothing to him, where a principle was involved. "God accepteth no man's person." "Not for an hour" did he "give place to them by subjection" (Gal. ii. 5, 6). "In nothing" did he think himself "a whit behind the very chiefest apostles." Yet his freedom and independence were not asserted without a consciousness that they rested upon a valid basis. He believed that he was illuminated, that he possessed "the Spirit," and that as the subject of a divine revelation he had a "knowledge" of the truth with respect to Christianity, which rendered it unnecessary to inquire of any one, to "seek counsel of flesh and blood," and in virtue of which the sacrifice of his liberty would be treason to Christ who had illuminated him. Accordingly, he says in a tone which borders on boasting, when he for the second time makes the declaration of his equality with "the

---

* A "wife," and not a "sister," who may be assumed to have travelled with him in a relation of reciprocal "Platonic affection," according to the apocryphal story of *The Acts of Paul and Thecla*. The apostle does not say, a sister *or* a wife, but "a sister, a wife." Mr. S. Baring-Gould (*A Study of St. Paul*, 1897) thus wonderfully "paraphrases" the passage, 1 Cor. ix. 5: "There is a difference between a wife and a female companion. It is much better to be attended by the latter and to live in Platonic affection, because then the time of the woman is not taken up with domestic affairs. But if one so living finds that his affection is ripening into love, by all means let him marry her. There is no harm in so doing. Yet the former is in my opinion under present circumstances most to be recommended"! Of the method of interpretation which reads into a passage ideas totally foreign to the thought of the writer, this is a most astounding example.

chiefest of the apostles": "Though I be rude in speech, yet not in knowledge" (2 Cor. xi. 6).

In his treatment of the question of marriage and the sexual relation, about which the Corinthian church had written the apostle, there is a manifest limitation of the point of view that is characteristic of him in the discussion of other matters. The whole matter is discussed from the standpoint of the illicit relations of the sexes. If this limitation was contained in the questions proposed to him, as may have been the case, this circumstance furnishes only a partial palliation of the defect. The general propositions are that it is good for a man to have no sexual relations with a woman; that if one have not the "gift" of continence, one may marry rather than permit oneself indulgence in illicit relations; that his own wish is that all men remain unmarried as he has remained; and that the father who does not give his daughter in marriage does better than the one who allows her to marry (1 Cor. vii. 1, 2, 7, 9, 37, 38). Nothing is said of the sanctity of the marriage relation, of the purifying influence of the chaste affection of husband and wife, of the blessedness of paternity, and of the inestimable uses of the home as a moral and social power. We cannot be limited in our judgment of a man by what he says on a given subject. We must also take into account what he does not say. The reason why Paul did not say more is evident. He wrote for the day and the hour. He wrote with reference to having his believers "unblamable in the day of the Lord." He saw everything in the blinding light of the approaching "glory" of the great day of the Parousia. Hence he gave no thought to the foundations of a permanent social order upon the earth. Another limitation appears in his treatment of divorce. The question is not considered from the point of view of the social order, but from that of belief and unbelief. He sets out with "the word of the Lord" (Christ) to the effect that divorce is absolutely unpermissible. Then he proceeds to say on his own authority that in case one of the parties to a marriage-contract is an unbeliever, the continuance of the relation may depend upon this one's choice, if she or he "be pleased to dwell with" him or her (1 Cor. vii. 12, 13), as if he thought "the word of the Lord" had no application to an "unbelieving" husband or wife. Upon the apparently unquestionable proposition that the children of these mixed marriages are "holy" he founds the doctrine that "the unbelieving husband is sanctified by the [believing] wife, and the unbelieving wife by the [believing] husband."

It is easy to see that the question is here treated, as is often Paul's manner, from the point of view of a *principle* which he regarded as once for all settled. The "holiness" of the children of mixed marriages is assumed, and thence is drawn the conclusion that both parents must be "sanctified," since if they were "carnal," that is, did not possess the Spirit, the taint of the flesh must descend to their offspring. Yet it appears from the questions in verse 16: "What knowest thou, O wife, whether thou shalt save thy husband? or how knowest thou, O man, whether thou shalt save thy wife?" that this reciprocal sanctification was not conceived as securing the salvation of the person so sanctified. It had no further consequences than to make the children "holy." The question of slavery is in like manner disposed of under a general principle, that of liberty in Christ. The believing slave is free anyway; is the freeman of the Lord (Christ), because "in the Lord" he has been "called." Let him not take it to heart that he is a slave, but if he have an opportunity to be made free, let him rather remain in bondage. Free and enslaved are alike servants of Christ. For the apostle this point of view dominates the whole discussion of the subject, and excludes consideration of it from any other. Being "bought with a price" (that paid by Jesus on the cross), slaves should regard themselves as Christ's servants, and not feel and act as if they were the servants of men (1 Cor. vii. 21–23).

In approaching the delicate subject of the claims of the women in the church in Corinth to an equality with men in the religious assemblies, the apostle praises the believers for having kept the ordinances which he had delivered to them, thus smoothing his way to the discussion of a difficult matter, which it seems had not presented itself elsewhere, since the custom in question was unknown to "the churches of God" (1 Cor. xi. 1, 16). Here again the method previously referred to is adopted. In taking ground against the claims of the women and the advocates of their cause whom they may be presumed to have had in a party among the men, he passes over the numerous practical considerations which he might have adduced, and rests his entire argument upon a theological doctrine. Accordingly, he begins with the declaration: "I would have you know that the head of every man is Christ, and the head of the woman is the man, and the head of Christ is God." He does not offer proof of this proposition, and appears to have expected it to be accepted on his authority. Incidentally, he establishes from Scripture the principle that the man is the head of the woman, when he says, "the man is not of the woman, but the woman of the man" (verse 8), evidently with reference to the story of woman's creation (Gen. ii. 21 f.). The two other principles in the proposition he probably derived from the Jewish theology, according to which the twofold account of the creation of man in Genesis (i. 26 and

ii. 7) was to be interpreted in the sense that one of them related the creation of the Messiah, Paul's "second Adam," and the other that of the progenitor of the human race, Paul's "first Adam" (1 Cor. xv. 46, 47). Since, according to Paul, Christ was "the image of God" (2 Cor. iv. 4), it is an easy step to the principle that God, the Creator of this second Adam, might be called his "head." It is not so evident, however, how the relation of Christ to man as his "head" was conceived. He says that the man is "the image and glory of God" (verse 7), which the woman of course is not. He is, then, in this respect like Christ; but being of the earth, earthy, and "natural" or "psychical," while Christ is the "heavenly," "spiritual" man, he is subordinate to him, and Christ may be called his "head." Such may have been the course of the apostle's thought.

We are especially concerned here, however, with calling attention to the apostle's method of dealing with the question that had been proposed to him. His reasoning from above downward does not appear to be very lucid when he comes to the particular application of it. It is not clear why a man dishonours his "head" (Christ) by praying covered, and the woman dishonours her "head" (the man) by praying uncovered; and the matter is not made any clearer by the declaration that "a man ought not to cover his head, forasmuch as he is the image and glory of God," but that the woman ought to have hers covered because she is "the glory of the man" (verse 7). The woman, being "created for the man," ought to "have power on her head," that is, a covering as the symbol of man's power over her or of her subordination. Yet the argument runs to the effect that man's subordination to his "head" (Christ) is shown by his being uncovered in worship. One cannot, moreover, but feel the extreme hardness and severity of the remark, that for a woman to pray or prophesy with her head uncovered is the same as if she were shaven, which can only mean, according to the custom of the time, that it is the same as if she classed herself among disreputable women. In view of the fact that the women in the Corinthian church who made the claim of equality with men in religious worship (and there appears to be no reason for supposing that an assertion of "equal rights" in general had been made) proceeded upon a doctrine of the apostle himself that in Christ there is "neither male nor female" (Gal. iii. 28), and that they were very likely sincere and devout, the harshness of this saying is set in a still more vivid light.

In the directions given to the Corinthians concerning idolatry and the eating of flesh offered in sacrifice to idols the apostle employs his favourite dialectical method, the argument from a principle which is followed to its utmost consequences; but it is interesting to observe here that at the end of the discussion the practical Christian idea of fraternal consideration for the welfare of others is made prominent. The fundamental doctrine is that as Christians the cup of blessing is "the communion of the blood of Christ"; and the bread is "the communion of his body"; just as in "Israel after the flesh" they who eat of the sacrifices are partakers of the altar (1 Cor. x. 16–33, viii. 4–13). Hence the absurdity of the idea that the Christians could at the same time "drink of the cup of the Lord and the cup of devils." Then, after turning aside from his argument to insert a threat in the questions: "Do we provoke the Lord [Christ] to jealousy? are we stronger than he?" he lays down the practical doctrine that while all things are lawful to him, "all things are not expedient; all things edify not," and gives the eminently Christian direction: "Let no man seek his own, but every man another's." His indifference on principle to the eating of flesh offered to idols is indicated in the teaching that the believers may "eat whatsoever is sold in the shambles, asking no questions," and that they may eat whatever is set before them at a feast of unbelievers; but if they are told that the flesh has been offered to idols, they are not to eat it "for his sake that showed it and for conscience' sake." One can hardly help feeling that there is an inconsistency here. For if the prohibition in question is at all a matter of conscience (whether the conscience of the weaker or that of the stronger be meant), the believer is inexcusable on moral grounds for not "asking questions" and ascertaining whether he is doing the forbidden thing or not. The reason given by the apostle why a Christian may eat whatever is offered in the market, "asking no questions for conscience' sake," is characteristic of his method. He quotes from Ps. xxiv. 1, "The earth is the Lord's and the fulness thereof," in a sense not intended by the psalmist, — all things are Christ's, and do not belong to idols or demons. But the second application of the quotation to the case where the eating is forbidden "for conscience' sake" is inept and forced.* Finally the matter is brought under a religious principle, and the injunction is given to the believers, "Whether, therefore, ye eat or drink, or whatsoever ye do, do all to the glory of God" (1 Cor. x. 31). Offence should be given to none, whether Jews or gentiles, and especially not "to the church of God," "even as I please all men in all things, not seeking my own profit but the profit of the many, that they may be saved" — a distinct disclosure of the chief aim of the apostle's life from the time he engaged in the service of Christ.

* Since "the earth is the Lord's and the fulness thereof," eat not of flesh sacrificed to idols when informed of its character, on account of the conscience of him who informed you!

In dealing with the question of spiritual "gifts," which had evidently caused no little trouble at Corinth, the apostle characteristically sets out from the general principle that "there are diversities of gifts, but the same Spirit." In all administrations of the church there is the one Lord Christ, so that the fact that there are different manifestations does not prejudice the principle that all have the Spirit. Those, then, who are gifted with the more striking and prominent charism of speaking "with a tongue" should not exalt their "gift" too much, and depreciate others, the expression of which was less obtrusive. Just as all parts of the body are essential to the unity and strength of the whole organism, so all the various gifts have their place in the body of Christ, the church. In assigning by a skilful and tactful course of reasoning the speaking with a tongue to its proper, that is, subordinate, place among the gifts he gives the practical interest predominance. All gifts should be so employed that "the church may receive edifying." The man who "prophesies" "speaketh unto men to edification and exhortation and comfort." But the ecstatic who speaks "with a tongue" only "edifieth himself." "Even so ye, forasmuch as ye are zealous of spiritual gifts, seek that ye may excel to the edifying of the church." He thanks God that he speaks with a tongue more than they all, yet he says that in the church he would rather speak five words with his understanding, that by his voice he might teach others, than ten thousand words in a tongue. The picture is forcible of a "whole church" raving together in this ecstasy, while "unbelievers" looking on say that they are "mad." "But if all prophesy, and there come in one that believeth not or one unlearned, he is convinced of all, he is judged of all." Finally, the sum of the whole matter is the practical precept, "Let all things be done to edifying" (1 Cor. xii. xiv.).

It must be conceded, however, that the concessions made to the merely external manifestations of the so-called "gifts of the Spirit" accord to them more recognition than is conducive to the welfare of the church, whether it be the church of the first or of any succeeding century.

The concluding portion of 2 Corinthians (x. 1–xiii. 10), which is so different in tone from the preceding chapters as to furnish strong support to the hypothesis that it originally had no connection with them, and is in fact a separate letter, reveals striking traits of the apostle's personality, and shows how unsparingly he could deal with refractory elements in his churches. He evidently regards it as an humiliation that he must boast of himself, of his revelations and privations and labours, and he exclaims: "I am become a fool in glorying; ye have compelled me; for I ought to have been commended of you." They had been receiving, some of them evidently with favour, his opponents, the judaisers, the ministers of Satan (2 Cor. xi. 15), and he says that "seeing that many glory after the flesh," he will glory also; for, he adds, "ye suffer fools gladly, seeing ye yourselves are wise" (verses 18, 19). This is a biting sarcasm. Since they listen to the boasting of other fools, his opponents, they will doubtless suffer him in their superior wisdom to make a fool of himself by boasting like the others. The irony is apparent in the correct rendering of xi. 4: "For if he that cometh [the judaiser] preach another Jesus whom we have not preached, or if ye receive another Spirit which ye have not received, or another gospel which ye have not accepted, ye bore it well"; did finely to take pleasure in a gospel hostile to mine. "You bear it," he tells them, "if a man bring you into bondage, if a man devour you, if a man take you [capture you], if a man exalt himself, if a man smite you on the face" (xi. 20). He fears that when he comes they will find him as they would not like to find him, and to "those who have sinned and to all others" he announces that if he comes again he "will not spare" (xii. 21, xiii. 2). Finally he tells them to examine themselves and see whether they be really Christians or "in the faith." They ought to know that unless they are "reprobates" Jesus Christ is in them, and he intends to let them see that he himself is at least not a reprobate. According to his profession (xii. 15), we must regard all this as the language of wounded affection.

The apostle's style is characteristic of the man in a greater degree than that of most writers, and this for the reason that he knew and would know nothing of the art of concealing himself. To him language was not "invented to conceal thought," but thought was invented to shape, to master, to crush language. His style is that of one who did not think of style because possessed and dominated by the ideas that he wished to express. All graces and artifices are foreign to it. The polished rhetoricians of the Greek schools would have been shocked at the way in which he treated their language. Renan's remark is doubtless somewhat extravagant, that "it is impossible to violate more audaciously, I will not say the genius of the Greek language, but the logic of human language." The genius of the Greek language could certainly not have consideration from one who could never get rid of the Hebrew idiom. He had not, moreover, the imagination which is essential to the production of a fine literary style. When we add to this that his letters were often dictated in haste and under great excitement, so that they have been compared to "a rapid conversation stenographically reported and reproduced without correction," it is a marvel that the blemishes are so few. His intense preoccupation with his theme, which rendered him regardless sometimes of the logical connection of his thought, could not but react upon his style, may, in fact, be said to a degree to have constituted it. Hence the want of sequence, the breaks and jerks, "the harshness and roughness which suggest that the thought is far too weighty for the language, and can scarcely find fit form for the superabundant matter it would express." It is this preoccupation often with a dogmatic idea which leads him to make sweeping statements without considering whether or no they are in accord with what he has elsewhere said. Hence the paradoxes or antinomies of his teaching, which must always remain stumbling-blocks to the theologians who study him with the presupposition that his writings contain a system of doctrine which is throughout accordant and consistent with itself. He had not time to consider whether he was consistent with himself or no, and as for formulating a doctrinal system or even writing a sacred and infallible literature, nothing was farther from his thought. It would be impossible for a man, in whose mind the Jewish theology and various Hellenistic speculations lay unreconciled, not to leave such an antinomy as that death is the penalty of sin, and that man is naturally mortal on account of the perishable nature of the flesh. But he was greater than all speculation, and all paradoxes, and all theologies. He could afford to perpetrate antinomies and to write in a style which, like himself, was both Hebraic and Grecian. It was because he was both Greek and Hebrew, and had a far-seeing vision, which looked beyond the making of a theology, and a great love that embraced mankind, that he became the conqueror of the world. It was because he saw in the cross the symbol of redemption for gentiles as well as Jews and in the Abrahamic promise an all-inclusive divine purpose, and because he was great enough and kind enough to become "all things to all men, that he might save some," that through him the gospel of Jesus became a religion for the world instead of the possession of a Jewish sect.

The portraiture of Paul's personality is not completed, or his influence accounted for by regarding him simply as a theologian and the author of a new interpretation, one may even say a transformation, of the gospel of Jesus. A sketch of his teaching and his missionary work furnishes only a bare outline, meagre and cold, until it is filled with the religious content which was the vital principle of his character, the mainspring of his activity, and the source of his power. He can never be understood until he is interpreted out of his personal experience, that is, until his interpreter recognises the fact that his doctrine, far from being an independent structure to be studied by itself apart from all living motives, is the attempt of a powerful intellect to put into an objective form what was most vital in his religious consciousness, to give an outward expression to an inward life in God. It could not be otherwise than that his religion was experienced to some degree in subordination to his thought, and took on the colour of his doctrine. Accordingly, while in its essence it reproduces the old, eternal experience of the human soul, in some of its forms and expressions it has the transient character of certain of his theological conclusions. The revelation of the Son of God in him (Gal. i. 15 f.) was a revelation of God's love for him and for mankind, which he interpreted in the sense that " God commendeth His love toward us in that, while we were yet sinners, Christ died for us " (Rom. v. 8). Through Christ the believer has " access " to God and " peace " with Him, and His " love is shed abroad in the heart " (Rom. v. 1 f.). The mystic fellowship with Christ, whose outward symbol is baptism, is a "newness of life," in the experience of which he conceived himself to be " dead to sin, but alive to God." Being made free from sin he would henceforth be "the servant of righteousness," and have his "fruit unto holiness" (Rom. vi. 3, 4, 11, 22). In his death with Christ to the flesh the old, sinful life with its fruitless struggle and bondage was put away, and in the gift of the divine Spirit was brought into his being a new religious principle which contained infinite possibilities of blessedness and of victory. By virtue of this indwelling power the "deeds of the body" are overcome, and that "life" is attained which is "hid with Christ in God," and which in the end overcomes "the last enemy," death. The summit of religious experience is reached in the "witness" of this Spirit with his spirit that he was a child of God; for "as many as are led by the Spirit of God, they are the sons of God." Here was a source of strength to him to do and dare and suffer all things. "If God be for us, who can be against us? He that spared not His own Son, but freely gave him up for us all, how shall He not with him also freely give us all things?" The love of God was not only shed abroad in his heart, but it also made him "more than conqueror," and was a protection round about him in which he lived and worked secure from the machinations of the "principalities and powers" of the realm of darkness, and from which "neither height nor depth nor any other creature" could separate him (Rom. viii. 13-16, 31-39). In this religious experience faith was a pivotal principle, "a new point of gravity." It was an indestructible trust in the love of God, through whom came the "atonement," and a confidence in the divine promise inclusive of gentiles as well as of Jews. Through this Paul conceived a new righteousness to be attained, "if not by way of the law, then by way of God" — a righteousness which if not expounded by him to our comprehension, was yet to him a reality and an inalienable possession. Yet the real spring of his life was "the Spirit of Christ," the love which "believeth all things, hopeth all things, endureth all things," and is greater than the faith that rests in God and the hope that lays hold on the coming kingdom.

CHAPTER III

THE CONVERSION

THE most important event in Christian history next to the birth of Jesus, the conversion of Paul, is involved in the obscurity that attaches to all spiritual processes which the subject of them cannot adequately explain to himself, much less to others. It does not appear from the apostle's own writings that he wished to make to others any disclosures as to the character and details of this great experience. Rather with a delicacy which the writer of Acts does not attribute to him he appears to shrink from such a proceeding, and we have only allusions to the fact of the change that throw little light upon its antecedents or its process. It is probable that the prominence of Paul in the early church may have been the occasion of more importance being attached to his conversion than he attached to it himself, or than was warrantable under the circumstances. The conversion of a Jew to Christianity was not so unusual at the time that there was any occasion for proclaiming the fact as a miracle; and if the church had never had the accounts of Paul's conversion in Acts, which show how the event was regarded a half-century or so after it happened, and how tradition had given the occurrence a legendary form and embellishment, no one would have thought of resorting to a miracle to explain it. It is worthy of note as a fact generally overlooked in the discussion of the matter that Paul does not anywhere mention a conversion, but says that Christ was "seen" of him and "revealed" in him (1 Cor. xv. 8; Gal. i. 16). Whether these events coincided with his first believing in Christianity or not he does not say. He does not tell us, and we do not know, but that these revelations and visions were subsequent to his acceptance of Christianity and connected with his call to the apostleship to the gentiles.

For the question why Paul became an apostle is legitimate, although the answer to it can be only conjecture. Many Jews were converted who do not appear to have thought of being apostles. Why, moreover, should he have felt called to be the apostle to the gentiles? According to his own statement this idea of a gentile apostleship was inseparably connected with the revelation of Christ in him; for his words are: "When it pleased God . . . to reveal His Son in me, that I might preach him among the heathen" (Gal. i. 15, 16). He says nothing here of a conversion to Christianity, but evidently has in mind the great theme which on this occasion was of paramount importance, — his call to the apostleship to the gentiles. In the entire connection of the passage in question, which is the one generally referred to as containing his own most important words on his "conversion," he speaks only of his apostleship, or rather of his call to the apostleship, declaring that he is "an apostle not of men, neither by man, but by Jesus Christ and God the Father, who raised him from the dead" (Gal. i. 1). He says furthermore that the gospel which he preaches is not after man, neither was he taught it, but by the revelation of Jesus Christ (Gal. i. 12). Weizsäcker's conclusion that since he uses the same terms in speaking of his apostleship and of his gospel, he must in that passage refer to his becoming a Christian or his acceptance of the gospel, is not valid. For his apostleship and his gospel were the apostleship and the gospel to the gentiles, and it is a gratuitous assumption that his distinctive apprehension of the gospel came to him at the moment of his conversion. We know that he did not immediately begin the gentile mission, but that he "went into Arabia, and returned again to Damascus" (Gal. i. 17).

If by the conversion of Paul one means his acceptance of his distinctive apprehension of Christianity, the gospel and the apostleship to the gentiles, one should hesitate to designate it with Weizsäcker as "sudden." It was essentially different from the change from an evil to a virtuous course of life of a man in whose consciousness there is an accumulation of good ethical influences and precepts which only await the right occasion to assert themselves. It was different from the ordinary conversion of Jews to Christianity. His "gospel" was fundamentally different from that of the Jewish Christians in general. The change that took place in him was radical, and this fact furnishes a presumption against its suddenness and in favour of the hypothesis that in its completeness it was the result of a series of impressions, influences, and reflections. Weizsäcker, in commenting on the passage in Gal. i. 15, 16, says that Paul in writing this "is conscious of no transition-period of wavering reflection and questioning, but the time of his persecution is immediately connected in his life with his belief and his apostleship" (*Apostol. Zeitalter*, 2te Aufl., p. 68). But it is evident that in this passage the apostle is not giving an account of his conversion with the intention of indicating the sequence of events in time. He says that he had persecuted the church, that he had been exceedingly zealous of the traditions of his fathers, and that when he felt called to be an apostle to the gentiles he "did not confer with flesh and blood." We must not put too strict an interpretation upon a mere allusion like this, which is devoid of all details. One is as much justified in reading into it a series of events as in binding the several stages inseparably together.

The same writer concludes from Paul's words in the first chapter of Galatians, that his conversion was independent of anything that he may have learned from men concerning Christ, and infers from the first verse that the certainty of the resurrection of Jesus was the content of the "revelation" that he received. But Paul's declaration that he did not receive his "gospel" from man does not exclude a knowledge gained in a natural way of the man Jesus, the Jesus "after the flesh," his claims, his work, his crucifixion, and his resurrection. That he should have persecuted the Christians without a very good knowledge of their beliefs is contrary to all that we know of his character and his conscientiousness. But if it be admitted that he was thus informed, it is evident that this knowledge could not have been without an influence upon him, and could not but have given rise in such a mind as his to "reflection and questioning." It must be questioned whether under such circumstances the "revelation" which Paul says he received was "the cause of the entire decision, entering suddenly and unexpectedly." We can easily conceive of the crisis as sudden, when the accumulated influences which induced it were ready to discharge themselves, and preceding "reflection and questioning" culminated, as in a logical and courageous mind they must, in the urgent pressure to a decision; but a sudden "revelation" that the Jesus whom he was persecuting in the person of his followers was the true Messiah, that he had been crucified "to deliver us from this present evil world" (Gal. i. 4), and that he had been raised from the dead, to one who had learned nothing of the matter "from men," and had not reflected and questioned with conscientious anxiety to know the truth, can only with difficulty be shown to be probable.

It is superficially apparent from the apostle's words in Galatians that he did not regard his undertaking of the apostleship to the gentiles as an act of his own self-determination, and his preparation for it as acquired in an altogether natural way, whether by his own study and meditation or by instruction from others. He says explicitly of his gospel that he "was not taught it," but that he had it "by revelation of Jesus Christ." These words, however, must be interpreted, and we have fortunately other sayings of his of a somewhat similar purport, which throw a little light upon them. It is important to ascertain as nearly as possible what psychological conditions he connected with the "revelations" that he claims to have received. We have already seen that in 2 Cor. xii. 1–4 he relates that he had "visions and revelations of the Lord" (Christ) under circumstances which undoubtedly indicate abnormal physical conditions, since he connects them with a disease, which he calls "a thorn in the flesh." He declares that he does not know whether when he had these visions and revelations he was "in the body or out of the body," and we can of course attach no objective importance to his reference to the current Jewish ideas of "the third heaven" and "paradise.". It appears, then, that some of the "revelations" that he had were received during a suspension of his normal consciousness. The numerous cases on record of similar phenomena render it hazardous to maintain that his experience was altogether exceptional and supernatural, and throw the burden of proof upon him who would support the affirmative of this proposition. The question is, what did Paul mean by a "revelation"? and we have in this passage from the second Corinthian letter the answer, that he sometimes meant what he experienced under conditions familiar to physicians who have studied abnormal physico-psychological phenomena. That he saw in these visions what he had never before thought of, is far from being as probable as that the revelations were an intensification of ideas prominent in his normal thinking. The mention of "the third heaven" and "paradise" is proof of this latter hypothesis, for these were ideas which he derived from his Jewish environment, and he does not intimate that these fictitious localities were made known to him in the revelations, but only "unspeakable words which it is not lawful for man to utter."

Another instance of a revelation is mentioned by the apostle in his account of his visit to Jerusalem to defend his gospel against the judaisers of that church. He says simply: "And I went up by revelation, and communicated to them that gospel which I preach among the gentiles" (Gal. ii. 2). From this bare statement we cannot determine whether the "revelation" in question was received under conditions similar to those implied in the passage in second Corinthians or not. One thing is, however, in the highest degree probable, and that is that the matter in question was one that had intensely occupied his thought and deeply moved him. The attitude toward his mission to the gentiles, which prevailed in Jerusalem, was a matter about which he was greatly concerned. It was the question whether the work which lay so near his heart was to be overcome and rendered futile by hostile influences, whether, in his own words, he "by any means should run, or had run, in vain" (Gal. ii. 2). Now it is manifestly impossible for us to determine whether or not, from his strictly theistic point of view, from which second causes were disregarded, and phenomena were attributed to direct divine intervention, he ascribed to a revelation from God a profound conviction respecting his mission, that was in fact the result of his earnest reflection. It is hazardous here to dogmatise either affirmatively or negatively, and we must leave the matter undecided with calling attention to the fact that neither the hypothesis of naturalism nor that of supernaturalism is susceptible of proof. The appeal to the apostle's use of the word "revelation" in the interest of the latter is ruled out, for the reason that it is precisely the meaning which must be attached to this term that is the question in debate.

In another passage, in which the apostle is not speaking of his conversion, but is defending his claims to the apostleship (1 Cor. ix. 1), he asks: "Am I not an apostle? have I not seen Jesus our Lord?" There is no cogent reason for applying this passage to his conversion. He may have "seen" the Lord in one of the visions mentioned in 2 Cor. xii. 1. But leaving this matter undecided, the question of moment is what he meant by having "seen" Christ. In 1 Cor. xv. 5–7, after mentioning various appearances of Jesus after his resurrection, he says: "And last of all he was seen of me as of one born out of due time." The probability that he refers here to the same experience mentioned in Gal. i. 16 as God's revelation of His Son in him is so great that it is not worth while to argue the case. Yet no one would assume on the ground of this latter passage that he had in mind anything but an inward manifestation, a conviction, which left the matter beyond all question that Jesus was the Son of God and the Saviour, in the sense peculiar to his gospel, the gospel of the cross and of the uncircumcision. For it was on this revelation that he grounded his apostleship to the gentiles. In the interpretation of "seen" ($\overset{\circ}{\omega}\phi\theta\eta$) recourse must be had to the apostle's doctrine of the resurrection-body. In 1 Cor. xv. 40, 44 he says that there are "terrestrial," that is, material, and "celestial" bodies, and that the body that is "raised" is a "spiritual body." He evidently did not believe in the "bodily resurrection" in the crude materialistic sense that the old body of flesh was raised. "Thou sowest not that body that shall be; . . . but God giveth it a body as it hath pleased Him" (1 Cor. xv. 37, 38). More especially he says in Phil. iii. 20, 21 that we look for the Saviour from heaven "who shall change our vile body, that it may be fashioned like unto his glorious body" or "his body of glory." It is hence evident that he did not think of the resurrected Jesus as possessing a body of corruptible flesh which "cannot inherit the kingdom of God," but as clothed with a spiritual corporeity. That he conceived this spiritual body to be visible to the eye of flesh is improbable not only on account of the "in me" of Gal. i. 16, but also from 2 Cor. iv. 6: "For God who commanded the light to shine out of darkness hath shined in our hearts to give the light of the knowledge of the glory of God in the face of Jesus Christ." The reference of this passage to his call to the apostleship, that is, to his profound "knowledge" of the gospel, cannot be doubted. The use of the plural, "our hearts," does not exclude this reference, for in 2 Cor. iii. 2 he says, "Ye are our epistle written in our hearts." In any case the experience described is plainly an inward one, and has no relation to a seeing with the eye of flesh, just as in 2 Cor. iii. 18 he says of himself and the believers generally: "But we all with open face beholding as in a glass the glory of the Lord [Christ], are changed into the same image from glory to glory, as by the Spirit of the Lord," that is, by Christ, who is the Spirit (2 Cor. iii. 17), and whose illumination and transformation of the apostle and of the believers is conceived as effected, not through the senses, but by the inward working of his power.

The change from a persecutor of Christianity to an apostle was not only an inward process, but also a conditional or dependent one, — a process determined by definite antecedents. Let this be stated as an hypothesis, and not as a dogmatic affirmation. We do not know enough about the matter to warrant dogmatism from any point of view, and we certainly cannot infallibly point out the assumed antecedents of the crisis. It is legitimate, however, to undertake to show the probabilities that are favourable to the hypothesis. Before all, then, no one will dispute the proposition that Paul's conversion to the religion of Jesus had its ground in his nature, as is the case with every man's conversion. Not every Jew persecuting the Christians would have had Paul's experience. Not every Jew converted from a persecutor to a Christian would have become an apostle. Not every Jew who might have become an apostle, would have become an apostle to the gentiles. Few will have the hardihood to affirm that God could have made of any Jew the great apostle to the gentiles. If He could have done it, we know very well that such is not His way. God's truth forces no man, but it transforms and shapes to divine ends him who has the native genius for it. The prophets and apostles are born God-endowed. No one can read the Epistle to the Romans without receiving a profound impression of the nature, the intellectual character of the author. Paul shows himself here to be preëminently a reasoner, a dialectician of a high order. The probability that he first learned to reason after he became a Christian is too slight to merit consideration. But the probability that such a man would have given up the religion of his race in which he was himself a zealot, and accepted in its most radical interpretation another which he was in the act of trying to exterminate, without reasons born of intense thought, few will for a moment entertain. A conversion without psychological antecedents is not now regarded as rational in enlightened Christian circles. We do not think the divine grace to be independent in its operations of subjective conditions, and we provide them with no small skill.

We shall not understand the conversion of Paul until we approach it from a similar point of view, that is, until we endeavour to ascertain what were the psychological conditions in his nature and in his thinking prior to the event. As to his nature, no one will dispute that he was thoroughly conscientious. He undoubtedly entered upon his persecution of the Christians with a good conscience, believing that as enemies of his religion and of God they ought to be exterminated. But conscience has its seditions and its revolutions from within, which are most radical and violent in the deepest and strongest natures. It is at least among the probabilities of the case, one may even say that it is an antecedent condition, without which his conversion, like that of any other man, is inexplicable, that Paul was tormented with conscientious scruples, and that they concerned his cruel persecution of the inoffensive Christians. The probability is raised to a certainty, when we consider that many years after he had not overcome these scruples, as is apparent from the humble confession: "For I am the least of the apostles, that am not meet to be called an apostle, because I persecuted the church of God" (1 Cor. xv. 9). That he saw and felt more keenly the wrong after his conversion than before may be conceded. But that he was conscious of it before that event, and that his scruples were among the causes that determined it, is in accord with human nature and with all we know about conversion.

That intellectual doubts accompanied the conscientious scruples is in the highest degree probable. The chasm that separated a persecuting Jewish zealot from a Christian apostle to the gentiles, is too wide to be bridged without an intellectual process. A conversion like that in question could be nothing short of a transformation of the entire inward man, mind, heart, and soul. A man like Paul can hardly be conceived to have become the enthusiastic preacher of the gospel of the uncircumcision without first giving himself a rational account of the matter. Much less, without being grounded in this conviction would he so persistently have adhered to it throughout his life. Nothing is more evident from his writings than that he regarded his peculiar apprehension of the gospel as a thesis which must be defended by argument and supported by reason. Shall we say, then, that he accepted the apostleship to the gentiles against a prejudice which even the original apostles of Jesus could not overcome, and first thought of the reasons for it afterwards? Such a construction of the matter were most unpauline. It is true that he does not tell us that he had reasoned on the matter prior to his conversion, and we have only an incidental hint as to his scruples of conscience. But "the light of the knowledge of the glory of God" which shone in his heart may well have been the white light of reason to a man so zealous as he was to "prove all things." That a man so enthusiastic as Paul was for righteousness and so intent upon reasoning should have accepted an entirely new theory of it without reasoning upon its grounds is not likely, when we consider how persistently and thoroughly he argues for it in the Epistle to the Romans. We have seen that as a Pharisee he believed in the Messianic kingdom, the condition of which was the righteousness of the people.

To a logical mind like Paul's the alternative was presented of either abandoning this great Messianic hope or of finding a new way of righteousness, — another way than the impossible righteousness of the law, which, even if he felt that he, the "blameless," had attained it, was far from being attained by the mass of his people. That in his acceptance of Christ was implied his belief in the new righteousness by grace, can hardly be doubted. For the question is legitimate here, why did he accept Christ at all? One will scarcely dare to affirm that he accepted him without any reason whatever. Was it because of a "revelation"? If so, the revelation must have had a content; and if that content was in part the theological doctrine of righteousness by faith without the works of the law, we have a choice between two interpretations of the matter — either this doctrine was supernaturally made known to him without his own reflection, or it was a discovery of his reason, which he called a "revelation." The way in which in his Epistles he seeks to buttress the doctrine on every side with argument, favours the latter alternative, and indicates that he did not think it could stand by authority. Two words in the passage in Gal. i. 16 reveal the apostle's consciousness at the time of his call to the gentile ministry and the grounds of his acceptance of the Christian faith. He says it pleased God to reveal *His Son* in him. He does not say, to reveal *Jesus*, and the thought undoubtedly is that his Christian belief rested upon his conviction that Jesus of Nazareth was the Son of God, the true Messiah. Without this belief Paul could never have become a Christian. He did not believe in Jesus because of his teachings, with which he shows little acquaintance, and so long as he thought him to have been a pretending Messiah ignominiously put to death, he persecuted his followers. The first verse of Galatians throws still more light upon the process of the change which took place in his thought. It cannot escape the observing reader that he is here intent upon stating the grounds of his apostleship to the utmost. Hence he does not stop with saying that he is an apostle, "not of men, but by Jesus Christ and God the Father," but he adds, *"who raised him from the dead."* Every one who has a slight knowledge of the apostle's doctrine knows that the resurrection of Jesus was one of its fundamental principles. By this Jesus was "declared to be the Son of God with power" (Rom. i. 4). Had Saul of Tarsus not been convinced of this, there would have been no apostleship to the gentiles.

Here, then, we have the key to the solution of the problem of the great apostleship. The exaltation of Jesus by divine power from the realm of death to heaven in a "body of glory" was to Paul indisputable proof that God recognised him as His Son. From this principle the step was easy by a process of reasoning from premises of the Jewish theology to the conclusion that his death was an atonement for the sins of men, and on this doctrine is founded that of the new righteousness by faith, the abolition of the law, the overthrow of sin and death, and by a marvellous stroke of religious genius the mystic union of the believer with Christ in the fellowship of the Spirit, the blessedness, the sonship, the victory. The Pharisaic doctrine of the last things furnished the idea of the great consummation, the coming of the glorified Messiah in his kingdom "with all his saints," the resurrection of the believers, Christ being the "first fruits," the "peace and joy" of the kingdom in which God should be "all in all." How, then, did Paul come to believe in the resurrection of Jesus? That he had heard of it cannot be doubted. That he did not believe it while he was persecuting the Christians is certain, for otherwise he would have been one of them. As a Pharisee, the doctrine of the resurrection "at the last day" was not new to him. But why should he have believed in this miracle of the special resurrection of Jesus? What he had witnessed at the martyrdom of Stephen, and perhaps of other Christians, may have made a strong impression upon him, and given him the idea of the glorified Jesus "sitting at the right hand of God" (Acts vii. 55). The transformation may have been completed by a vision of Christ (1 Cor. xv. 8), which, in the conditions to which he was subject, would be regarded by him as representing an objective reality according to 2 Cor. xii. 1-4.*

---

* According to the generally accepted chronology of Paul's life and work, his conversion was in the year 34 or 35 of our era. This chronology is based upon the dating of the appointment of Festus as procurator in the year 60 or 61. Harnack dates Festus' appointment in the year 56 and the conversion accordingly in the year 30. A detailed discussion of this matter is remote from the purpose of this work, and it is sufficient to remark that Harnack's data are not of a character to place his conclusion beyond question. For a discussion of Harnack's construction the reader is referred to an article by Professor F. W. Christie in *The New World* for September, 1897. See also Heuduck, *Die Chronol. der neutest. Schriften*, in *Evan. Kirchenzeitung.* 1897, No. 3 f., and Schürer, *Zur Chronol. des Lebens Pauli*, in *Zeitschr. für wissenschaftl. Theol.* 1897, i. pp. 21-42.

PART II

THE MISSIONARY

CHAPTER IV

THE FIRST YEARS—GALATIA AND THE GALATIAN EPISTLE

THE man Paul could not but become Paul the apostle. He could not, however, be simply an apostle, a Jewish-Christian apostle, but must of necessity become the apostle to the gentiles. To be this lay in his nature, which permitted him to do nothing by halves. The call of God, who revealed His Son in him, that he "might preach him among the heathen" (Gal. i. 15), was the objective apprehension and expression of a subjective necessity,—a necessity of his nature, a requirement of his reason and conscience. His Epistles show, as we have seen, the method of his thinking to have been the treatment of a subject from the point of view of its fundamental principle, which he followed out to its logical consequences. The death of Christ as an atonement for sin was the central thought of his Christian belief, and we have seen that without this apprehension of it, that is, if he had regarded it as only a martyrdom for a principle, he could never have become a Christian. To him the cross must symbolise "the end of the law" and the overthrow of the Jewish dispensation with its bondage and its whole system of righteousness by works. Accordingly, a Christianity which was only another form of Judaism was impossible to him. This is clear from his declaration that "if righteousness come by the law, then Christ is dead in vain" (Gal. ii. 21). The logical conclusion from these premises to such a mind as Paul's was that the law being abolished, Jews and gentiles, those "under the law" and those "not under the law," were on an equality in the Christian dispensation. Christ was "the end of the law" not to Jews only, but to all who should believe. "If ye be Christ's," he writes to a gentile church, "then are ye Abraham's seed, and heirs according to the promise" (Gal. iii. 29). This is the logical side of the apostleship to the gentiles. It has also its emotional side.

That Paul had an irresistible natural impulse to defend and propagate his convictions is evident from his own confessions. The man who before his conversion to Christianity was a Jewish zealot and persecutor could not become a merely passive believer in the new religion. He felt that he was born to be an apostle, a missionary, an evangelist. He designates himself as one "called to be an apostle of Jesus Christ by the will of God" (1 Cor. i. 1). "Necessity is laid upon me," he says, "yea, woe is me if I preach not the gospel" (1 Cor. ix. 16). The matter demanded haste, and he set himself to the task with eager interest and unquenchable zeal. "The time is short" to him, for the Lord Christ would soon come to establish his kingdom, and he was zealous to "present" to him on that great day a multitude of believers as his "crown," his "joy" (1 Thess. ii. 19). His was not a nature capable of enjoying alone the blessedness of the new faith and its promises. Christ died for all, and the apostle's hope was that the Master's kingdom when he came might be universal. With the love of Christ for all men he grieved especially over his "brethren according to the flesh" because of their blindness, and we have a revelation of the great missionary's heart in the words: "Brethren, my heart's desire and prayer to God for Israel is that they might be saved" (Rom. x. 1).

With all his zeal for the gentile mission the salvation

of the Jews lay near the apostle's heart. He could not forget that for them the Messiah's kingdom was primarily intended, and that the Messiah was "of the seed of David according to the flesh." His eager desire for the evangelisation of "Jew and Greek" alike is expressed in the words: "For whosoever shall call on the name of the Lord shall be saved. How then shall they call on him in whom they have not believed? and how shall they believe in him of whom they have not heard? and how shall they hear without a preacher? and how shall they preach except they be sent?" (Rom. x. 13-15). His dream of the kingdom of Christ so ardently expected and longed for was that it should not only contain "the fulness of the gentiles," but that in it also "all Israel" would be "saved" (Rom. xi. 25, 26). Attention has already been called to the fact that it was far from the apostle's thought to be the founder of a system of theology. The ruling impulse of his life was to carry the gospel of Jesus, his gospel, the Pauline good news of universal grace, far and wide, up and down in the earth. "I have planted," he says, and to put the seed of Christian truth in new soil was the mission to which he was "called." "According to the grace of God which is given unto me," he writes to the Corinthians, "as a wise master-builder I have laid the foundation, and another buildeth thereon" (1 Cor. iii. 10). He conceived Christ to have wrought by him wondrous things "to make the gentiles obedient by word and deed." With the true spirit of the pioneer he sought out new fields, and strove "to preach the gospel, not where Christ was named," lest he should "build on another man's foundation" (Rom. xv. 18, 20), but where the good tidings had not been proclaimed.

To a man of such impulses and ambitions the appropriate gifts could not have been wanting. For what is a "call" but the inward cry of capacities and powers for an opportunity to fulfil their destiny? We have no means of forming an adequate conception of the apostle as a preacher. The discourses attributed to him in Acts cannot be exact reproductions, but must be compositions based upon what he was reputed to have said, and embellished according to the fancy of the writer. But we may conclude from many passages in his Epistles that, notwithstanding the charge of his enemies that "his bodily presence was weak, and his speech contemptible" (2 Cor. x. 10), he was a speaker of no little fire, passion, and persuasion. In Rom. vii. and viii. are manifested graphic power and moving pathos, and in 1 Cor xiii. he attains to lyric beauty and classic completeness. It is the inward man, the conviction, the earnestness, the pent-up fire, that moves, and is mighty "to the pulling down of strongholds"; and if a man have these qualities he may be a power even with a fragile body and an unprepossessing exterior. Whatever advantage in convincing, moving, and controlling men belongs to him who has the courage of his convictions was certainly on the side of the apostle as a missionary. The boldness with which he preached his gospel of liberty and his fearless defence of it against the judaisers could not but captivate and hold to his cause a class of minds whose support was essential to its success. To this was joined the intensity that sprang from the concentration of his thought upon one theme which he made central in his ministry — that of the cross. "For I was determined," he writes to the Corinthians, "to know nothing among you save Jesus Christ and him crucified" (1 Cor. ii. 3).

There was one preëminent qualification, moreover, to which, however we may seek to explain it psychologically, the apostle's power as a preacher was largely due. He believed that his word was not his own, but that he spoke by the authority of the Spirit. A superhuman power, now conceived as the Spirit of God, now as Christ, was to him not only the source of his "gospel," but also a constant inspiration. "I can do all things," he declares, "through him who strengtheneth me" (Phil. iv. 13). To the Corinthians he writes: "And my speech and my preaching were not with enticing words of man's wisdom, but in demonstration of the Spirit and of power" (1 Cor. ii. 4). Again in the same chapter (vv. 12, 13) he says: "Now we have received not the spirit of the world, but the Spirit which is of God, that we might know the things that are freely given us of God; which things we also speak, not in the words which man's wisdom teacheth, but which the Holy Ghost teacheth, comparing spiritual things with spiritual." The power which a man with such a consciousness of communion with the unseen world, whose gaze was fixed upon the things that are invisible and eternal, could wield over the simple-minded who were predisposed to a belief in the supernatural, is not easily conceived by us at this distance and in this age.

This inner light, this "revelation," this "witness" of the Spirit with his spirit (Rom. viii. 16), was the source of the apostle's religious life and experience. Here was the basis of his religious belief, his "seat of authority," on which he placed the utmost reliance, not indeed without dogma, but through and beyond all dogma. His theism, his doctrine of Christ, of the atonement, and of the resurrection, were all lifeless to him without this direct illumination of his consciousness from above, without the divine witness that he was a son of God, and without the mystic fellowship with Christ in which he became one with him. This independence of external authority, of tradition, and of human counsel and experience, which would have been hazardous to a man without Paul's religious genius and sobriety of judgment, was to him indispensable, and wanting it he could not have undertaken his mission. For his "gospel" was not that of the original apostles. He must, then, have a new one, or he had none. Whence was he to derive it? Not from the tradition of the teaching of Christ of which he knew but little. He had no recourse but to his own consciousness illuminated by the Spirit and glowing with the spiritual baptism of immediate fellowship with Jesus. We find no evidence of any speculation of his on the psychology or philosophy of this experience. "The light of the knowledge of the glory of God" which had dawned in his mind he ascribed to the immediate operation of the Spirit, or to the indwelling Christ. The speculative and dialectic interest, which was so strong in him where questions of doctrine were concerned, did not lead him upon this holy ground. We may well hesitate to venture upon it and to attempt an analysis and definition of that which to him was unanalysable and indefinable. Let it suffice us here to note that this consciousness of divine quickening and guidance made him very bold, and produced an astonishing self-reliance.

When the light of his new gospel dawned upon Paul — an event which, he implies, occurred at Damascus — instead of seeking for information and instruction as to the personality, life, and teachings of Jesus from those who had had intercourse with him, he boasts that he "conferred not with flesh and blood," but "went into Arabia, and returned again to Damascus." He does not specifically mention a reason for this action, but the natural inference from his words (Gal. i. 16, 17) is that he did not feel the need of such a conference. The evident intention, the motive, of the passage is a distinct declaration of his independence of human teachers and of the knowledge of Christ which the apostles might have given him. Weizsäcker's remark that "the most probable explanation [of this procedure] is that the external relations, dangers, which immediately threatened him on account of the step he had taken, made it necessary," is not based upon any legitimate inference from the apostle's own declaration. It was not until three years later that he went up to Jerusalem, and during this period, passed between Arabia and Damascus (for that he was in Arabia all this time is an unwarrantable assumption), he must have matured his purpose, and formed his plans for his life work. Why he three years later decided to go to Jerusalem he does not inform us; but we shall not err in assuming that it was not to seek instruction in the gospel from the original apostles or from any one of them. This would be contrary to the manifest intention of his words. The same reason that restrained him from seeking an interview with them immediately after his conversion must, on the assumption of his honesty, be operative at a later period. If his "revelation" was sufficient, he could not at any time be false to it.

What the motive of this visit to Jerusalem was, is in the absence of any intimation regarding it by the apostle himself purely a matter of conjecture. We may positively say that he did not think that in taking this step he was prejudicing his position as "an apostle not of men, neither by man, but by Jesus Christ and God the Father." His refraining for three years from seeking counsel of man was sufficient to show his independence and his consistency with his claim of an adequate revelation from above. His mention of the limitation which he imposed upon himself in Jerusalem as to intercourse with the apostles can hardly have been made without a purpose. He says he saw

Peter, and abode with him fifteen days, but that he saw no other of the apostles, but only James, the brother of Jesus. Was his motive in going to Jerusalem perhaps to ascertain the attitude of these two prominent leaders of the church in that city toward his mission to the gentiles? If he came to any understanding with them at this time on this subject, we may conclude from subsequent events that it was not a radical and thorough one. That their opposition to him was not violent is probable from the fact that he does not intimate that there was any, but says that afterwards when he carried on his mission in "the regions of Syria and Cilicia," and "the churches of Judea" heard that their former persecutor was a preacher of "the faith which he once destroyed," "they glorified God" in him (Gal. i. 22, 23), although "the pillar-apostles" in Jerusalem are not necessarily included in this statement. The mission to Jerusalem appears to have been a private and confidential one in any case, and the inference is legitimate, that Paul wished to avoid the irritation to which a public discussion of the grounds of his new gospel might have given rise, and that his procedure indicates "how much there yet was to be overcome, how much yet lay between Paul and the believing Jews in Jerusalem." The presumption is a very natural one that he here learned something of the events of the life of Jesus and of his teaching, although neither the former nor the latter occupies a very prominent place in the writings that he has left. For a discussion of the account of the first years of Paul's work given in Acts, the writer of which omits all mention of the journey into Arabia and the three-years' interval, and brings him directly from Damascus to Jerusalem, the reader is referred to Chapter VII., in which the relation of that book to the Epistles is considered. In regard to the matter in question, it will suffice to quote here Weizsäcker's remark, that "the narrative of Acts is as clearly and completely excluded by Paul himself as it possibly could be."

In one point the account in Acts agrees substantially, however, with a statement made by the apostle himself, that regarding his narrow escape from death at Damascus: "In Damascus," he says, "the governor under Aretas the king kept the city of the Damascenes with a garrison, desirous to apprehend me; and through a window in a basket I was let down by the wall, and escaped his hands" (2 Cor. xi. 32 f.). The account in Acts omits mention of Aretas and the governor and the garrison, and ascribes the persecution to "the Jews" (Acts ix. 23–25). This happened, according to this narrative, "some days" after the conversion, and since the journey to Arabia is here omitted, we cannot learn from it whether it was before or after it; and since, moreover, in the passage in 2 Corinthians the incident is simply mentioned without reference to its connection with other events, it is impossible to assign it a definite place in the apostle's career. Paul says in Galatians that after going to Arabia he returned to Damascus. It is hardly probable, accordingly, that the persecution and escape occurred prior to the departure for Arabia, since he would not be likely to come back to Damascus where he would be exposed to so great a danger. The peril and escape are more probably assigned to the period subsequent to his return from Arabia, and there seems to be no good reason for the conjecture that they find their place during a third visit to Damascus after the fifteen days spent with Peter in Jerusalem; a visit of which the apostle makes no mention, and for which he can hardly be said to leave room, when he says, "afterwards I came into the regions of Syria and Cilicia" (Gal. i. 21).

Of this period of the apostle's work, occupying fourteen

years, we have unhappily no details. He simply says that he was employed in these regions, and "was unknown by face to the churches of Judea," which "glorified God" in him when they heard that he, the former persecutor, was "preaching the faith that he once destroyed" (Gal. i. 22–24). The natural inference from this is that he was undisturbed in his work in Syria and Cilicia by interference from Jerusalem. That he was here occupied with the gentile mission is probable, one may almost say certain; from what we know of him and from the predominant purpose of his life according to his interpretation of the "call" of God "by his grace" (Gal. i. 15). Hausrath's contention that during this period he was a preacher of the circumcision, a Jewish-Christian apostle, carrying on a mission in the synagogues acceptable to the Jerusalem authorities, is not well supported, to say nothing of its antecedent improbability. There is not the slightest intimation of such a mission in the section in Galatians under consideration. On the contrary, in immediate connection with the mention of his mission in Syria and Cilicia, the apostle gives an account of his journey to Jerusalem to communicate to the leaders of the Jewish-Christian church "the gospel" which he preached "among the gentiles," "lest by any means," he says, "I should run or had run in vain" (Gal. ii. 2). The natural reference of this passage is to the preceding fourteen years. In fact we cannot find any other period of his life to which it relates, for the "had run" implies a mission prior to the conference in question. The appeal to the passage in Gal. v. 17: "And I, brethren, if I yet preach circumcision, why do I yet suffer persecution," cannot sustain the contention.

For there is no reference here to any particular period of the apostle's ministry. The argument of the passage is that his preaching of uncircumcision is an offence to the

Jewish-Christian opponents who were troubling the Galatians, an "offence of the cross"; if he continue to promulgate circumcision this offence would disappear so far as they are concerned, and this offence being taken away, their persecution of him ceases. The only purpose of the passage is to make it apparent to the Galatians that he is persecuted solely because he is not a preacher of circumcision, and it does not by any means follow from these words that, during fourteen years of his ministry or indeed at any time since he became a Christian apostle, he had been an advocate of a teaching directly opposed to that "gospel" to which he had been especially "called." The hazard of hanging upon a single passage of somewhat doubtful interpretation the doctrine that the apostle did not really begin the mission of his life till after fourteen years of judaising, is too manifest to require farther argument. His declaration, moreover, that "to those under the law" he was "as under the law" cannot fairly be pressed into the support of the position in question. In being "all things to all men" the apostle never compromised his fundamental doctrine, otherwise his journey to the conference in Jerusalem and the Epistles to the Galatians and Corinthians are inexplicable. The fact that during at least a part of this period of fourteen years he was undisturbed by the church in Jerusalem, and that the Christians in Judea "glorified God" in him, indicates only that the attention of the apostles at the head of the Jewish-Christian organisation was not at first directed to the peculiar character of his work, and that the questions which called him to the conference were not agitated until later, that is, until toward the end of this mission in Syria and Cilicia. The "irrepressible conflict" was, however, inevitable.

That Paul was true to his gentile mission during this

period is apparent from the mention of Titus in Gal. ii. 3. This Greek was in all probability one of the converts made during the mission, and Paul took him to the conference in Jerusalem as an uncircumcised Christian according to his gospel, where he must have been an offence to the judaisers, who apparently brought a pressure upon the apostle to have him submit to the Jewish rite. But Paul writes in a tone of triumph to the Galatians that Titus was "not compelled to be circumcised." This reference to a single instance may be regarded as an indication of the general principle of his mission in the regions in question, and proves that here as elsewhere, in this earlier period as well as later, he accepted as Christians men of gentile birth without imposing Jewish rites upon them, and thus proceeded in accordance with the great principle of liberty in Christ, without which there could have been no mission to the heathen. It is significant of the point of view and purpose of Acts that Titus is not even mentioned in that book. The writer of it could find no place in his construction of primitive Christian history and of the relation of Paul to the original apostles for the bold procedure of taking an uncircumcised Greek believer into the stronghold of the circumcision. It appears that the apostle was not alone in his mission in Syria and Cilicia. The mention of Barnabas in Gal. ii. 1 as his companion on the journey to attend the conference in Jerusalem implies the participation of this Jewish Christian in his missionary work. He received also with Paul at the close of the conference "the right hand of fellowship, that we should go unto the heathen" (Gal. ii. 9). From the fact that when afterwards Peter came to Antioch, and after him "certain came from James," and induced him to withdraw from the relations which he had had with the gentile Christians, "other Jews dissembled likewise with him" (Gal. ii. 12), it appears that the church in Antioch was not composed entirely of converts from the heathen, but in part of Jewish Christians. This may be regarded as an indication of the general results of the mission in these regions. To say nothing of the apostle's ardent interest in the conversion of his "brethren according to the flesh," it is not probable that he should have made no effort to urge Jews to his apprehension of the gospel.

The understanding at the conference that Paul and Barnabas were to "go to the heathen," and the original apostles "to the circumcision," should not be so rigidly interpreted as to exclude the effort on both sides to bring any willing hearer into the Christian communion. The principle for which Paul contended was the freedom of his converts from the bondage of the law. The difficulty of organising purely gentile-Christian churches composed, as they must be, of men who had had no traditions connecting them with the antecedents of Christianity and no knowledge of the Scriptures, on which the apostolic preaching founded it, must have appeared to a man of Paul's insight insuperable. The Messiahship of Jesus could have little significance to men who were not familiar with the great Jewish hope in the Deliverer who was to come and with the prophetic writings of the Old Testament. Paul's doctrine of the atonement would also be with difficulty appreciated by minds not schooled in the Jewish theology, although heathenism did not wholly lack points of contact with it. It must, then, be regarded as the great good fortune of the mission to the gentiles that the churches founded by it contained a nucleus of converts from Judaism. It was also its good fortune that the man who conducted it was a Hellenist in sympathy with the thought of those whom he sought to win, and with a mind hospitable enough to receive and appropriate in his teaching certain ideas with which they were familiar, or in his own words, able to become "to those without the law as without law." In the hands of purely Jewish propagandists the gentile mission would have been a failure. A Jewish Christianity could not become a world-religion.

It is related in Acts that the disciples were first called Christians in Antioch (xi. 26) — a statement which there is no good reason for doubting. In connection with this, however, the construction of the history of this period which the author makes is open to question as to its accuracy. The manifest purpose is to make it appear that the missionary work in Syria was watched over and directed by the authorities in Jerusalem. That the church in Antioch was founded by "men of Cyprus and Cyrene" who fled from Jerusalem on occasion of "the persecution that arose about Stephen," and who there preached "unto the Grecians the Lord Jesus," is not incredible or improbable. The mission in Antioch may have been begun independently of Paul, and that it was a gentile Christian mission is evidently implied in the narrative in Acts xi. 20. But the account of the relations of Paul to the Jerusalem authorities given in this section is in the highest degree improbable from his own statement of the matter which we must regard as the historical source. He represents that the attitude of the church in Jerusalem toward his work in Syria and Cilicia was such that he was apprehensive that he "should run or had run in vain," and that the situation required that he should go up there, and set before the apostles the character and grounds of his mission. The legitimate inference from this is that during these fourteen years he had been the real representative of the gospel to the gentiles in those regions, and that this was his mission, and not one carried on chiefly by Barnabas and others to which the Jerusalem church stood as a foster mother.

But the writer of Acts, after relating that Paul's visit to Jerusalem, instead of being a private one to Peter, was a public one in which he was with the apostles, "coming in and going out at Jerusalem," and "speaking boldly in the name of the Lord and disputing with the Grecians" (Acts ix. 27–29), says that instead of his acting independently "the brethren brought him down to Cæsarea, and sent him forth to Tarsus." Here he is left until Barnabas, the representative of the apostles, goes and brings him to Antioch (Acts xi. 25, 26). In all this the motive to assign him a subordinate part is manifest, as is the attempt to make it appear that the gentile mission in Syria was watched over by the mother-church, and that such cordial relations existed between the two that relief was sent by the adherents of the former to the latter during a famine which a "prophet" from Jerusalem had foretold would extend "throughout all the world." To complete the series of improbabilities, Paul is made one of the messengers to carry this contribution to Jerusalem, although he says that until he went up there to the conference he was personally unknown "to the churches of Judea" (Acts xi. 30; Gal. i. 22); and plainly indicates that he did not make the journey after his first visit until he went for that purpose.*

Paul went to Jerusalem, then, to defend his mission as the self-conscious representative of a cause and a work which he thought to be in jeopardy from that source. He returned to his labours with a consciousness of victory. The apostles had accorded him "the right hand of fellowship," because they were convinced that "He who wrought effectually in Peter to the apostleship of the circumcision was mighty in him toward the gentiles" (Gal. ii. 8). We must not, however, draw too sweeping a conclusion from

* See Chapter VII.

this recognition that "grace was given" to Paul for his work. We may well believe rather that, as is the case in compromises generally, the whole question at issue was not ventured upon. A complete accord was in the nature of the case impossible. Paul's "revelation" had not been vouchsafed to Peter and James and John. They had not learned from Jesus that his death was "the end of the law," and that "if righteousness come by the law, Christ was dead in vain." That Paul demanded of them the full recognition of his gospel is improbable. To make such a demand were to lose his cause. He doubtless asked for what he actually obtained — the recognition of his freedom to preach his gospel to the gentiles as a missionary. He does not intimate that he secured a recognition of his apostleship, the claim to which he was afterwards so strenuous to maintain, when it was disputed by men who from the Jewish-Christian side came into his churches to oppose him (1 Cor. ix. 1–5).* If it was accorded to Paul that his gentile converts should not be subjected to circumcision, the full observance of the law was doubtless reserved for the Jewish-Christian believers. A complete accord between the two parties to the controversy would have required a recognition of the principle that the way of salvation was the same for Jewish and gentile converts, either by the observance of the law or by its non-observance on both sides. But subsequent events show that no such agreement was reached. Paul certainly did not yield his doctrine that salvation is without the works of the law, and the apostles did not abandon their doctrine that the law was the way of life. We cannot think of them as admitting that righteousness is not "through the law," that they who are under the law are under a "curse" (Gal. iii. 10), and that in a Christian experience it "is found to be

* It is significant that the writer of Acts studiously avoids this recognition.

unto death" (Rom. vii. 10). In "the right hand of fellowship that he should go unto the heathen" was not implied the settlement of the question as to the relations of Jewish-Christian and gentile converts in churches composed of both. We have no intimation that this important matter was discussed at all.

If Paul understood the compact to mean that both classes should associate on an equality, and eat at the same table, it is evident that James did not so construe it (Gal. ii. 12). That a Jew should overcome the deep-seated repugnance of his race for the uncleanness of heathenism required his endowment with the "grace" of Paul, just as his recognition of the doctrine that Christ was "the end of the law" was impossible without the great apostle's religious insight and genius. That Paul in this matter had "the Spirit of Christ" no one will now dispute. In his doctrine that in Christ "there is neither Jew nor Greek," and that the spiritual relation of man to God is one of inward union of the human with the divine will in independence of outward forms, he rescued from Jewish Christianity, and preserved for mankind our most precious inheritance in Jesus. That he was glad to accede to the request to "remember the poor" among the Jewish Christians is in accord with his doctrine that "all are one in Christ Jesus" (Gal. ii. 10, iii. 28). However defective the compact in question was, on account of insuperable prejudices and opposing irreconcilable points of view, it is of vast importance in so far as the recognition of the Pauline mission laid the foundations of a Christian church for the world.

The incompleteness of the Jerusalem compact became soon after apparent at Antioch, where Peter joined with other Jewish Christians in eating at the same table with the gentile converts, but withdrew from this fellowship when emissaries "from James" apparently brought the influence of that leader to bear upon him (Gal. ii. 12). The situation was critical for both parties. The authorities in Jerusalem could not but see that for Peter to make such a concession was practically the abandonment of the principle for which they contended. On the other hand, Paul's cause was in peril, for the contagion of Peter's "dissembling" extended to "the other Jews" in the church at Antioch, and "Barnabas also was carried away with their dissimulation" (Gal. ii. 13). The procedure of Paul in the emergency reveals the leading traits of his character, decision, the courage of his convictions, inflexibility, inexorable logic. Not to take a decided position now was to lose his cause and to be false to his "gospel." The vacillation of Peter filled him with indignation. He had him at a great disadvantage, and he did not fail to improve his opportunity. He charges him with hypocrisy for having fellowshipped the gentile Christians apparently on principle, and immediately changed his policy, because "he feared them who were of the circumcision." Whether Peter in previous interviews had substantially adopted Paul's interpretation of Christianity or no is not important here. Paul's charge "to his face" before the assembled church was well founded on the fact that he had freely associated with the gentiles at first, and had retreated through fear. He had acted according to the Pauline principle that "there is nothing unclean of itself" (Rom. xiv. 14), and had then been intimidated, and driven into a course of conduct which was a declaration that he regarded his gentile brethren as unclean. He had suffered the spirit of Christ which had ruled him for a time to be driven out of his breast by the fear of man. From Paul's pointed question, which exposes Peter's inconsistency: "If thou being a Jew livest after the manner of the gentiles [as he had done there in Antioch] and not as do the Jews, why compellest thou the gentiles to live as do the Jews?" it may be inferred that the latter had endeavoured to force the gentile believers to accept the Jewish rites.

This of course aggravated Peter's offence in the eyes of Paul. Perhaps he had justified his withdrawal by the declaration that the gentiles were by nature "sinners," unclean, from the Jewish point of view. In any case Paul takes up this thought, and says: "We Jews by nature, and not [as you say] sinners of the gentiles, knowing that a man is not justified by the works of the law, but by the faith of Jesus Christ, even we have believed in Jesus Christ, that we might be justified by the faith of Christ, and not by the works of the law; for by the works of the law shall no flesh be justified" (Gal. ii. 14-16). The inference from these words is that of the two, Paul alone had acted consistently with the profession of Christian faith. Why should one call oneself a Christian at all, if one is still to attain righteousness in the old way of the law? But, the apostle continues, in seeking this new righteousness by faith, in disregarding the works of the law, and in living like gentiles and with them we are not "sinners," are not unclean, otherwise Christ is "the minister of sin" (Gal. ii. 17). The seeking after justification through faith in Christ, the practical overthrow of the law, is no sin, but "if I build again the things which I destroyed [seek to restore the law and attain righteousness by works] I make myself a transgressor" (Gal. ii. 18). By restoring the law, which was done away in Christ, by seeking righteousness as Peter would have it sought, he would put himself in the way of becoming a transgressor, because there is transgression only where there is law (Rom. iv. 15). But "through the law," he adds (by reason of the fact that according to the law the penalty of sin is death), "I am dead to the law . . . I am crucified with Christ" (Gal. ii. 19; see Rom. vii. 4). To do otherwise is to "frustrate the grace of God."

It would be unjust to charge James, and Peter in following him perhaps through fear of excommunication, with a violation of the agreement made with Paul in Jerusalem. For, as has already been pointed out, that agreement did not contemplate and provide for a situation like that in Antioch, where the relations of Jewish and gentile Christians in a mixed church were concerned. The rupture in Antioch showed the hollowness of the compromise, showed that in fact there could be no adjustment of differences so radical. The gentile church was not born of the compact in Jerusalem, which was adapted only to men who do things by halves, but of the conflict in Antioch, out of which the great apostle who never did anything by halves came forth at last the victor.

Among the missionary-fields of the apostle which have an imperishable record in his Epistles that of the churches of Galatia is one of the most important. It is remote from our purpose to enter upon a discussion of the question of the exact location of these churches, that is, whether they lay in the Roman province in which were the cities of Derbe and Lystra or in the northern region inhabited chiefly by Celts. The greater probability appears to be in favour of the former hypothesis, but the decision of the question does not affect the character of Paul's missionary work and the conflict in which he was involved on behalf of the Galatian churches. We have already seen that Paul declares explicitly in Galatians that the first fourteen years of his work succeeding his visit to Peter in Jerusalem were passed in "the regions of Syria and Cilicia," after which he went up to Jerusalem for conference with the apostles. On the contrary the writer of Acts records a mission of "Barnabas and Saul" in Cyprus, Pamphilia, Pisidia, and Lykaonia (Acts xiii., xiv.), prior to the conference in Jerusalem. Since Paul could not have included these regions in "Syria and Cilicia," it is probable that the order of time in Acts is not historical, and that we have here one of the many deviations of this book from the course of events indicated in the Epistles. Although the legendary character of many of the events recorded in these chapters is evident, the account of the journey appears to have an historical basis in the names of the cities visited, and it is not improbable that we have here such a narrative of the beginnings of the Galatian churches as might have been written at the end of the first or the beginning of the second century by such a writer from the fragmentary sources at his disposal. There is no reason on the ground of intimations in the Epistle to the Galatians for assuming that the churches of that name were founded prior to the conference in Jerusalem. The words in Gal. ii. 5: "To whom we gave place by subjection, no, not for an hour, that the truth of the gospel might continue with you," do not contain such an implication, for the entire fortune of the gentile mission was at stake in the contest, and a special application is made to the Galatians in the Epistle as gentiles whose interest in the issue did not depend upon the time of their conversion. Gal. iv. 13 contains a reference to two visits to these churches prior to the writing of the Epistle. "Ye know how," the apostle writes, "through infirmity of the flesh I preached the gospel to you at the first," that is, the first time. The sources at our disposal do not make this matter clear beyond question, and we cannot do better than resort to Weizsäcker's conjecture that the second visit was on the return journey of the first missionary tour recorded in Acts xiv. 21-26, or that it occurred on the second missionary journey (Acts xvi.).

The Epistle to the Galatians is exceedingly bare of references to the external conditions of the churches, such as their locations, the journeys made in founding them, and the attendant circumstances and incidents. The internal situation was the urgent matter that called the Epistle forth, and with this it is intensely occupied. Apart from this particular exigency, however, occasional intimations occur which throw light upon the antecedents of the converts and the character of the mission. There is no reason for doubting that the Galatian churches were composed chiefly of converts from heathenism. This appears from the words: "Howbeit, then, when ye knew not God, ye did service unto them which by nature are no gods" (Gal. iv. 8). Not the existence, but the divinity of the beings formerly worshipped, is here denied. They belong to "the weak and beggarly elements," that is, elementary powers mentioned in the next verse which were associated with the Jewish observance of "days and months and times and years" (verse 10) as the spirits of the heavenly bodies (Gal. iv. 3). In iii. 13, "bought us off from the curse of the law," "us" apparently refers to the Jews, but the immediately following words, "that the blessing of Abraham might come on the gentiles," denotes that not Jewish-Christian, but gentile-Christian readers were in the writer's mind. To these simple-minded idolaters Paul, detained among them by his infirmity, preached his gospel of theism, of the one true God, and of the great redemption through Jesus Christ, of the sonship into which they were born by reason of their acceptance of the atonement, of the Spirit which as sons they receive (iv. 6), of the love of God, who sent His Son to deliver them "from this present evil world" (i. 4), of the faith through which they received the Spirit that by works could not have been theirs (iii. 2), and of the liberty to which through Christ they were called (v. 13).

That the question of "another gospel" had been touched upon in his preaching either on his first or second visit is clear from i. 9: "As we said before, so say I now again, if any man preach another gospel . . . let him be accursed," and an echo of the contest with the judaisers is plainly heard in the words: "For I testify again to every man that is circumcised that he is a debtor to the whole law" (v. 3). Here "before" and "again" indicate that he had in his original teaching warned them against the enemies of his gospel who might come to "spy out their liberty" and "bring them into bondage" (ii. 4).

The unhappy situation which called forth the Epistle full of energy and passion soon intervened. "I marvel," he writes, "that ye are so soon removed from him that called you into the grace of Christ unto another gospel" (i. 6). From the question: "Am I therefore become your enemy, because I tell you the truth?" we may infer that his opponents had so represented him to the churches. He doubtless knew to whom the disturbance of the faith of his converts was chargeable, but he does not definitely indicate him or them in the Epistle. In immediate connection he speaks of one and more, "he who troubleth you" and "they who trouble you" (v. 10, 12). There can be no question as to the source from which the "trouble" came and as to the authorisation of those who had made it. The rupture at Antioch had doubtless made the judaisers in Jerusalem more than ever determined to employ every means in their power to uproot the Pauline gospel. We have, indeed, no proof that James or Peter or John sent emissaries among the Galatians to antagonise the apostle by sowing disaffection among his converts. But that such a work should have been undertaken without the sanction of those in authority is extremely improbable. When the men went to Antioch to set Peter right from the Jerusalem point of view, Paul distinctly says that they came "from James," and this circumstance furnishes a presumption in favour of a similar authorisation in the case in hand.*

What was the message which these emissaries brought, and what were their arguments? The Galatians believed that in becoming Christians they had an inheritance in the kingdom of Christ. So Paul had doubtless taught them. If they were sons of God (iv. 5), then they were "heirs," who would at Christ's coming in his kingdom be "glorified together" with him (Rom. viii. 17). The judaisers doubtless endeavoured to convince them that they were not really God's people and could not be until they entered the ancient and only true household of faith through submission to Jewish rites (vi. 12, 13), and observed the Jewish forms, days, etc. (iv. 10). The note of personal sensitiveness and defence in the Epistle indicates that his claim to the apostleship had also been impugned. Hence the earnest defence of his position, the reference to the "revelation" that he had received, and the assertion of his independence. To this attack upon him we owe the account of the contest with Peter in Antioch, for which

---

* The Epistles to the Galatians and the Corinthians are unintelligible on the theory of Paul's relation to the Jerusalem apostles put forth by Lightfoot in the dissertation, *St. Paul and the Three*, in *St. Paul's Epistle to the Galatians*, 1866. He sees in Paul's earlier visit to Jerusalem the purpose of obtaining "instruction in the facts of the gospel," and accordingly a "recognition of the authority of the elder apostles." This is an improbable motive to attribute to one who expressly declares that he did not confer with flesh and blood. As to recognising the "authority" of the apostles, nothing is more evident than that he nowhere admits their superiority to himself. Dr. Lightfoot's teaching, moreover, that in the conference "the Three" admitted in Paul "a perfect equality" with themselves, is not supported by the facts which the Epistles disclose. There is no evidence that they recognised him as an *apostle*. On the contrary, James sent emissaries to Antioch to compel Peter to act in direct antagonism to him, as one without coördinate authority.

the writer of Acts found no place in his scheme of the history of primitive Christianity. A few words in the Epistle indicate the power wielded by the apostles in Jerusalem, and show the grounds of Peter's fear of "those who were of the circumcision," when he withdrew from the gentiles at Antioch. Paul charges the emissaries who disturbed the Galatians with striving to constrain them to be circumcised, "lest they [of the mission] should suffer persecution for the cross of Christ" (vi. 12). This plainly shows not only that they had orders to go among the Galatians on this mission, but also that they did not dare refuse for fear of the authorities. To suffer persecution "for the cross of Christ" meant for Paul to suffer it for advocating his gospel that in the cross the law was done away. This throws light on a difficult passage already considered: "If I yet preach circumcision, why am I yet persecuted" (v. 11)? in which, it has been conjectured, he employs substantially the words of his opponents who may have represented to the Galatians that Paul could not be preaching the right kind of gospel from the point of view of the only competent authorities, for if he were, why would these authorities be against him?

The answer of the apostle to his opponents is a vindication of the principles of his own gospel. After pronouncing a curse upon those who pervert the truth as it is in Jesus and showing the grounds on which his apostleship rests, he makes clear to the Galatians the real significance of accepting Judaism. It is no light matter to assume the yoke of the law, for "he who is circumcised is a debtor to do the whole law" (v. 3). He that is under the law is "under a curse," for it is written in the law itself that every one is cursed "who continueth not in all things which are written in the book of the law to do them" (iii. 10). Judaism in its observance of years and days and months is no better than the heathenism out of which they had come, but like it is a subjection to the weak and beggarly elemental powers, which are "no gods." If they accept circumcision, "Christ is become of no effect," and they are "fallen from grace," having rejected the gospel of grace whose righteousness is not that of works. He shows them that all that the judaisers claim for themselves as inheritors of the promise to Abraham belongs also to the gentiles on the condition of faith, and that in Christ there is neither Jew nor Greek (iii. 14-29). Against all the requirements of the judaisers and the perils of accepting them he lays down the one injunction: "Walk in the Spirit, and ye shall not fulfil the lusts of the flesh"; for if they are led by the Spirit they are not under the law (v. 16, 18). "The fruit of the Spirit is love, joy, peace, longsuffering, gentleness, goodness, faith, meekness, temperance." Against those who do these things the law can make no charge (v. 22, 23). This brief Epistle is one of the most important documents of primitive Christianity in so far as it reveals the condition of parties, the personality and struggles of Paul, and the powers with which he had to contend. If it is one-sided in its judgment of the law and incomplete in its exposition of the apostle's gospel, it was not written with the purpose of expounding either. It doubtless in a good degree attained its end as a defence of the author and an exhortation to the churches. On the south-Galatian theory it was written at Antioch soon after the council in Jerusalem, and subsequent to the second visit to Derbe and Lystra. Those who support the north-Galatian hypothesis place the composition at Ephesus in the year 55, a date which must be changed to 50 if Harnack's construction be adopted.

CHAPTER V

PHILIPPI, THESSALONICA, CORINTH

THE beginning of Paul's missionary work in Europe was made in Philippi of Macedonia, an inland city with a harbor, Neapolis, opening into the Ægean Sea on the north. It is related in Acts that after he had "gone through Phrygia and the region of Galatia" on his second missionary journey, he was "forbidden of the Holy Ghost to preach the word in Asia," and that in a "vision in the night" a man of Macedonia appeared to him and "prayed him saying, Come over into Macedonia, and help us" (xvi. 6, 9). The mission in Philippi is mentioned by Paul himself in 1 Thess. ii. 2, where he speaks of sufferings there which appear to have left a deep impression upon him and of going thence to Thessalonica. His companions on this mission were Timothy and Silas (Acts xv. 40, xvi. 1–4, xvii. 14, 15; 1 Thess. i. 1, iii. 2; Phil. i. 1, ii. 19). The account in Acts of the apostle's work in Philippi is very meagre, but a portion of it is important, since it is based upon the "we-sections," which were probably fragments of a journal kept by one of his companions. The limits of these sections are not precisely determinable, and we do not know with how much freedom the writer of Acts employed them. Weizsäcker assigns in chapter xvi., verses 10–24 and 35–39, to the "we-sections." It is not certain that there was a synagogue here, although that there were Jews is evident from Acts xvi. 13: "On the Sabbath we went out of the city by a river-side where prayer was wont to be made." In any case, there is no mention here in this doubtless most trustworthy source of Acts of an attempt to preach to the Jews — a procedure which is elsewhere so regularly recorded as to give rise to the suspicion of a purpose on the part of the writer to make it appear that the gentile mission was secondary to that to the Jews in the apostle's thought.

Here a woman "named Lydia, a seller of purple, of the city of Thyatira, who worshipped God, heard," was converted, and baptized with her household (Acts xvi. 14). From the circumstance that she "worshipped God" the inference is not to be drawn that she was a proselyte to Judaism (see the case of Cornelius, Acts x. 1, 2-28, 35, xi. 1, 18, xv. 7). In the Epistle to the Philippians two other women are mentioned, Euodias and Syntyche (Phil. iv. 2). Mention is also made of the casting out of an unclean spirit from "a certain damsel" (Acts xvi. 16-18), which may be regarded as an example of the "miracles" of which Paul speaks as the signs of his apostleship (2 Cor. xii. 12) and as among the "gifts of the Spirit" (1 Cor. xii. 28).* The story of the imprisonment and the miraculous

* That Paul should have believed himself to be possessed of supernatural powers is not surprising when we consider his doctrine of the Spirit. The "gifts" bestowed by this indwelling divine principle were conceived by him to be supernatural in the sense that they came from God, and were not explicable as productions of the natural human faculties. His entire theology, his teaching of salvation, of Christology, and of eschatology, proceeds, moreover, upon premises of the divine interference. It is true that he does not often appeal to outward "signs" as an evidence of his apostleship, but rather to his "call" and to the fruits of his mission (Gal. i. 1; 1 Cor. ix. 1 f.; 2 Cor. iii. 2 f.). His call, however, was conceived to be supernatural and effected by a revelation by God of His Son in him (Gal. i. 16), and his message he regarded as of the same origin (1 Cor. ii. 10-16). The speaking with a tongue, in which he thanked God he was proficient above all the Corinthian Christians, he thought to be one of the gifts of the Spirit (1 Cor. xii. 10, xiv. 18). He appears accordingly to have believed that an apostle possessed in a greater measure than other Christians the supernatural powers common to all of them as πνευματικοί or those having the Spirit. This idea is implied in the expression,

deliverance is invalidated not only by its legendary features, but by the improbability that Paul should have allowed himself to be ill treated when the mention of his Roman citizenship would have prevented such a procedure, as is apparent from the account itself (Acts xvi. 37, 38). "Only one thing stands here," says Weizsäcker, "not as the kernel of the narrative, but as the condition of its origin, that during his sojourn in Philippi Paul was in great distress . . . and was obliged to flee." When five years later (58, according to the generally accepted chronology) he went from Ephesus the second time into Macedonia, giving "much exhortation" to the believers (Acts xx. 2), he says that he had no rest, "without were fightings, within were fears" (2 Cor. vii. 5; see also i. 16, ii. 13), but the character of his opponents is not mentioned. A visit to Philippi is doubtless implied.

About ten years after the establishment of the church in Philippi Paul wrote a letter to the believers here from his prison in Rome. That in the interval other letters were written them is probable, but the canonical Epistle to the Philippians is the only one that has been preserved, and is our sole source of information as to the relations of the apostle with this church. From this we learn that these relations were undisturbed by such unhappy complications as those in the Galatian churches. There is no intimation

---

"signs of an apostle." That the gift to perform "miracles" as well as various wonderful works was thought to be possessed by others than apostles is evident from 1 Cor. xii. 8–10, 28. The Epistles of Paul furnish no data for forming a conception of the nature of these "signs" ($\sigma\eta\mu\epsilon\iota\alpha$) and "mighty works" ($\delta\upsilon\nu\acute{\alpha}\mu\epsilon\iota\varsigma$). They were phenomena of an age in which ignorance of the natural forces gave free scope to the invoking of supernatural powers for their explanation. Events doubtless similar received a like explanation one hundred years later by Justin Martyr (Apol. ii. 6; Dial. 30, 39). Compare the account in Acts xx. 7 ff. of the resuscitation by the apostle of a young man supposed to be dead.

that the judaising opponents found their way to the believers here. In the Epistle he thanks God for their "fellowship in the gospel from the first day until now" (Phil. i. 5). He exhorts them to maintain unity without intimating that deplorable divisions had taken place among them: "Stand fast in one spirit, with one mind striving together for the faith of the gospel" (i. 27). He commends them for having "always obeyed," not only in his presence, but also in his absence (ii. 12), and calls them "dearly beloved and longed for," his "joy and crown" (iv. 1). That he saw the need of exhortations regarding their relations to one another perhaps on account of the self-exaltation of some may be inferred from ii. 4–10, where he counsels them to consideration of one another, and enforces his admonition by reference to the example of Christ who "made himself of no reputation, and took upon him the form of a servant, and was made in the likeness of men.". The kindly relations existing between him and the Philippians are indicated by the fact that he received more than once support from them, notwithstanding his boast that he earned his bread with his own hands (1 Thess. ii. 9; 1 Cor. iv. 12, ix. 4–18). He tells the Corinthians that what was lacking to him "the brethren from Macedonia supplied" (2 Cor. xi. 9), and writes to the Philippians themselves that they had "once and again" sent to his necessities (iv. 15, 16), and out of his imprisonment he "rejoices in the Lord" that now at the last their "care for him hath flourished again" (iv. 10), and in ii. 25 he mentions Epaphroditus as their messenger who had come to him and ministered to his wants.

The Epistle contains numerous exhortations to unity, indeed, and it is apparent that information had reached the apostle of certain divisions, "murmurings, and disputings." He beseeches Euodias and Syntyche that they be "of the same mind in the Lord," and admonishes the believers generally to let their moderation be known unto all men, for "the Lord is at hand," as if personal strife and passion were trivial in view of the great consummation of the Parousia (iv. 2, 5). But we are not warranted in supposing that any such conflict existed in the church as divided the churches of Galatia, or that if there was a Jewish-Christian party in it they had taken the extreme ground that the gentile Christians must submit to Jewish rites. Opponents actual or possible from whom danger existed or was threatened are mentioned in severe terms with a warning against them in iii. 2, 18. They are "dogs," and "enemies of the cross of Christ," "evil workers," and "of the concision," while the Christians are "the circumcision," that is, represent the true circumcision of the heart, and "have no confidence in the flesh." The most probable reference in these passages is to a Jewish influence from without, from which danger was apprehended. The want of unity which evidently attracted the apostle's attention may very likely have been between Jewish and gentile Christians. But the distinct expression of Paul's gratitude for the "fellowship in the gospel" excludes all deep-seated doctrinal differences.

From Philippi Paul and his companions went by way of Amphipolis and Apollonia to Thessalonica, where according to Acts xvii. 2 he immediately devoted himself to a Jewish-Christian instead of a gentile mission. On the contrary, the apostle afterwards wrote to this church as if it were composed of converts from heathenism: "Ye turned," he says, "to God from idols to serve the living and true God" (1 Thess. i. 9). Again he writes them that, just as the churches of God which are in Judea had been persecuted by the Jews, so they have suffered from their own countrymen (ii. 14). Distressed after his arrival in Athens about the condition of the Thessalonians, when he "could no longer forbear," he sent Timothy to them to "establish and comfort" them in their faith (1 Thess. iii. 1, 2). This "brother and minister of God" brought him in Corinth "good tidings of their faith and charity," so that he was "greatly comforted" in all his affliction and distress (verses 6, 7). This first Epistle gives important information as to the situation in Thessalonica on the condition that its genuineness is established. It has been contested on grounds which can hardly be regarded as sufficient to warrant its rejection. The account of the founding of the church sounds, indeed, like a narrative made to persons who knew nothing of the matter rather than to those who already had a knowledge of it, and the reference to the church as "ensamples to all that believe in Macedonia and Achaia" has been thought to denote a later period. The distinctive Pauline doctrines of faith and justification, of the law, and of the atonement are not referred to in the Epistle, or at least receive no detailed exposition. But the internal evidences of Pauline authorship far outweigh the indications to the contrary. The apostle's style and mode of thought are distinctly evident, especially in the greeting, the exhortations, and the concluding words. The doctrine of the resurrection as the ground of the believers' hope at the coming of Christ, when "God will bring with him" those "who are asleep in Jesus" reminds us of 1 Cor. xv. 22, 23 (1 Thess. iv. 14, v. 10). The wrath of God and deliverance from it through the death of Christ (i. 10, iv. 9 f.) are distinctly Pauline conceptions (see 2 Cor. v. 15; Phil. iii. 10; Rom. xiv. 7-9).

Pfleiderer calls attention to "a still more compelling reason against a later authorship" in the expression of the apostle's expectation that he would survive the coming of Christ, contained in the words, "we who are alive and remain unto the coming of the Lord" (iv. 15). "This no one could have written after Paul's death." This Epistle was written from Corinth by Paul, Silvanus, and Timothy perhaps within a year after his mission in Thessalonica, probably about 54 or 55, if we assume 34 or 35 as the date of his conversion, instead of 30 according to Harnack. Although it is a joint letter (i. 1), the apostle frequently takes occasion to speak in his own name, and it bears throughout the impress of his personality. The report which Timothy had brought, while on the whole encouraging, as we have seen, evidently impressed the apostle with the conviction that the church needed certain exhortations as to Christian conduct. There was something "lacking" in their faith and in their "love toward one another" (iii. 10, 11). He would have them "abound more and more" in accordance with the precepts he had given (iv. 1, 10). There is a plain intimation that some of them had gone astray and needed to be admonished to "abstain from fornication" and from defrauding one another (iv. 3, 6). Some were troubled as to the future fortune at the coming of Christ of those of their friends who had died, and he tells them that when Christ shall descend from heaven "the dead in Christ" will be raised, since Jesus himself had been raised from the dead (iv. 14–17). The "unruly" needed to be warned, the "feebleminded" comforted, and the "weak" supported, and these offices the brethren should themselves perform (v. 14). Those who "laboured among" them and were "over them in the Lord" were not duly esteemed, and all the believers were apparently not "at peace" among themselves (v. 12, 13). It is evident in the note of personal defence that charges against Paul had been made in some quarters, perhaps from the heathen opponents, which he thought ought to be answered. Hence his disclaim-ing of "deceit," "flattery," "covetousness," etc. (ii. 4, 5, 6, 9).

The second Epistle to the Thessalonians furnishes no new information of importance regarding the conditions in the church at Thessalonica even on the hypothesis of its genuineness. It is, however, very doubtful that it came from the hand of Paul. The slight deviations from Pauline usage in words and forms of expression are hardly sufficient to support an argument against its genuineness. But the indications of imitation both in the substance and form are suspicious, and Schmiedel concludes that the turns of expression are to such a degree drawn from the first Epistle as would have been impossible for Paul himself without a fresh reading of it. The so-called "little apocalypse" (ii. 1-12) is almost certainly spurious on account of its disagreement with what the first Epistle teaches as to "the last things" or the Parousia. According to ii. 5 Paul had "told" the Thessalonians that certain definite signs would precede the second coming of Christ, the appearance of "the man of sin," "the son of perdition" (ii. 3 f.). If this is genuine, he must have taught them orally the direct opposite of what he wrote them in the first Epistle. For in this he says that the day of the Lord will "come as a thief in the night" (1 Thess. v. 2), and tells them that they know this perfectly, as if he had so taught them. "Sudden destruction" will come upon those who "cry peace and safety." This certainly means an unexpected coming of the great day, and is incompatible with such preceding signs as are mentioned in the second letter. In the first Epistle he declines to tell them anything about the "times and the seasons" of the advent, since they knew well that its coming is without warning, like that of a thief.

In the second letter, on the contrary, he enters into this

very question, and warns the believers against thinking that the day is "at hand," and plainly tells them that they will know by certain signs when to expect it. The warning against being misled by spurious letters purporting to come from the apostle (ii. 2) is suspicious. There is no trace of such letters written during the lifetime of the apostle, and the improbability against the existence of them is great. An intensifying of the first Epistle is manifest in several features of the second, particularly in all that relates to the catastrophe of the end. Here we have Christ "taking vengeance in flaming fire," and instead of the "sudden destruction" of 1 Thess. v. 3 which would come upon those who cry peace and safety, the second letter tells of a punishment with "everlasting destruction" to be visited upon "those who know not God, and obey not the gospel of our Lord Jesus Christ" (i. 8). As if, moreover, the evil tendencies in those who are to "perish" were not sufficient to compass their ruin, the writer represents that "God will send them a strong delusion, that they should believe a lie, that they all might be damned" (ii. 11, 12). The hypothesis of a genuine letter consisting substantially of i. 1–4 and ii. 13 — iii. 18, which was interpolated prior to the year 70, can hardly be sustained, since it leaves such a fragment as Paul would hardly have written. The portions omitted on this hypothesis constitute the kernel of the Epistle.

Of the succeeding fortunes of the Macedonian churches Acts gives us no information, although it mentions a visit of the apostle to that region (xx. 1–3). But the second Epistle to the Corinthians written thence throws some light upon the conditions existing there four or five years after the founding of the churches. He wishes the Corinthians to know of "the grace of God bestowed upon the churches of Macedonia, how that in a great trial of affliction the abundance of their joy and their deep poverty abounded unto the riches of their liberality" (2 Cor. viii. 1, 2). The natural inference from his words is that the distress was so great that he could not find it in his heart to ask them to contribute to the collection that he was making for the needy Christians. He says, however: "To their power I bear record, yes, and beyond their power they were willing of themselves, praying us with much entreaty that we should receive the gift, and take upon us the fellowship of the ministering to the saints" (2 Cor. viii. 3, 4). "Not as we hoped," he says, "but first gave themselves to the Lord and unto us by the will of God." So freely and liberally did they give, that he calls their generosity a giving of themselves. The apostle wishes that through the visit of Titus to the Corinthians in the interest of the collection "the same grace" may be completed in them also. With Titus Paul sends from Macedonia two companions to the Corinthians, one of whom he calls "the brother whose praise is in the gospel throughout all the churches." The other he designates as "our brother, whom we have oftentimes proved diligent in many things" (2 Cor. viii. 18, 22). Conjecture as to who these men were is fruitless. In Acts xx. 4 mention is made of two men from Thessalonica as companions of Paul on his journey with the collection, Aristarchus and Secundus, but we cannot certainly connect these with the two mentioned in 2 Cor. viii. 18, 22.

According to 1 Thess. iii. 1 Paul was in Athens when he sent Timothy to Thessalonica to establish the church and comfort them concerning their faith. In 1 Cor. xvi. 15 he speaks of "the house of Stephanas" as "the first fruits of Achaia," and in 2 Cor. i. 1 he addresses "the church of God which is at Corinth with all the saints who are in all Achaia." That in Achaia there were believers outside of

Corinth is accordingly probable. We are not warranted, however, in assuming a ministry in the Pauline sense and the founding of a church in Athens. That Paul while in Athens was inactive and silent is hardly probable from our knowledge of him, and the mention of Dionysius and the woman Damaris (Acts xvii. 34) has the appearance of being derived from an historical source. The historical value of the account as a whole is, however, doubtful. That Paul's spirit should have been "stirred within him" at sight of a "city wholly given up to idolatry" is not improbable; but why on this account he should have disputed "in the synagogue with the Jews and with the devout persons" is not apparent (Acts xvii. 16, 17). The address attributed to the apostle on Mars' Hill, to say nothing of the impossibility of its being reproduced with anything like accuracy forty or fifty years later, does credit to the invention of the author; but we miss in reading it the distinctive Pauline traits. It contains no message of salvation through Christ, who is represented simply as the agent of divine judgment; and the summons to repentance, because God "will judge the world," is more after the manner of John the Baptist than of Paul. In any case, whatever one may think of the discourse as Pauline or unpauline, it is improbable that so important an event as a ministry in Athens, discussions with Greek philosophers, and an address to the enlightened Athenians on Mars' Hill would not have been mentioned by the apostle, if it ever occurred.

Of the church in Corinth, the history of which is of the greatest importance for a knowledge of the mission among the gentiles, of the personality and methods of Paul, and of his relations with the Jerusalem authorities, we should know nothing of value if we had no other source of information than Acts (xviii. 1-19). The writer of this book, for reasons about which it is useless to speculate, tells us nothing of the inner history of the church, nothing of the parties and their conflicts, nothing of the Epistles or of the occasions that called them forth, and nothing of the skilful dealing of the apostle with the trying emergencies which confronted him there. That he should have been unacquainted with the Pauline Epistles appears incredible, and his omissions here as well as his passing over in silence of the important episode of the conflict of Peter and Paul at Antioch constitute one of the unsolved problems of his problematical work. From his narrative it would appear that Paul was primarily occupied with a mission to the Jews, and did not think of preaching to the gentiles until the Jews rejected him. This is not in accord with Gal. i. 16, and has not the slightest support in the Corinthian Epistles. Not only are the omissions noteworthy, but the brief account of the mission leaves much to be desired regarding the matters with which it deals. Paul goes immediately to a Jew of Pontus lately come from Italy, and stays with him because the two are of the same handicraft, tentmakers. Of this Aquila and his wife Prisca ("Priscilla" is a diminutive) we are not told whether they became Christians or not, and if we may infer that they did, whether or no they were converted by Paul. The apostle goes at once to the synagogue, and "reasons" there "every sabbath," how many sabbaths, we are not told. But during all this time it would appear that he was reasoning about something else than Christianity, for he did not "testify that Jesus was Christ," until "Silas and Timothy came from Macedonia," when he was "pressed in spirit," and took up the subject of his mission. There is no intimation that during this period he had thought that he was the divinely appointed apostle to the gentiles (Acts xviii. 1–6). Only when the Jews "opposed themselves, and blasphemed," did he "shake his raiment," and declare that he would "go to the gentiles."

It is from the Corinthian Epistles (57-58) that we learn whatever may be known of the founding of the church in Corinth and of its internal history during the first years of its existence. The apostle writes that the gospel of the Son of God was here preached by himself and Silvanus and Timothy (2 Cor. i. 19); that he was the founder of the church (1 Cor. iii. 6); that the Christians here are his "work in the Lord" (1 Cor. ix. 1); and that though they "have ten thousand instructors in Christ, they have not many fathers," for in Christ Jesus he begot them in the gospel (1 Cor. iv. 15). He says that his message to them was only "Jesus Christ and him crucified" (1 Cor. ii. 2); that he was with them "in weakness and fear and much trembling," "not in enticing words of man's wisdom, but in demonstration of the Spirit and of power" (1 Cor. ii. 3-5); that he could not speak unto them "as unto spiritual, but as unto carnal," feeding them as babes with "milk" (1 Cor. iii. 1-3); and that in his preaching he had nothing to glory of, for a "necessity was laid upon him" (1 Cor. ix. 16). The church was composed chiefly of the common people, "not many wise after the flesh, not many mighty, not many noble" (1 Cor. i. 26), although from the requirement to give bountifully (2 Cor. ix. 6) it may be inferred that some were at least not poor. That the mission began among the gentiles is apparent from the mention of Stephanas as the "first fruits" whom and his household Paul himself baptized (1 Cor. xvi. 15). The apostle writes to the believers here as if they were chiefly converts from heathenism. "Ye know," he says, "that ye were gentiles, carried away unto these dumb idols, even as ye were led" (1 Cor. xii. 2); yet there were evidently some converts from Judaism (1 Cor. vii. 18, ix. 20, xii. 13). It is noteworthy that in his account of the beginnings of his ministry in Corinth he makes no mention of the persecutions and perils related in Acts. His timidity and "fear" are to be ascribed to his want of confidence in himself as a public speaker, who could not employ the rhetorical methods to which the people in this cultivated community were accustomed. He could rise above all personal deficiencies only by the power of the word which he had to speak.

What the substance of the apostle's message to the Corinthians was may be learned chiefly from the first Epistle, although, from the fact that it was written in answer to questions that arose after he had left them, we must conclude that it treats of some matters not included in his oral teaching. "The gospel which he preached to them," he says, was that of the death of Christ "for our sins," his resurrection, and his manifestation to the apostles and last of all to himself (1 Cor. xv. 1–8). By this gospel they will be "saved," if they keep in memory what he preached to them. He also delivered to them what he had "received of the Lord" respecting the last supper (1 Cor. xi. 23–25). The kernel of his gospel, however, was evidently that apprehension of the cross which was to the Jews a stumbling-block and an "offence" to the Jewish Christians. So we must doubtless understand 1 Cor. i. 23. That in a message to idolaters, however, the preaching of the one God occupied the foremost place, and was made fundamental to the entire message is antecedently probable, and indications are not wanting in the Epistles that this was the course pursued. He writes to the believers what he must before have preached to them that "an idol is nothing in the world, and that there is none other God but one." Though "there be gods many and lords many," "to us," he declares, "there is but one God, the Father, of whom are all things, and we in Him" (1 Cor. viii. 4–6). He tells them that formerly they "were carried away unto these dumb idols" (1 Cor. xii. 2). But the way to this one God was shown to be through Christ, and he was preached among them as "the Son" (2 Cor. i. 19). It was God who established the preachers along with the hearers, who anointed them, and sealed them, and gave them "the earnest of the Spirit"; but this was done "in Christ" (2 Cor. i. 21, 22). Through God Christ Jesus in whom they are is made to them "wisdom and righteousness and sanctification and redemption" (1 Cor. i. 30). Jesus died for all, that they who live should not henceforth live to themselves, but to him who died for them and rose again," and if any man be "in him," he is a new creation; old things are passed away; behold, all things are become new" (2 Cor. v. 15, 17). In Christ the believer comes into a spiritual fellowship in which new and noble ethical motives prevail. The body has become a ."member of Christ," and should not be debased to unholy uses, is "the temple of the Holy Ghost" which is in them, which they have of God, and they are not their own. They are "bought with a price," and should glorify God in their spirit and their body "which are God's" (1 Cor. vi. 20).

The organisation of the little religious community, which probably assembled in a private house, as in Ephesus (1 Cor. xvi. 19), is not clearly defined in the Epistles. Intimations are, however, not wanting, which throw some light upon the matter. Among these nothing appears to favour the supposition that men were appointed to governing positions with official titles, according to the representation in Acts to the effect that it was the apostle's custom to "ordain elders" in every church (Acts xiv. 23). Paul does not intimate that he assumed such a function in his churches. On the contrary, the organisation appears at first to have had a much simpler form than the writer of Acts supposes, who looked upon the matter from the point of view of a later time. In 1 Cor. xii. 28 the apostle enumerates certain classes of persons whom "God hath set in the church," and mentions successively apostles, prophets, teachers, miracles, gifts of healing, helps, governments, diversities of tongues. None of these appear to have been formally "ordained," and the natural inference from the passage is that each one took upon himself, probably with the tacit consent of the others, such functions as his gifts fitted him to perform. When the apostle calls attention to irregularities in the church, he mentions no titled functionary with authority to control and to check extravagances, but appeals to the little community as a whole (1 Cor. v. 3–5; 2 Cor. ii. 6), which elects its envoys, and in which there are no distinctions of rank, sex, or race (1 Cor. xii. 13, xvi. 3). The relation of the organisation to that of the heathen cult-associations cannot be precisely ascertained, but it is probable that, while similarities may have existed, the needs of the church were the determining factor. Under "governments" may be included a presiding officer, but there is no indication that a title belonged to him, and the supposition is not improbable that the persons first converted took an active part in the management of affairs, and thus naturally attained a leadership either by tacit common consent or by election.

There must in any case be assumed the freedom of a self-governing body to adapt itself to circumstances and provide for such needs as its situation and development made apparent. In Corinth the first convert appears to have held a prominent position in the church when the first Epistle was written, for the apostle exhorts the believers as follows: "I beseech you, brethren (ye know the house of Stephanas, that it is the first fruits of Achaia, and that they have addicted themselves to the ministry of the saints), that ye submit yourselves unto such and to every one that helpeth with us and laboureth" (1 Cor. xvi. 15). These words indicate that there were leaders in the church who had "addicted themselves to the ministry of the saints," but they are not mentioned with an official title, and nothing is intimated as to their appointment. Rather the voluntary performance of certain duties appears to have been preliminary to the attainment of a position which warrants the apostle in requiring others to "submit" themselves to them. The Thessalonian church presents an analogous situation in the apostle's exhortation: "We beseech you, brethren, to know them who labour among you, and are over you in the Lord, and admonish you; and to esteem them very highly for their works' sake" (1 Thess. v. 12, 13). Here "labour among you" and "are over you" denote special and prominent activities without any indication of such a title as "elders" (πρεσβύ-τεροι) or of an "ordination" by the apostle himself. It is evident that similar conditions existed in Ephesus, to which Rom. xvi. 1-20 was probably originally written, where separate organisations perhaps meeting in private houses appear to be addressed and greeted through their presiding officers. In Rom. xii. 8, "he that ruleth, with diligence" doubtless refers to such a leading personage. Here the position appears to belong to one who was supposed to have the requisite "gift," and he is mentioned along with those who have the gifts of prophecy, ministry, exhortation, teaching, and giving, as if each one assumed his position, and performed its appropriate duties in the interest of all according as he was regarded by all to be qualified by special endowment. The mention of "bishops and deacons" in the address of the Epistle to the Philippians doubtless denotes a later development, or the terms ἐπίσκοποι and διάκονοι may signify no more than is implied in "those who are over you" (προϊστάμενοι) and "those who labour among you" (κοπιῶντες) of 1 Thessalonians.

The first Epistle to the Corinthians was occasioned by internal conditions in the church which arose shortly after Paul's departure from Corinth for Ephesus, and was written from the latter city, when he was contemplating a visit to them (1 Cor. xvi. 2–8). An intervening visit is maintained by some authorities, upon the discussion of whose reasons for the contention we cannot here enter. He had in any event received information as to the situation from various persons. Some dependents of "the house of Chloe" had told him of "contentions" (1 Cor. i. 11). Stephanas, Fortunatus, and Achaicus had visited him (1 Cor. xvi. 17), and Apollos had come, and was with him when the Epistle was written (1 Cor. xvi. 12). A letter that has not been preserved he had also written them, in which he says expressly that he had charged them "not to company with fornicators" (1 Cor. v. 9). He had also had a letter from them to which he refers with a special indication of its subject-matter (1 Cor. vii. 1). As to the relation of Apollos to the "contentions" which had arisen in the church, we have no definite information. In mentioning the party "of Apollos" Paul throws no blame upon him, as if he had endeavoured to form a faction opposed to him. On the contrary, he speaks of him as having "watered" where he had "planted" (1 Cor. iii. 6). A very natural explanation of the situation is that given in substantial accord by Pfleiderer and Weizsäcker to the effect that Apollos had imparted instruction of a more philosophical character than that of the simple gospel which Paul had preached to the Corinthians as "babes," and that, schooled as he was in the Alexandrian method of interpretation, he had made somewhat hazardous flights in the regions of allegorising. That a certain class of minds should have been captivated by a ready teacher of this sort is in accordance with the nature of things, and they may naturally be assumed to have gone beyond their teacher to the extent of perverting his teachings, and to have grouped themselves into a party bearing his name. The letter which the apostle had received from the Corinthian church prior to the writing of the first Epistle contained questions concerning marriage, the eating of flesh offered to idols, and spiritual gifts, and the indications point to divisions of opinion on these subjects. His treatment of these matters, so far as it shows his personal qualities as a man and a missionary, has been considered in a preceding chapter, and we do not need here to enter upon the subject.

The matter of the party-divisions is not treated by the apostle in such a manner as to indicate that a serious rupture had occurred which had separated the church into hostile camps. That the influence of Apollos had led some to declare themselves of his party would naturally lead the friends of the Pauline teaching, or rather we should say, method (for there is no reason for supposing a radical difference of doctrine) to array themselves on the side of their first teacher. Thus the origin of these two factions is easily accounted for. It is not so clear why others should have taken Peter as their party-name, for there is no reason for thinking that he had been in Corinth, and nowhere in the Epistle does Paul express himself about him as if he were an opponent in this field. His attitude toward the question which he discusses with so much vehemence in Galatians indicates that it had not here assumed such a form as there. The existence of a party of Peter cannot, however, be denied, and the most obvious explanation of the fact of its existence is the supposition that the judaisers had found their way into the church, and were exerting an influence hostile to Paul and his gospel. The reference to circumcision in 1 Cor. vii. 18 shows that the question was discussed, although it may not have been "the open question of the day," and although there is no reason for concluding from what the apostle says about it that a distinct demand had been made on the part of a Jewish-Christian party for the subjection of the gentile Christians to the rite.

But that the advocates of views distinctively opposed to those of the apostle were on the ground is indicated not only by the existence of the party of Peter, but by pointed references to them in the second Epistle as the preachers of "another Jesus" and "false apostles" (2 Cor. xi. 4, 13). Since Peter was the acknowledged head among the apostles in Jerusalem, it is natural that those of the Corinthians who were favourable to the Jewish-Christian interpretation of the gospel should call themselves, or be called, the party of Peter. That those who instigated this party were not of Corinth, but came with authorisation, is indicated in the reference of Paul to "epistles of commendation" which were brought by "some" (2 Cor. iii. 1). There can be little doubt that to this party is to be traced an influence tending to overthrow the authority of Paul. Such an influence was evidently exerted. This is an unavoidable inference from his defence of himself. He speaks of being "judged" by the Corinthians, and says it is a small matter, that of their judgment. He has one who judges him, and that one is Christ. The admonition to judge nothing before the time, until Christ came, is a reproof of their plainly-implied censure of him. Whether or no Weizsäcker's opinion have sufficient exegetical support to justify it, that the Corinthian church proposed to call the apostle to account, and had appointed a time for a hearing, the inference is warranted that a party was busy in opposition to him. The question mooted may have been his claim to apostolical recognition. In fact his words show this plainly. "Am I not an apostle?" he asks. "Have I not seen Jesus Christ our Lord? are ye not my work in the Lord?" The opponents, the judaisers who denied his apostleship, are definitely enough indicated in the words: "If I be not an apostle unto others, yet doubtless I am to you, for the seal of my apostleship are ye in the Lord" (1 Cor. ix. 1, 2).

A third party, that "of Christ," appears to be denoted in 1 Cor. i. 12, and perhaps, as Schmiedel maintains, one cannot on strictly exegetical grounds deny its existence. But not without good reasons does Pfleiderer argue that the expression, "I am of Christ," is to be understood as the common cry of the three other parties in the sense that "each made for itself the chief or even exclusive claim of belonging to Christ on the ground that it confessed to faith in him according to Paul or Apollos or Peter." In this interpretation he follows Röbiger who, he thinks, has assigned the Christ-party to its proper place — "the realm of shadows, of historical phantoms" (*Urchristenthum*, p. 90). The passage presents exegetical difficulties, but the question in the following verse, "Is Christ divided?" may very well be interpreted in the sense, Are there three doctrines which can be called Christian, that of Paul, that of Apollos, and that of Peter? Can you all say that you are "of Christ," while you confess to three forms of Christian doctrine? Apart, however, from the exegetical question, it is difficult to explain the existence of such a party beside the other three. It is conceivable that the adherents of the party of Peter might claim that the original apostles, having been personally with Christ, were rather entitled to be called Christians than Paul and his supporters, and that such an idea was current and had come to Paul's knowledge appears from his question,

"Have I not seen Christ?" This ground of the attack of the judaisers upon Paul's claims to the apostleship has already been referred to, and it is difficult to discover a basis for a party of Christ in distinction from the Petrine. Besides, it is worthy of note that apart from this one passage of difficult and doubtful interpretation no reference is made by the apostle in the Epistle to this so-called Christ-party. On the contrary, when he in another place mentions the subject of party-divisions, he says nothing of this fourth faction while explicitly naming the other three: "Let no man glory in men; for all things are yours, whether Paul or Apollos or Cephas or the world or life or death or things present or things to come; all are yours; and ye are Christ's, and Christ is God's" (1 Cor. iii. 21, 22). Moreover, the question, "Is Christ divided?" (1 Cor. i. 13) is appropriate on the supposition of the three parties, those of Paul, Apollos, and Peter, but has no application to a party of Christ. The passage in 2 Cor. x. 7: "Do ye look on things after the outward appearance? If any man trust to himself that he is Christ's, let him of himself think this again, that as he is Christ's, even so are we Christ's," which Weizsäcker adduces in support of the theory of a Christ-party, doubtless relates to Paul's claim to apostolical authority which was disputed by the judaisers, and is accordingly adapted to the party of Peter. In the next verse he says: "For though I should boast somewhat more of our authority." The sense is the same if we translate the first clause of the former verse with Schmiedel: "Look upon what lies before your eyes." To have authority as an apostle and to be Christ's are here one and the same.

Before despatching the first Epistle Paul had sent Timothy to Corinth, to bring them into remembrance of his ways which are in Christ, as he taught everywhere in every church (1 Cor. iv. 17). He promises himself to "come shortly" to them, and asks them whether he shall come "with a rod or in love and in the spirit of meekness." It appears that Timothy's mission was ethical rather than doctrinal, for the apostle says: "I beseech you be ye followers of me. For this cause I have sent Timothy," etc. The "ways" into remembrance of which he was to bring them relate to his walk and conversation, and the mission denotes his solicitude as to the morals of the church. To this matter he devotes in fact a section of the first part of the Epistle, which includes the first six chapters. In chapters v. and vi., namely, he addresses himself to the moral shortcomings of the church in respect to fornication of which he had written them in a previous letter, and in respect to going to law with one another before heathen magistrates. In the second part of the Epistle, from chapter vii. to the end, which is "in some sort a new letter," he attends to the questions addressed to him in the letter from the church — marriage, virgins, flesh offered to idols, women in the church, the so-called "gifts of the Spirit." He returns to the matter of his personal defence, his apostleship, inserts the hymn to love, treats of excesses in the observance of the Lord's Supper, and finally discusses the matter of the resurrection (chap. xv.). This was a vital question, and he addresses himself to its discussion with a manifest sense of its importance.

The feeling, force, eloquence, and argumentative skill displayed render this chapter one of the most noteworthy and masterful productions of the apostle's genius. He regards his entire mission as standing or falling with this doctrine of the resurrection of the dead. The resurrection of Jesus, which was a central thought in his teaching, was for him an assurance of the resurrection of those who believed in him, and of their entrance into his kingdom when he should appear. Accordingly, he argues that "if the dead rise not, then is Christ not risen; and if Christ be not risen, then is our preaching vain, and your faith is also vain" (1 Cor. xv. 13, 14). From the question: "How say some among you that there is no resurrection of the dead?" it is evident that his argument was occasioned by reports of the doubts of some persons in the church as to the resurrection, their denial of it in fact. This denial could not have come from Jewish-Christian believers, and hardly from those who were of the party of Paul. If they belonged to any one of the parties it was that of Apollos, though we are not warranted in supposing that Apollos had so taught them. The denial may have arisen from the revolt of gentile-Christian thought against the supernaturalism of the doctrine of the resurrection (Weizsäcker), or from opposition to the materialism which belonged to the Jewish doctrine of the bodily resurrection (Pfleiderer). The apostle evidently endeavoured to overcome the materialistic objection by a spiritual doctrine, teaching that the resurrection-body is "incorruptible" and "celestial," and that "as we have borne the image of the earthy, we shall also bear the image of the heavenly" (1 Cor. xv. 40-49).

From this Epistle one obtains a tolerably good idea of the difficulties which were encountered in the attempt to establish the pure morality of the gospel among a people accustomed to the laxity of the heathen mode of life. The apostle and his gospel could not have been subjected to a greater trial than just here in this city of license. A strange Christianity that of the Corinthian church must have been at the time the first Epistle was written — a Christianity of which we can scarcely form a conception; a mixture of lofty ideas dimly apprehended with "the weak and beggarly elements of the world," of Jewish theology, Pauline mysticism, and the Alexandrian speculations and allegorising of Apollos, of conflicting notions as to the flesh and the Spirit, continence and license, marriage and celibacy, circumcision and uncircumcision, the authority of Paul and that of Jerusalem, theism and polytheism; a conflict of old customs and habits with new principles half understood, of the "puffed-up" spirit of self-assertion and dogmatism with the modesty that waits to be instructed, of the sense of decorum with the loud demand for the unveiled "prophesying" of the women, of a sound feeling of the fitness of things with a heathenish glee and gluttony at the Supper of the Lord; and a babel of a many-voiced speaking "with a tongue," which led the looker-on to think the church was "mad." The situation might well dishearten as brave and great a man as Paul, not only as to local success, but also as to the entire future of the cause of Christ. Who could have foreseen that out of such crudeness and elemental fermentation could come the Christendom of the nineteenth century? It needed the courage, the hope, the divine patience of the great apostle, the sure insight and faith of a religious genius, who looks upon "the things that are not seen," to undertake the mighty task of bringing order out of this chaos. Not by violence and rough compulsion could the task be achieved, but only by the ideal and by the love that "hopeth all things, endureth all things." He who could at the same time assert authority and charm with the spirit of Christ might venture. This Paul could do, and he has left us the first Epistle to the Corinthians as an evidence of his skill and mastery.

That the first Epistle did not, however, altogether produce its intended effect is evident from the second, if we assume that in its existing canonical form it is the second. The difficulties instead of being removed appear to have taken on a more intense and aggravated form. That Timothy on his return had reported the result of the first letter is probable, as well as that he had brought information regarding the condition of the church. In any case the situation seemed sufficiently serious to require that Paul should at once carry out the purpose of visiting them, of which he makes mention in the first Epistle (1 Cor. iv. 21, xi. 34, xvi. 5–8). The indications are that the visit, suddenly resolved upon, was short, and that he soon returned to Ephesus. The visit is proved by references to it in the second Epistle which also contains intimations of his experiences in the course of it. In 2 Cor. xii. 13, speaking of a contemplated visit, he says: "Behold, the third time I am ready to come to you." In xiii. 1, 2 he writes again of a third proposed visit, and tells the believers there that, just as when he was with them the second time, so now in his absence he warns "those who have sinned" that if he comes again he "will not spare." These words cannot fairly be interpreted as referring to intentions to visit them which were never carried out. The words: "But I determined this with myself that I would not come to you again in heaviness [sadness], for if I make you sorry, who then is he that maketh me glad" (2 Cor. ii. 1, 2), taken in connection with, "I call God for a record upon my soul [to witness against my soul] that to spare you [out of consideration for you] I have not yet come to Corinth" (i. 23), cannot by any fair interpretation be referred to his first visit. They plainly indicate a second in which he had had painful experiences. Not only was there, then, a second visit with distressing accompaniments, but a second letter following our first and prior to our second canonical Epistle is distinctly referred to. "I wrote this same to you," he says, "lest when I come I should have sorrow from them of whom I ought to rejoice;" "For to this end did I write, that I might know the proof of you, whether ye be obedient in all things" (2 Cor. ii. 3, 9).

There can be no doubt that this letter was written after the apostle's second visit, and had reference to the humiliating and grievous circumstances which accompanied it. "Out of much affliction and anguish of heart," he says, "I wrote unto you with many tears" (2 Cor. ii. 4). Just as he intimates that this visit had been a sorrowful one, so he says of the letter that follows it: "For though I made you sorry with a letter, I do not repent, though I did repent, for I perceive that the same epistle hath made you sorry, though it were but for a season" (2 Cor. vii. 8). These words cannot be referred to our first canonical Epistle, and no more characterise its general tone than what he says about his second visit describes his first mission. It appears, then, that four letters were written by Paul to the Corinthians: 1. The one preceding our first canonical Epistle (1 Cor. v. 9); 2. Our first canonical Epistle; 3. An intervening one between our two canonical Epistles; 4. Our second canonical Epistle, unless the second part of this, x. 1–xiii. 10, was No. 3. Between our two canonical Epistles was a visit of Titus to the church, who was doubtless sent by the apostle with reference to the painful incidents connected with the latter's second visit, and who brought him a report in Macedonia whither he had come from Ephesus (2 Cor. vii. 6, 13). It is not improbable that he was the bearer of letter No. 3. He could hardly have been sent in any case without a writing from the apostle. On his relations with the church, see 2 Cor. vii. 7, viii. 6, 16.

The first part of our second Epistle doubtless contains references to the situation which occasioned the apostle's second visit to Corinth, and with which the letter that followed it dealt. He speaks of a man who had "caused grief," and been punished "of many," that is, probably, by the majority of the church. Now he should be forgiven, and Paul himself is ready to forgive (2 Cor. ii. 5-10). Again in another place he relates how Titus had told him of the "mourning" of the church and writes of his having made them "sorry with a letter," of their "repentance," of their "clearing" of themselves, their "indignation, zeal, revenge," and says that the letter in question was written neither on account of him who did the wrong, nor on account of him who was wronged, but that his care for the church might be apparent (2 Cor. vii. 8-12). The reference of this to the case of the incestuous person (1 Cor. v. 1-5) is hardly satisfactory. The punishment which Paul had determined on for him was nothing less than his delivery to Satan for the destruction of his flesh, and we should not without good reason assume the apostle to have so far changed his attitude and purpose as to be ready to forgive him; and there appears to be no other reason for this explanation than the interpretation of the second Epistle out of the first.

The indications which we have rather point to an occurrence on Paul's second visit in which he had been grossly maltreated by some one, and are moreover to the effect that the church supported this person, and had afterward perhaps under the influence of the apostle's second letter "repented," and shown "their indignation" against the offender. Those who favour the hypothesis already referred to that it was proposed by some of the apostle's enemies in Corinth to put him on trial, think that the plan was carried out on his second visit, and that in the course of the proceedings the apostle was deeply offended, "wronged" by some one. In any case the references to the matter in second Corinthians indicate a personal offence against him, which he was ready to forgive after the punishment inflicted "of many" (2 Cor. ii. 6). It is not improbable that the second letter, which doubtless dealt with this matter, gave rise to the remark to which he refers that "his letters indeed are weighty and powerful, but his bodily presence is weak" (2 Cor. x. 10). To what extent the opposition and maltreatment were represented by the Jewish-Christian party we are unable to say. The indications in the second Epistle are not precise enough to warrant any positive conclusions regarding the matter, but the definite reference to a second visit and a second letter render its explanation in connection with these highly probable.

That between the writing of our first and second canonical Epistles the opposition to the apostle on the part of the judaisers was largely developed and much intensified is evident from the tone of 2 Cor. x–xiii., the second division of the letter. There is a reference to them in the first part where he asks: "Do we need, as some others, epistles of commendation to you?" and perhaps in the words: "But if our gospel be hid, it is hid to them that are lost" (2 Cor. iii. 1, iv. 3). It is difficult to determine to what extent this portion of the Epistle is addressed to an opposing party in the church; probably that "of Peter" instead of that "of Christ," but the apostle seems to have had them in view, while his invective is directed against intruders of the Jewish-Christian propaganda who doubtless were known by him to have sympathisers among the believers. They appear to have charged that he was no real apostle, that with his bold letters and contemptible personal presence he was not worthy of consideration, that there was nothing to be feared from him, and that a man was of small account who went about working at a wretched handicraft for his support. He retorts upon them with a fine irony, and says that he will not make himself "of the number of those who commend themselves," and "measure themselves by themselves." The charge is plainly implied that these judaisers have come into his field and "boast of other men's labours," and he says that he proposes to preach the gospel in regions beyond Corinth, and not to "boast in another man's line of things made ready to his hand" (2 Cor. x. 15-18). The self-commendation of his opponents is not to be accepted. The one commended by the Lord (Christ) has alone the true commendation. He is apprehensive lest the false teachers "corrupt" the minds of the believers "from the simplicity that is in Christ," just as the serpent beguiled Eve (xi. 3).* Against the charge that he was "rude in speech" he sets the assertion that he is not deficient "in knowledge," and in order to "cut off occasion from them who desire occasion" he defends himself against the "offence" which his opponents found in his working with his hands to support himself (xi. 7-12). Then in the climax of his invective he charges "the false apostles," who "transform themselves into ministers of Christ," with being ministers of Satan, "transformed as the ministers of righteousness" (xi. 13-15).†

* The comparison is appropriate only in the sense that Eve was through the serpent (identified with Satan, verse 14, Rom. xvi. 20) made unfaithful to her husband, as the Corinthians are in danger of being made unfaithful to Christ, to whom they are "espoused" (verse 2). Paul may have had in mind the Jewish tradition that Satan or his angel seduced Eve to commit adultery. How early this tradition was current we do not know, but Irenæus was acquainted with it among the Ophites. Paul's implied reference to it here would be doubtful if he always kept to the Bible in his illustrations, as we have seen that he did not. See Everling, *Die paul. Angel. u. Dämonol.*, p. 51 ff., and Schmiedel on the passage.

† Dr. McGiffert makes a discrimination between judaisers and judaisers, and thinks that those who worked against the apostle in Corinth are to be distinguished from his opponents in Galatia and Antioch, for the reason that in the Corinthian Epistles Paul does not openly "expose their purpose" (p. 315). But the strong terms which he employs in 2 Corinthians in denunciation of

The tone and contents of the section of our canonical second Epistle included in x. 1–xiii. 10 furnishes considerable support to the hypothesis that we have here the principal part (the introduction being absent) of the letter referred to in 2 Cor. ii. 4, vii. 8, the next letter following our first Epistle or No. 3 of the whole series of four letters written to the Corinthians. The difference between this section and the preceding portion is so marked in the attitude and feeling of the apostle toward the church as to render the supposition extremely improbable that he could have expressed himself in such a way in one and the same letter. In v. 12 he says he does not commend himself again to the church, but gives them occasion to glory on his behalf, so that glorying in him they may answer those who glory only in appearance, that is, the judaisers; while in the second part (xii. 11) he says he is "compelled" by their attitude toward him to "become a fool in glorying." The entire submission of the Corinthians to his requirements, so that he is "filled with comfort," and repents of the severity with which he had written them, since they have "cleared themselves" by their compliance is acknowledged in vii. 4–15; while in xii. 20, 21 he fears that when he comes he will not find them such as he would, and will be "humbled" among them on account of their "envyings," "wraths," etc., against which he will be obliged to proceed with such severity that they will find

them appear to indicate that he had no less persons than his old enemies in mind. Besides, what is more likely than that the judaisers with "letters of commendation" probably from the Jerusalem authorities, should in Corinth have charged that Paul was no real apostle, while asserting that their sponsors were the only true apostles, since they had been with Jesus? The fact that Paul, as Dr. McGiffert says, "defends his apostolic character" in opposition to them denotes what sort of enemies they were, and what was the nature of their antagonism. A Jewish-Christian contention apart from the question of the Jewish rites is hardly supposable.

him as they would not. The supposition that this section is substantially the letter written after his second visit to the church, and that the preceding portion (i.-ix.) was written later, that is, after he had received favourable news from them, has been supported by a considerable number of authorities, and most recently by Schmiedel.*

Our two canonical Epistles to the Corinthians are among the most important of the existing writings of the apostle, especially in what they show of his character and of his dealing with the most trying and critical emergencies arising from the contact of Christianity with heathenism. They are also of no small doctrinal importance, although the circumstances and the readers did not require such an expounding of his opinions on the law and the atonement as we find in Romans. For his doctrine of Christ and of the last things they furnish an abundant material, and of his ethics we learn more from them than from any other source, particularly as to marriage and divorce, the relations of the sexes, and social purity. We learn here more than anywhere else of his physical and mental condition, of his "visions and revelations," of his seeing of the Lord, of the place that he would assign to women in the Christian community, of his attitude toward idolatry, and of his dealing with the matter of the "gifts of the Spirit." Not a little do we find in them too of his method of interpretation, and of his style as a writer they furnish a striking example. The spiritual apprehension of the resurrection is expounded in detail and with graphic power. The great missionary here openly confesses himself to those whom he loved and for whom he suffered. In his timidity, his hesitation before his great task, his humiliation at the hands of his enemies, his outbursts of

* Dr. McGiffert must now be reckoned among the supporters of this hypothesis (*The Apostolic Age*, p. 313).

indignation, his irony and scorn, his devotion to his spiritual children, his wrestling with himself, his anguish, and his tears, he stands before us in unveiled exposure. The Epistles are, moreover, of great value on account of the vivid picture which they present of the fortunes of primitive Christianity in its ethical and religious relations with modes of life so foreign to its principles and spirit as those that prevailed in Corinth. Not less important, too, are they than Galatians in what they show of the attitude and methods of Paul's unwearied opponents, the judaisers; and if in his opposition to them he expresses himself with more bitterness and severity than we can approve, we shall do well to remember that he was human, that the cause of his life was at stake, and that in the classic hymn to love is revealed the deep and permanent mood of his spirit — a mood without which his success would have been impossible.

CHAPTER VI

EPHESUS — ROME

PASSING in our study of Paul's missionary work from Corinth to Ephesus is like going out of light into darkness. The vividness with which the Corinthian Epistles delineate the relations of the apostle to the church, and the bold relief into which they throw his personality, invest these writings with an interest that makes the meagreness of the information concerning the mission in Asia the more keenly felt. Of his work here during nearly three years we have only the most unsatisfactory intimations. In first Corinthians he says he will "tarry at Ephesus until Pentecost" (1 Cor. xvi. 8). We have seen that after this letter was written he made a second journey to Corinth, whence he doubtless returned to Ephesus. In second Corinthians which was written in Macedonia after he had left Ephesus he says: "For we would not have you ignorant, brethren, of our trouble which came to us in Asia, that we were pressed out of measure, above strength, insomuch that we despaired even of life" (2 Cor. i. 8). How extensive a missionary work is implied in "the churches of Asia salute you" (1 Cor. xvi. 19) we do not know. The so-called Epistle to the Ephesians affords no information as to Paul's relations with the church in Ephesus. This fact is in itself unfavourable to its genuineness. That after his extended labours there and the perils to which he was exposed, he should have written as long a letter as this without the personal reminiscences in which his Epistles addressed to churches

which he had founded abound is highly improbable. The deviations apparent in it from the style and thought of his unquestionably genuine writings throw doubt upon it from another source. It is, moreover, doubtful whether it was addressed to the Ephesian church, for according to the conclusions of textual criticism the words "in Ephesus" in the first verse "were either originally not there at all, or were very early stricken out," from which circumstance the conclusion is drawn that "the Epistle was indeed accepted, but was not regarded as directed to Ephesus." *
All the later indications go to show that the apostle's work in Ephesus left no permanent results. The words which the writer of Acts puts into his mouth when on the last journey to Jerusalem he avoided Ephesus and addressed "the Elders" of the church at Miletus, having sent for them to come to him there: "And of your own selves shall men arise speaking perverse things to draw away disciples after them," are probably a prophecy after the event (Acts xx. 30). The author of second Timothy represents that "all they who are in Asia are turned away from" the apostle (2 Tim. i. 15). The strange occurrence of numerous greetings in the last chapter of Romans, an Epistle addressed to a church which the apostle had never visited, and where he could hardly have had twenty-five or thirty personal friends, has led, as has before been remarked, to the supposition that this portion of that letter (xvi. 1-20) was addressed to the Ephesian believers.

If this supposition be correct, we know that the church of Ephesus was in existence at least until toward the end of Paul's work. The fragment is a recommendation of Phebe of Cenchrea, the harbour of Corinth, and the references to the various persons are such as only one could

* For a discussion of the Epistle in detail the reader is referred to the author's volume in the *International Handbooks to the New Testament.*

make who knew not only them but also their situation, their households, etc., and had had personal relations with them. Rome being excluded, the most probable address of this letter of commendation is Ephesus. The mention of Epænetus as the first fruits of Asia (not Achaia) favours this supposition, as does also that of Prisca and Aquila, who are represented as here in 1 Cor. xvi. 19, and as having a church in their house in Ephesus. Whether this was originally the conclusion of a letter to the Ephesians or a complete writing intended according to the first verse to commend Phebe to the various persons mentioned we can only conjecture. The latter supposition is not at all improbable. How the letter came to be connected with Romans we cannot tell. It has been conjectured that Phebe was the bearer of the Epistle to the Romans as well as of the short letter of commendation to friends of the apostle in Ephesus, and that she went from the latter city to Rome. The verses 21–24, whose position is variously given in different MSS., are believed by some authorities to have been the concluding greeting to the Romans. If they were written by a transcriber on a sheet on the other side of which was Phebe's letter to Ephesus, the incorporation of the latter with Romans is not strange in the course of copying (so Lipsius). These conjectures arise out of the improbability already mentioned that Paul should have sent these greetings to Rome, and proceed upon the supposition that both letters were written from the same place (Corinth) by the same hand. The concluding verses of the chapter (25–27) are of doubtful genuineness. The different concluding formulas of the Epistle (xv. 33, xvi. 20, 24) show that in the process of transcribing the end of the letter was early confused; and the insertion of the greetings doubtless contributed to this result.

That the apostle was exposed to some great peril while

in Ephesus we have seen from the passage 2 Cor. i. 8. In the letter of commendation (Rom. xvi. 4) he says of Prisca and Aquila that they have for his life "laid down their own necks," that is, probably, exposed themselves to great danger in order to save him. Again in 1 Cor. xv. 32 he says: "If after the manner of men I have fought with beasts at Ephesus, what profiteth it me if the dead rise not? Let us eat and drink, for to-morrow we die." These are all vague allusions, and we cannot be certain that they relate to one and the same event. The last is the most definite, and yet expositors do not agree as to its interpretation. If there was an actual contest with beasts in the arena, which could be possible only if he were condemned by the authorities of the city on some grave charge, it is in the first place improbable that he would have come out of it alive, and in the second place, exceedingly strange that he should not have mentioned the peril in 2 Cor. xi. 23–27. Notwithstanding these objections, Holsten and Weizsäcker maintain the literal interpretation of the passage, the latter expressing himself with rather more positiveness than the circumstances warrant. If Paul was a Roman citizen (Acts xvi. 37, xxii. 25), he could not, even if condemned to death, have been so executed by the Ephesian authorities. A difficulty in the way of a figurative interpretation of the passage lies in the word employed for "fought with beasts" (ἐθηριομάχησε) which according to usage denoted a contest with beasts in the arena, and was not applicable to an encounter with them in case of meeting them on a journey. This difficulty Krenkel seeks to overcome by supposing that there was a sort of secret language among the Christians in which "wild beast" (θηρίον) signified the Roman power according to the current interpretation of the four beasts in Daniel ii. and vii. Whether this view be tenable or no, the objections against the literal rendering can hardly be overcome, and we must be content with the only fact that stands indubitable, namely, that in Ephesus the apostle was exposed to a mortal peril. We may also assume that the Corinthian Christians knew enough of it to enable them to understand and correctly interpret the expression "fought with beasts." Weizsäcker's conjecture that a fighting with beasts in the arena drew public attention to the apostle, and was thus the occasion of the opportunity referred to in 1 Cor. xvi. 9: "A great door and effectual is opened unto me," is not supported by any hint in the Epistles, and certainly not in Acts, where the episode is not mentioned. In 2 Cor. i. 8-11 the apostle refers after he had left Ephesus to a "trouble which came to him in Asia," in which he was "pressed out of measure, above strength," insomuch that he "despaired even of life." The time of his writing of this was far enough from that of the reference in 1 Cor. xv. 32 to exclude the probability that he had the same peril in mind. Yet what this second danger was is uncertain. It may have come from a renewal of the persecutions, or it may have been a dangerous illness (see 2 Cor. iv. 10; Gal. vi. 17; Phil. iii. 10). In any case, the deliverance was as from death.

We learn little more of the Ephesian church and of Paul's relation to it from any source. The information furnished in Acts is unsatisfactory even if trustworthy. As usual this book tells us nothing of the inner history of the church, and nothing that covers the indications of perils to which the apostle himself makes reference. The affair with the silversmith, Demetrius, may have an historical basis (Acts xix. 23-41), but the situation of the apostle in this difficulty is not represented as excessively perilous. He is surrounded with the protection of "certain of the chief of Asia," or at least is saved from going into danger by their counsel. An officer of the city addresses the crowd, and the matter ends in the confusion and failure of those who wished to harm him and his companions. There is nothing here that corresponds to the critical situation which Paul characterises as a fight with beasts. We learn nothing from Acts, moreover, of the circumstances under which Prisca and Aquila for the apostle's life "laid down their own necks," nor do we find an intimation of a situation in which these friends exposed themselves for him, or Andronicus and Junias became his "fellow-prisoners" (Rom. xvi. 7). The salutations in Phebe's letter (Rom. xvi. 3-16) throw little light on the affairs of the church in Ephesus. We learn from the names and from the designation "kinsmen" that several of the persons were of Jewish descent. Two of these, Andronicus and Junias, he calls "apostles" (verse 7), a use probably of the word in the wider sense (Acts xiv. 14), and says of them that they were "in Christ" before him. They were evidently Christian missionaries temporarily located in Ephesus. Then there are the "kinsmen" Herodion (verse 11) and Mariam (verse 6) and of course Prisca and Aquila. Among those greeted we find especially mentioned certain persons as "helpers," as those who "labour in the Lord," "laboured much in the Lord," etc., a designation very likely denoting such prominent positions in several little communities, perhaps meeting in private houses, as that assigned to Stephanas in 1 Cor. xvi. 15. These labourers in Christ may also have been helpers of the apostle in missionary work. If in verse 6 we adopt a well-authenticated reading (ϵἰς ὑμᾶς) the woman here mentioned is designated as one who bestowed much labour on the church instead of on the apostle. We learn from greetings sent to persons of certain households that there were some slaves among the converts. Every one interested in following the apostle's work will regret that so great an obscurity hangs over the scene of a labour long continued and full of perils.

We have arrived at the end of Paul's distinctive missionary work as the apostle to the gentiles; and yet we are not at the end of his mission, for he appears in another relation as a missionary to the Jewish Christians. He never forgot the compact made in the conference at Jerusalem that he would "remember the poor" (Gal. ii. 10); and it is an evidence of his magnanimity that, although he was harassed and crippled in his gentile mission in Galatia and Corinth by Jewish-Christian emissaries, who sowed discord and threatened to destroy his work by undermining his influence, he never abandoned the purpose of a collection for the needy Christians in Jerusalem, but carried it out, not as a matter of contract, but as a privilege. His frequent references to the matter show how near it lay to his heart. In Rom. xv. 26, 27 he says: "For it hath pleased them of Macedonia and Achaia to make a certain contribution to the poor saints who are at Jerusalem. It hath pleased them verily, and their debtors they are. For if the gentiles have been made partakers of their spiritual things, their duty is also to minister to them in carnal things." We may infer that in this characteristic style he urged the collection upon his churches as a "duty." He also urges it upon the ground that it will not only "supply the want of the saints," but will likewise be "abundant by many thanksgivings unto God" (2 Cor. ix. 12), that is, will cause thankfulness to God to abound in the recipients, and will accordingly have a religious result. From Ephesus he writes to the Corinthians that he has "given order to the churches of Galatia" concerning the collection, and exhorts the believers in Corinth that "upon the first day of the week every one lay by him in store, as God hath prospered him," that all may be in readiness when he comes. His purpose at this time appears to have been to send from each church to Jerusalem as the bearer of the gift some one "approved by letters," instead of going himself (1 Cor. xvi. 1-3). Later he writes them of "the grace of God bestowed on the churches of Macedonia, how that in a great trial of affliction the abundance of their joy and their deep poverty abounded unto the riches of their liberality" (2 Cor. viii. 1, 2), and urges the Corinthians that they, according to their previous "readiness to will," now show "a performance also out of that which they have" (verse 11).

It must have been with no little hesitation that Paul finally himself undertook to go to Jerusalem as the bearer of the collection. He must in so doing put himself into the hands of the men who "both killed the Lord Jesus and their own prophets," and had "persecuted" him, "forbidding him to speak to the gentiles that they might be saved, to fill up their sins always; for the wrath is come upon them to the uttermost" (1 Thess. ii. 15, 16). The we-source of Acts represents that at Tyre certain disciples said to Paul "through the Spirit that he should not go up to Jerusalem" (Acts xxi. 4), and in Cæsarea the prophet Agabus foretold as the word of "the Holy Ghost" that if he went he would be "delivered into the hands of the gentiles" (verse 11). The former statement must be taken with some allowance, for the apostle was not accustomed to disregard the express commandments of "the Spirit." At any rate, neither warnings nor entreaties could shake his resolution. He was "ready not to be bound only, but also to die at Jerusalem for the name of the Lord Jesus" (verse 13).

According to Acts the "brethren" in Jerusalem, the Jewish-Christian believers, "James and all the elders," received Paul "gladly," but counselled him, in order to appease the multitude of believing Jews "all zealous of the law," to perform a Jewish rite so as to show that he "walked orderly, and kept the law." That he should have taken steps to do this, as Acts represents, is simply incredible (Acts xxi. 17–24).* The writer of Acts is more interested in representing Paul as ready to sacrifice his principles to please the Jewish brethren than he is to report the real object of the apostle's mission to Jerusalem. He makes no mention in this connection of the important fact that this object was to bring the collection that he had gathered for the poor of the church, and in the preceding account of his resolution to go to Jerusalem and of the journey thither there is no intimation of his benevolent purpose. Before the time for the completion of the ceremony, however, the Jews, among whom appear to have been some of his old enemies from Asia, fell upon him, and "went about to kill him," and he was saved from their wrath only by the interference of the "chief captain of the band" and his soldiers (Acts xxi. 27-34).

The unconcealed hostility of the Jewish-Christian believers is unmistakable in the terms in which Paul is asked to assume the Nazarite vow. He is told that there are "many thousands" of them, and that, when they hear that he is there, "they must needs come together." They have heard that he teaches the Jews among the gentiles "not to circumcise their children," etc., and the manifest implication is that he will be in peril unless he joins in the performance of a Jewish rite in order to appease them (Acts xxi. 20). It is no wonder that emissaries could be found in Jerusalem to go to Galatia and Corinth. To this Acts here bears unconscious testimony, although the book makes no mention of this interference from any quarter.

* See Chapter VII.

It does not appear, moreover, that of these "many thousands" any interfered to save the apostle, who had come with a gift of love to their poor, from the hands of the Jews who would have killed him. After he was a prisoner in the hands of the Romans, these zealots for the law, these "enemies of the cross of Christ" to whom the Pauline apprehension of the cross was an "offence" (Gal. v. 11), continued their work among his believers, whom he warned against them out of his imprisonment "even weeping" (Phil. iii. 18, cf. verses 2, 3). If at this distance in time and in this age of toleration and indifference to dogma, we cannot join with him in calling them "dogs," we can at least sympathise with him in proportion as we share his noble passion for liberty. We shall do well to consider, however, that these men were doubtless as sincere and conscientious as he was in regarding him as an enemy of Christ and a perverter of his gospel, while he denounced them as "false apostles" and ministers of Satan. The situation illustrates the persistence and indomitable force of dogma in a dispensation which was according to the poetic fancy of an evangelist heralded with the announcement of "peace and good-will," but which under the conditions of human nature could not "bring peace."

Paul went to Rome as a prisoner on his appeal to Cæsar, and not, as he had hoped and expected to go, as a missionary. From Corinth he had written to the church in Rome that he had often purposed to come to them, that he might have some fruit among them also, as among other gentiles, and that so far as in him lay he was ready to preach the gospel to them (Rom. i. 13-15, xv. 25, 32). This city was not destined to be a field of his personal missionary labours, yet it was made a missionary field of his by the great Epistle. This, then, calls for consideration in an account of his missionary activity, more especially since, having been written to a church that had had no communication from him, it probably shows more than any other of his letters his method of presenting his message. It is most distinctively a gospel-Epistle, an Epistle of the Pauline gospel, in which the development of his religious and theological theme is not disturbed by questions of administration and the dealing with practical affairs. Conjectures as to when and by whom the church in Rome was founded are fruitless. We also know with certainty almost nothing of its composition, that is, whether it was preponderatingly gentile-Christian or Jewish-Christian. The former supposition is supported by such passages as i. 13, 14, xi. 13–32, and especially by the fact that the apostle grounds his writing of the Epistle upon his apostleship to the gentiles in i. 5, where the correct rendering is "grace and apostleship for obedience to the faith among all the gentiles." On the other hand, not a little of the argument of the Epistle is adapted especially to Jewish Christians (iii. 1–8, 31, iv. 1, vi. 15, vii. 7, 13, xi. 1, 11). The readers are sometimes addressed as knowing the law or formerly under it (vii. 1–5), and such passages as ix. 1–5 and x. 1 would be inappropriate unless Jewish-Christian readers were among those for whom the Epistle was intended. These doubtless constituted a portion, probably a minority, of the church. In any case, there is no evidence in the letter that they had to the apostle's knowledge attempted to force the gentile Christians to accept their interpretation of Christianity. While the argument of the Epistle bears in some parts an analogy to that of Galatians, the note of antagonism to Jewish Christianity which we discern in the latter is here wanting, and the treatment of the law in general is milder and more conciliatory. It was evidently written out of a different mood and for different conditions.

The object of the Epistle is clearly indicated. The

apostle intended to visit the church in Rome in which he was deeply interested, making mention of it in his prayers (i. 9–13), and he wrote in order to prepare the way for his coming to impart to them "some spiritual gift to the end that they may be established" (i. 11), that is, may be instructed in the Pauline gospel. The Epistle indicates that he was cognizant of difficulties to be encountered in Rome, a Jewish-Christian opposition, or at least a prejudice, to be overcome, and it was written with this end in view. There may have been a conciliatory purpose in his mention of his mission on account of the collection for the needy Jewish Christians in Jerusalem (xv. 25-29), and the exhortation to unity (xii. 3, 16, xiv. 1–20, xv. 5–9) is naturally connected with his proposed visit. The Epistle does not, accordingly, constitute an exception to the letters of Paul in general which are writings directed to special local occasions and exigencies, and is not to be regarded as a purely dogmatic treatise addressed to the world at large.

As to its contents the Epistle may be considered in three grand divisions: 1. The exposition of the gospel of the righteousness of God through faith and not through the works of the law (i.–viii.); 2. Proof that this gospel is not prejudiced by the failure of the Jews to accept it (ix.–xi.); 3. Exhortations adapted to the conditions in the Roman church and a statement of the reasons for writing the Epistle (xii.–xv.). After the introduction (i. 1–15) the theme of the letter is stated to the effect that the gospel is "the power of God unto salvation to every one that believeth, to the Jew first and also to the Greek," etc. (i. 16, 17). Then follows a proof of the futility of striving for righteousness by works on the ground of the failure of Jews and gentiles alike to attain it, their sinfulness, and their exposure to the wrath of God (i. 18–iii. 20). The atonement is shown to be the basis of the only true righteousness, that by faith (iii. 21-26). There follows, then, the declaration that the Jews have nothing to boast of in respect to an advantage over the gentiles (iii. 27-30). This equality of Jews and gentiles is in accord with the Old Testament, and is established by the typical faith of Abraham (iii. 31-iv. 25). "Being justified by faith we have peace with God," "justified by the blood of Christ, we shall be saved from wrath through him," and we "joy in God through our Lord Jesus Christ through whom we have now received the atonement" (v. 1-21). The Romans are exhorted not to let sin reign in their bodies, having come into fellowship with Christ, but to overcome the impulses of the flesh, since they "are not under the law, but under grace." "The wages of sin is death, but the gift of God is eternal life through Jesus Christ our Lord" (vi.). Under the law, man is under the power of sin (vii.).

The mystic fellowship with Christ frees from "condemnation," and the Spirit dwelling in the believer assures him of his resurrection. God's "predestinated" cannot be separated from His love (viii.). The second division begins with a declaration of the apostle's solicitude and sorrow on account of the Jews (ix. 1-5). The Jews' idea of the divine promises is invalid, because God is not limited in His promises to the natural descendants of Abraham, but "hath mercy on whom He will, and whom He will He hardeneth," making "one vessel unto honour and another unto dishonour" (ix. 6-29). Israel failed to attain righteousness because seeking it by works and not by faith. The true righteousness is by faith through Christ (ix. 30-x. 21). God has not, however, "cast away His people," but "there is a remnant according to the election of grace." As to the others, their exclusion is only temporary, and when "the fulness of the gentiles be come in, all Israel shall be saved," for God hath concluded them all in unbelief, that He might have mercy upon all. Then follows praise of God for "the depth of the riches of His wisdom and knowledge" (xi.). The third part consists of exhortations, a warning against self-exaltation, the recommendation of brotherly love, unity, and conciliation, an admonition to obey "the powers that be," the injunction to owe no man anything, but to love one another, for "love is the fulfilling of the law," and the grounding of these teachings on the doctrine of the near approach of the day of the Lord (xii., xiii.). Then follow some admonitions regarding divisions in the church; the relation of the strong to the weak in faith and of Jewish and gentile Christians; a mention of the reason for writing the Epistle and of the collection for the needy Christians in Jerusalem; a communication of his plan to visit the Romans (xiv., xv.); the letter for Phebe probably addressed to the church in Ephesus (xvi. 1-20); greetings (xvi. 21-24); and a doxology, probably by another hand (xvi. 25-27).

This Epistle written to prepare the Romans for his intended visit to them is the most complete exposition of the apostle's gospel that we possess. Its purpose manifestly was not only to instruct the gentile Christians of the church in Rome in the fundamental doctrines of his mission, but also to overcome the opposition of the Jewish Christians whom we can see in the lines of the letter that he had constantly in mind. In his argument he places himself upon their ground, adopts their point of view, and employs their premises and forms of thought in order to overthrow their pretensions. From the point of view of the law and righteousness by works he brings home to their consciousness the fact of universal sinfulness which they cannot deny. "For circumcision verily profiteth if thou keep the law; but if thou be a breaker of the law thy circumcision is made uncircumcision" (ii. 25). Since none of you keep the whole law, your righteousness by works is a fiction. He proves to them from their Scriptures that "there is none righteous, no not one" (iii. 10). As to Abraham, his faith was "counted to him for righteousness," and his circumcision was "the seal of the righteousness of the faith which he had yet being uncircumcised, that he might be the father of all them that believe, though they be not circumcised" (iv. 11). Thus the history of this patriarch is made to support the gentile gospel. The law, by which they expect to be saved, only makes sin abound, and though "ordained to life," is on account of the flesh really "unto death" (vii. 8–24).

The logical consequence of the Jewish doctrine of atonement the apostle shows to be the transfer to the believers of the atoning efficacy of the blood of Christ, whom God "set forth to be a propitiation through faith." Thus the law which man cannot fulfil is satisfied, "redemption" is secured, and a new righteousness "imputed" on account of faith, becomes the possession of the believer, who in mystic fellowship with Christ has the witness of the Spirit that he has become a child of God and an heir of the divine promises (iii. 20–28, vi. 3–8, viii. 9–18). The greatness of the conception of doctrine in the Epistle is apparent in its historical significance. Two great periods of human history are set over against each other — the Adamic order of sin and death, and the Christ-order of righteousness and life. In the former ruled the flesh with its fatal consequences of transgression and destruction. In the latter Christ is king victorious over death, "the end of the law," the beginning of a new order of life, which will be consummated in the resurrection of those who believe and in the glory of the kingdom. Over against Judaism and Jewish Christianity this doctrine is a new conception of the world, a new interpretation of history, a new philosophy of religion, which had its temporary place in the development of Christianity — a second gospel which prepared the way for the first to the conquest of the world.

In his account of Paul's journey from Cæsarea to Jerusalem the writer of Acts follows his we-source beginning with chapter xxvii. Of the sources of the preceding narrative (xxii.-xxvi.) we know nothing, but the impression which it makes upon the reader is that its vividness is due "not so much to the knowledge as to the art of the narrator." If the sources were tradition, the fancy of the writer, and his own invention of the discourses, such a picture as is presented might well be the outcome. That the apostle should have delivered such an address as represented before the mob in Jerusalem, in which he gives an account of his conversion, has been declared to be "unthinkable" (Weizsäcker). It is at least improbable (Acts xxii. 1-21).

Improbable also it is that Paul should have said before the sanhedrim that he was called in question on account of the hope of the resurrection of the dead (Acts xxiii. 6), when he knew very well that the gentile mission and his attitude toward the law (Acts xxi. 28) had excited the Jews against him; and it is equally unlikely that Pharisees and Sadducees should have forgotten their animosity toward him, and fallen into a strife over this question, the former supporting Paul because he agreed with them on this point. Felix is represented as keeping Paul in prison and often "communing" with him in the hope of getting money from him (Acts xxiv. 26)! Festus, in order that he may have some "certain thing to write" to Rome, calls together along with Agrippa and Bernice a grand assembly of "the chief captains and principal men of the city," before whom Paul delivers an extended discourse, in which he again tells of his conversion with the important variation from his previous account of it that he represents Jesus as making an extended speech to him out of heaven, which concludes with the announcement that Paul is sent to the gentiles "to open their eyes, and to turn them from darkness to light, and from the power of Satan unto God, that they may receive forgiveness of sins and inheritance among them who are sanctified by faith that is in me" (Acts xxvi. 1–18)!

Festus succeeded Felix in the year 61, according to the generally accepted chronology, and there is no reason for supposing that he delayed sending Paul to Rome on his appeal to the Emperor. The two-years imprisonment in Cæsarea, however, remains a problem in view of the fact that according to Acts Felix could not have believed the apostle "worthy of death or of bonds." The reasons given why he detained him are trivial. The account of the voyage to Rome given in the trustworthy we-section of Acts shows interesting traits of the apostle's personality. After the author brings him to Rome, however, he has little more to tell. He leaves him there in comfortable imprisonment living in his "hired house" under the guard of a soldier (Acts xxviii. 16, 30). That he must have known of the tragic fate of his hero one cannot but believe, and it is one of the many problems of the book why he tells us nothing of it. The epistle of Clement of Rome to the Corinthians, written at the end of the first or the beginning of the second century, leaves no doubt that he suffered martyrdom.

Thus ended the earthly career of the man who among the apostles and early followers of Jesus is eminently entitled to be called great. Intent upon carrying the message of the cross far and wide in the earth, zealous, intense, and courageous, he was the foremost of missionaries. His life in the service of his Master was a succession of conflicts, and was passed amidst conditions of hardship, sacrifice, and labour at a wretched handicraft for his own support. Under the circumstances his achievement must be regarded as remarkable, although the number of his converts was not large, and many of the little churches which he founded early disappeared, and have left no record in the history of Christianity. His passion for liberty and his fearless defence of his convictions against tendencies which would have resulted in stifling Christianity in its cradle, denote a championship of principles to whose success and supremacy is due all that is most precious and fruitful in human civilisation. His apostleship of the gentiles was the apostleship and the gospel of humanity, of freedom from the yoke of formalism, and of the love that "hopeth all things." Whatever may be the fortune of his dogmatic interpretation of Christianity in the judgment of mankind, his spiritual interpretation of it, his idea of the mystic fellowship with Jesus, and his conception of the life that is hid with Christ in God, will be cherished by the devout wherever the religion of the Master shall be most deeply understood. His ethical zeal, his life of devotion, of heroic sacrifice, of single-eyed service, of unflinching fidelity, will remain as an ideal and inspiration to the generations to come. His ideas and conflicts as well as certain traits of his personality isolated him in his life, and rendered him a solitary figure in primitive-Christian history. Alone, a unique and majestic figure, he went to his death amidst the decay of the mightiest pagan civilisation — yet not to death, but to the resurrection and the life which in the order of God belong to the true, the brave, and the good.

CHAPTER VII

THE PAUL OF THE ACTS AND THE PAUL OF THE EPISTLES[*]

IN the history of apostolic Christianity no subject is of more importance than the part taken by the apostle to the gentiles in the activities of the time, and the relation which he held to the "pillars" of the church in Jerusalem respecting the burning question as to the conditions on which the converted heathen should be admitted into the community of expectant believers, to whom the coming of their Lord from heaven would, they believed, secure the complete fruition of the kingdom of God. The difficulties of the problem, which are evident from the difference of opinion on important points still apparent after an exhaustive discussion during nearly three quarters of a century, arise from the relation of the two sources of information on the subject, the Acts and the Pauline Epistles. That these two sources differ widely both in some matters which they have in common and in incidents and circumstances contained in one of them alone no one will undertake to dispute. The historical trustworthiness of the only canonical account of the fortunes of the apostolical church has accordingly been the centre about which the conflict of opinion has raged most violently. It has been maintained that this ostensible history is in fact a "tendency-writing," the author of which, having a certain theory of the relations of the parties in the early church to establish, invented situations and suppressed facts in the interest of his manifest purpose; that remote from the events

[*] *The New World*, June, 1897.

and depending on sources not altogether good he has idealised the history, and given the colour of his own time to important episodes; and that (as Spitta has recently done) by assigning various portions of the book to sources of different degrees of credibility a tolerably consistent history can be constructed from the best of them, and the difficulties diminished by the assumption of the author's defective information. Adherents of the apologetic school have proceeded upon the assumption of the general trustworthiness of the history in Acts, and have employed the expedients and arts of the harmonist in order to bring it into accord with the Pauline Epistles. Sympathy with this procedure is apparent in some details of the treatment of the subject by a few representatives of the critical tendency, particularly Keim and Pfleiderer (see the former's *Aus dem Urchristenthum* and the latter's *Das Urchristenthum*).

Paul's relation to the heads of the church in Jerusalem and his attitude toward the Jewish ceremonial observances are matters of great importance in forming a judgment of his character and work and of the course of affairs in the history of apostolic Christianity. He himself lays so much stress upon the former that we are not justified in passing lightly over it, and in a judgment upon the latter is involved something more than the consistency of his conduct with principles which he clearly enunciated. Great difficulties present themselves in the attempt to reconcile his own positive affirmations regarding these matters with the accounts of them in Acts. In writing to the Galatians of his conversion, which he thought to be the revelation of God's Son in him for the express purpose that he might "preach him among the gentiles," he declares in a manner which shows that he regarded his independence of men and his immediate authority from God as involved in the statement, that he "conferred not with flesh and blood," neither went up to Jerusalem to the apostles, but went away into Arabia, then returned to Damascus, and after three years went to Jerusalem to visit Peter tarrying with him fifteen days and seeing no other of the apostles, but only James, the Lord's brother (Gal. i. 16, 17). To this fragment of biography he adds the emphatic declaration: "Now, touching the things which I write unto you, behold, before God, I lie not." On the contrary, the writer of Acts betrays a purpose to bring Paul after his conversion with all possible despatch into relations with the apostles in Jerusalem, as if to make it appear that he sought there the very recognition which he himself takes pains to affirm that he did not want. Omitting mention of the journey to Arabia he represents Paul as betaking himself immediately to the synagogue in Damascus and there preaching Jesus to the Jews, as if he had no thought of a mission to the gentiles. The Jews, displeased with the proclamation of Jesus as "the Son of God," attempt to kill him, and he escapes with difficulty and repairs to Jerusalem, where he tries to "join himself to the disciples," who, it appears, were suspicious of him, and received him only through the intervention of Barnabas.

That these two accounts convey, or were intended by their writers to convey, the same conception of Paul's movements directly after his conversion and of his relations with Jerusalem, cannot be successfully maintained. They are not so related that one can be said to supplement the other, so that the two can be combined into a consistent and probable narrative. The purpose of the writers, so far as it can be judged by their reports, was not to relate the same course of events. Either the author of Acts did not know of the journey to Arabia, — in which case he could not have read the Epistle to the Galatians, — or knowing it he omitted mention of it for a purpose not far to seek. He evidently did not intend that the inference should be drawn from his narrative that Paul allowed three years to elapse from his conversion before seeking the acquaintance of the original apostles or endeavouring to "attach" himself to them. The term of his residence in Damascus is given as "a considerable number of days" (ἡμέραι ἱκαναί), and this answers all the requirements of Paul's own account of the episode in 2 Cor. xi. 32, 33. The sojourn in Arabia and the return to Damascus are excluded by the immediate sequence of the mention of the journey to Jerusalem. The supposition that the persecution in Damascus occurred, according to the meaning and intention of the writer of Acts, after Paul's return from Arabia, or three years after his first arrival in that city, is contrary to the evident sense of ἡμέραι ἱκαναί, and requires a reading into the passage of a sense which was manifestly not intended, and which only the interest of a violent harmonising could suggest. It is, moreover, rendered improbable by the subsequent events in Jerusalem recorded by the writer of Acts himself. For he represents the apostles in Jerusalem as suspicious of Paul and ignorant of his conversion, so that the good offices of Barnabas were necessary in order that he might succeed in his effort to "attach" himself to them, — a condition of affairs which has not been too strongly characterised as "unthinkable" three years after the great event on the road to Damascus and a ministry in the synagogues of that city. Damascus was not so remote from Jerusalem, and intercourse between the two cities so infrequent, that the apostles can be supposed not to have heard of the conversion of the vehement persecutor of the Christians. Moreover, the account in Acts of this first visit of Paul in Jerusalem does not accord with that of the apostle himself in other particulars. Paul represents that he went up to Jerusalem to visit Peter, and that during the fifteen days of his sojourn there he saw no other one of the apostles, but did see James, the brother of Jesus, who was not an apostle (Gal. i. 18, 19). On the contrary, it is explicitly stated in Acts that when he came to Jerusalem he endeavoured to "attach himself to the disciples," that they were "*all* afraid of him," and that Barnabas "took him and brought him to the apostles" (ix. 26, 27). As Paul's declaration that the object of his journey was to visit Peter, and that he saw no other one of the apostles, was not without an intention in connection with the assertion of his independence, so the writer of Acts, if he was not ignorant of the facts, could hardly have related without a purpose ("tendency") a story of directly the opposite purport, — that Paul on his arrival in Jerusalem did not simply visit one of the twelve, but endeavoured to "attach" ($\kappa o \lambda \lambda \hat{a} \sigma \theta a \iota$) himself to the apostles in general, and was taken to them by Barnabas to this end. Again, the apostle's declaration that immediately thereafter he was "unknown by face to the churches of Judea" (Gal. i. 22) is irreconcilable with the statement in Acts that he was introduced to the apostles, and conducted for some time an active ministry in Jerusalem (ix. 28, 29); and especially with the words which the writer puts into the mouth of Paul in one of the accounts of his conversion, that immediately after that event he preached repentance "both to them of Damascus first and at Jerusalem and throughout all the country of Judea and also to the gentiles" (xxvi. 20).

It is evidently necessary to an understanding of the influences which determined the history of primitive Christianity as well as to a knowledge of Paul's motives and character and actions to make a right choice between these two accounts, since no combination of them into a consistent whole can be fairly made. The testimony of the apostle must not assuredly be rejected in the face of his asseveration of truthfulness (Gal. i. 21). His genuine Epistles must be regarded as a first-class source outranking in trustworthiness the record of Acts, of whose writer and his means of information we are, to say the least, not accurately informed. In any case we are compelled to believe that he was either ignorant of important facts or capable of suppressing them in the interest of a theory of primitive-Christian history or of seeing them inaccurately through the medium of a later time. It is also inadmissible to read the record of Acts into the statements of Paul regarding his relations with, and his attitude toward, the original apostles, since to do so is to modify his testimony to the extent that it is practically invalidated. In like manner, the story in Acts cannot be interpreted by inserting into its framework the historical incidents mentioned in Galatians without reaching a result which is opposed to the manifest intention of the writer of that book. Nothing is gained by this attempt to maintain the credibility of an author whose work is admitted by many of those who engage on his side to contain not a few unhistorical and improbable accounts. The injury to a sound hermeneutics resulting from such a procedure has no compensation. After making all due allowances for Paul's zeal as an "advocate" (see W. W. Fenn, *Lessons on the Acts*, p. 50), we cannot impugn his testimony in any important particular without attacking his character for integrity; and this any one should hesitate to do on the authority of a writing composed perhaps from forty to fifty years after the events in question occurred, from sources about which we must remain uncertain. If Paul on his first visit to Jerusalem after his conversion did not go solely to visit Peter, and if it is not true that he saw no other of the apostles, but sought to "attach" himself to the twelve, then is Galatians rather than Acts a "tendency-writing," if not worse, and important consequences must follow for our construction of the history of apostolic Christianity.

The report in Acts of other journeys of Paul to Jerusalem is not favourable to the trustworthiness of that record, or to the correctness of the writer's conception of the relation of the apostle to Judaism. The account of the journey undertaken in order to carry "relief to the brethren that dwelt in Judea" (xi. 29) is manifestly incorrect according to Gal. ii. 1, for it supposes a connection with Jerusalem which Paul could not have omitted to mention in that context without exposing himself to the charge of evasion or concealment. The unmistakable meaning of his words is, that he did not go up to the holy city after the visit recorded in Acts ix. 26-30 (Gal. i. 18-20) until fourteen years afterward, but was unknown in the mean time to the churches in Judea (Gal. i. 22). This second visit, mentioned in Gal. ii. 1, is identical with that recorded in Acts xv. 2, and here incorrectly appears as the third. Meyer's expedient, that in the journey recorded in Acts xi. 29 Paul did not go as far as Jerusalem, is scarcely worthy of refutation (see Mr. Fenn, *ut supra*, p. 64). A journey to Jerusalem is intimated in Acts xviii. 22 (ἀναβάς) which has caused no little perplexity to the commentators. In verse 21 Paul appears in great haste to get away from Ephesus, though for what reason does not appear, unless the words are genuine: "I must by all means keep this feast that cometh in Jerusalem." They are wanting in ABESin., and some other MSS., and are omitted by Lachmann and Tischendorf; but most MSS., the Syrian included, retain them, and they are defended by Zeller, Ewald, De Wette-Overbeck, Hilgenfeld, and

Meyer. Their omission in the cases mentioned is accounted for by Meyer with great probability on account of the uncertainty of the sense of ἀναβάς (verse 22); but that the reference here is to Jerusalem is regarded by Weizsäcker as unquestionable. The words "and went down to Antioch" (verse 22) can hardly signify anything else than a journey from Jerusalem to Antioch. The entire account is involved in great uncertainty, and Holtzmann very properly remarks on the improbability of Paul's making a journey to Jerusalem at this period of "open conflict." The intention of the author of Acts, however, to represent that such a journey was made, is scarcely to be doubted, whether its purpose was to attend a Jewish festival or to "salute the church." The supposition that he was misinformed or confused by his sources can alone save him from the charge of a definite intention to bring Paul as frequently as possible into friendly relations with the church in Jerusalem, regardless of historical accuracy. Such an intention is probable in xix. 21, where Paul is represented as having "purposed in the spirit . . . to go to Jerusalem," without any apparent motive in the midst of his successful activity in Ephesus, where "mightily grew the work of the Lord and prevailed." This view of the matter is supported by the apparent interest of the writer in making the apostle seem to have been zealous in the observance of Jewish ceremonies, when he puts into his mouth the declarations that he went up to Jerusalem to worship and to present offerings in the temple, and that, "after the way which they call a sect," he served the God of our fathers, "believing all things which are according to the law" (xxiv. 11, 14, 17); and when he represents him, according to the most probable rendering, as "having shorn his head in Cenchrea, for he had a vow" (xviii. 18).

More befitting the Paul of the Acts than the Paul of the Epistles is the account of a procedure of his in Jerusalem in connection with a Nazarite vow (Acts xxi. 21-24). Paul is here informed by "the elders" that the Jewish Christians, who were "all zealous for the law," had been told that he was teaching the Jews who were among the gentiles to forsake Moses, and neither to circumcise their children nor to walk after the customs; and is advised by them to take four men who had a vow on them, purify himself with them, and be at charges for them, that they may shave their heads, that all might know that the accusations against him were false, and that he was walking orderly and keeping the law. This Paul is represented as having done without a word of objection, as if he were himself a zealot for the law! Since he is said to have acted on the advice of the elders in order to invalidate the charge that he was teaching the Jewish Christians not to circumcise their children and observe the customs, the question arises whether he could have regarded this charge as a calumniation to be answered by such a subjection of himself to a Jewish ceremonial. The Paul of the Acts, the Paul of the so-called apostolic council, as reported by the author of that book, may have made the unresisting concession here related if the words of the elders, probably by the mouth of James, can be regarded as a commentary on the decree of that council: "That thou thyself walkest orderly, keeping the law. But as touching the gentiles who have believed, we wrote," etc. (verses 24, 25). For the import of this plainly is that Paul and other Jewish Christians were bound by the terms of the council, as Jews, to observe the law, while the gentiles were exempted. But could the historical Paul, the Paul of the Epistles, ever have accepted such a principle? Could he have deemed himself calumniated by the charge that he taught his Jewish converts not to circumcise their children? Must not he have opposed on principle the subjection of the offspring of Christian parents to this rite, he who solemnly declared to the Galatians, "I, Paul, say unto you that if ye receive circumcision, Christ will profit you nothing" (Gal. v. 2)? Would he not have thought them, if circumcised, to be as truly "debtors to do the whole law" as he affirmed that the gentile converts would be? It is futile, as Zeller has shown, to quote 1 Cor. vii. 18 f., for according to Paul's gospel of uncircumcision the children of Jewish-Christian parents were born ἐν ἀκροβυστίᾳ (see 1 Cor. vii. 14), and hence the injunction μὴ περιτεμνέσθω was applicable to them. It is evident that more was involved for Paul in the advice of the elders than the mere performance of a Jewish rite, more than a matter which he could have "deemed indifferent." The central principle of his gospel was at stake, since he was asked to refute a charge which, according to his entire teaching, was false; and if such a counsel was given him he must have resented it as an insult, and have felt that to follow it were a degradation. But, conceding that he had connived at the circumcision of the children of the believing Jews of the dispersion or permitted it, one cannot but think with Holtzmann that it involved a sort of mental reservation, an ambiguous proceeding, or, at least, anything but a grand mode of action, to make use of such a fact in Jerusalem as a last resort for the support of the assertion that all which they had heard of his undermining of the law was nothing, and for the promotion of the idea that he "walked orderly, keeping the law." Under the circumstances, Paul's tame and humiliating acceptance of the advice of the elders can be regarded according to the record as nothing short of an acknowledgment that he was, contrary to 1 Cor. ix. 20, ὑπὸ τὸν νόμον as a φυλάσσων τὸν νόμον. For "all apologetic efforts go to pieces upon the fact that no act of accommodation, but a confession is reported, and turn moreover into charges as well against James as against Paul, to the effect that the advice of the former was unsatisfactory, unfitting, untimely, and the following of it on the part of the latter a 'weakness and undue haste'" (*Hand-Commentar*, i. p. 407). Apropos of the fact that Calvin thought that he must excuse the one as well as the other for participation in the superstitious vow, Hausrath remarks that it is rather credible that Calvin on his death-bed should have vowed a golden robe to the Mother of God than that Paul should have gone in the way indicated.

The account of the circumcision of Timothy by Paul (Acts xvi. 1–4) presents similar difficulties. Timothy, according to the report, was a convert to Christianity, whose father was a Greek. His mother, however, was a Jewess, and he had not been circumcised. Paul wanted him as a companion, and performed the Jewish rite upon him, "on account of the Jews that were in those parts." To one whose knowledge of Paul's character and principles is derived entirely from Acts, this narrative, related as if the proceeding were a matter of course, would present no serious difficulty. But the case is quite different when we undertake to judge of it with the Paul in mind who vehemently rebuked Peter in Antioch for "dissimulation," and wrote the account of his determined opposition to the circumcision of Titus in Jerusalem. Meyer expresses the opinion that Paul could not have performed the rite on this occasion if the request had been made by Jewish Christians, but might have done it "on account of the Jews," so that they should not take offence at his having as a companion an uncircumcised man who was on one side of Jewish parentage. But it is not apparent why he should yield to Jews what he would not concede to Jewish Christians, and in fact refused to them in the case of Titus. If he was willing to be as a Jew to Jews in order that he might gain some of them, can he be supposed to have carried this accommodation so far as to perform the rite of circumcision upon a Christian companion out of deference to Jewish prejudice? The judgment must turn upon the question whether for Paul a principle was at stake in the case. Professor Pfleiderer remarks on the subject that such a condescension of Paul's constitutes so striking a contrast to his inflexibility regarding Titus, shortly before in Jerusalem, that a doubt of the correctness of the account seems justified. The apostle, he says, was always unyielding where questions of religious principle arose out of legal externalities; while, where this was not the case, he judged the latter as religious ἀδιάφορα,* and made no objection.† This scholar finds a solution of the difficulty in the supposition that the writer of Acts has placed here an event which occurred early in Paul's ministry, when according to Gal. v. 11, the apostle may have favoured circumcision. But, to say nothing of the absence of grounds for the assumption of a displacement of the narrative, the passage referred to does not necessarily imply that Paul advocated circumcision at the beginning of his ministry, or ever as an apostle. The passage is equivalent to, "If I were still preaching circumcision, I should not still be persecuted." ‡ But it is very doubtful whether the apostle could have regarded such a matter as among ἀδιάφορα, or things indifferent, either before or after the episode concerning Titus. The proceeding is in direct

---

* ἀδιάφορα, things indifferent.

† *Das Urchristenthum*, p. 585 f.

‡ εἰ περιτομὴν ἔτι ἐκήρυσσον, οὐκέτι ἂν ἐδιωκόμην. See Meyer, *Commentar, in loc.,* and Lipsius, *Hand-Commentar,* ii. p. 59.

opposition to the doctrine: "If any one is called in uncircumcision, let him remain uncircumcised" (1 Cor. vii. 18). One can hardly think of Paul as circumcising a believer "on account of the Jews" when he held that the rite implied the obligation to keep the whole law, and that Christ profited him nothing on whom it was performed. The question has well been raised why the apostle whose ministry was to the gentiles should be believed to have made such a concession "on account of the Jews." About to depart on a journey, why should he regard the prejudice of "the Jews that were in those parts"? If the "inconsistency" of Paul is to be easily assumed, he should not at least be charged with it unless a good reason for it can be shown. Not without grounds has doubt been cast upon this narrative, which probably does not belong to the "we-source," because of the writer's apparent purpose to represent Paul as chiefly associating in his ministry with those to whom the unbelieving Jews, zealots for the law, would take no exception. His omission of any mention of Titus and of the apostle's inflexible opposition in Jerusalem to the demand for his circumcision is noteworthy in this connection, and can with difficulty be explained on any other hypothesis than that of an intention to disregard facts not in accord with his conception of Paul's character and work.

This writer's account of the apostle's work as a missionary is in fact hardly reconcilable with the spirit and aim of Paul as he represents himself in the Epistles. Not to dwell upon the fact that, according to Acts, it is not the apostle to the gentiles, but Peter, who was the real founder of the mission to the uncircumcised (Acts x. 1 f.), the ministry of the former is generally represented as primarily to the Jews. In most cases his preaching to the gentiles is set forth as merely incidental and as occasioned by the hostility of the Jews to his message. It is made to appear that the redoubtable advocate of the gospel of the uncircumcision, who said of himself that God had revealed His Son in him in order that he might preach the good news to the gentiles (Gal. i. 16), goes to them for the reason that his own people reject and persecute him (Acts xiii. 46). At an advanced period in his ministry he is made to say to the unbelieving and blasphemous Jews: "Your blood be upon your own heads; I am clean; *from henceforth* I will go unto the gentiles" (xviii. 6). Yet repeatedly thereafter he pursues the settled policy, "as was his custom," of beginning his ministry at various points in the synagogues. Some exceptions to this procedure are, indeed, to be noted (xiii. 7-12, xiv. 6, 7, 21, xvii. 11. 12, 17-34), but in the first instance Sergius Paulus is only incidentally converted after the synagogue had been favoured with a ministration. The theory of the author of Acts is carried out with striking consistency and vigour to the very end of Paul's work as he records it, so that in Rome his relations with the Jews are at first unconstrained, until, rejected by a portion of them, he hurls at them a condemnatory prophecy, and declares that the "salvation of God is sent unto the gentiles" (xxviii. 23-28). Thus the writer represents from first to last that the origin of the Pauline gentile church is due to the obstinate unbelief of the Jews. On the other hand, it must be conceded that Paul was profoundly interested in the conversion of his "brethren" to the Christian faith. But, according to his own declarations on the subject, the method should have been the reverse of that pursued if the representation in Acts is correct; for the Jews were to be incited to "jealousy" by the prior acceptance of the gospel on the part of the gentiles, the "fulness" of whom was first to be brought in (Rom. x. 16-21, xi. 5, 11-16, 20, 23, 25-31.

See Holtzmann, *ut supra*, p. 316). Single instances of beginning his ministry first among the Jews are not of so much importance as the "suspicious regularity" (Weizsäcker, Holtzmann) of the procedure according to Acts, where it appears as a "principle" of his mission (xiii. 46, 47, xviii. 6, xxviii. 26-28). On this theory "the principal difference between Paul and the original apostles is that he turned to the gentiles when the Jews would not hear him," in direct contravention of the agreement reached in Jerusalem between him and them (Gal. ii. 9), according to which they were to undertake the ministry to the Jews, and he that to the gentiles.

For an estimate of the two representations of Paul in question, his doctrinal teachings as given in the respective sources furnish important data. We should expect to find in a history of the apostle, which a considerable portion of Acts ostensibly is, an account of his method of presenting his peculiar apprehension of Christianity, or at least specimens of his missionary preaching in which his distinctive doctrines would be given emphatic expression. It is true that some of his speeches in Acts are apologetic, and do not furnish occasion for such an exposition. But opportunities for it are not wanting, and where they occur we are invariably disappointed by the contrast between the Epistles and the addresses in this history. In Antioch of Pisidia he delivered an address to the Jews in the synagogue, in Athens to gentiles, and at Miletus to Christians; yet in neither of these does he go beyond the average Jewish-Christian profession of faith,—the one God, Christ the Messiah, and the resurrection (xiii. 16-41, xvii. 22-31, xx. 17-35), just as elsewhere he testifies of repentance and conversion, and "reasons of righteousness and temperance and the judgment to come" (xxii. 1-21, xxiv. 10-21, xxvi. 2-23). In all the speeches of the apostle reported in Acts, there is little that indicates the vigorous champion of the new gospel of grace who has impressed the stamp of his originality on almost every page of the Epistles. The Pauline terminology is, indeed, employed in xiii. 39 (δικαιοῦται), but according to Holtzmann "this passage presents instead of a full Paulinism in the sense of Rom. i. 17, vi. 7, viii. 3 a negative conception of justification, *i.e.* absolution, and presupposes like Luke xviii. 14 that a certain though unsatisfactory measure of it is to be found as the ground of the law." An intimation of the doctrine of justification by faith is contained in xvi. 31, and possibly in xx. 21; yet the fact is significant with reference to the relation assumed in Acts of Paul and the original apostles to Christianity that, as has been repeatedly pointed out, the distinctive "watchwords" of Paulinism are put into the mouth of Peter, who represents himself as "a good while ago" chosen of God to preach the gospel to the gentiles (Acts xv. 7-11). But if the apostles in Jerusalem felt, as Peter here represents, that the law was "a yoke upon the neck of the disciples" which neither they nor their fathers "were able to bear," it is not easy to see what ground for controversy there was between them and Paul. It is precisely this controversy, however, that the writer of Acts is studious to ignore. He may not, as the older Tübingen school supposed, have drawn the portraits of Peter and Paul with a conscious "tendency," but may rather, perhaps, as Dr. Pfleiderer remarks, have "made Peter speak like an ecclesiastical Jewish Christian, and Paul like an ecclesiastical deutero-Paulinist of his own time. Because these two tendencies had then come so near each other to the point of indistinguishability, it was very natural that their typical representatives should appear much closer together than they in reality once stood" (*Das Urchristenthum*, p. 581).

M

The conference which Paul held with the apostles in Jerusalem on his second visit to that city concerning the central question of the church at the time, that of the circumcision of the gentile converts, has already been referred to in the course of the preceding discussion. The two accounts of this event (Gal. ii. 1-10, Acts xv. 1-35) are, if not controlled by opposite aims, at least from widely different points of view. The veritable course of affairs in this conference, the attitude of Paul and of "those in authority" (οἱ δοκοῦντες) in Jerusalem respecting the question in debate, and the actual outcome of the council, are matters of the gravest importance for the history of apostolic Christianity. It was not without good reason that the keen insight of the great founder of the Tübingen school saw in this passage of Galatians the right point of departure for the critical study of the literature of the primitive church. The question, whether this literature could have been what it is if the account in Acts is correct, must be determined by a careful analysis of that report, and a comparison of its statements with those made by the apostle himself on the subject.

It is, first of all, of paramount importance to ascertain as nearly as possible Paul's point of view and feeling respecting all that was involved in the journey to Jerusalem, and it will not be denied by the ardent supporters of the credibility of Acts that the most trustworthy source for this information is found in his own declarations in Galatians. Now it is manifest to the student of the first two chapters of this Epistle that the apostle is concerned before all with the assertion of his independence of men, especially of the "pillars" in Jerusalem, in all that related to his credentials as a preacher of the new gospel to the gentiles (Gal. i. 1). He also declares specifically that no man taught him this gospel, but that he had it "through revelation of Jesus Christ" (Gal. i. 12). It is with the one end in view of making prominent the original character of his authority as an apostle that he mentions his conversion, wrought by God for the sole purpose of sending him to the gentiles, and emphasises the fact that he did not thereupon go to Jerusalem "to them that were apostles before" him, but only after three years, and then solely to visit Peter, seeing no other of the apostles. After having disregarded during fourteen years those "reputed to be somewhat" in Jerusalem, and apparently shown himself disposed to ignore them indefinitely except in an especial emergency, he went up at length "by revelation." There is no intimation in his account that those in authority there had paid any more attention to him than he had to them,—that they had molested him, or in any way interfered with his work. Nothing is known of the character or contents of the "revelation," but the mention of it in the connection is important, as Weizsäcker has pointed out,* since it indicates, like the "revelation" of his conversion, a consciousness of direct authority from above and independence of external constraint. Whether, according to Acts, he was sent to Jerusalem by the church in Antioch, or no, is not a matter of moment, but it is of the greatest consequence whether he went to argue a question which had been discussed in that church, before an apostolic tribunal whose authority he who "took not counsel of flesh and blood" could recognise in the matter in dispute. It is not expressly declared, but is probably implied in the account in Acts, that the question of salvation without circumcision remained unsettled after "no small dissension" in the Antiochian church, and could only be settled by an appeal "to the apostles and elders" in Jerusalem. But in view of the spirit and feeling mani-

* *Jahrbücher für deutsche Theologie*, 1873, p. 195.

fested by Paul in his account of the affair, and of the connection in which he places it, his acceptance of such a mission is unthinkable on any just estimate of his character. He to whom the gospel of the uncircumcision had come by "revelation of Jesus Christ," and who for fourteen years had not recognised the authority of "those reputed to be somewhat," could not thus have compromised himself even out of deference to the wishes of the "brethren" in Antioch. Had such a humiliating proposition been made to him, could he have let slip the opportunity of declaring in the Epistle to the Galatians his indignant rejection of it? It is altogether unmistakable, from what he says of the matter in this Epistle, that he could not have gone to Jerusalem to seek a human authorisation for a gospel which he believed to be divinely authenticated to him. His own words comport well with his sense of dignity and authority: "I went up by revelation, and I laid before (ἀνεθέμην) them the gospel which I preach among the gentiles" (Gal. ii. 2). The journey was evidently undertaken with the purpose of compelling, of winning by a contest if necessary, the recognition of the "pillars" of the church; but he does not by a word cast the least doubt upon his own conviction of the rightness of his cause, or intimate that he could be strengthened in his assurance of it by anything that the apostles might say. Probably a knowledge on his part of a feeling hostile to him in Jerusalem, and of an influence against him issuing thence, must be assumed as the occasion of the experience which he calls a "revelation." At any rate, he went up with the "proud conviction" that in his gentile mission he was not running and had not run "in vain," and that the presentation of the matter to the apostles would at least secure him from any further interference with his work on their part.

That the apostle did not make this journey in a spirit of compromise, or to secure a "supplementary authorisation" of his gospel, or to bring for decision before a higher tribunal a question debated in Antioch, is apparent from the fact that he took with him the uncircumcised Greek Titus "as a living example" of the principle of his mission. This circumstance, the mention of which did not accord with the purpose of the writer of Acts, he places before the Galatians with an unconcealed pride, and adds that he did not yield for an hour to the demand that the Jewish rite should be performed upon his companion, "that the truth of the gospel might continue" with them (Gal. ii. 5). He stakes the principle of his mission on this contest, which he glories in having brought to a victorious conclusion, and which had its chief significance for him and his cause on account of "the false brethren who came in privily [among his churches] to spy out their liberty." That Titus was not circumcised at all, whether by compulsion or voluntarily, is too evident from the tone and context of the account to warrant discussion. The reason is manifest why the writer of Acts, who records the circumcision of Timothy "on account of the Jews," should have omitted mention of this episode on which Paul lays so much stress. It does not accord with the point of view of that book to give prominence to any conflict between Paul and the Jewish-Christian leaders in Jerusalem. But that a bitter conflict arose in the case in question is evident from the sketch in Galatians. That the apostle, moreover, regarded it as of great importance, and as denoting a crisis, an epoch, in Christian history, there can be no doubt. Its significance certainly depends in no small degree upon the part taken in it by "those in authority." Paul's condensed statement of the matter leaves us in uncertainty on this point. He doubtless means to be understood as declaring that a pressure was brought to bear upon him in Jerusalem for the circumcision of Titus. The passage is very difficult, and has received widely different interpretations. If we read "on account of the false brethren," etc. (διὰ τοὺς παρ. ψευδ.), in close connection with the foregoing, the sense may be that the demand was made by reason of these persons, assumed to be present in Jerusalem; while, if we separate them as in the revised version, it may be that Paul's attitude and struggle were with reference to them in his several churches.[*] But, in any case, he does not say that "the false brethren" made the demand, and he certainly could not mean to imply that he resisted the requirement because *they* made it, as if he would have acceded to it under different circumstances. Whether he was required by performing the act in question to bear public testimony against his gospel by the whole church in Jerusalem, by few, by many, or by the apostles themselves, he does not tell us. Perhaps Lipsius goes too far in saying that it results "with certainty" from the account that the apostles at first required the circumcision of Titus.[†] It is certain, however, that the demand came from a source which Paul deemed of so much importance as to justify emphatic mention. It is also of no little significance, as Weizsäcker has pointed out (*ut supra*, p. 304), that he gives as the sole reason why the requirement was not carried out his own opposition to it, and does not intimate that he had support in his resistance from any quarter. The fact that the pillar-apostles yielded in the end does not necessarily carry with it the implication that they did not at first join in making the demand.

Not only did Paul successfully resist the demand in question, but he secured from the three chief apostles, Peter,

---

[*] So Lipsius in *Hand-Commentar, in loc.*
[†] Article, "Apostel-Convent" in Schenkel's *Bibel-Lexicon.*

James, and John, a recognition of his mission to the gentiles. He does not intimate, however, that fellowship was extended to him on behalf of the whole church in Jerusalem, or that he had that of the other believers there. An important question arises here respecting the relation of these three men to the rest of the Christian community in the holy city, in which is involved the significance of apparently ironical expressions of the apostle's regarding the former. If these chiefs did not join in the demand respecting Titus, they at least did not prevent it, and were perhaps unable to do so. From this point of view, Paul's words with reference to them, "those reputed to be somewhat," "whatsoever they [once] were, it maketh no matter to me," may be significant of the fact that they were not masters of the situation, and could not control their followers. On the other hand, if they favoured the requirement, or counselled his acquiescence in it for the sake of harmony, these expressions may denote, in view of his successful resistance, his superior authority and his triumph over them. Another question arises, which is of still greater importance, because it involves the trustworthiness of the account in Acts xv. : Were the transactions in question "privately" conducted before "those who were of repute," or before a veritable council of "the apostles and elders"? If we leave without discussion Weizsäcker's opinion that the writer of Acts had Galatians as a source for his narrative, it is in any case evident that, besides omitting the account of the strife about Titus, he has given a graphic delineation of an event of which Paul gives no intimation, — a formal council in which speeches were made, and a decree was agreed upon. Paul's statement is simply that he went up to Jerusalem, and laid before "them" his gospel, "but privately before them who were of repute." The former "them" has no immediate antecedent, and the probably correct interpretation is that, when he used it, he had in mind the apostles, but qualified it immediately by saying that he meant only those who were recognised as their leaders. It is upon this private conference that he lays the entire stress, and no place can be found in his account (Gal. ii. 2-10), without the greatest violence, for such proceedings as those recorded in Acts. The author of this book, looking at the matter from the point of view of his time, could see nothing so fitting as an ecclesiastical council, and he accordingly knew nothing of a private transaction, a compact of the chief apostles with Paul, a right hand of fellowship. The supposition of a formal council encounters the difficulty involved in Paul's silence about it. If it was held after a private conference, which he explicitly mentions, it would be significant as giving a public sanction and authority to whatever compact was made in the latter. Accordingly, he could not have omitted to give it prominence in his account of the proceedings, for to do so would have strengthened his position. It is unthinkable that in such a council the chief apostles should not have been conspicuous, and equally unthinkable that Paul should have said nothing of their attitude and words. A private conference after the council could have no significance unless it were held in order to reverse the formal decree, in which case the latter would be made a farce.

The attitude and relation of Paul toward the apostles in Jerusalem, as set forth in the two accounts, present a contrast which is of no small historical significance. According to Acts, he goes up as a delegate, along with others, to lay before an ecclesiastical council the question of the circumcision of the gentile converts, which had been discussed in Antioch, where it would appear that he was not himself recognised as an authority on the subject. Arrived in Jerusalem, he does not go before his peers, the apostles, to defend his gospel and assert his rights as one who, having "seen the Lord" and had a "revelation," acknowledged no superior among them, but he submits to present the vital question of his mission to an assembly composed of "the apostles and elders," according to one statement, and according to another, of "the apostles and elders and the whole church," as if the matter at issue were one on which he could accept a majority vote as decisive. In this council he is no conspicuous figure. He has no cause to argue. There is no contest over the question for the defence of which he would have given his heart's blood. He does not appear as the redoubtable antagonist of those "reputed to be somewhat" for the exposition of his gospel of liberty and for the arraignment of those who would bring his gentile converts into bondage. No words of his are reported, but he is consigned to obscurity with the remark that together with Barnabas he rehearsed "what signs and wonders God had wrought among the gentiles by them." Finally, he meekly receives the decree of the council, and departs to publish it among the gentile churches. On the contrary, according to the account in Galatians Paul went to Jerusalem, not because he was sent to appeal a case to a council, but by reason of an inward intimation which he regarded as a "revelation." He was not "appointed" together with certain others, but apparently chose his own companions, and had the boldness to take with him the Greek Titus into the stronghold of the circumcision. On arriving there he does not go before an assemblage of the church to receive instructions, but lays privately before those whom he regarded as his equals, not his superiors, the gospel which he preached by direct divine authority among the gentiles. He resists the demand for the circumcision of Titus, and wins his cause alone. The result is that "those who were reputed to be somewhat" imparted nothing to him, but rather derived from him the conviction that he "had been intrusted with the gospel of the uncircumcision." When about to depart he receives no decree satisfactory to "the apostles and the elders and the whole church," but the right hand of fellowship which he had won from the pillar-apostles, accompanied with the request that he should remember the poor, a thing which he "was zealous to do." These two accounts are so opposed in spirit and evident intention that an inward, essential reconciliation of them is impossible. An external harmonising of them appears, accordingly, superficial and trivial. The construction of a "composite" portrait of the Paul of history and the Paul of fancy serves rather the ends of amusement than of instruction.

That the historical Paul is represented in the account of these events in Galatians is probable from some circumstance incidental to them. It is difficult to explain his journey to Jerusalem at all, to find an adequate motive for it, unless the implications of it were such as he sets forth. He would hardly have taken all the trouble of such a journey unless an object of great moment were to be achieved. This could have been nothing less than a conference, a contest, with the chief apostles. Why should he go up and lay before them the gospel that he preached if he believed them to be already favourable to it? A subordinate disaffected party, which the apostles could very well hold in check if they were friendly to his cause, would hardly be worthy of such an effort. Again, it will not be disputed that Paul's account of the affair with Titus is historical. Yet he speaks of an influence brought to bear upon him which was of the nature of an attempted compulsion. A pressure that he could so designate could have come only from an authoritative source. Accordingly, the presumption is very strong that the apostles not only, as we have seen to be probable, gave him no support in this contest, but also either joined in the demand, or lent their influence to those who pressed it upon him. They would have this concession on his part, until they saw they could not obtain it, as the condition of the sort of "fellowship" which he at length gained as the result of the contest. All this would have been very improbable, the journey to Jerusalem, the contest, the note of triumph in Galatians, if the attitude of the apostles is correctly represented by the speech of Peter at the "council," as reported in Acts. For he is there represented as saying not only that he was himself the divinely appointed agent of the gentile mission, and that God made no distinction between Jews and gentiles, but also that it was a tempting of God to require circumcision, and thus put a yoke upon the neck of the disciples which neither the Jewish fathers nor their descendants were able to bear. "But we believe," he declares, "that we shall be saved through the grace of our Lord Jesus" (xv. 7-11). These remarks, which the author of Acts composed and put into the mouth of the chief of the apostles of the circumcision, contain, as far as they go, a confession of the Pauline faith. If they represent the supposed council, and there is no intimation of a dissenting voice, it is difficult to see any reason for Paul's journey, or how the demand respecting Titus could have been made. Peter's subsequent demeanour in Antioch in eating with gentiles furnishes no presumption in favour of his having acknowledged the essentials of the Pauline gospel in Jerusalem. In fact, his immediate retreat at the command of James shows that he stood upon no liberal conviction in the matter. The speech put into the mouth of James is even more improbable from what we know of him, and both cannot be better characterised than by saying that they are well adapted to the harmonising purpose of the writer of Acts or at least to his historical point of view.*

The story of a decree of a council in Jerusalem which Paul submitted to receive, and to go about promulgating

---

* Dr. McGiffert, whose work on *The Apostolic Age* comes under the writer's notice as this book is going through the press, expresses the opinion (p. 209) that "there is nothing improbable in the supposition that Peter and James made such addresses as are ascribed to them in Acts xv.," although he casts doubt upon one-half of Peter's speech. Apart from the fact that the rejection of a part of the speech throws suspicion on the rest, and favours the theory that the whole of it is a composition of the writer of Acts, it should be remarked that the section, of the genuineness of which Dr. McGiffert is doubtful (verses 9 and 10), is precisely that part of it which is important to the question that was under discussion. Peter, for example, is represented as having said:

(Vs. 8) "And God who knoweth the hearts bare them [the gentiles] witness, giving them the Holy Ghost, even as he did unto us;

(Vs. 9) "And put no difference between us and them, purifying their hearts by faith.

(Vs. 10) "Now therefore why tempt ye God to put a yoke upon the neck of the disciples which neither our fathers nor we were able to bear?

(Vs. 11) "But we believe that through the grace of our Lord Jesus Christ we shall be saved even as they."

The eighth verse contains only a general declaration as to the bestowal of the Spirit, and the eleventh is a confession of faith in the Pauline "gospel," in accordance with the manifest purpose of the writer of Acts to make Peter speak like Paul. But if we allow the genuineness of these words, it is evident from Peter's conduct at Antioch that he did not interpret salvation by "grace" in the Pauline sense, or he could not, as Paul charges, have endeavoured to "compel the gentiles to live as do the Jews" (Gal. ii. 14). Without verses 9 and 10 Peter's speech is emptied of significance, and may as well be left out of account altogether.

As to the speech ascribed to James, to say nothing of the improbability of its having been reproduced with anything like accuracy fifty years afterwards, together with the long quotation from the Old Testament, the declaration: "My sentence is that we trouble not them who from among the gentiles are turned unto God," stands in direct opposition to the bitter "trouble" which James soon after prepared for the gentiles in Antioch, when he sent the emissaries to Peter. James appears in history in a better light, so far as honesty is concerned, on the supposition that he made no such speech at the council as Acts represents.

among his churches, has against it every probability in the case. It does not at all comport with the spirit of independence and the consciousness of an authority not derived from men, that constitute the nerve of Paul's account of the matter in Galatians, that he should passively have received such a decree, which denotes an acknowledged jurisdiction of the Jerusalem church over the gentile mission. The sense of his own autonomy is plainly implied in the declaration that those who were reputed to be somewhat imparted or communicated nothing to him (οὐδὲν προσανέθεντο Gal. ii. 6), together with a depreciation of the authority which they assumed, or which was assumed for them. Moreover, despite the fact that Paul asserts one of the results of the conference to have been that the apostles made of him "only" the modest request that he should "remember the poor" (Gal. ii. 10), the account in Acts represents certain "necessary things" to have been required in the decree, — Jewish prescripts as to food, abstinence from "things sacrificed to idols, and from blood and from things strangled" (Acts xv. 29). Apart from its direct contradiction of Paul's declaration, the decree implies, as Weizsäcker remarks, a purpose to so regulate the deportment of the gentile converts that the Jewish Christians could associate with them. Yet, if such a decree was actually promulgated, Peter's subsequent difficulty in Antioch is inexplicable, — a matter about which Acts has for obvious reasons nothing to say. It is, moreover, irreconcilable with the existence of such a decree that Paul nowhere in his Epistles takes the least notice of it, particularly when, as in 1 Cor. viii. 1 f., x. 28 f., he discusses the question of the eating of things offered to idols. Here he might very effectively have quoted the decree of the "council," and could in fact hardly have refrained from doing so, if such a document had been in existence. But he does not even enjoin the abstinence in question on the ground that the eating of such things is wrong in principle, but recommends it for the sake of the weaker brethren who "have not knowledge."* The decree of the council has, then, no historical basis, and with it falls the entire account in Acts of the transactions in Jerusalem, of the false position of the original apostles, the humiliation of Paul, and the distorted view of his character and mission.

In any case, however, even on Paul's own account of it, the issue of the conference must have been quite unsatisfactory. In the attempt to reconcile irreconcilables, only a "preliminary expedient" was reached. The "right hand of fellowship" had small significance. There was a division of the work, and each might go to his own. But neither party was convinced that the other was right. For the original apostles to concede that uncircumcised gentiles might sit with Jews in the kingdom, which Christ was about to establish at the Parousia, was in fact to admit that the rite was not necessary to the latter. Accordingly, the conjecture appears probable that this matter was not really determined in their minds at all, and that the "expedient" was "preliminary" also in the sense that the Lord would settle that question at his coming. In the "right hand of fellowship," then, Paul received recognition neither of the truth of his gospel nor of his own claim to the apostleship. The gospel of the circumcision was still to be preached, and Jerusalem was

---

* Regard is had to him that is weak and to the one who may have indicated to the believer that the flesh was offered to idols: "For if any man see thee who hast knowledge sit at meat in the idol's temple, should not the conscience of him that is weak be emboldened to eat those things which are offered to idols?" (1 Cor. viii. 10). Again he says: "If any man say to you, This is offered in sacrifice to idols, eat not for his sake that showed it, and for conscience' sake" (1 Cor. x. 28).

the centre to which the gentile converts might send their offerings. On Paul's part, the gospel of the apostles could not be accepted as that of Christ, and stood over against his own in irreconcilable opposition. He was destined to go his way alone, and alone to contend and to triumph. His cause prevailed, because in the nature of things the victory belongs to the spirit over the letter, to liberty over bondage, to Jesus over Judaism.

PART III
THE TEACHER

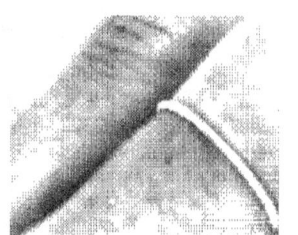

PART III

THE TEACHER

CHAPTER VIII

THE LAW*

A KNOWLEDGE of Paul's apprehension of the law, his interpretation of it, and his attitude toward it, is necessary to an understanding of his thought and an appreciation of his mission. His gospel to the gentiles

* The chapters in this third part, which is devoted to an elucidation of the teachings of the apostle, have not been arranged in accordance with the hypothesis that his theological doctrine is to be regarded as a *system*, the different parts of which can be related to one another under the notion of dependence or of development. He was, indeed, the first among the followers of Jesus to give to Christianity a theological or doctrinal expression; but to do this was not his primary purpose. He was before all and essentially a missionary, and his work as a teacher was subordinate to his work as a travelling herald of the cross. The elaboration of a system of theology was incompatible with the conditions of his activity and with the circumstances amidst which his Epistles were written. These were all writings of the occasion, called forth by the exigencies of his missionary work, and adapted to the needs of his churches. In them, it is true, are distinctly emphasised the pivotal doctrines of his "gospel": Christ, the Son; his death as an atonement for sin; the mystic fellowship of the believer with him; his resurrection as evidence of his divine sanction; the abolition of the law; the new righteousness by faith; and the Christian's sonship of God, which was to be consummated at the early coming of Jesus in his kingdom and glory. These cardinal doctrines, however, which were doubtless the burden of his preaching as a missionary, find in his writings no systematic elaboration, but are presented according to the requirements of the occasion, with varying emphasis, and with different forms of expression which sometimes reveal the most astounding paradoxes. The theory which has been advocated by some of the apostle's expositors, that his teaching reveals a progressive development, must be taken with some grains of allowance. One must in particular be cautious about accepting the doctrine to which Dr. Matheson (*The Spiritual Development of Paul*) unreservedly commits himself that Paul during many years after his conversion was a preacher of the circumcision — an idea irreconcilable with the fact that he distinctly declares the was aggressive as toward the advocates of the permanent validity of the law, and no small part of his work consisted in a justification and defence of his position against Jewish-Christian contentions and interference. Hence his theology was to a large degree polemical, and was wrought out in a contest which turned upon this question of the law. His mission was necessarily an apology for an attitude toward the traditional opinions and prejudices of his race, which excited as much surprise and indignation among his opponents as among us it elicits admiration of his courage and genius. The more this limitation must in the nature of the case give a temporary and transient significance to much of his thought, the more do his occasional bold flights beyond it reveal his greatness. If, because he was a Jew, and could not wholly free himself from his environment, his theology is in some respects Jewish, yet because he was a Christian and a thinker of profound spiritual insight, he gave the world the gospel of liberty, and revealed the heights and depths of universal religious experience. The prominence accorded to the law in his writings is externally apparent in the circumstance that the word (ὁ νόμος or νόμος) occurs more than one hundred times in the four great Epistles. The word

---

conviction of his call to be the apostle to the gentiles to have been one of his first experiences of the new religion. That the exigencies of his mission may have elicited differing forms of expression for his fundamental doctrines is not improbable; but that they occasioned any modifications of the original "gospel" which was given in the "revelation" of the Son of God in him is not apparent from his writings, and may be regarded as a groundless theory. For the reason, then, that the doctrine of Paul is not regarded and treated as a system of theology, coherent and consistent throughout, it has been thought expedient to place first in this part of the book two chapters which contain an elucidation of some words belonging to the Pauline terminology, a knowledge of which is necessary to an understanding of his teachings — a chapter on the apostle's use of the term "The Law," and a chapter on the sense in which he employs the terms "Death," "Life," and "Salvation."

is employed in general (νόμος with or without the article) of the Mosaic law. The attempt to establish a difference in the meaning of the word according as the article is present or absent (Volkmar, Holsten, Lightfoot, and Gifford) has not been successful, and it is significant that the two acutest investigators, Holsten and Volkmar, who have undertaken to maintain a discrimination of this kind have arrived at directly opposite conclusions.* Fine distinctions between the Mosaic law and law in general are not Pauline. The apostle was too much a theist to recognise any law that was not God's, and too much a Jew to discriminate in general between God's law and the Mosaic. In Gal. iii. 23, 24 he says, for example: "We were shut up under the law" (νόμος without the article); "wherefore the law (νόμος with the article) was our schoolmaster," etc., where the Mosaic law is in both cases unquestionably meant. Also in Rom. ii. 23–27 the frequent recurrence of νόμος and ὁ νόμος denotes no change in the point of view, which is throughout that of the Mosaic law. In "breaking the law" (τοῦ νόμου) and "a breaking of the law" (νόμου) two conceptions of "law" are not implied.

The law, then (νόμος or ὁ νόμος), denotes in Paul's usage for the most part the law as laid down in the Pentateuch. This was so well understood by himself and assumed to be understood by the readers addressed that the qualification, "of Moses," is not generally employed. Once he says: "It is written in the law of Moses" (1 Cor. ix. 9), and twice in Romans "the law of God" is used with reference undoubtedly to the same Old Testament legislation (Rom. vii. 22, viii. 7). That the purely legislative portion of the Pentateuch is not meant is evident from Gal. iv. 21–28,

* For a discussion of this matter in detail, upon which it is remote from the purpose of this work to enter, the student is referred to Grafe's monograph, *Die paulinische Lehre vom Gesetz*, pp. 2–7.

where he asks those who "desire to be under the law" if they do not "hear the law," and then quotes from the historical part of the so-called "Thora" or book of the law, a section of the story of Abraham. Not only the entire Pentateuch, legislative and historical, but the whole Old Testament is included under the term "law." In Rom. iii. 19, after several quotations in preceding verses from various parts of the Old Testament, he refers to them as "whatsoever things the law saith," and in 1 Cor. xiv. 21 a quotation from Isaiah is introduced with the words: "In the law it is written." The term "law" or "the law," then, generally means in Paul's usage according to the connection the Mosaic legislation from the point of view of the Mosaic authorship of the Pentateuch, the historical portions of these five books, or the entire Old Testament revelation, which along with his Jewish contemporaries he regarded as the word of the divine Spirit. It is doubtful whether Grafe is justified in his conclusion that Paul employs "the law" in "an extended signification" denoting "the natural moral consciousness of the heathen," when he says that they "do by nature the things contained in the law" (Rom. ii. 14) and have "the work of the law written in their hearts." "The law" here is only that of the Old Testament revelation, and what they have "written in their hearts" corresponds to it. When they "do by nature the things contained in the law," they conform to the standard of the written legislation. If they are "a law to themselves," it is because in their conscience is an analogon of the Mosaic law. The several passages in which "the law" denotes simply a norm or standard, "law of the mind," etc., contain their own explanation.

It must also be borne in mind that by "law" or "the law" the apostle means generally the entire Mosaic legislation and the Old Testament revelation without making a distinction between the ritual and ethical portions. If, as Holsten maintains, he had regarded the ritual prescripts as no real part of the law, but only as "traditions of the fathers," he could not have been so strenuous with regard to merely outward forms in his polemic against Judaism. To him the rite of circumcision carried with it the obligation to keep "the whole law." It was, then, a part of the law, and was not in his thought discriminated from it as one of the "traditions." As Grafe remarks, the whole law in all its parts was to him of divine ordination. This fact, however, does not carry with it the exclusion of such a discrimination as may be made in emphasising now the ritual and now the ethical contents of the law. When he says that the whole law is fulfilled by love (Rom. xiii. 8, 10) he evidently refers to the ethical requirements, and to the gentiles who have the law written in their hearts, and fulfil what the law requires without written prescripts, the ritual prescripts are of course not applicable.

It is a still greater error to suppose that the apostle in his depreciation of the law as a means of attaining righteousness and in his demonstration of the futility of "works of the law" had in mind only the ritual and ceremonial prescripts. The attempt to carry out such a discrimination would introduce confusion into the interpretation of his Epistles, and obscure all his teaching. The impossibility of keeping the law is emphasised with such intensity, and elaborated with so much feeling as to denote unmistakably a profound moral interest. No one can read attentively the seventh chapter of Romans without receiving such an impression. "The law is spiritual," he says, "but I am carnal, sold under sin." "The commandment is holy and just and good." This he could not have said of the ceremonial law. On the contrary, he sets the ethical prescripts over against the tendencies and impulses of the "carnal" man. The "delight in the law of God after the inward man" is certainly not declared with reference to anything but the ethical requirements of the law, against which the other law of the fleshly nature contends, so that the man in whom the hopeless conflict is waged feels himself bound to a "body of death." The observance of the ritual prescripts of the law might indeed be regarded as burdensome, but Paul could not have spoken of it as an impossibility, and when he says that every man who is circumcised is "a debtor to do the whole law" (Gal. v. 3), he does not mean the ritual part of it. The inclusion of the ethical requirements of the law in the general term, "the law," is, moreover, evident when we consider how much stress he laid upon the matter of attaining righteousness by "the works of the law." It is irreconcilable with his depreciation of all ceremonial forms to suppose that he could have connected them alone with righteousness, and that by the expression, "justified by the law," he could have meant justified by keeping the outward prescripts. One would hardly undertake to maintain that he attached no other significance to the death of Christ with reference to the Old Testament economy than that it rendered the ritual observances ineffective. On the contrary, when he says that "if righteousness come by the law then Christ is dead in vain (Gal. ii. 21), he evidently includes in the general term all that the ancient economy of Israel signified to the Jew. The same interpretation of the term is required in the declaration: "I had not known sin but by the law; for I had not known lust, except the law had said, thou shalt not covet" (Rom. vii. 7); and he certainly could not have said that the ceremonial law "was our schoolmaster to bring us unto Christ" (Gal. iii. 24). The antithesis of law and grace, which runs through all his theology, would be flat if not meaningless, if he intended to convey by it only the opposition of the gospel to the Mosaic ritual, and did not rather set over against each other the two historic dispensations, that of the old Covenant and that of the new righteousness by faith (Rom. vi. 15).

It is only from this point of view that we can rightly understand the apostle's conception of the place of the law in the divine order, his interpretation of its significance. His attitude toward it was so directly and fundamentally opposed to that of the Jews and the Jewish Christians that it is no wonder that they assumed a position of irreconcilable antagonism to him. From their point of view, which was that of all the teachers of the Old Testament, the law was given in order to be obeyed, and because through obedience to its requirements righteousness was attainable. This was the ancient historical significance and object of the law, which underlay all the admonitions and exhortations of lawgivers and prophets. Paul undertook the hazardous task of denying this hallowed traditional doctrine, and set over against it the teaching that " by the works of the law no flesh shall be justified," and that a law had not been given which could have imparted life, otherwise the new plan of salvation through Christ would not have been devised (Rom. iii. 20; Gal. ii. 21, iii. 11, 21). To him the old order of the law of works was not simply overshadowed by the new order of righteousness by grace, but it was done away. It came to an "end" in Christ for "every one that believeth" (Rom. x. 4). That by "the works of the law" he does not mean mere legalism, but includes the entire ethical code is evident from his declaration that "the commandment was ordained to life," and that "the man who doeth these things [keeps the requirements of the law] shall live by them," that is, shall find "life" in them (Rom. vii. 10, x. 5; Gal. iii. 12). This he could not have said of the Mosaic ritual prescripts alone. He did not deny that the ethical precepts of the law, "the law" as a whole in fact, were intended to produce righteousness, and that they might produce righteousness if observed. But his contention was that the law would not produce righteousness, because, on account of the flesh, man could not keep it. It does not appear to be a logical conclusion from his theism and his doctrine that the Old Testament was the divine and authoritative word of the Spirit, to teach that the law which "was ordained to life" was "found" by him, Paul, "to be unto death," that is, that the result of a divine ordinance was directly opposite to its original intention. Such inconsequences, however, show the difficulties and the hazards of his position. If we may regard the graphic delineation of the struggles of the natural man to attain righteousness under the law against the fatal tendencies of the flesh as a chapter out of his own life (Rom. vii.), the opinion that his experience contributed to the doctrine of the impossibility of this sort of righteousness is well founded. He saw too that Jews and gentiles were all alike incapable of attaining it, and were "treasuring up wrath against the day of wrath" (Rom. ii. 5); and as if this fact were not manifest enough to the open eye, he proceeds to establish it by a series of citations from the Old Testament to the end that "every mouth may be stopped, and all the world may become guilty before God" (Rom. iii. 10-19). The old order shows by its results its inadequacy to produce righteousness.

The apostle reached the conclusion that righteousness by the works of the law is impossible from two points of view, one theoretical and the other practical. Theoretically he argues from the premises of his Christology. If Jesus was the Christ, the Messiah of God, then his mission must have a profound historical significance. He must have established a new order of life, a new righteousness. "The last Adam" stood historically over against the first as the founder of a new dispensation. The old order has, then, no longer any utility. The fact that another was instituted showed its inadequacy. The main argument, however, was from the cross backward to the law. Christ's death was not an ignominy, but a glory, and its glory it was that it abolished the old economy of the law and sin and death, and established the new way of grace and of life. The law was against the whole race, and held over them one and all its awful judgment of death as the penalty for the sins which were accumulating into an appalling record. As the representative of the race Christ paid this penalty of death once and for all. As many as have faith in this atonement become free from the law, of which Christ is "the end to every one that believeth," and are made partakers of the new righteousness, which is not of works, but of faith. This is the doctrinal kernel of the apostle's gospel. As a new philosophy of religion it had no standing unless the righteousness "by the works of the law" were null and void. Both could not stand, and with relentless logic he declared the abolition of the old order. His Christianity with its "glorious liberty" was at stake. To him, if "the works of the law" stood, the cross must go down in darkness and shame. "If righteousness come by the law, then Christ is dead in vain" (Gal. ii. 21).

From the practical side the apostle saw the inadequacy of the law to effect righteousness in the power of the flesh as he experienced and observed it. Although "the law is spiritual," man is "carnal," and through this carnality the law is found to be "weak." It commands, but can furnish no inward impulse that is able to overcome the resistance of the flesh, so that the result of the unequal contest is that "the law in the members warring against the law of the mind" brings the "wretched man" "into captivity to the law of sin." "The carnal mind is enmity against God, for it is not subject to the law of God, neither indeed can be." Far from being able to deliver the carnal man from the stress of this conflict, the law rather conspires with the flesh to effect his complete overthrow. "The commandment works all manner of concupiscence. For without the law sin was dead." "When we were in the flesh, the motions of sin *which were by the law*, did work in our members to bring forth fruit unto death" (Rom. vii. viii.). On this line of argument the apostle's logic brings him to the conclusion that the law, which thus incites to sin, and alone "revives" it out of its sleep of death, was given for this very purpose. We have seen that he has declared it to have been in its intention "unto life," but to have been "found to be unto death." Yet from the fact that it provokes to sin, he argues teleologically, that is, from its actual effect to its intention, that it was given for this very purpose. He makes no attempt to reconcile these conflicting conclusions, and betrays no consciousness of the contradiction. "The law entered that the offence might abound" (Rom. v. 20). To the question, "Wherefore serveth, then, the law?" he answers, "It was added for the sake of transgressions" ($\tau\hat{\omega}\nu$ $\pi\alpha\rho\alpha\beta\acute{\alpha}\sigma\epsilon\omega\nu$ $\chi\acute{\alpha}\rho\iota\nu$), in order to give to actions which otherwise would not be formal sins the character of transgressions, not to increase them, not to bring them to knowledge, since they must first exist as transgressions before they can be known as such, and least of all to check them, which is opposed to the meaning of $\chi\acute{\alpha}\rho\iota\nu$ and to the plain sense of Rom. v. 20. "Where there is no law, there is no transgression," and "I had not known sin but by the law" (Rom. iv. 15, vii. 7), are passages which denote the result of the law, while in Rom. vii. 13, the law is the occasion of sin, and sin works death.

Thus the law is "found to be unto death" in the sense that it is the occasion of sin, whose penalty is death.*

It did not, however, suit the apostle's grand style of thinking to leave the matter in this merely individual relation. To him the law has also an historical significance in the divine economy. Not only does it result in bringing home to every man the conviction of his inability to attain a righteousness by its "works," a righteousness of his own, but it also has a part in the development of God's plan of salvation for mankind, according to which all men were "concluded under sin, that the promise by faith of Jesus Christ might be given to them that believe." They were "kept under the law, shut up unto the faith which should afterwards be revealed"; so that "the law was our schoolmaster to bring us unto Christ, that we might be justified by faith" (Gal. iii. 22–24). "Heirs of God" men are, indeed, through faith; but "the heir, as long as he is a child, differeth nothing from a servant . . . but is under tutors and governors until the time appointed of the father. Even so we, when we were children, were in bondage under the elements of the world," until "the fulness of the time was come," when "God sent forth His Son" (Gal. iv. 1–3). Under this bondage to the flesh and the law the "wretched man" cries out to be delivered from "this body of death" (Rom. vii. 24). "In this sense," remarks Grafe, "one may ascribe to the law a negative

* The distinction must be kept in mind between sin as carnality, as a tendency inhering in the flesh and entailing its consequence, death, even upon those who did not, between Adam and Moses, sin against a positive commandment, and sin as a transgression of the law. Paul conceived the law to have been given because of the former condition for the sake of realising the latter. It was not the law, which is "good," he says, that slew him, but sin becoming by the law "exceedingly sinful." Without this discrimination Dr. McGiffert's remark is likely to be misleading, that the law was given "in consequence of sin." (*The Apostolic Age*, p. 138.)

preparation for the New Testament economy of grace. A positive causal relation between law and salvation Paul denies throughout." In Rom. iii. 21 "the righteousness of God," that is, the righteousness of faith which belongs to the new dispensation, is declared to be "without the law" (χωρὶς νόμου), an expression which excludes the law from any part in the attainment of righteousness, and which is in contrast with "by the law [διὰ νόμου] is the knowledge of sin" in the preceding verse. In like manner the apostle says that "the promise [to Abraham] that he should be the heir of the world" "was not through the law, but through the righteousness of faith" (Rom. iv. 13). This temporary and transient institution was destined to be "done away," to be "abolished," and to find its "end" in the coming of the new dispensation (Rom. x. 4; 2 Cor. iii, 11, 13, 14).

In view of these sweeping declarations one reads at first with astonishment Rom. iii. 31: "Do we then make void the law through faith? God forbid; yea, we establish the law." This is introductory to a proof that the righteousness by faith, that is, without "the works of the law," is testified to by the law itself. In this demonstration is evident the flexibility of the term "the law" in the apostle's usage. While in the passages quoted in the preceding paragraph he plainly intends by the term to denote the law as legislation, that is, the ceremonial and ethical requirements, with the purpose of showing that by the attempt to observe these the attainment of righteousness is impossible, he here (iii. 31–iv. 25) proceeds to show from "the law," that is, from the historical part of the Pentateuch, that his position is supported in the Old Testament. One might suppose that a Jewish or a Jewish-Christian logician would object to this mode of argumentation as an artful avoidance of the question in debate. To the apostle, however, the whole Old Testament economy is "the law," and he appears to have thought that he could make out his case and "establish" that which he had vehemently rejected by a single historical instance of "righteousness by faith" in the person of a representative Israelite. Accordingly, he appeals to the case of Abraham, whose faith was accounted to him for righteousness, and argues that the law which came four hundred and thirty years afterward could not annul and make of no effect the promise which was made to Abraham, and which "was not to him or to his seed through the law, but through the righteousness of faith" (Rom. iv. ; Gal. iii.). To this argument a Jew might have answered that it is a grasping at words, and is not based upon historical facts. In fact the imputation of righteousness on account of faith in the Pauline sense is not implied in the story of Abraham, to whom it was simply reckoned as an evidence of his piety that he believed in God's promise that he should have a numerous posterity despite his old age (Gen. xv. 6). Moreover, that nothing is known in this connection of righteousness without works is apparent from the fact that the commandment is given to Abraham to circumcise himself and "every man child that is born in the house or bought with money of any stranger," and that accordingly he was circumcised when he was ninety-nine years old (Gen. xvii. 10-27). According to the Pauline doctrine that he who is circumcised "is a debtor to do the whole law" (Gal. iv. 3), Abraham's righteousness by faith without works is not historically apparent.

The law is also shown to be inferior to the promise to Abraham on account of the different way in which it was given. The inheritance was given directly to Abraham by God through His promise. The law, on the other hand, which was "added for the sake of transgressions," "was ordained by angels in the hand of a mediator." Then follows the passage which has been a riddle to interpreters: "Now a mediator is not a mediator of one, but God is one" (Gal. iii. 18-20). The idea evidently is that the subordination of the law to the promise is shown in the fact that it was given through a "mediator," Moses, who stood between the author of the law and the people, and mediated its transmission, while in the giving of the promise God, who is one, acted as one, and communicated it without a mediator to Abraham. The place and function of the "angels" in the transaction are, however, not apparent, unless the law was conceived as given by them to Moses. But it is probable that Paul had in mind Lev. xxvi. 46: "These are the laws which the Lord made between him and the children of Israel in Mount Sinai by the hand of Moses." It is to be noted that he does not say that God was the author of the law, yet we know from other passages that this was his doctrine. The idea that angels were the medium of the giving of the law appears to have been a current Jewish tradition. We find it in the speech put into the mouth of Stephen in Acts (vii. 53), in Heb. ii. 2, and in Josephus, *Ant.* xv. 5. Such is the apostle's argument; but it is not apparent how the law becomes subordinate because it was not communicated to the people directly, but to Moses, their representative. In the account of the giving of the law in Exodus nothing is said about "angels" having a part in the transaction, but God speaks directly to Moses amidst the most terrific accompaniments of solemnity and majesty. In fact, Yahweh would not give the law in any other way than through Moses, and "the people and the priests" are ordered not to "come up unto Yahweh," lest He "break forth upon them" (Ex. xix. 24). Paul seems to have written not with immediate reference to the account of the Sinaïtic legislation in Exodus, but rather with the Jewish tradition about the law as "ordained by angels" before his mind. His interpretation from the point of view of the Old Testament narrative of the giving of the law is altogether fanciful and superficial.

The apostle undertakes to show by another reference to the giving of the law through Moses that it was of a transitory character. "The children of Israel," he says, "could not steadfastly behold the face of Moses for the glory of his countenance, which glory was to be done away." He argues that "if that which is done away was glorious," "that which remaineth" is much more glorious. Accordingly, he says, "we use great plainness of speech; and not as Moses, who put a veil over his face, that the children of Israel could not look steadfastly to the end of that which is abolished" (2 Cor. iii. 7, 11–13). There is no intimation, however, in the narrative referred to (Ex. xxxiv. 33–35) that Moses veiled his face in order to conceal from the people whom he represented the fading away of the "glory," or that the people could not look upon his face because of its splendour. On the contrary the writer says that they saw the face of Moses, that it shone, and that he spoke to them in this condition, being himself ignorant of it (verses 29–32). Paul appears to have understood that Moses, conscious that the light on his face faded away, put on a veil, in order that the people should not interpret this waning of the "glory" as a symbol of the transient character of the law. The Old Testament writer does not seem to have thought of this, and it did not occur to him to represent the great lawgiver as capable of coming forth from the presence of Yahweh and deceiving the people as to the nature of the sacred legislation.

Paul appears to have recognised the fact that his doctrine of the abolition of the law had its ethical perils. This freedom in Christ from obligation to the law might be abused in the interest of license. That his opponents made the most of this is apparent from his attempts to parry the objection. "But if," he asks, "while we seek to be justified by Christ, we ourselves also are found sinners, is therefore Christ the minister of sin? God forbid" (Gal. ii. 17). This is the ethical side of his contest with the Jewish Christians; and that such a conflict of opinion existed is evident not only from occasional references to it in his Epistles, but from the fact of the constant opposition to which he was exposed. His teaching that the law was given to increase transgression in order that grace might the more abound (Rom. v. 20, 21) was met with the derisive answer, "The more sin, then, the more grace." Accordingly, the apostle declares the damnation of those men to be just who "slanderously report" him to say, "Let us do evil that good may come" (Rom. iii. 8). Again he asks, "What shall we say then, shall we continue in sin that grace may abound" (Rom. vi. 1)? Jewish-Christian opposition and misinterpretation did not, however, deter him from the bold assertion and defence of the doctrine that liberty in Christ meant unqualifiedly deliverance from the law as the rule of life. He could not logically take any other ground; for if "Christ was the end of the law to every one that believeth," then the law is no longer the standard or rule of life for believers. Without this practical application his entire contention would have been a mere strife about words. The fundamental proposition is that "where the Spirit of the Lord [Christ] is, there is liberty" (2 Cor. iii. 17). This liberty is deliverance from the law — a doctrine which is laid down in unmistakable terms in the declaration that, "if ye be led by the Spirit, ye are not under the law" (Gal. v. 18).

The law was conceived as adapted only to the natural, carnal man, and served the purpose of making the offence "abound" which was stimulated by the flesh. The Christian, being the possessor of the Spirit, was exalted above the law and lived in a higher realm. "They that are Christ's have crucified the flesh, with the affections and lusts" (Gal. v. 24), and have now no longer any practical relation to the law, which binds the carnal man with chains of steel. The exhortation to them is: "If we live in the Spirit, let us also walk in the Spirit" (Gal. v. 25). They are "dead to the law," that they may "live unto God" (Gal. ii. 19). Accordingly, the apostle writes to the Romans: "Now are we delivered from the law, that being dead wherein we were held, that we should serve in newness of Spirit and not in oldness of the letter" (Rom. vii. 6), that is, in the new condition of being impelled by the Holy Spirit, in opposition to the bondage of the law. He who is led by the Spirit is a son of God (Rom. viii. 14), and owes allegiance to no law but "the law of the Spirit of life in Christ Jesus" (Rom. viii. 2). Although the ancient ordinances may be "spiritual" and "holy and just and good," the Spirit is supreme, and has its own law. He who possesses it is no longer in "bondage" to old ordinances and dispensations, but is driven by it whithersoever it "listeth."* That this was not conceived as a condition of moral indifference and laxity, but of the highest ethical-spiritual life, is manifest, and the apostle very naturally repudiated with indignation the charge that his doctrine contained a principle of license. The "sons of God," "led by the Spirit," or impelled by this supernatural agency, cannot go astray. Under the law a man painfully produced only "works," and of these not enough

---

* "Wer darf mir Halt gebieten? Wer dem Geist
Vorschreiben der mich führt? Der Pfeil muss fliegen
Wohin die Hand ihn seines Schützen treibt."
—SCHILLER, *Jungfrau von Orleans*, ii. 4.

to effect righteousness. In the Spirit he bears "fruits," against which the law can make no complaint (Gal. v. 22, 23). This doctrine undoubtedly has its ethical perils, and to Paul's opponents it must be granted that they were not altogether wrong. There is wanting a test of the actual possession of "the Spirit," and the ordinary man, puffed up with sense of an inward illumination, may sin against all laws human and divine.

The moral hazards of this teaching have doubtless furnished the motive of the contention on the part of some expositors that Paul had in view only the abolition of the ceremonial law. This position has an apparent support in passages in which he speaks of love as the fulfilling of the law, mentioning once a portion of the decalogue (Gal. v. 14; Rom. xiii. 9, 10), and particularly in the words: "That the righteousness of the law might be fulfilled in us who walk not after the flesh, but after the Spirit" (Rom. viii. 4). It should be borne in mind, however, that when Paul addresses Christians, he speaks to them as not "under the law," but "under grace." He did not regard love as one of "the works of the law," and it would be a denial of one of the fundamental tenets of his theology to maintain that he thought it could be produced and practised under the law. If it is the fulfilment of the law, it includes all righteousness; and he explicitly declares that "if righteousness come by the law, Christ is dead in vain," and that "if there had been a law given which could have given life, verily righteousness should have been by the law" (Gal. ii. 21, iii. 21). On the contrary, to him love is one of "the fruits of the Spirit" (Gal. v. 22). It is not conceived as a matter of obedience, but as a product, a "fruit," of the indwelling Spirit. Rom. viii. 4 must be interpreted from the same point of view. "The righteousness of the law" is accomplished in the believer not by his "works," but by the power of "the Spirit." All that is vital in the law the Spirit impels its possessor to do, for there is no essential difference between the law, which was given by the Spirit, and the rule of life which the Spirit fulfils in him in whom it resides. But the two kinds of life are separated "by the whole diameter of being," and what is brought forth in him who is "under grace" is precisely that which "the law could not do" (Rom. viii. 3). The law is "the ministration of death," "the letter" that "killeth" (2 Cor. iii. 6, 7), not because its contents are not "spiritual," but because it is simply a law, a letter, commanding and threatening and punishing with death, an external authority furnishing no inward quickening.* But the Spirit is a productive power which dwells within (1 Cor. iii. 16, vi. 19; 2 Cor. i. 22), and "sheds abroad the love of God in the heart" (Rom. v. 5). Through this, which "helpeth our infirmities," are freedom, spontaneity, and life.

If despite this repudiation of the law the apostle says that "the doers of the law are justified," and admits that gentiles without a written code may "do the things contained in the law" (Rom. ii. 13, 14; see also verses 26, 27), it should be borne in mind that in these passages he does not appear to deny that in rare cases it might be kept, and that he who kept it was completely justified. Yet the absolute declaration that "by the works of the law shall no flesh be justified" is not reconcilable with that concession.

---

* In view of the estimate of the law given in Romans, the teaching that it is "spiritual," "holy, just, and good," and of the declaration that "the doers of the law shall be justified" (Rom. ii. 13), the following words from Dr. Matheson (*The Spiritual Development of Paul*, p. 98) are plainly a misinterpretation of the apostle: "Paul felt that a man might be legally blameless and a deep-dyed sinner still. He felt that he might keep the law without even offending in a single point, and yet be at that moment in the gall of bitterness and the bonds of iniquity."

Perhaps Rom. ii. 13 may be regarded as conditional in the sense, "if any are doers of the law," as verses 25, 26, and 27 certainly are. It should be said besides that the points of view from which the law is judged in Galatians and in Romans are not altogether accordant. The characterisation of the lapse of the Galatians to the observance of the law as a return to "the weak and beggarly elements of the world," hardly agrees with the declaration in Romans that the law is "spiritual" (Gal. iv. 3, 9; Rom. vii. 14). Some allowance must undoubtedly be made for the circumstances under which the two Epistles were written, the readers, and the objects in view. Moreover, apparent and real inconsistencies will not trouble the student of Paul who bears in mind that he is not reading a systematic theologian, but a man whose temperament and special dogmatic or practical purpose are always to be considered. Finally, the recognition of the fact that the apostle's attitude toward the law was that of an extremist whose method was uncompromising, and whose judgments were harsh, will lead to a fair estimate of the position of his opponents. They could plead both the spirit and the letter of the Old Testament, and might well maintain that the doctrine that the law was not given to effect righteousness, but to make sin abound, was a perversion and a false judgment of the whole economy. The difficulties and hazards of Paul's contention are manifest in the propositions that the law was given to produce "life," and that it was "a ministration of death," in the attempt to reject the law as a way of righteousness by an appeal to the law itself, and in the strained and artificial interpretation by which he sought to support his argument from the case of Abraham's righteousness by faith, from the ordaining of the law through "angels," and from the veil over the face of Moses.

CHAPTER IX

THE PAULINE TERMS, "DEATH," "LIFE," AND "SALVATION"

THE terms "Death," "Life," and "Salvation" are of so much importance in the doctrine of Paul as to warrant a detailed consideration of them in connection with an exposition of his thought. The first may be regarded as set over against the other two in an opposition which can be removed only by the triumph of the powers of goodness. Two great dispensations of the divine economy are accordingly represented by these terms — the dispensation of sin and its consequences, at the head of which was the progenitor of the human race, Adam, and the dispensation of redemption, whose great Head was the Lord from heaven, the last Adam, Christ. The first Adam was simply the progenitor of physical life, "became a living soul" ($\psi v \chi \acute{\eta}$), was "of the earth, earthy," and in the progressive order according to which the lower form of existence precedes the higher he was only "natural" ($\psi v \chi \iota \kappa \acute{o} \varsigma$). The last Adam, however, became a life-giving Spirit. He was from heaven, and, "as we have borne the image of the earthly," Paul says to the believers, "so also shall we bear the image of the heavenly." If by the first Adam death came into the world, by the last Adam came "the resurrection of the dead" (1 Cor. xv. 21, 45-49). The drama of human existence is thus conceived as a conflict between these opposing powers. Against the "god of this world" and all the forces of dissolution and destruction is arrayed the divine Son with his great atonement and his revelation of grace, and the destiny of each individual is decided according as he shall through faith appropriate the life-giving Spirit, or remain in bondage to "the law of sin and death" (Rom. iii. 28, vi. 11, viii. 2).

The meaning of the term "Death" ($\theta\acute{a}\nu a\tau o\varsigma$) in Paul's theology has been the subject of no little discussion, and an examination of the principal passages in his Epistles in which it occurs is necessary in order to determine its sense. The doctrine that death is the consequence of sin, a result following according to the relation of cause and effect, is laid down by the apostle with an explicitness which leaves no doubt as to his meaning. In Rom. v. 12-14 the introduction of this dread power into the world is attributed to the transgression of Adam, the apostle of course assuming the literal truth of the story of Eden. Accordingly, he says: "Therefore, as through one man sin entered into the world, and death through sin, and so death passed unto all men, for that all sinned; for until the law sin was in the world, but sin is not imputed when there is no law. Nevertheless, death reigned from Adam to Moses even over those who had not sinned after the likeness of Adam's transgression." Here the meaning evidently is that in the divine order of human existence death is the inevitable consequence of sin, and that its sway in the world originated in the first transgression in Eden. Since that event its reign has continued over all men, inasmuch as all have sinned, whether like Adam in violation of an express commandment or otherwise.

Attention has been called in a preceding chapter to the influence of Paul's environment upon his thought; and it is of interest in this connection to note that a doctrine similar to this appears in the Jewish theology, the documents of which are, indeed, much later, but the substantial contents of which very likely existed in his time. Weber declares it to have been a capital and fundamental idea of the Synagogue that death was caused by Adam's fall, and has since reigned in the world, and will reign until the Messiah removes it.* To the question of the angel why the first Adam died the answer is given : "Because he did not keep my commandments." Likewise in the Wisdom of Solomon it is declared that "God created man for immortality, and made him to be an image of His own being, but through the envy of the devil death came into the world" (i. 13 ff. ii. 23). Also in Sirach xxv. 23 it is said that "of the woman came the beginning of sin, and through her we all die." The apostle's doctrine that "in Adam all die" is so closely related to these sayings as to indicate its origin in the current Jewish thought.

That the θάνατος of Rom. v. 12 is primarily physical death there can be no doubt, not only on account of the analogy of the Jewish theology, but also because the word is employed without any indication that other than its literal sense is intended. The contrast of "justification of life" in which the word is placed in verse 18 does not invalidate this interpretation of it, since, as will be shown later, the prevailing Pauline conception of "life" is that of a transfigured corporeity not subject to death. In verses 13 f. Paul proceeds to establish the doctrine that the death of all men is consequent upon Adam's sin by arguing that "death reigned from Adam until Moses," through whom the law was given, even over those who had not sinned, as the progenitor did, against an express commandment, doubtless on the ground that those who "have sinned without law shall also perish without law" (Rom. ii. 12); although the declaration that "sin is not imputed where there is no law" (Rom. v. 13) is irreconcilable with this "reign" of its penalty "from Adam to Moses."

That Paul's doctrine of death as the penalty of sin has

* *System der altsyn. palästin. Theol.*, p. 238.

its roots in the Old Testament as well as in the Jewish theology is evident from Gen. ii. 17, where death is threatened in connection with the prohibition of the fruit of the tree of the knowledge of good and evil. Yet 1 Cor. xv. 47, "The first man is of the earth, earthy," doubtless implies the natural mortality of Adam and consequently of his descendants. The first man as "natural" ($\psi\nu\chi\iota\kappa\acute{o}\varsigma$) must according to the analogy of the apostle's teaching be regarded as subject to death, since "life" and "incorruption" belong only to those who through Christ, the "life-giving Spirit," have entered into a supernatural relation to God (Rom. vi. 8, viii. 11), or have received the adoption as sons (Rom. viii. 14–17; Gal. iii. 26, iv. 5–7). That the death in question is primarily that of the body is evident from the declaration that "he that is dead is justified from sin" (Rom. vi. 7). This doctrine of the Jewish theology that "all the dead are atoned by death" (Weber, *System*, etc. p. 311) is here applied by the apostle as a proof of the teaching that those who have died symbolically with Christ in baptism are freed from sin, having died to it, since Christ's representative satisfaction of the law, the payment of its penalty on the cross for the race as its Head in the new order of "life," is available for all who through faith and baptism come into mystic fellowship with his passion. The conclusion must not be drawn, however, that he taught the certain resurrection of all men to life; for according to the Pauline theology only those would rise at the second coming of Christ (the Parousia) who in their lifetime had come into spiritual union with Jesus, who having "died to sin" for all received those alone into the fellowship of his resurrection who had become "members" of him. Those who died without thus possessing the Spirit, which is the "earnest" of the resurrection, paid the penalty of sin by dying absolutely, that is, without hope of living again

(1 Cor. i. 18; 2 Cor. ii. 15; Rom. viii. 11, 23; 1 Thess. v. 3). This sense of "death" is apparent in the passage: "Yield yourselves unto God as those who are alive from the dead" (Rom. vi. 13), where the condition of subjection to death or to "perishing" in exclusion from the resurrection is conceived as that of all men who have not come into spiritual fellowship with Christ. This is apparent from verses 21 and 23, where the "end" of their former mode of life and "the wages of sin" are declared to be "death." To be "alive from the dead" is to pass from the condition in which "sin reigns in the mortal body" (verse 12), and with sin its consequence, death, into that of "life," which is that of those in whom the Spirit abides that insures the final overcoming of death, the quickening of the mortal body (Rom. viii. 11), or the resurrection at the Parousia.

A similar anticipation of death occurs in Rom. viii. 10, where the apostle says to his readers that if Christ is in them the body is dead because of sin, but the Spirit is life because of righteousness. Here the actually accomplished death of the body is of course not meant, but its condition of subjection to death because of sin whose "wages" it is — a condition from which he hastens to say it will be delivered through the Spirit that dwelleth in them. An analogous application of the idea of dying occurs in Rom. vii. 9, "And I was alive apart from the law once, but when the commandment came, sin revived, and I died; and the commandment which was unto life I found to be unto death." The human race, for whom Paul is here speaking, since he could not himself at any time have lived apart from the law, was "alive," that is, without consciousness of the law, prior to a positive commandment, and hence not knowing sin. But it is obvious that Paul does not mean that when the law came those who were its subjects at once "died" ($ἀπέθανον$), but that the death which sin entails became operative in them, and would take its dreadful course working their "destruction," unless through faith in "the last Adam," who abolished death, they should fulfil the condition of attaining "life."

It is plainly a doctrine of the apostle's that the body is the seat and organ of sin, and carries in it the seeds of death during its life. Sin "reigns in the mortal body," and commands obedience to its lusts (Rom. vi. 12). The "members" (μέλη) are "instruments of unrighteousness." "The body of sin," that is, the body in which resides the power of sin, may be "done away" or "destroyed" (Rom. vi. 6). "The deeds of the body" may be "mortified" by the Spirit (Rom. viii. 13). The body is also capable of "redemption," that is, transformation into or being "clothed upon" with the "spiritual body" or "body of glory" at the Parousia (Rom. viii. 23). It is "vile," and its "change" is earnestly desired as a deliverance into freedom and glory, in which condition it will be conformed to the resurrection-body of Christ (Phil. iii. 21). This doctrine receives a graphic expression in Rom. vii. 9–24, where the apostle represents the man who is under the law as powerless to do the good that he would, as delighting in the law of God after the inward man, but seeing a different law in his members which wars against the law of his mind, and brings him into captivity to the law of sin that is in them. Hence the longing for that transfigured corporeity which should never die, the incorruptible "body of glory," and the cry to be delivered from "this body of death," whose impulses lead to the "destruction" of the whole man.

It is very doubtful whether Paul ever employs the words "death," "dead," and "die" in the sense of moral or spiritual death, as they have come to be used in our current theological terminology. Rather he appears always to have in mind physical death as the penalty of sin, with the supplementary idea of "perishing" or the deprivation of the resurrection-life. Accordingly, he sets over against death the life of the resurrection instead of a moral-spiritual renewal in 1 Cor. xv. 21: "For since by man came death, by man came also the resurrection of the dead." The counteracting of the death "in Adam" by Christ is not simply a spiritual transformation of the spiritually dead, but the delivering of the man who dies in Christ from hades and the clothing of him with a "body of glory" for the new kingdom. "For this corruptible must put on incorruption" (1 Cor. xv. 53). The "God who quickeneth the dead" is He whose indwelling Spirit will give life to the "mortal body" (Rom. viii. 11). When the apostle declares himself to be "a savour of death unto death" to them that are "perishing" (2 Cor. ii. 16), he means that to the unbelievers in his gospel, who are in a condition which if persisted in will end in the hopeless fate of those who will not be raised at the Parousia, his message will bring precisely this result. Accordingly, Christ is the source of death or of life according as he is rejected or accepted. A similar conception is contained in the words: "The sorrow of the world worketh death" (2 Cor. vii. 10), that is, the sorrow which those whose only stake is the sensuous well-being of the world, that of unbelievers, whose minds "the god of this world has blinded," works out the fate which awaits them, death, "perishing" the Messianic ἀπώλεια.

No other meaning of "death" is required in the passage: "Know ye not that to whom ye present yourselves as servants his servants ye are whom ye obey, whether of sin unto death or of obedience unto righteousness" (Rom. vi. 16)? In the two parallel clauses Paul has in view the end "unto" (εἰς) which the two sorts of obedience lead, as in verses 21 and 22 he declares that "the end" is in the one case "death" and in the other "eternal life." Two opposite awards will be adjudged at the Parousia. Those who have been the servants of sin will then be found to have died never to live again, while the servants of obedience will receive the reward of righteousness or resurrection to "eternal life." This interpretation will at once be seen to be the only correct one by those students of Paul who have apprehended the prominence in his thought of the great consummation which was to be effected when Christ should presently come in power and glory to bring the existing world-order to an end. A similar anticipation of the result of sin is apparent in the words: "For when we were in the flesh, the sinful passions which were through the law wrought in our members to bring forth fruit unto death" (Rom. vii. 6). That moral or spiritual death is not intended here is evident from the fact that those in whom this destructive power is working are represented as already "in the flesh," that is, in a state of subjection to sin, while the condition which will result is the "fruit" yet to be borne of the sinful passions, which is nothing else than death or "perishing" in the underworld. The same idea is conveyed in the words: "The commandment which was unto life, this was found to be unto death," and, "Did that which was good become death unto me? God forbid! But sin, that it might be shown to be sin, by working death to me through that which was good" (verses 10, 13). There are two opposing powers which are of world-historical significance to the race and of tragic significance to each individual, — "the law of sin and death" and "the law of the Spirit of life in Jesus Christ." The latter sets "free" from the former the man who fulfils the required conditions. The Parousia will reveal the result of the conflict between the two in the precise terms of "life," "resurrection," and "glory" on the one hand, and of "death," "perishing," and "destruction" on the other, according as men have believed or have not believed.

Such is also the fateful significance of the words: "The mind of the flesh is death" (Rom. viii. 6). The works of the flesh enumerated in Gal. v. 19 result precisely in excluding those who "practise such things" from inheritance in the kingdom of God — an exclusion which is simply and only "death" in its ultimate form. The futurity of this consummation is plainly expressed in the words: "If ye live after the flesh ye are sure to die" (Rom. viii. 13). Here the form of expression in the use of μέλλετε unmistakably shows what we have seen to be frequently implied, how the apostle looked forward to the completion of the course of sin, when at "the end" the work of death would be made manifest in the irrevocable fortune of those who should then be found to be without "the life-giving Spirit." The reference to the future contained in μέλλετε excludes moral-spiritual death; and mere physical dissolution, to which all men are subject on account of sin, is of course not meant, but the secondary and final result of sin, from which all may escape by faith. The final overthrow of death is the issue of the conflict between it and the powers of life. "When this corruptible shall have put on incorruption, then shall come to pass the saying that is written, Death is swallowed up in victory" (1 Cor. xv. 54). The resurrection of the believers and the "change" of the living Christians (1 Cor. xv. 51 f.) denote the victory over death. In the kingdom death would have no dominion. The saints clothed with incorruption would die no more. Paul has left us no data for determining whether the destruction of death at the Parousia (1 Cor. xv. 26) was conceived as extending to the realm of the underworld. So far as the kingdom is concerned, this "last enemy" is certainly conceived to be destroyed, for it is a kingdom of "life." If the annihilation of the underworld is implied (Rev. xx. 14), "the whole creation" would be delivered from "the bondage of corruption," and become a suitable abode for the children of God.

The foregoing interpretation of "death" furnishes the key to the meaning which Paul attaches to its opposite, "life" ($\zeta\omega\acute{\eta}$). As death is the dissolution of the body and Messianic or eschatological "destruction" ($\dot{a}\pi\acute{\omega}\lambda\epsilon\iota a$), so life is not primarily moral and spiritual, but Messianic and eschatological. The Pauline "life" includes the potential or actual incorruptible corporeity of the coming kingdom of God which the Parousia and its eternal life would reveal. In the words: "If Christ be in you, the body is dead because of sin, but the Spirit is life because of righteousness" (Rom. viii. 10), the body is represented as a prey to death on account of sin, as "the wages of sin," while the spirit possessing righteousness by reason of the fact that Christ dwells in it is "life," or has already the life-principle which will manifest itself at the Parousia in the "quickening of the mortal body" according to the following verse. Thus Paul does not regard the moral-spiritual life which the believers possessed by reason of their fellowship with Christ or of the indwelling of the Spirit as an end in itself, but considers it with reference to the great consummation at the Parousia, that is, eschatologically. This is apparent in the section Rom. vi. 4-8, where the being buried with Christ in baptism, in which "the old man was crucified with him," carries with it the obligation to "walk in newness of life," because this fellowship with him in his death implies a participation in his resurrection. Being dead with Christ the believers will at "the end" "live with him." Their "life" in the present has not only its real significance, but also its motive, in the future consummation, where they will be "glorified together with him." Accordingly, the apostle proceeds to say that Christ in his death "died unto sin once, but in that he liveth he liveth unto God." In like manner, the believers should reckon themselves to be dead to sin, but alive to God (verses 10, 11). Having paid the penalty of sin for men in his death he now lives in his resurrected state the eternal life that is not subject to death. He has now the incorruptible "body of glory," and the completion of the believers' fellowship with him will consist in their possessing new spiritual bodies "conformed" to his. In their possession of the Spirit they have the "earnest" or pledge of "the redemption of their bodies." The ζωή which they have by virtue of their mystic union with Christ is potentially the Messianic eternal life, and the term must not be emptied of this signification.

Likewise in the passage previously quoted (Rom. viii. 2): "The law of the Spirit of life hath made me free from the law of sin and death," "life" is the opposite of all that "death" meant to the apostle. Over against the dissolution of the "mortal body" and the "perishing" in the underworld is placed the resurrection with its attendant blessedness in the kingdom. If "the mind of the flesh," to be carnally minded, "is death," "the mind of the Spirit," the being spiritually minded, has the earnest of a share in the "glory" presently to be revealed. Those who by the Spirit mortify the deeds of the body shall "live," for "the Spirit beareth witness" with the spirit of the believers that they are "children of God; and if children then heirs," whose great fortune it is that in the Parousia they "will be glorified with him" (Rom. viii. 6–17). It is this triumphant end that Paul always has in mind when he writes of the Christian's possession of the "life" which was in Christ victorious over death. Those who "seek for glory and honour and incorruption" or immortality, will receive as their award just this, that is, "eternal life" (Rom. ii. 7). Theirs will be an "eternal weight of glory" and the putting on of "incorruption" (2 Cor. iv. 17; 1 Cor. xv. 53). The "fruit" of the believers' "being made free from sin" is "sanctification, and the end eternal life" (Rom. vi. 22). Over against the reign of death "through the trespass of one" is set the future "reign in life" of those who "receive" the offered grace and "the gift of righteousness" (Rom. v. 17). The writer of 1 Timothy expresses the apostle's idea in the declaration that if the believers "endure" they "will also reign with Christ" (1 Tim. ii. 12). In like manner the "Justification of life" which the believers receive through Christ (Rom. v. 18) is the justification that leads to life, that is to the "eternal life" in the kingdom (verse 21).

The foregoing interpretation is supported by the doctrine of the resurrection which predominates in 1 Cor. xv. Here the dying in Adam and the being made alive in Christ are contrasted as physical death with its secondary conception of perishing in the case of unbelievers and the resurrection to existence in the spiritual body of those who accept him. The first man was only a living soul ($\psi v \chi \acute{\eta}$) doomed to death, as are all those who inherit only from him, while the last Adam was made "a life-giving Spirit" ($\pi v \epsilon \hat{v} \mu a$), and those who through faith become "members" of him will be raised at his coming and "bear the image of the heavenly." No careful student of Paul can have failed to observe the prominence of the eschatological factor of his Christology. To this his interest in the ethical aspects of the life of Jesus is subordinate. Just so the believer's relation to him at the end or in "the day of the Lord" has everywhere the chief place in the apostle's thought. As the life of their Lord was consummated in the resurrection, so will theirs be. Burdened and groaning in this tabernacle of flesh, they long to be clothed upon with "the building from God," the "celestial body," and this swallowing up of what is mortal will be the crowning and completion of "life." They have sown to the Spirit, and their glorious harvest will be eternal life (Gal. vi. 8).

The passages discussed in the foregoing pages show the great significance which death and life have in the apostle's thought. In them he sees the consummation of human existence under the divine order of award in connection with the plan of redemption. The ultimate result of sin is death, the end of righteousness is life. The terrible evil that came into the world through Adam carried with it, so long as sin was left to do its awful work unchecked, not only the dissolution of the body, but also the "destruction" of those who had no hope of the resurrection at "the last day." On the other hand, the principle which came into the world through "the last Adam" was destined to counteract in those who should come into fellowship with him the power of death, is the greatest good, and the consummation of their fortune. This is "life," the resurrection, the putting on of incorruption, the entrance into the "glory" of the Messianic kingdom. While death and life are conceived as states beginning in the present world, they receive their chief prominence either in an actual or an implied reference to "the end." Here will be the supreme reward, and all the appointments of religion exist for its realisation. All that is to be hoped for at the end, all that can be conceived of blessedness, yea all that it hath not entered into the heart of man to conceive of things reserved for the believers, and all that is to be reaped in the great harvest of joy in the time to come, the Messianic age, is included in the "life" on which the apostle dwells with exhaustless interest. For the sake of securing this blessedness Christ died and rose triumphant, for this are all the steadfastness, the hoping, the enduring, the waiting for the coming of the Lord, and for this is the Spirit bestowed which is the earnest of the redemption of the body. To this faith looks forward beholding the things that are unseen and eternal; for by faith the believer is united in mystic fellowship with Christ, through which he has the assurance that he will "live" and "reign" with him. Hence "life" and not "righteousness" is the preëminent possession. The latter is subordinate to the former, and a means for its attainment. The "gift of righteousness" serves to secure to those who receive it the Messianic blessedness, and they will "reign in life." Righteousness is the means through which "grace reigns unto eternal life."

The meaning of "salvation" ($\sigma\omega\tau\eta\rho\iota\alpha$) in the apostle's terminology is implied in several of the passages quoted in the foregoing discussion. Like the terms "life" and "death" it denotes, indeed, a condition in the earthly state of existence, but its predominant sense is not that of a moral and spiritual order of life, but rather that of a final deliverance from that dreaded evil, that greatest of calamities, the Messianic "perishing" or "destruction." In a word, its significance is eschatological. It either expresses or implies in the connection in which it is employed a participation in the glorious Messianic kingdom. Those who are to be saved are the living believers and the Christians who in the touching Pauline phrase had "fallen asleep." The former will be "changed" into an incorruptible corporeity, and the latter raised from the dead with spiritual bodies. The former will not "anticipate" the latter (1 Thess. iv. 13–18; 1 Cor. xv. 52–58). This doctrine is grounded upon the principle that "flesh and blood cannot inherit the kingdom of God" (1 Cor. xv. 50). The kingdom was to be one of "incorruption." The living believers would, accordingly, escape the "tribulation and anguish" which were appointed for the wicked who should survive until the Messianic judgment. As to how the transformation of the bodies of the living saints was to be effected the apostle gives no intimation. Perhaps he regarded the teaching that the bodies of those who were "Christ's at his coming" would be "quickened" through the Spirit dwelling in them as including all that needed be said upon the subject. That salvation was to be the portion of the living and the dead believers on the great "day of the Lord" is evident from the declaration: "For God appointed us not unto wrath, but unto the obtaining of salvation through our Lord Jesus Christ, who died for us, that, whether we wake or sleep [at the time of his coming], we should live together with him" (1 Thess. v. 9, 10). This passage accords with the declaration that at the coming of Christ, with which salvation was associated in the mind of the apostle, "We that are alive, that are left, shall with them [the raised] be caught up in the clouds to meet the Lord in the air; and so shall we ever be with the Lord (1 Thess. iv. 17). Then when the wicked shall in vain be saying, "Peace and safety," and "sudden destruction" shall come upon them, and they shall in no wise escape (1 Thess. v. 3), the believers will receive salvation or deliverance from the dread Messianic ἀπώλεια, the overthrow, the perishing; for, "being now justified by his blood, shall we be saved from the wrath of God through him" (Rom. v. 9). The end to which the apostle looks forward amidst his tribulations lies beyond the confines of "this present evil world," to "deliver" believers out of which Christ died (Gal. i. 4), and his gaze is steadfastly fixed upon the heavenly kingdom that is to come in the joyful day when the Lord shall appear. Salvation is deliverance from the bondage to the clogging flesh, "the body of death," into "the glorious liberty of the children of God." Accordingly he declares: "Our citizenship is in heaven; whence also we wait for a Saviour, the Lord Jesus Christ, who shall fashion anew the body of our humiliation that it may be conformed to the body of his glory, according to the working whereby he is able to subject all things unto himself" (Phil. iii. 20, 21). It was "in the day" of this Saviour expected from heaven that the salvation of the believers was to be consummated. A Christian guilty of incest might be delivered over to Satan "for the destruction of his flesh," but the apostle hopes for the salvation of the offender's "spirit" "in the day of the Lord Jesus" (1 Cor. v. 5). An anticipation of "the end" is implied in the words: "For the word of the cross is to them that are perishing foolishness; but unto us who are being saved it is the power of God" (1 Cor. i. 18). Here the condition of being exposed to the Messianic "perishing" at the last day on the one hand, and that of hope for the Messianic deliverance and entrance into the kingdom of God on the other, are contained by implication in the participial form of expression either, says Meyer, as a certainty or as a process of development. So the declaration that "the body is dead because of sin" means that the body is certain to die under the universal law of death, and the phrase "by which ye are saved" (1 Cor. v. 2) must be understood as implying a condition which will in the end result in salvation. "The day [of the Lord] will declare" the work of each teacher, "because it is revealed in fire." When the fire shall have "proved" the work, and it shall be burned up, the man will suffer loss, but he himself will be saved, "yet so as through fire." So the character and the work of men are regarded as conditions in which is involved either the "destruction" or the "salvation" of their souls and bodies when, at the great judgment of the

Parousia, God "shall judge the secrets" of their hearts. The emphasis is, however, not placed by the apostle on the present moral-spiritual state as something complete and sufficient in itself, but is thrown forward to the consummation which is to be effected in the future when the salvation or destruction will be accomplished in fact by the final award of "life" or "death." Accordingly, he admonishes the Corinthians that they "judge nothing before the time, until the Lord come, who will both bring to light the hidden things of darkness, and make manifest the counsels of the hearts ; and then shall each man have his praise from God" (1 Cor. iv. 5).

The blessedness of Christian "salvation" that is to be the portion of believers is a glorious fortune to which they are exhorted to look forward, "waiting for the revelation of our Lord Jesus Christ, who shall also confirm you unto the end, that ye be unreprovable in the day of our Lord Jesus Christ" (1 Cor. i. 7, 8). It will consist, in part, in the "fellowship" (κοινωνία) of God's Son, Jesus Christ (verse 9), which is a participation in the glory of the divine sonship, in the "eternal life" of the Messianic kingdom. If this adoption as sons (υἰοθεσία) has its beginning in this life, its consummation is looked forward to as a bodily and spiritual event of the great "day of the Lord." "And not only so, but ourselves also who have the firstfruits of the Spirit, even we ourselves groan within ourselves, waiting for our adoption, *to wit*, the redemption of our body" (Rom. viii. 23). Not only is the putting on of "incorruption" included in this "fellowship" with Christ, not only will believers appear when their salvation is consummated in the "glory" of his transfigured body, but those for whom this great fortune is reserved are promised a higher blessedness appropriate to their divine sonship. Hence the admonition : "Walk worthily of God, who calleth you into His own kingdom and glory" (1 Thess. ii. 12). "The image of the earthy" will not alone be put off, and that of the "heavenly" put on, but as sons they will become "heirs of God, joint-heirs with Christ," in the dominion and eternal joy of the kingdom soon to come (Rom. viii. 17; 1 Cor. xv. 49). Since the believers having suffered with Christ will be "glorified with him," the apostle exclaims, looking forward to the realisation of the joint-heirship: "Let us rejoice in hope of the glory of God" (Rom. v. 2). This "hope" receives the expression appropriate to an assured fact in the words: "For whom He foreknew He also foreordained to be conformed to the image of His Son, that he might be the firstborn among many brethren; and whom He foreordained them He also called; and whom He called them He also justified; and whom He justified them He also glorified" (Rom. viii. 29). The being "conformed to the image of His Son" is doubtless the "adoption," "the redemption of our body" spoken of in verse 23, the future "glory which shall be revealed" (verse 18) when the believers shall enter into the kingdom clothed with "incorruption." The glorification which is actually in the future, is spoken of as already accomplished (ἐδόξασε), so certain is the apostle of its consummation.

The "glory" and "incorruption," which are among the chief goods of salvation as conceived by the apostle, are set in strong contrast with the earthly conditions of existence. With the latter he associates qualities and states which he regards with extreme repugnance, while he looks forward to the former with eager longing and inextinguishable hope. Here the believer is bound to "the body of death" which he "buffets and brings into bondage" (1 Cor. ix. 27). It is a "body of humiliation" (Phil. iii. 21) which at death is sown in "corruption," "dishonor," and "weakness" (1 Cor. xv. 43). On the great day of salvation this will be transformed into a "body of glory." It will be raised in "incorruption," "glory," "power," and as "a spiritual body." The living believers, will be "changed" (1 Cor. xv. 51), and the groaning creation will be delivered from the bondage of corruption into "the liberty of the glory of the children of God" (Rom. viii. 21), so that the kingdom of God and the theatre of its manifestation will contain nothing that has the taint of death. The supreme blessedness of this condition of salvation will consist in a clearer vision of God than is possible to the believer while he is in the tabernacle of flesh. "For now we see in a mirror, darkly; but then face to face. Now I know in part; but then shall I know even as also I have been known" (1 Cor. xiii. 12). "As it is written,

> Things which eye saw not, and ear heard not,
> And which entered not into the heart of man,
> Whatsoever things God prepared for them that love him."

CHAPTER X

THE DOCTRINE OF SIN*

IN the writings of Paul no explicit doctrine of sin, its origin, nature, and operations, is distinctively set forth as a part of a complete theological system. In fact there is no Pauline system of doctrine to which a teaching concerning sin could have an articulate relation in the sense of dogmatic construction. The currents of the apostle's thought centre in soteriology, and the classical passage regarding the entrance of sin into the world (Rom. v. 12-19) is one of the members of an antithesis, the two terms of which are Adam, the head of the old order of sin and death, and Christ, the founder of the new order of righteousness and life (see also 1 Cor. xv. 45-50). It would, however, be a mistake to conclude from this circumstance that his teaching regarding sin is of slight importance to his doctrine as a whole. On the contrary, it is of such fundamental significance that a right understanding of it is essential to an adequate comprehension and a due relating of other aspects of his thought. The profound interest of the apostle himself in the subject is evident from the prominence given to it in the opening chapters of the Epistle to the Romans and from numerous passages in the four great Epistles.†

* *The American Journal of Theology*, April, 1898.

† See in particular Rom. iv. 7, 8, v. 12-21, vi. 1, 2, 6, 7, 10, 11, 12-14, 22, 23, vii. 5, 7-9; 1 Cor. xv. 3, 17, 56; 2 Cor. v. 21; Gal. i. 4, ii. 17, iii. 22.

Sin is conceived by Paul under a twofold aspect, (1) as a principle and a power in the individual and in human life and history (ἁμαρτία) and, (2) as an act in violation of the divine law (παράβασις, ἁμαρτάνειν). The former may be regarded as its objective and the latter as its subjective aspect. The term ἁμαρτία has not, however, throughout an objective reference, but sometimes expresses in the plural number concrete acts of disobedience, as when sins are said to be "covered" (Rom. iv. 7), or "taken away" (Rom. xi. 27), and when Christ is said to have "died for our sins" (1 Cor. xv. 3; see also 1 Cor. xv. 17 and Gal. i. 4). Sin as a category, a general term, a principle, is spoken of as a subject to which certain predicates may be attached quite as if it were conceived as a personal agent. It has come into the world, where it has dominion, works concupiscence, slays, comes to life, deceives, does the wrong which the better self rejects, holds men in bondage, and is a force which has a "law" (Rom. v. 12, 21, vi. 14. 17, vii. 9, 11, 20, 23, 25). The universal sway of this power in human life and history is a capital proposition of the apostle's which he undertakes to establish by an induction from observed facts of sinfulness, by individual experience, and by Scripture (Rom. chaps. i. ii.; iii. 10–12, 19, 23, vii. 23). He makes no exception in favour of the Jews who, equally with the gentiles, are "included under sin." In this respect he is not in accord with the Jewish theology, striking agreements with which are not wanting elsewhere in his thought, as will appear in the course of our inquiry. For the Jewish theology maintained not only the possibility of sinlessness in man, but also that some men were actually without sin, for example, the Patriarchs, Elijah, and Hezekiah.[*]

[*] See Weber, *System der altsynagogalen Palästinischen Theologie*, pp. 52 f., 223 f.

How Paul thought sin (ἁμαρτία) as a power and principle to be connected with human nature is a problem which must be considered before we can further pursue the investigation of the subject in hand. The discussion of this question requires a glance at one or two points in his doctrine of man or his anthropology. In the apostle's physical anthropology the outward man (ὁ ἔξω ἄνθρωπος) is regarded as a material organism, the substance of which is flesh (σάρξ). This is the perishable part of man's nature, which "cannot inherit the kingdom of God," the "corruptible," which in the resurrection "must put on incorruption" (1 Cor. xv. 50, 53, 54). A man may speak of it as belonging to himself and as that of which he is in part composed (Rom. vii. 18, "my flesh," vii. 14, "I am fleshly," σάρκινος, of flesh). Bodily or physical descent is "according to the flesh" (Rom. ix. 5, 8; Gal. iv. 23; 1 Cor. x. 18), and to live the bodily life is to "be in the flesh," while the material support of the physical being is designated as "carnal things" (2 Cor. x. 3; Rom. xv. 27). The matter constituting the body cannot, however, be regarded as lifeless, and accordingly Paul employs the term ψυχή for the life-principle, and it has been truly remarked that σάρξ and ψυχή are so closely related in his anthropology that the one conception is not to be thought of without the other. Inseparable in life, they are together devoted to corruption. The closely related sense of the two terms is shown by the use in the same signification of the adjectives σάρκινος and ψυχικός, and by the extended application of both words with πᾶς to denote all men * in accordance with Old Testament usage (see also σῶμα ψυχικόν, "natural body," *i.e.*, body of flesh, as contrasted with the spiritual body," 1 Cor. xv. 44). The flexibility of words in the Pauline terminology (a fact too often overlooked in

* πᾶσα σάρξ, πᾶσα ψυχή.

the study of the apostle's thought) is apparent in the frequent employment of "flesh" in the sense of "body" or "members" and *vice versa*. Accordingly, we find "body of sin" and "flesh of sin" (Rom. vi. 6, viii. 3), and "flesh" and "body" in substantially the same sense.*
Yet the employment of "body" where "flesh" would be entirely inappropriate and even self-contradictory shows that the two terms are not in the Pauline usage throughout synonymous.

The discrimination maintained by Lüdemann,† Pfleiderer,‡ Holtzmann,§ Schmiedel,|| and others that $\sigma\acute{a}\rho\xi$ denotes the "substance" and $\sigma\hat{\omega}\mu a$ the "form" of the outer man is tenable so long as it is not applied with too much "vigour and rigour." For Paul undoubtedly conceived the resurrection-body, the $\sigma\hat{\omega}\mu a\ \pi\nu\epsilon\upsilon\mu a\tau\iota\kappa\acute{o}\nu$, as having a form identical with that of the $\sigma\hat{\omega}\mu a\ \psi\upsilon\chi\iota\kappa\acute{o}\nu$, but a different substance, since it was to be a "body of glory," "fashioned like unto" that of the risen and ascended Christ (1 Cor. xv. 44, 49; Phil. iii. 21). While the body is said to be "mortal" (Rom. vi. 12), as it must be when conceived simply as consisting of corruptible flesh, it is declared to be capable of "redemption" (Rom. viii. 23), *i.e.*, of being saved from "perishing" in death, and of being "quickened" (Rom. viii. 11), on condition that the Spirit of Him who raised up Christ from the dead dwelt in its possessor. It is noteworthy that such affirmations are nowhere made of the flesh. The discrimination in question is supported by the frequent antitheses of "flesh" and all that pertains to and partakes of it and the divine Spirit and its operations and ministry. "He that soweth to his flesh [not body] shall of the flesh reap corruption; but he that

---

* Rom. viii. 13; 2 Cor. iv. 4, 10, 11, v. 6, x. 2, 3; Phil. i. 22, 24.
† *Die paulinische Anthropologie.* § *Neutest. Theol.*
‡ *Paulinismus.* || *Hand-Commentar.*

soweth to the Spirit shall of the Spirit reap life everlasting" (Gal. vi. 8).* The contention that σάρξ denotes the whole man empirically constituted and conscious of his opposition to the law fails in view of the antithesis of the outward and the inward man, and is irreconcilable with the distinction made with unmistakable clearness between the self (ἐγώ) and the sin dwelling in the flesh, and between the "law in the members" and "the law of the mind" (νοῦς) in Rom. vii. 17-23.

In the ethical signification of σάρξ in the anthropology of Paul we find the relation of sin to human nature, and it is precisely in the conflict already mentioned between the outward and the inward man that the kernel of the problem lies. Leaving on one side for the present the consideration of the question how sin came to exist in man (a question which Paul does not definitely answer), it will be sufficient to indicate the part of his nature to which it is assigned. There is certainly no want of precision in the apostle's declarations on this point. In speaking of the law as calling sin into activity he says that in man (for he must here be regarded as personating mankind in general), "that is, in his flesh, dwelleth no good thing," and when, a little further on, he asserts that it is not the man, that is, the essential ἐγώ, who does the wrong, but sin that dwelleth in him, it is evident that sin as a power and principle is equivalent in his thought to the "no good thing," or evil of the preceding verse, and that, accordingly, it has its seat in the flesh. The physical sense of σάρξ in this connection is apparent from what immediately follows, when

* The terms of these antitheses are such as "flesh" (σάρξ, for which we cannot think of Paul as here using "body") and "Spirit" (πνεῦμα), "corruption" (φθορά), which pertains to the flesh, and "incorruption" (ἀφθαρσία), "the natural" (τὸ ψυχικόν) and "the spiritual" (τὸ πνευματικόν), "fleshly" (σαρκικά), and "mighty" (δύνατα), etc. (Rom. i. 3, 4, ii. 28, 29, 1 Cor. ii. 14, 15; 2 Cor. i. 12, x. 4; Gal. iv. 29).

he proceeds to contrast the outward and the inward man, and represents the subject as delighting in the law of God after the inward man, but finding in his "members" another law warring against the law of his mind and bringing him into captivity to the law of sin which is in his members. The conclusion of this much misunderstood passage is: "So then with the mind (νοῦς) I myself serve the law of God, but with the flesh (σάρξ) the law of sin," where σάρξ must evidently be interpreted by "members" in the preceding verse (Rom. vii. 17–25). This interpretation is supported by the fact that Paul often connects sin with the body regarded as the form which the flesh assumes in the earthly life of man. "The body of sin" (Rom. vi. 6) signifies the physical organism or the "members," so far as it is controlled by sin, and is parallel with "the flesh of sin" or "sinful flesh" (Rom. viii. 3). "This body of death" (not "the body of this death") in Rom. vii. 24, and the σῶμα νεκρόν of Rom. viii. 10 correspond with "mortal flesh" in 2 Cor. iv. 11. Compare also "live after the flesh" and "mortify the deeds of the body" in Rom. viii. 13 and "crucify the flesh" in Gal. v. 24.

The misinterpretation of σάρξ as something different from the material substance of man's earthly body is due in part to the erroneous idea that the apostle's thought on the subject moved entirely within the circle of the Old Testament anthropology. His conception includes, indeed, the essential notion of flesh בָּשָׂר expressed in the canonical Hebrew writings, which, according to Wendt,* is that of "living beings with the accessory notion of the absolute weakness and transitoriness of their nature over against the power and living operation of God." But he passes altogether beyond the Old Testament idea in associating with the σάρξ an element of sinfulness which Wendt

* *Die Begriffe Fleisch und Geist*, etc.

is unable to find in any of the writers of that literature.*
Paul "would have remained," says Holtzmann, "within
the Jewish representation if, according to his apprehension, just as the inward man, reason, heart, conscience,
would gravitate to the good, so the outward man, or rather
the flesh of which it consists, would also gravitate to the
bad."† But for the apostle the flesh, while not itself sin,
contains impulses, desires, and lusts which are in direct
opposition to the good, which "war against the law of the
mind," and bring man into captivity to the law of sin that
is in his members (Rom. vii. 23).

Whether in this position Paul was on the ground of the
later Jewish theology or that of Hellenistic ethical dualism
or that of the first Christian anthropology, which was his
own, is a question which has received contradictory answers. There is probably truth in all three positions.
While the radical metaphysical dualism of Greek thought
finds no expression in his writings, the Hellenistic influence
is probably apparent in his ethical dualism of the νοῦς and
the σάρξ, which, with the substitution generally of σῶμα,
τὰ πάθη, and related terms for σάρξ, is frequently found in
Philo. In his idea of the flesh in relation to the mind,
which would serve the law of God, he appears to be in
accord with the Hellenistic Wisdom of Solomon, according
to which the body is an encumbrance to the νοῦς. His
doctrine of the flesh bears, again, a close analogy to the
weaker dualism of the later Jewish theology, according to
which, while the soul is pure by nature, the body is impure,
not simply as perishable, but because it is the seat of the
evil impulse called the *jeser hara*, which is to it what the
leaven is to the dough — a fermenting, impelling power.‡

* See Dickson, *Paul's Use of the Terms Flesh and Spirit*, p. 112.
† *Neutestamentliche Theologie*, ii. p. 38.
‡ Weber, *System*, p. 221.

This is counteracted, however, to some degree by the good impulse which resides in the soul, and which in exceptional cases was thought to have been so strengthened by religious exercises as completely to overcome the *jeser hara*. The idea, finally, that the flesh, not constituting a part of the real personality of man, is doomed to perish, while the body may, by means of the indwelling divine Spirit, be "quickened" into a σῶμα πνευματικόν, is a distinctively original feature of the Pauline anthropology. The "redemption of the body" is a specifically Christian conception, and rests upon the central doctrine of the Pauline theology that Christ became in his resurrection the head of a new order of the Spirit and of life, which was intended through faith to overcome the Adamic order of sin and death.

The interpretation of σάρξ which finds it to denote not the substance of the physical or "natural" body, but "the weak and creaturely side of our nature" is objectionable, because it separates the apostle's physical and ethical anthropology at the foundation. It yields a result which is altogether vague and confusing and a definition which itself needs to be defined. What is this weak and creaturely side of human nature in view of the fundamental distinctions of the outward and the inward man? Paul employs no language which naturally yields itself to this interpretation. He says in so many words: "Let not sin, therefore, reign in your mortal body, that ye should obey it in the lusts thereof," where σῶμα means the flesh as organised in the psychical or natural body. So long as the Christians were in this physical body, and had not yet the σῶμα πνευματικόν (spiritual body), they were in danger of yielding to its "lusts" and of making their "members" instruments of unrighteousness on account of the "infirmity" of their "flesh" (Rom. vi. 12, 13, 19). The law in the members which wars against the law of the mind (Rom. vii. 23) is the mode of operation of the lusts of the flesh proceeding with the fateful regularity of a natural necessity. With the lusts of the flesh and the lusts of the body as interchangeable terms there can be no question that the σάρξ is conceived as the body organised for its temporal existence. (Compare Rom. vi. 12 and xiii. 14.) "The likeness of sinful flesh" (σαρκὸς ἁμαρτίας) in which Christ is said to have appeared (Rom. viii. 3) evidently has reference to his physical being as a man, and not to "the weak and creaturely side of his nature," however we may interpret the difficult ὁμοίωμα (likeness). It was, moreover, "in the flesh" of Christ on the cross that the judgment of condemnation upon sin was executed. It is only when we regard the flesh not as a vague "side of human nature," but as a definite part of it, that the opposition of the σάρξ and the πνεῦμα, *i.e.*, the divine Spirit, which occupies so conspicuous a place in the apostle's theology, has a clearly defined significance. In this grand ethical antithesis the outward, psychical, sarkical man, the earthly, material man, with stormy passions and fateful lusts, is conceived as at warfare with the inward man, the νοῦς and the human πνεῦμα, in which the Spirit of God finds an abode.

The conflict is represented in the apostle's thought as one power, one substance, contending against another power and substance, each having its spontaneous and contradictory impulses and desires. The issue of the tragic contest is determined according as on the one hand "the lusts of the flesh," "the law in the members" (Rom. vii. 23; Gal. v. 16), or on the other the forces of the divine πνεῦμα preponderate: "For if ye live after the flesh ye shall die; but if ye through the spirit do mortify the deeds of the body ye shall live" (Rom. viii. 13). The fundamental relation of the physical and ethical sides of the apostle's anthropology is apparent in the employment already mentioned of the attributive terms derived from σάρξ, σάρκινος, consisting of flesh as to the outward man, and σαρκικός, morally fleshly so far as the subject is determined in his activity by the lusts of his sarkical nature. Because he is σάρκινος, fleshly as to the physical substance of his being, he is σαρκικός, fleshly, as to the quality of his ethical life, *i.e.*, living in the flesh, he walks according to the flesh, unless the divine Spirit intervenes, and "cuts the causal nexus" between the nature which is σάρκινος and the actions which are σαρκικά (Rom. iv. 12; 2 Cor. x. 3). A few terse words in the pathetic and impassioned passage, Rom. vii. 14–25, indicate the relation between the flesh, as such, and sin — a relation inseparable, except through the supernatural intervention of the divine πνεῦμα — "But I am of flesh (σάρκινος), sold under sin," where the relation of the two clauses evidently is that the former gives the reason for the latter — because I am of flesh, I am sold under sin, doomed like a slave to its dread dominion, so that even "the law of the mind" is ineffective against the fatal "law in the members."

The objection to the interpretation of σάρξ herein defended on the ground of 2 Cor. vii. 1, "Let us cleanse ourselves from all filthiness [defilement] of the flesh," rests upon an erroneous idea of the relation of sin to the flesh in the thought of the apostle, and upon a misapprehension of the passage itself. Dickson's difficulty is thus disposed of,[*] who errs and confuses the whole matter in supposing that in the interpretation which he opposes sin and the flesh are identified, instead of the latter being regarded as the seat of the former. The judgment of Dr. Schmiedel that the words are "certainly unpauline," results from a too rigorous application of the term "flesh,"

[*] *Loc. cit.*, pp. 310, 313.

as distinct from the "body," conceived to mean the flesh as organised in the human earthly existence.* "The flesh," he remarks, "*is* defiled, and hence one can only speak of a cleansing of it when in conversion it should be set free from sin. . . . In fact, then, it comes to this: that this power of sin is suppressed in Christians through the Spirit of God; removed out of the flesh it is not." "Only the body," he says further, "is the temple of the Holy Spirit and capable of holiness" (1 Cor. vi. 19; vii. 34).

But it is an error to suppose that Paul makes a rigorous distinction between the σάρξ and the σῶμα and its "members" in relation to the seat of sin. What difference exists in his thought between "the law in the members" and the uniform and necessary working of the lusts of the flesh? The body, which may become the temple of the Holy Spirit, is the body of flesh, and those who are not " in the flesh," since the Spirit of God dwells in them, who have "crucified the flesh" (Rom. viii. 9; Gal. v. 24), are in peril of yielding their "members as instruments of unrighteousness" (Rom. vi. 13). To be "holy both in body and spirit" (1 Cor. vii. 34) is the same thing as to be cleansed from all defilement of the flesh and spirit, and to have the members as "instruments of righteousness." If, however, the meaning of the passage were necessarily, "Let us cleanse ourselves from all defilement that may come to the flesh and spirit," then defilement of flesh might be regarded as unpauline, since the flesh is by nature already defiled. But if we may render it in the sense that the apostle exhorted the Corinthians to cleanse themselves from all defilement which inheres in the flesh as the seat of sin, and may taint the spirit through its connection with the flesh, then the passage is in accord with the Pauline doctrine that even the believers,

---

* *Hand-Commentar*, on the passage.

whose flesh had been crucified with Christ, were still in peril from it (Rom. vi. 12, 13, 19).

In view of all the foregoing considerations, the judgment of Holtzmann does not appear to be expressed with too much vigour when he says: "When a writer so plainly gives his readers to understand that by 'flesh' he really means flesh, and nothing but flesh; that for the elucidation of his meaning he speaks occasionally of 'deeds of the body' (Rom. viii. 13, actually not different from 'the works of the flesh,' Gal. v. 19), and of 'the law of sin in the members' (in them dwells sin, as in the flesh, Rom. viii. 18, 23), then it is not he, at least, who is to blame, but the determination of his theological expositors to misunderstand him, ... when to his words the only sense which they can have is continually denied, and from the throughout clear and unitary conception which they express is derived an understanding that is arbitrarily changing, contradictory, and with difficulty intelligible."* The objection which is raised on the ground that in Gal. v. 19 ff., referred to in the foregoing quotation, other sins are mentioned than those proceeding immediately from the σάρξ literally regarded, is invalid, because it would be manifestly unjust to such a thinker as Paul to require that if he regarded the sensuous nature as the seat of sin, its manifestations must be directly related to the body alone, and not allowed a wider range into the domain of thought and feeling. It has already been pointed out that the apostle thought man to be sold under sin," in bondage to it, because he was σάρκινος or of flesh. But the "sin" in question in this passage is sin in general, and not sin specifically related to the physical nature. The physical basis is not, however, lost sight of, and in fact the list of "works of the flesh" in the passage

* *Neutestamentliche Theologie*, ii. p. 40.

under consideration begins and ends with offences of a directly sensuous character. Man, being by nature σάρκινος, becomes ethically σαρκικός or carnal in the entire scope of his activity, and this sarkical quality of his acts exists precisely and only because he is "of flesh." Moreover, are we able to determine categorically, with our present knowledge of psychical phenomena, what connection "hatred, wrath, and strife" have with the physical nature, or dare we affirm dogmatically that they have none?

The latent sin which has its seat in the flesh is brought into activity, "revived" (Rom. vii. 9), through the agency of the "law." By the term νόμος or ὁ νόμος Paul understands primarily the Mosaic legislation, moral and ceremonial, includes under it, however, the Old Testament Scriptures generally, and recognises an inward law where no outward commandment has been given in Rom. ii. 9: "For when the gentiles, who have no law, do by nature the things contained in the law, these not having a law [*i.e.*, according to the Jewish idea of the law as an express injunction], are a law unto themselves." This last view of law, which was current among the Greeks, has an important relation, as will appear further on, to the apostle's doctrine of the entrance of sin and death into the world. With all his depreciation of the law, Paul concedes so much to the genius of his race out of which it sprang as to declare it to be "spiritual" and "holy, just, and good." It is, however, ineffective in spiritual results, because man is "of flesh" (σάρκινος, Rom. vii. 14). It cannot stop the course of sin and produce righteousness, because it is "weak through the flesh" (Rom. viii. 3), powerless against the lusts of the σάρξ, by whose force its divine ordinances are swept aside, so that it is totally inoperative "to make alive" (ζωοποιῆσαι, Gal. iii. 21). Though man may "delight in the law of God" according to the νόμος τοῦ νοός (the law of the mind), the other law in his "members" overcomes the good impulses of the "mind," and he can only cry out in impotent despair: "O wretched man that I am, who shall deliver me from this body of death?" (Rom. vii. 24.) Thus he finds the commandment, which was ordained to life, to be unto death (Rom. vii. 10).

But Paul does not stop here in his exposition of the relation of the law to sin. Not only is it unable to "make alive," *i.e.*, although "spiritual" and "holy," to effect righteousness, but it also actually produces subjective sin or transgression, since through it comes the knowledge of sin, the consciousness that the impulses of the flesh which without the law take their inevitable course by natural necessity, are in fact sinful. "The motions of sin" are "by the law," and without it man would never have known sin, for "I had not known lust [as such] except the law had said 'Thou shalt not covet'" (Rom. vii. 5, 7). It is through "the commandment" that the sin which was as such before inoperative "took occasion," and "wrought all manner of concupiscence." "For without the law sin was [is] dead" (Rom. vii. 8). This is a general proposition regarding sin and the law, and is to the same purport as the declaration that "sin is not imputed where there is no law" (Rom. v. 13). Without the law, by which the apostle probably means an express commandment, the lusts of the flesh in their nature sinful, partaking of ἁμαρτία, pursue their natural course blindly, and the man is "alive" (lives), but "when the commandment came, sin revived" and the man "died," *i.e.*, became subject to death (Rom. vii. 9). Whether if "the commandment" had not come man would have lived forever in this merely animal existence without moral consciousness is a question which Paul neither raises nor answers, and which we may pass by for the present at least. It should, however, be remarked that if he had in mind the human race prior to the giving of the law through Moses, he is not consistent with himself in giving this alone a place in the scheme; for he recognises for the gentiles an inward law and a conscience according to which they are held responsible (Rom. ii. 14-16). Perhaps there hovered before his mind the Adamic legend of the innocent childhood of the race or the thought of the childhood of the individual before the dawn of conscience. In any case the ὁ νόμος in verse 12, which evidently means the Mosaic law, and the occurrence of "commandment" (ἐντολή) repeatedly in verses 9-13, which he does not employ to designate the inner law (Rom. xiii. 9; 1 Cor. vii. 19, xiv. 37), create a difficulty for which there appears to be no solution without violence to the natural sense of the passage. We might, indeed, suppose the apostle to have regarded the law of the conscience unenlightened by divine revelation as carrying an ἐντολή by implication, but this is a gratuitous expedient, and the probability is that the question in hand did not present itself to him at all.

Paul's teaching regarding the entrance of sin into the world is one of the most difficult and most disputed points of his theology; yet, as before remarked, he does not set out to formulate a specific doctrine on the subject. The matter involves the questions: whether he means to teach that sin first made its appearance in the world through Adam's transgression, whether in that transgression was implied a "fall" of Adam in the traditional sense of the term and a radical change of human nature, whether in the sin of the progenitor as the federal head of the race all men sinned, and whether sin is to be regarded as belonging originally to the divine order of human existence or as chargeable to man's free activity. The classical passage on the subject is the much-disputed Rom. v. 12-19, which opens with the declaration that "as by one man sin entered into the world, and death by sin, and so death passed upon all men, for that all sinned;" the thought is here broken off to be resumed in the eighteenth verse, where the parallel between Adam and Christ is carried out. That the apostle does not here mean that sin came into the world through Adam as a man having the fleshly nature (σάρκινος), and thus beginning an order of life in which sinfulness or sin as an objective power was to prevail, is evident from the fact that in verses 17, 18, and 19 he speaks of Adam's "offence" and "disobedience." He has in mind, then, Adam's transgression of the divine commandment in accordance with the account in Genesis. Through this transgression, he declares, death (physical death without hope of resurrection except through "the last Adam," the "life-giving spirit," 1 Cor. xv. 45) passed upon or unto all men, for that all sinned.

The *crux interpretum* of this passage is the expression ἐφ' ᾧ πάντες ἥμαρτον, which can only mean, "inasmuch as [because] all sinned" (2 Cor. v. 4; Phil. iii. 12), and the central question is whether Adam's sin is regarded as the sin of all, or all are declared to have sinned individually. The former interpretation is without support in the Greek text since ἐφ' ᾧ does not mean "in whom," and since to supply "in him" after "sinned" is to read a new idea into the passage. The simple statement is that "all sinned" as the reason why all are subject to death, and Paul never employs the verb "to sin" (ἁμαρτάνω) in any other sense than that of individual transgression. Accordingly, the meaning is not that all men became sinful at the same time with Adam and through his sin. Nevertheless, the expression "by one man" must have its rights, so that the sin of Adam shall not be cut off from connection with the sin of his posterity, and the transgressions of the latter for which they suffer death be regarded as independent of his "offence." Otherwise the argument of the entire section would be destroyed, which draws a parallel between Adam and Christ as the respective heads of the two world-orders of sin and death and righteousness and life; and as men do not and cannot attain salvation without connection with, "the last Adam," so they are not conceived as bringing destruction upon themselves or as being naturally subject to death independently of "the first Adam." "As in Adam [*i.e.*, on the ground of Adam] all die, so in Christ shall all be made alive." "For as by one man's disobedience many were made sinners, so by the obedience of one shall many be made righteous" (1 Cor. xv. 22; Rom. v. 19).

If, however, under the new order men do not become righteous simply because of the righteousness of Christ and without their own choice, neither under the old order did Paul think them to be subject to death without their own acts of sin. Each representative head is conceived only as the occasion of the results of his work, on the one hand in the tragic order of death, and on the other in the blessed order of life — the occasion indispensable to all that follows in either order. It may be questioned whether Pfleiderer does not state the case too strongly when he says that the sin of Adam's posterity is regarded as "the necessary consequence" of the sin of the first man (*Paulinismus*, 2te Aufl., p. 54). It does not necessarily follow from the employment of the aorist ἥμαρτον that the sinning of all is conceived as contained in that of Adam, although this sense must be conceded as grammatically possible. It is not, however, the only grammatically defensible sense. The aorist is technically not used for the perfect, and "have sinned" may be an incorrect translation if one will be excessively exact. But strict accuracy is not always observed in the use of the aorist, and this tense is often employed when a connection with the present closely analogous to our perfect is intended. It would not be regarded as a gross inaccuracy to translate in Luke i. 1, ἐπεχείρησαν "have taken in hand," or to make one invited guest say in xiv. 19, "I have bought a field," and another, "I have married a wife." (So in each case the Revised Version.) Moreover, Paul himself says: "For all have sinned and are come short of the glory of God" (Rom. iii. 23), where ἥμαρτον certainly does not denote such a definite past act filling only one point of time as is claimed for it in the passage in question, but means that all began to sin in some past time and have continued sinning till at the present, as before, they are in the condition mentioned. The perfect tense could not express this idea more clearly. In fact the perfect of ἁμαρτάνω is rarely used in the New Testament and not at all by Paul except in the participial form, while the aorist is repeatedly employed in connections in which our perfect would be the accurate equivalent (Luke xv. 18, 21; Rom. ii. 12; 1 Cor. vii. 28, "If thou marry, thou hast not sinned" ἥμαρτες). In almost every place except Rom. v. 12 the revisers have rendered the aorist of ἁμαρτάνω by the perfect tense. Why not there?

The apostle's teaching on this subject has a point and vividness which are doubtless due to his own experience of sin and to his conversion, and it may be regarded as his original contribution to hamartiology. The doctrine was certainly remote from the Jewish point of view and even antagonistic to the thought and feeling of a Jew that sin became exceeding sinful by the commandment, and that the law was given for the express purpose of making "the offence abound" (Rom. v. 20, vii. 13). The sin that is in the flesh is brought to life through the presence of the commandment, and rushes forth into every forbidden field simply because of the prohibition. The objective sin becomes subjective, the "material sin" becomes "formal." All that Paul says, however, on the law and sin is incidental to a purpose to which any specific doctrine of sin was for him subordinate, to show, namely, that righteousness is unattainable through the law. If the law can do nothing but make men sinners and expose them to death and the wrath of God, it certainly does not open a way to eternal life. The entire observance of its requirements is impossible. The more a man knows of it the wider yawns the chasm within him between ideal and achievement, between what the law of his mind requires and what the law in his members fatally compels him to do.

It is an error, however, to suppose that Paul thought the law to be imperfect as a law or an incomplete disclosure of the divine will. The Old Testament was to him the perfect word of God. Accordingly, if the law was a pedagogue to lead men to Christ, it had this office in the sense that it was intended to hold them in subjection, convict them of sin, show them their inability to save themselves by their own works, and fling them at last upon Christ who abolished the old law and revealed the new law of the Spirit and of life. He therefore, as Weizsäcker remarks, "accepted the paradox involved in the two propositions, that the law contains the commands of God by whose fulfilment man obtains life and righteousness, and that as a matter of fact its only effect was to produce the knowledge of sin." The solution of this paradox is superficial according to which the law is conceived as "spiritual" and given "unto life," but performs a transitional function in producing the knowledge of sin and in showing to man the impossibility of salvation by works, in order to prepare the way for salvation under the new dispensation, and so in fact to fulfil its original purpose. An incidental result of the law, that Paul himself discovered, does not invalidate its original intention, which he declares in the most precise terms to have been "to life" (εἰς ζωήν); and yet in the same breath he asserts that he had found the law to be "unto death" (εἰς θάνατον, Rom. vii. 10). A divine ordinance produces a result directly the opposite of its original intention! Verse 13 does not resolve the paradox, for although he there says that not the law which is good is the occasion of death to him, but rather sin, the responsibility still falls upon the law, since it was given in order that sin might abound. If "the sting of death is sin," "the strength of sin is the law" (Cor. xv. 56).

To the question which one of the two terms of the antinomy under consideration is supported by the historico-religious facts relative to the law the apostle himself furnishes the only valid answer when he says that this was given "unto life." From the point of view of the Old Testament the law was unquestionably given not to make "sin abound," but to produce righteousness. Obedience is not therein enjoined by the voice of teachers and prophets from age to age as if it were an impossibility, but as an achievement within the power of men. Actual righteousness achieved by conforming through good works to the will of God is not enforced by unremitting warning and exhortation as if it were an unattainable ideal, but as a possible accomplishment of which many shining examples exist. It is hardly necessary to add that the teaching of Jesus in this regard is in accord with that of the illustrious representatives of the genius of the old Hebrew morality and religion (Matt. v. 19, vii. 21, viii. 50, xix. 16–21; Luke xvi. 29). Even Paul himself occasionally shows that he had in fact "profited in the Jews' religion" (Gal. i. 14), and echoes the mighty voice of his race, when he for the moment loses sight of the dogmatic purpose which led him into the antinomy in question (Rom. ii. 6–13; 1 Cor. iii.

13, v. 10; Gal. vi. 7). Another obscurity appears in the connection in which the apostle here speaks of "the law" as occasioning sin in connection with the flesh, and declares that without it no formal sin could exist. That he has in mind, as before remarked, the Mosaic law, and includes its moral precepts is evident from the words: "I had not known lust except the law had said, 'Thou shalt not covet'" (Rom. vii. 7). Yet he recognises sin as existing in an aggravated form among the gentiles "who have not the law," and speaks of sinning "without law" (Rom. ii. 12, 14). His intense preoccupation with polemical dialectic, and the impetuous rush of his thought toward the end that this proposed for him furnishes the only explanation of such paradoxes, which are stumbling-blocks to those only who are wanting in insight into the nature and the absorbing aims of the great apostle.

The interpretation which we have given to Rom. v. 12 is the only one consistent with verses 13 and 14 in which the apostle proceeds to establish the proposition that all individually sinned: "For until the law sin was in the world; but sin is not imputed when there is no law. Nevertheless death reigned from Adam until Moses even over them that had not sinned after the similitude of Adam's transgression." This does not mean, as Lipsius will have it,* and as Meyer maintains, that individuals were not punished by death for their actual sins but by reason of the objective transference of the sin of Adam. This might be Paul's meaning in accordance with his doctrine that "without the law sin is dead" (Rom. vii. 8), if a sin that is "dead" be punishable, but why should he take the trouble to state the obvious fact that sin which is not sin in fact and in form is not "imputed"? Meyer's remark on this point, which is irreconcilable with his

* *Hand-Commentar*, on the passage.

interpretation of the passage as a whole, is that "in the absence of the law the action which in and by itself is unlawful is no *transgression* of the law and cannot, therefore, be brought into account *as such*." *

But that these "actions" performed under the universal reign of ἁμαρτία were regarded by Paul as individual sins is evident from Rom. i. 19–32, ii. 12. They were violations of the inner law by those who knew "the judgment of God that they who commit such things are worthy of death" (Rom. i. 32). Besides, in the passage in hand he says of those who lived before the giving of the formal law that they had "sinned," although not like Adam by violating an express outward commandment. This certainly is not a sinning "in Adam." The death, then, that "reigned from Adam until Moses," reigned over all because

* The difficulties presented in the words, "Sin is not imputed where there is no law," are exceedingly perplexing whether the non-imputation be referred to God, or to the individual conscience. The sinning of men between Adam and Moses is explicitly declared, and with equal explicitness the apostle affirms that those who sin against the innner law *know* that they are "worthy of death." Hence there can be no non-imputation in the sinners' conscience, and if they are "worthy of death" their sin must be imputed by God. Bovon objects to the interpretation herein supported that it makes Paul in the passage in question (Rom. v. 13, 14) "withdraw with one hand what he gives with the other" (*Théologie du nouveau Testament*, ii. p. 268). It would not, however, surprise any one who is familiar with the Pauline paradoxes if this hypothesis were found to be necessary to the solution of the difficulties which according to any explanation inhere in the section. It is futile to adduce the words "sin is not imputed where there is no law," in support of the doctrine that according to Paul the men over whom death reigned from Adam to Moses bore the consequences, not of their own sins, but of the transgression of the progenitor; for the apostle expressly says that these men "sinned" in a particular way, and is, moreover, debarred by his own declarations from affirming that their sins were not "imputed" because there was no "law" in the case. He declares unequivocally that those who "have not the [Mosaic] law are a law unto themselves," and that they have the "accusing" and "excusing" "conscience." It is hardly legitimate for an expositor to take advantage of a paradox of the apostle's in order to support a theory of his meaning in a given passage.

"all sinned." Meyer remarks that the Rabbinical writers derived universal mortality from the fall of Adam, all having sinned in him, and thinks that Paul's doctrine may have had its roots in his Jewish training. According to Weber, however, the Jewish theologians found an antinomy in the two propositions that death came as the consequence of Adam's sin, and that sin is not inheritable. They concluded accordingly that death has power over the individual only on the ground of his own sin.* Paul's teaching also was that death came into the world as the penalty of Adam's offence, and that since penalty can be conceived as inflicted only where there is actual sin, the death of his descendants, sin not being transmissible, was due to the fact that all had sinned. The death of innocent children is not taken into the account.

The difficulties which inhere in the Pauline doctrine of the origin of sin are not, however, cleared up by the passages thus far considered. It cannot be denied that in Rom. v. 12 ff. the apostle speaks of sin as though it had no existence in the world prior to Adam's transgression, and as though through the principle of solidarity "by some sort of continuity" the descendants of the progenitor were subject to sin and death through him. Such expressions as "By one man's offence death reigned;" "By the offence of one judgment came upon all men to condemnation," and "By one man's disobedience many were made sinners" (Rom. v. 17, 18, 19), indicate that Adam's act is conceived not as the act of an isolated individual from which no consequences follow to others, but as one fraught with such far-reaching tragic results as can proceed only from the head of the race, just as Christ's act of atonement extended to the whole series of his descendants in the spiritual order. In other words, the

* *System*, pp. 240 f.

teaching appears to be that just as grace could not "reign through righteousness unto eternal life" except "through Christ," "sin," and so "death" as its consequence "reigned" primarily "by one" (Rom. v. 17, 21). If in these passages the origin of sin in the descendants of Adam appears to lie outside themselves, it is not in 2 Cor. xi. 3 placed in the progenitors themselves, but in the serpent or Satan, in which evil personality Paul evidently believed (Rom. xvi. 20; 1 Cor. v. 5, vii. 5; 2 Cor. ii. 11, i. 14).

To the question raised by Sabatier[*]: "Why, then, did not the apostle say that sin entered into the world with Satan and by him?" the inquiry may be proposed to determine what he does mean to say here if not precisely this. For, according to Sabatier himself, he here follows the Adamic legend in Genesis as an "authority," and that recognises no sin either objective or subjective in the progenitors except through an outward seduction. On the other hand, according to a series of passages already quoted and elucidated, the apostle regards the origin of "formal" sin in the individual as due to "material" sin residing in the flesh in connection with the law which provokes and calls it into activity. He certainly ascribes to all the descendants of Adam an indwelling principle of sin which is "dead" until the law brings it to life. And this, too, despite the principle of solidarity and some sort of causal connection of the first sin with that which reigned in the world subsequent to Adam, he appears to regard as the natural condition of man. The first man Adam was only a "living soul" (ψυχή), was "earthy" (χοϊκος), and had not the spiritual quality of "the second man from heaven," otherwise he would not have sinned. In the divine order "that is not first which is spiritual, but that which is natural," and the ψυχή and the πνεῦμα represent the antithetic

[*] *L'Apôtre Paul*, 3me ed., 1896, p. 384.

K

orders of life (1 Cor. xv. 45 f.). "The natural (ψυχικός) man receiveth not the things of the Spirit of God" (1 Cor. ii. 14), *i.e.*, he is essentially σαρκικός because he is "of the flesh" (σάρκινος), and "no good thing" dwells in him, namely, in his flesh, but rather sin ready to manifest itself when the "occasion" is presented "through the commandment," and to "bring forth fruit unto death."

It is a natural conclusion from these premises that one at least of the apostle's doctrines of the origin of sin was that it resided primarily in the nature of man and in "the first man Adam" as well as in his descendants. If this conception, so far as Adam is concerned, does not appear in the account of the first sin in Genesis, which he seems to accept in ascribing sin to the temptation or deception of Satan, then there is in this regard if not an antinomy at least a gap in his thought which he has not formally filled. That he believed the children of Adam to have "all sinned" in the same way and for the same reason, *i.e.*, because they had like him the evil impulse in the flesh, is evident from the foregoing considerations. There is, then, no solution of the antinomy which is contained in this proposition and in the other that sin and death came to men through Adam, except on the assumption that their fleshly nature, their evil impulses, were inherited from him. But Paul nowhere intimates the doctrine that either the nature of Adam or that of his descendants underwent a change by reason of the first transgression. We must conclude accordingly, that his teaching, as we have it, furnishes no means of resolving this paradox.

That the traditional doctrine of the fall of man is not taught by Paul is not only based upon exegesis, according to which such a teaching would be incompatible with the idea that man was originally "earthy," *i.e.*, the opposite of "spiritual," but also upon the natural and obvious philosophy of the matter derivable from the reasoning of the apostle. For assuming the premises from which he proceeds, the Eden-legend, the absence of fleshly or sinful impulses in "the first man" leaves the beginning of sin inexplicable. That this difficulty inheres in the Genesis-story, and that Paul appears once to have overlooked it, need not enter into the consideration. Enough, that it is a fundamental principle of his thought that only the man can be superior to the flesh and sin in whom dwells the life-giving Spirit imparted through Christ. Sin inheres in the flesh of the psychical or natural man, and it is from the fleshly nature that sin proceeds, that is, it is grounded in the original constitution of man. Sin did not make man fleshly through "the fall," but he sinned first, and has always sinned, because of the flesh. The law is spiritual, but man is carnal, sold under sin. According to the inner man he aspires and strives toward the service of God in which his mind delights, but the law in his members brings him into captivity to the law of sin and death which is in his members, so that he does what he would not and what he hates. "In no place," says Weizsäcker, "where the antithesis of flesh and Spirit is broadly discussed is there any hint that the flesh, considered in its moral aspect, is a secondary growth (*ein Gewordenes*). It is only its full moral influence that is to be thought of as a later development. . . . But the law is incapable of attaining its object. It was weak on account of the flesh (Rom. viii. 3). After all this there can hardly be a doubt that for Paul the antithesis of flesh and Spirit ultimately rests on the nature of the flesh, that is, on the natural quality of man."*

We are thus led to the conclusion that according to a fundamental doctrine of Paul's man cannot be regarded as

* *Apost. Zeitalter*, p. 131.

naturally immortal. It was "by man" that death came, by "the first man," who was "earthy" and as such by nature doomed to corruption (φθορά). "In Adam all die." Life, incorruption, the glory of the blessed in the Messianic kingdom, the resurrection, pertain only to those who, through having accepted Christ, have "the earnest [pledge] of the Spirit," and who can hopefully wait for "the redemption" of their bodies (Rom. viii. 23). Even believers, though possessing "the Spirit," are conceived as subject to physical death, and it was only when Christ should come for the resurrection that the dead would be "raised incorruptible," and the saints then living would "be changed" (1 Cor. xv. 52). Incorruptibility belongs only to the kingdom of God, which "flesh and blood cannot inherit." The body, which is mortal by reason of having the flesh as its substance, becomes triumphant over death only when "quickened" by the indwelling Spirit of God. This is only another way of saying that the body of the believer conceived as a form will have at the resurrection an incorruptible spiritual substance, and will become like that of Christ in his exalted state a "body of glory." With this principle, which cannot be removed from the apostle's theology without leaving it a soulless body, it is not easy to reconcile his doctrine that death came into the world in consequence of Adam's transgression, that "by one man's offence death reigned by one" (Rom. v. 17), and that "death passed upon all because all sinned." Death is "the wages of sin," and the doctrine that it is imposed as a divine judgment for sin could not well be more explicitly expressed than it is in the words: "Therefore as by the offence of one judgment came upon all men to condemnation," etc. (Rom. v. 18), where the "offence" is the sin on account of which "death reigned" (verse 17).

We have, then, the two propositions over against each other, (1) that man being "of flesh" and "earthy" is naturally mortal, and (2) that his mortality is by reason of the divine judgment upon sin. It is true, as Sabatier remarks, that Paul does not say that "the physical law of death did not exist in the world before the sin of Adam." Neither does he say explicitly that Adam was by nature immortal, and would not have died if he had not sinned. But this proposition and its opposite are legitimate deductions from two series of passages. The same inconsistency existed in the later Jewish theology, which taught that Adam was created mortal, and yet in consequence of the fall became subject to death.* The Pauline antinomy cannot be solved; it can only be explained, as it has been, by supposing that two ways of regarding the subject were in the apostle's mind without reconciliation: the Pharisaic-Jewish, according to which death was a positive punishment of the definite transgression of Adam, and that corresponding to the old Hebraism as well as to Hellenism, according to which death was the natural consequence of the perishableness of all earthly material (so Pfleiderer,† Holtzmann,‡ Schmiedel, § and others).

The passage concerning "the groaning creation" (Rom. viii. 19-22) is in accord with the ancient Hebrew tradition recorded in Gen. iii. 17 as well as with the later Jewish theology. The latter taught that the earth had its part in the curse of Adam, so that not only human nature, but also the inanimate creation, underwent a change in consequence of the fall. The earth brought forth harmful insects, and the course of the planets was altered as a result of Adam's sin; their path was lengthened and their speed retarded.‖ An echo of this idea appears to be the

---

* Weber, *System*, pp. 214, 238. † *Paulinismus.* ‡ *Neutest. Theol.*
§ *Hand-Commentar.* ‖ Weber, *System*, p. 216.

teaching that "the whole creation groaneth and travaileth in pain together until now," in "earnest expectation" waiting "for the manifestation of the sons of God"—the glorious revelation of their sonship which would be effected at the Parousia, "the restoration of all things." That this condition of the creation is not conceived as inhering in its original constitution, but as imposed upon it from without, is evident from the expression, "on account of him who subjected" it, whether this one be man effecting the result through sin, or God who did it "because His counsel and will had to be thus satisfied." The sin which struck man with mortality brought a malediction upon nature.

The objection to this construction of the Pauline theology, according to which sin is conceived as arising out of the natural fleshly impulse of human nature in conjunction with the divine law, that it makes God the author of sin, though not "scientific" from the point of view of exegesis, but dogmatic, may well have a brief consideration, because its discussion will throw light upon the apostle's hamartiology. If man was originally of "flesh" ($\sigma\acute{a}\rho\kappa\iota\nu o\varsigma$), "earthy" ($\chi o\ddot{\iota}\kappa\acute{o}\varsigma$), and "psychical" ($\psi\nu\chi\iota\kappa\acute{o}\varsigma$), so that sin must immediately "revive" when the commandment comes, and if the power of this inherent $\dot{a}\mu a\rho\tau\acute{\iota}a$ was so great that its desolating sway has been universal, it would appear to be a valid inference that sin is a part of the divine order (Rom. ix. 13, 17, 18, xi. 7, 8, 32; Gal. iii. 21, 22), a necessary result of the infirmity of the human constitution. In fact, according to the strenuous theism of Paul God is the Author of everything (Rom. xi. 36; 1 Cor. viii. 6). It is He who created "the first man," the psychical, earthly one (Rom. ix. 20–22), and He also created the last Adam, "the life-giving spirit," who was destined conditionally to restore all that the former had devastated.

The apostle knows nothing of an absolute human freedom. On the one hand, the psychical man is powerless under the servitude to the flesh and its indwelling sinfulness (Rom. vii. 14, 23). "The carnal mind is not subject to the law of God, neither indeed can be" (Rom. viii. 7).

Thus man cannot liberate and save himself; but on the other hand, his salvation is effected by the supernatural intervention of the mighty Spirit of God by whose power his spiritual life is just as certainly determined as his sinful activity was governed by the indomitable "carnal mind." The sons of God are "driven," impelled, determined in their living by the Spirit of God.* If the unregenerate man is determined in his activity by the compelling flesh, the believer, who has the Spirit, acts under the compulsion of this supernal power, this masterful over-soul. "Since the days of the prophets no one had so strongly felt the constraint of the divine thought upon man as Paul. If in general man regards the operations of his being as his free actions, believes that he pushes, and is pushed, is like a stone which is thrown, and thinks it flies, much more did the apostle clearly feel the flight of his spirit to be a cast from the hand of God." † Yet the apostle employs in unmistakable terms the language of freedom and responsibility. He condemns men for their transgressions, and exhorts them to the activities of obedience and righteousness quite as if he regarded them as free agents and moral beings in the libertarian sense. If all this denotes an antinomy in his thought, it is one which still lurks in our thinking, and which theistic philosophy has not yet been able to resolve.

The dark picture of the natural man's servitude to the flesh and of his inability to do right is relieved by the doctrine of the ἔσω ἄνθρωπος, so that Paul cannot be charged

* πνεύματι θεοῦ ἄγονται, Rom. viii. 14.
† Hausrath, *Neutestamentliche Zeitgeschichte*, iii. p. 113.

with teaching the traditional dogma of total depravity. The flesh is not the whole man despite Holsten's acute reasoning. There is a delight in the law of God after the inner man, and the mind ($νοῦς$) renders a spontaneous service to the divine order of virtue, struggling against the fleshly impulses which reign in the members (Rom. vii. 22 f.). While according to the apostle's philosophy of salvation the $νοῦς$ is unable without the divine $πνεῦμα$ to attain righteousness, and appears to be represented in Rom. vii. 13-23 as consenting to the law that it is good and serving it so far at least as a recognition of its demands and a desire to fulfil them are concerned, but still doing what it hates, there is on the other hand in passages written without the doctrinal preoccupation which often leads him into extreme statements a recognition of man's ability to "do by nature the things contained in the law," even when the subjects are gentiles who have only the inward law. It would indeed be a fruitful inquiry that should enable the expositors of Paul to determine to what extent a manifest polemic-dogmatic interest on his part in connection with the antinomies of his thought should incline them to regard one or the other member of them as expressing his deepest conviction. There is, however, only an apparent antinomy in his teaching on the subject in question, and the importance of the right anthropological point of view to a comprehension of his doctrine is here apparent. The $νοῦς$ is a part of man, and is to be distinguished from the divine $πνεῦμα$ which is elsewhere represented as striving against the flesh. The activity in the direction of the good which he here ascribes to the $νοῦς$ renders his teaching on the subject of man's moral ability essentially different from Augustine's.

The dreadful consequences which Paul attaches to sin indicate the deep earnestness which underlay his teaching regarding its nature and operations. As has already been pointed out, the judgment upon sin is conceived as an immediate decree of God, a divine condemnation. The hard and impenitent heart treasures up "wrath" that will break forth "in the day of wrath," *i.e.*, at the judgment of the Parousia which will manifest the divine "indignation and wrath," and bring "tribulation and anguish" upon evildoers, then to be overwhelmed by the might of Him who "taketh vengeance" (Rom. ii. 5, 8, 9, iii. 5, v. 9. See also Eph. v. 6). This terrible judgment conceived and executed by almighty power denotes the dread significance of "death" ($\theta\acute{a}\nu a\tau o\varsigma$) which is so frequently mentioned as the penalty of sin. This means not only the going out of existence of the physical body, of soul ($\psi v\chi\acute{\eta}$, life-principle of the flesh) and body, but also the exclusion of the individual from participation in the resurrection, his hopeless tarrying in the underworld, hades, the realm of the dead, if not the absolute destruction of his personality. The words "corruption" ($\phi\theta o\rho\acute{a}$), "destruction" ($\dot{a}\pi\acute{\omega}\lambda\epsilon\iota a$) and their corresponding verbs ($\phi\theta\epsilon\acute{\iota}\rho\epsilon\sigma\theta a\iota$ and $\dot{a}\pi\acute{o}\lambda\lambda\upsilon\sigma\theta a\iota$) do not mean simply punishment and to punish, and do not convey the mere idea of temporal overthrow, but their proper sense is exclusion from existence as ordinarily understood and in particular from the life of believers who alone, since they had "the Spirit," could hope for resurrection. It is not of great moment whether the terms signify the absolute extinction of being or simply exclusion from the resurrection, for according to the ideas of the time the sad and gloomy existence of shades in the underworld was scarcely to be preferred to annihilation. The Jewish theology believed in the destruction of the wicked in gehenna with discrimination against some.[*] For Paul's use of the words see in particular Rom. ix. 22; 1 Cor. iii. 17. Such

[*] Weber, *System*, pp. 374, 375.

being the apostle's view of the fate of the wicked, it is evident that the doctrine of their endless punishment has no support in his writings, but that his thought on the matter is rather expressed by the αἰφνίδιος ὄλεθρος (swift destruction) of 1 Thess. v. 3.

The Pauline doctrine of sin considered by itself presents a gloomy view of human nature, life, and destiny — the indomitable flesh with its debasing appetites and passions; the law in the members in endless warfare against the law of the mind; the inward man which delights in the law of God engaged in a doubtful struggle with the powers of evil; and the universal reign of death in whose awful harvest the wicked are gathered to destruction. A full view of the apostle's thought requires a consideration of his doctrine of redemption, from which a gleam of hope is thrown upon this darkness, and in which the despairing exclamation "O wretched man that I am!" is answered by the cry of triumph, "Thanks be to God who giveth us the victory through our Lord Jesus Christ."

CHAPTER XI

SALVATION — ATONEMENT

TO Paul salvation was inseparably connected with participation in the approaching kingdom of God which Christ at his second coming (Parousia) was to establish. In this respect his conception of soteriology is in accord with that of the other New Testament writers (Matt. xxv. 31-46; Mark xiii. 24-37; 1 Tim. vi. 14; 2 Tim. iv. 1, 8; 2 Pet. iii. 10-14). He reminds the Thessalonians that they had turned "from idols to serve the living and true God," not as an end sufficient in itself, but with a view to an ulterior though not remote consummation, viz.: "to wait for His Son from heaven, whom He raised from the dead, even Jesus, who delivers us from the wrath to come" (1 Thess. i. 10). This deliverance from the "wrath" which would be manifested against unbelievers in the great day of Christ's Parousia constitutes the nerve of salvation from the Pauline and the general New Testament point of view. This was the inheritance of the New Testament writers from Judaism, to which "the age to come," the Messianic age, held all the blessedness and glory that God purposed to bestow upon His people. Accordingly, to Paul he that is to be "saved" will be "saved in the day of the Lord Jesus" (1 Cor. v. 5). The Romans are admonished to exercise brotherly love and keep the commandments as "knowing the time, that it is now high time to awake out of sleep; for now is our salvation nearer than when we believed," that is, became believers. "Salvation" is not thought to be consummated in the practice of the moral virtues or the keeping of the commandment in which all the others are "comprehended," but is to be realised in the near future, the Messianic "age to come"; and because the great "day is at hand," the apostle says, "let us *therefore* cast off the works of darkness, and let us put on the armour of light" (Rom. xiii. 8–13). From this point of view the "promise," the "inheritance," and the glory of the approaching kingdom appear not only as a hope and encouragement, but also as a motive.

As Christ was to come to usher in and establish the kingdom, as he then would claim his own to reign with him, so he is conceived as the sole and indispensable agency of salvation. The glorious deliverance which will be effected at the coming of the kingdom depends unconditionally upon his previous relation to those who are to enjoy it. Their title to the inheritance comes only "through" him. The kingdom is one of righteousness, and he must be righteous who becomes a member of it and a participant in its blessedness. This was not an original Christian idea, but was derived from the Messianic doctrine of Judaism. Paul made it his own, however, and he declares that "the kingdom of God is righteousness and peace and joy in the Holy Ghost." Now the Pauline doctrine of salvation takes its departure from two propositions which to its author were indisputable, namely, that no man is by nature righteous and therefore fitted for the kingdom, and that no one can of himself obtain righteousness. On the one hand, "Jews and gentiles are all under sin" (Rom. iii. 9), and on the other, "by the deeds of the law there shall no flesh be justified" (verse 20), that is, the righteousness which is requisite for admission to the kingdom is unattainable by the utmost endeavour to observe the requirements of the law as they are laid down in the Old Testament. The only righteousness that can avail is that which is "of God," that is, bestowed by God, and the condition of attaining this is "faith in Jesus Christ." All may be justified freely by the grace of God through the redemption that is in Christ (verses 22, 24). The sum of the whole matter is expressed in the words: "Therefore we conclude that a man is justified by faith without the deeds of the law" (verse 28).

It is evident, then, that since "all have sinned, and come short of the glory of God," the relation between God and man is abnormal and discordant, and that the entire fortune of the kingdom of God, or in other words, the destiny of the human race, depends upon the establishment of right relations between them, that is, upon the extent to which the mission of Christ should realise its purpose. A reconciliation must be effected, an atonement made, before man, the "servant of sin," who cannot alone free himself from his bondage, can become a subject of the kingdom of God. Paul does not appear ever to have raised the question why God chose this means of saving man, that is, the intervention of Christ, or whether He might not have accomplished the same result in another way, by a general and unconditional pardon, for example. It was enough for him that according to the "revelation" that he had had this was God's plan. When it pleased God to reveal His Son in him (Gal. i. 15, 16), the Christ that he saw was the resurrected and glorified Christ, and in the resurrection he recognised God's seal confirming the Son as the Saviour of the world and transforming the opprobrious cross into a symbol of redemption. Accordingly, Menegoz has admirably remarked that " Paul's faith in the expiatory sacrifice of Christ was not the conclusion of a process of reasoning on the relation between the mercy and justice of God, but on the contrary, the apostle's ideas on the justice and mercy of God were founded on his faith in the expiatory death of Christ."

The entire Pauline scheme of salvation through Christ hinges upon his death, and no greater violence can be done to this teaching than to interpret it in the sense that the office of Jesus was simply a reconciliation of man to God through the moral influence of his life. From this point of view the death on the cross has no other significance than that, as an inevitable consequence of Jesus' devotion to duty, it may serve as an example and an ethical impulse to men in the interest of a similar consecration. This interpretation, which springs from a rationalistic motive or a motive to make the apostle's teaching correspond with what seems rational to the expositor, is without exegetical support. The attempt to maintain it is made in total disregard of the most explicit declarations of the apostle, in which the entire stress in defining the work of Christ is laid upon his death, or these declarations are not accorded their legitimate force and meaning. The central significance of the death of Christ appears unmistakably in such passages as the following: "When we were yet without strength, in due time Christ died for the ungodly"; "While we were yet sinners, Christ died for us"; "We were reconciled to God by the death of His Son"; "Being now justified by his blood, we shall be saved from wrath through him" (Rom. v. 6–10); "For in that he died, he died unto sin once"; "If we have been planted together in the likeness of his death" (Rom. vi. 5, 10); "Who was delivered for our offences, and was raised again for our justification" (Rom. iv. 25); "Whom God set forth to be a propitiation through faith in his blood" (Rom. iii. 25); "If righteousness come by the law, then Christ is dead in vain" (Gal. ii. 21); "Who died for us, that whether we wake or sleep [are living or dead at the time of the

Parousia — cf. 1 Thess. iv. 13-17] we should live together with him" (1 Thess. v. 10); "For the preaching of the cross is to them that perish foolishness; but unto us who are saved it is the power of God"; "We preach Christ crucified"; "I determined not to know anything among you save Jesus Christ and him crucified" (1 Cor. i. 18, 23, ii. 2).

These passages show unmistakably that to the apostle the death of Christ was vital and essential in his redemptive work. There is besides no evidence that he attached a fundamental importance to the moral qualities of the life of Jesus or to his example. In Rom. v. 10, "For if when we were enemies we were reconciled to God by the death of his Son, much more being reconciled, we shall be saved by his life," means that, just as the believer's justification and reconciliation have been effected by the death of Christ, so his future salvation, his deliverance from the wrath of God and his participation in the glory and blessedness of the coming kingdom, will be brought about through the resurrection of Jesus. The fact that Jesus now lives, and will come again gives him assurance of the consummation of his salvation. The "obedience" of Christ which is set over against the disobedience of Adam, and represented as the means of counteracting it by making many righteous (Rom. v. 19) does not relate to his ethical conduct or to the influence of his example, but to his subjection of himself to the death of the cross, which though voluntary on his part was yet in accordance with the will of God: "Who gave himself for our sins, that he might deliver us from this present evil world [age, the 'evil' time preceding the Parousia and 'the age to come'] according to the will of God" (Gal. i. 4). Accordingly, the apostle says of Christ that he humbled himself, and became obedient unto death, even the death of the cross (Phil. ii. 8). It is significant, moreover, that when he enforces upon the believers the practice of brotherly love, he does not adduce the life of Jesus as an example, but cites only the fact of his death "for all" as a reason why "they who live should not henceforth live to themselves, but to him who died for them, and rose again." No one familiar with the self-sacrificing life of Jesus and holding it in high regard as an example could instead of using illustrations drawn from it resort to an Old Testament quotation as he does in Rom. xv. 2, 3 : " Let every one of us please his neighbour for his good to edification ; for even Christ pleased not himself, but as it is written, the reproaches of them that reproached thee fell upon me." *

The object of the death of Christ, as Paul conceived it, was to counteract the effects of Adam's sin and thus restore the normal relations between God and man. This thought is clearly defined in the words : " Therefore as by the offence of one judgment came upon all men to condemnation, even so by the righteousness of one the free gift came upon all men unto justification of life" (Rom. v. 18). This act of righteousness which in the following verse is called "obedience," that is, compliance with the will of God on the cross, was an atonement for all men objectively considered and subjectively for as many

* In Rom. viii. 3, God's sending of His Son " in the likeness of sinful flesh," and thereby condemning sin in the flesh, is interpreted by Dr. Stevens (*The Pauline Theology*, p. 231) as "certainly" implying "that the overthrow of the dominion of sin in the flesh was conditional upon the sinlessness of the life of Jesus." But "in the flesh" should be connected with "condemned." The condemnation of sin was in the flesh of Christ on the cross. In his death was executed the judgment of condemnation upon it, and the benefit of this representative suffering of the death entailed in the divine order upon sin accrues to men in so far as through faith they come into that mystic fellowship with the death of Christ, whereby they ideally die to that to which he died. Thus, and thus only, "the righteousness of the law may be fulfilled" in them, since by reason of his atonement and their appropriation of it they are no more "after the flesh, but after the spirit" (verse 4).

as through faith lay hold on the salvation thus offered, and so become subjects of the divine decree of "justification" which assures them "life," yet, not merely the moral-religious quality of life in the present existence, but superiority to death, the resurrection, and participation in the blessedness of the kingdom at the Parousia. The necessity of an atonement was conceived to be based upon the relation of hostility between man and God, the removal of which could alone save the race from "destruction." Unless a new principle of "life" were introduced, the "death" which had come into the world through Adam's sin would continue unmitigatedly its dreadful work, until all would "perish," as some were destined to be destroyed in "the day of the Lord" (1 Thess. v. 2, 3). The relation of hostility is expressed in various terms. In Rom. v. 10, the apostle says: "For when we were enemies, we were reconciled to God by the death of His Son"; and again: "The carnal mind is enmity against God, for it is not subject to the law of God, neither indeed can be" (Rom. viii. 7). The condition of the natural man, the man who is not "in the Spirit," is one in which it is impossible to "please God" (Rom. viii. 8, 9).

The hostility in question is of the nature of an active opposition expressing itself in disobedience and in a course of life which cannot meet with the divine approval. An enmity of man from the divine point of view, as passive enmity, certainly belongs to this general conception of hostility, and if it is not implied in the passages in hand, is unequivocally expressed in Rom. xi. 28, where "enemies" of God are contrasted with those who are "beloved" of Him. The hostility of God to the natural man, who is controlled by the carnal mind, is expressed by the term "wrath." Because the law induces transgression, the apostle says that it "worketh wrath." "The wrath of

God is revealed from heaven against all ungodliness and unrighteousness of men." The evil-doer "treasures up wrath against the day of wrath and revelation of the righteous judgment of God" (Rom. i. 18, ii. 5, iv. 15 ; cf. 1 Thess. i. 10, ii. 16). There is an apparent incongruity in the fact that in Rom. xi. 28 the Jews are represented as at the same time objects of God's hostility and of His love. The same must be said of the conception of God's wrath toward sinners in general, which to the apostle is not incompatible with His love for them that is preëminently manifested in the mission of Christ, for "God commendeth His love toward us in that while we were yet sinners, Christ died for us" (Rom. v. 8). This dual state of feeling is not, however, foreign to our experience, and the apostle's representation of the matter doubtless belongs to the general anthropopathic conception of the age. It must not be forgotten that he thought of God's relation to man in accordance with the judicial idea of Judaism, to which the law was inexorable.* It was an expression of God's attitude toward sin, and must take its inevitable course of retribution unless an atonement was provided. The thought never appears to have occurred to Paul that God could arrest the penal operation of the law on any other condition, but must allow it to proceed in its remorseless infliction of death and destruction.

But though God is conceived as unable to arrest the fatal course of the law, though His "wrath" must have

---

* The "Jewish basis" must not be disregarded. "Ancient thought in general, but in particular the religious consciousness of the later Judaism, regulated the relations between the Deity, who represented the moral requirements and avenged the transgression of them, and men, from the axiom that on the one hand compensation must be made to requiting justice for guilt incurred, a sacrifice must fall, but on the other, an innocent person may intervene for the atonement of the offence, and thus take the penalty upon himself."—Holtzmann, *Neutest. Theol.* ii. p. 109.

its work upon the transgressor under the natural order, His love for man is manifested in the fact that He originates the scheme by which man may be delivered from the impending "destruction." He "sends His Son," and the Son, whose glorious estate was such that he is represented as being " in the form of God," " made himself of no reputation, and took upon himself the form of a servant, and was made in the likeness of men," that through obedience unto death on the cross he might effect the great redemption (Rom. v. 8; Phil. ii. 7, 8). It is unwarrantable, then, so to rationalise the Pauline doctrine of the atonement that it shall appear that of the two parties in the hostile relation one only, man, was "reconciled" through a change of disposition or the abandonment of his enmity. The atonement proceeds from God, and is a transaction conceived in heaven without man's participation. Christ does not come to effect by his teaching and example such a change in the moral disposition of men that they shall be reconciled to the divine order. This is a secondary result. Primarily the law must be satisfied. Then those men who accept through faith this atonement are "freely justified by His grace"; but only "*through the redemption that is in Jesus Christ*" (Rom. iii. 24). Far from proceeding from men, the atonement comes to them through the office of Jesus, " by whom we have now *received* the atonement " (Rom. v. 11). "God was in Christ reconciling the world unto Himself" (2 Cor. v. 19). Not only is the initiative on His part, but the process is defined as His in that He does "not impute their trespasses unto men." Accordingly, if, when in the following verse Paul prays the Corinthians to "be reconciled to God," their change of disposition completed the transaction, then it were idle to speak of God's part in not imputing their trespasses.

According to the Pauline doctrine, men's trespasses are

no longer reckoned as theirs when they have accepted Christ by faith, because he has made the atoning sacrifice which satisfies the demands of justice, and does away with the law, so far as it can have any claims upon them after they have fulfilled the conditions. The penal operation of the law ceases for them, and since this is the expression of the divine "wrath," it may be said that God has for them laid aside His wrath. Accordingly, the atonement as the apostle understood it implies a change of attitude on God's part; and, indeed, this may be regarded as the most important factor in the transaction. He conceives and institutes the atonement. He provides for the satisfaction of the law, and offers this means of reconciliation to men. They have only to accept it through faith and enter into the mystic fellowship with Christ by being "baptized into his death" (Rom. vi. 3, 4). Then they will receive "the Spirit" and the "adoption as sons," will henceforth be under "the law of the Spirit of life in Jesus Christ," and may look forward with joy to the resurrection and the blessedness of the approaching kingdom. If the idea of a change of disposition and attitude in God is repulsive to our theistic philosophy, this is no good reason why we should maintain that it does not belong to Paul's theology, which must be ascertained by exegesis and not by *a priori* reasoning. The result of exegesis is that he believed that God's "wrath" was directed against the sinner, and that it would pursue him to "destruction," unless an atoning satisfaction intervened. If he thought there was any other way in which the constant grace and love of God could come to the relief of man in the bondage to sin, he does not give any intimation of such an idea.

How according to Paul Christ effected the salvation of men is explicitly expressed in the words: "Christ hath redeemed us from the curse of the law, having been made a curse for us; as it is written, cursed is every one that hangeth on a tree" (Gal. iii. 13). Here is evident the emphasis heretofore pointed out which he places upon the death of Christ. It is by means of the death on the cross that man's redemption is effected. The idea here is plainly that of vicarious expiation. By his death on the cross Christ paid the price of the deliverance of men from bondage to the law, whose curse rests upon all that are subject to it, since being unable to fulfil its requirements they must bear its penalty of destruction. "Redeemed" ($\dot{\epsilon}\xi\eta\gamma\acute{o}\rho\alpha\sigma\epsilon\nu$) means "bought off," and the thought is that as the representative head of the race Christ by his death in which he became a curse for us purchased our ransom. The law, conceived as a power which even God cannot disregard, demands the penalty of sin, and Christ is doubtless here conceived as paying for the human race that penalty to the law, for the apostle cannot have thought of him as buying off mankind from God or from the devil. The citation from Deut. xxi. 23 relates to the requirement that the body of one hanged for a crime worthy of death should not be left over night upon the tree, lest the land be defiled, "for he that is hanged is accursed of God." Paul regards Christ in suffering this accursed death as bearing the curse of the law in his capacity as the redeeming Messiah, instead of being a rejected and abandoned outcast who by the fact of his crucifixion was branded with a curse, as he must have thought of him before his conversion. Lipsius' opinion that these words from Deuteronomy were of fundamental importance for Paul's whole theology is hardly well taken, although he concedes that this point of view does not appear in Romans, and Dr. Everett has made too much of a passing allusion to the curse that in Israel attached to a particular mode of executing criminals.*

* *The Gospel of Paul.*

The fact "of fundamental importance" for Paul was that Christ suffered death, the penalty of the law, and thus satisfied its demands "once" as the head of mankind, so that all might be redeemed from its curse. The cross is made prominent in his teaching generally not because under the Old Testament order a curse attached to hanging, but because it happened to be the instrument of Christ's death.*
The passage in question must be interpreted in connection with verse 10: "For as many as are of the works of the law are under the curse of the law," that is, he who undertakes to attain salvation by keeping the law is under its curse, and will "perish." But Christ (verse 13) redeemed men from this curse, by taking upon himself the penalty of the law, death, and thus becoming a curse for them. The law being thus satisfied was abolished, Christ became through his atonement "the end of the law," and the new dispensation of "the Spirit" and "life" was introduced. This interpretation is supported by other passages which represent the Christians as redeemed in the sense that a "price" has been paid for them: "Ye are bought with a price" (1 Cor. vi. 20, vii. 23). Similarly Christ is said to have been "made of God unto us wisdom and righteousness and redemption" (1 Cor. i. 30). Here "redemption" is used in the sense of the payment of a ransom (Ex. xxi. 8). Paul does not use the word in the weaker sense of "setting free from" except once, and then in connection with the body (Rom. viii. 23). The words in Col. i. 14: "In whom we have redemption through his blood" express the Pauline idea. The blood of Christ is the ransom (λύτρον) which releases man from the curse of the law. Pfleiderer has appropriately pointed out the futility of

---

* One would hardly attempt to maintain that Paul's doctrine of the atonement would have been different if Jesus had been put to death through any other instrumentality than the cross.

raising such questions as, "To whom was the price of redemption paid?" "Why was there need of paying a price?" "Can Christ's death be regarded as a satisfactory price or equivalent for man's redemption?" "Paul himself doubtless never found any occasion for raising such dogmatic questions, because he did not proceed from *a priori* dogmatic reflections on the necessity or possibility of a saving atonement, but from given facts and theories, which he simply related to one another, interpreting the one in the light of the other."

It should be borne in mind that the apostle's doctrine of atonement is due to the circumstance that instead of being a rationalising Christian philosopher of the nineteenth century he had been educated in the school of ancient thought and particularly in the Jewish theology, where any one may learn what he had learned that "the suffering and death of the righteous have an atoning power to make satisfaction for their own sins and for those of the whole people." Believing that Christ had died for men, he could not but interpret his death as he had been accustomed to regard atonement in general. That the law or the righteousness of God of which it is an expression must be satisfied, and that man could render a satisfaction only by his death in the sense of "everlasting destruction," were the two premises from which he set out. The conclusion was inevitable that man could be "saved" from "perishing" only by a representative satisfaction rendered by "the second Adam," "the man from heaven."

A prominent feature of the atonement as held by Paul is doubtless that of sacrifice, "construed," as Holtzmann concludes, "from the premises of expiation and recompense." He finds here the influence of the later Jewish ideas of "exchange," "substitution," and "satisfaction." The reaction of the sacrificial death of Christ is expressed in the non-imputation of their sins to those for whose benefit the satisfaction of the law was effected through the sacrifice (2 Cor. v. 19). Such is probably the doctrine of Rom. viii. 3 : "For what the law could not do in that it was weak through the flesh, God sending His own Son in the likeness of sinful flesh and for sin condemned sin in the flesh." The end in view is the deliverance from the power of sin and death and the fulfilment in the believers of the righteousness of the law (verses 2, 4) through the atoning effect of Christ's death. This the law could not do on account of the power of "the flesh." It could enjoin, and declare the penalty of sin, but had not the strength to break its power. Man could not attain righteousness under it, could not free himself from its "bondage," because by reason of his inability to fulfil it the account was constantly running up against him. His deliverance came through Christ "in the likeness of sinful flesh." Without the flesh he could not accomplish man's deliverance. His appearance, if that were possible, in the "glory" of his heavenly state as a teacher of spiritual truth, the exercise of moral influence to quicken the faculties of men, would not meet the conditions of the problem as it presented itself to Paul. The penalty of sin must first be paid before "the law of the Spirit of life" could become operative. Death is that penalty, and it must be paid, and can only be paid in the flesh. To save man from death with its attendant "everlasting destruction," a substitute, a representative of the race, must die "in the flesh." Hence we must interpret "the likeness of sinful flesh" not in the sense that Jesus had a flesh merely similar to that of man yet without the natural impulses which belong to the flesh in the Pauline sense of the word. If he was "without sin," it does not follow that he was without sinful impulses, which indeed are implied in the synoptic story of the temptation and in the Epistle to the Hebrews. Paul, it is true, nowhere represents him as undergoing a struggle with temptation, neither does he imply that he was conceived and born otherwise than after the natural manner. "Born of the seed of David according to the flesh" is his formula (Rom. i. 3). "He was made to be sin for us" (2 Cor. v. 21) in the fact that he suffered the penalty of sin, yet he was not made, and did not become, according to Paul's thought, a sinner.

Now the purpose for which God sent Jesus in the flesh is declared to be the condemnation of sin, its condemnation "in the flesh." This cannot on the one hand mean that God through the sinless life of Jesus pronounced a condemnation of sin, or exhibited sin in an eminent manner as condemnable, or on the other that his condemnation of sin was simply the ethical overcoming of it by Christ. Sin was already condemned by the law so far as the announcement of its wrong and its penalty is concerned, and the idea of overcoming is not conveyed in "condemnation" (κατάκριμα) or in the verb (κατακρίνειν). Besides, it were an awkward expression to say that God overcame sin in the moral victory of Christ. The apostle's thought is that God condemned sin in the flesh of Christ by executing upon him in the flesh the judgment of condemnation originally pronounced upon sin, that is, death. That this death was substitutional, the act of one appointed to perform it as the representative of mankind, is clear, not only from the analogy of the apostle's thought, but also from the connection of the passage in question. The design of this offering was "that the righteousness of the law might be fulfilled in us who walk not after the flesh, but after the Spirit"—in us who could accomplish no righteousness by obedience to the law, and could come into the liberty of "the law of the Spirit of life" only after Christ by his death had become "the end of the law" by satisfying its demands.*

That the death of Christ was regarded by Paul as representative is evident from 2 Cor. v. 14: "Because we thus judge, that if one died for all then were all dead" (correctly, "then all died"). Pfleiderer regards this passage, rightly interpreted, as "the key to the Pauline doctrine of salvation." Christ is so identified with the human race that his real death is ideally the death of all. Accordingly, "for" in the usage of Paul when he is treating of the relation of Christ's atonement to man does not mean "for the benefit of," but denotes the representative character of the transaction on the cross, "the head of every man" (1 Cor. xi. 3) performing an act in which all participate. This conception of solidarity was familiar to the ancients, and appears in Paul's doctrine of the relation of the first

---

* Holsten, whose posthumous work (*Das Evangelium des Paulus*, Theil. II., die paulinische Theologie) comes to the writer's hand as this book is going through the press, admirably remarks (pp. 54, 55): "Through the substitutional atoning death those who were destined to salvation were unburdened of their sins and their punishment. . . . Here Paul's logical thought transcended the ideas of Peter and the Jewish Christians. Peter saw in the death of the Messiah on the cross a death for our sins; but he did not go beyond the negative notion of the forgiveness of past transgressions. For real, positive righteousness he held fast the principle of the law, the actual fulfilling of its commandments by those whose sins were forgiven. . . . His principle of salvation was the connection of faith and works ($\pi i\sigma\tau\iota s$ $\kappa a i$ $\ell\rho\gamma a$). This was the essence of his gospel of the circumcision; and because the gospel was bound to the law, it could be preached only to the Jews, to whom the law was given. But here appeared the illogicalness of Peter's thinking. If the believers should acquire righteousness by keeping the law, and could they do this after the death of the Messiah, then they might have done it before his death. In that case, then, his death was superfluous (Gal. ii. 21). . . . Paul therefore drew the conclusion: This death as a death for salvation is not only forgiveness of sin, but also bestowal of righteousness [by the decree of God] without man's acts of obedience to the law. . . . Thus the Jewish idea of righteousness passes over into the Pauline conception of justification, *justitia* into *justificatio*, although the word $\delta\iota\kappa a\iota o\sigma\upsilon\nu\eta$ remains."

and the last Adam to mankind — the one standing at the head of the order of sin and death, the other at the head of the order of righteousness and life, so that, "as by one man's disobedience many were made sinners, so by the obedience of one [unto death] shall many be made righteous" (Rom. v. 19). It is evident that by the expression, "all died," Paul does not mean that all actually died; and it is certain also that he did not have in mind a gradual moral conquest of evil. A process of ethical growth in accordance with the natural order was not in his thought. The process as it presented itself to him was supernatural. Christ, the supernatural representative of the race, "the man from heaven," died for all, and in his death all men suddenly, supernaturally died in an ideal sense. In dying he put off the flesh, the seat of sin, destroyed "the body of sin," "died unto sin once" (Rom. vi. 6, 10), to the law and all legal limitations (Rom. vii. 4), to distinctions of race, and to the world (Gal. iii. 28, vi. 14). The result of this substitutional death is the dying of all men in similar relations, so that the apostle could speak of them as "crucified with" Christ (Rom. vi. 6; Gal. ii. 20).

The interpretation of this passage should not be confused by raising such a question as, "If Paul held that Christ died representatively for all men, how could he then say that all men died, since his death in their stead should render theirs unnecessary?" For Paul does not think of men as dying the kind of death that Christ died. In becoming a "curse" for them, he received in his flesh the penalty of sin, which is death, broke the power of sin when its sentence of condemnation was executed upon him, and having satisfied the law abolished it. Men are thus delivered from the law and from sin and from death the consequence of sin or from the "perishing" which is the deprivation of the resurrection and of the "life" of the kingdom. This deliverance is their ideal dying in the death of Christ. Their "old man is crucified with him, that the body of sin might be destroyed," and having thus died they are "freed from sin." Its penalty was paid by Christ in his death, and by virtue of their participation in it they are freed from sin (Rom. vi. 6–8). While it is evident that according to the passage in question man has nothing to do in the atonement, the entire transaction being conducted by God and Christ, it must not be interpreted in the sense that the advantage accrues to all men unconditionally. In fact, all men did *not* die with Christ. The benefits of his sacrifice accrue only to those who believe on him. Upon all others "sudden destruction" will come in "the day of the Lord" (1 Thess. v. 2, 3). In the same sense must the words be understood: "Being now justified by his blood, we shall be saved from wrath through him" (Rom. v. 9). The atonement is devised of God, performed by Christ, and offered to men. Those who actually "receive" it are the "we" so often employed by the apostle to designate the believers. These are "justified by his [Christ's] blood," and are saved from the wrath of God expressed in the remorseless operation of the law. Those who do not receive the proffered grace remain "enemies," are shut out from the fellowship of the life in Christ and in the Spirit in their earthly existence, and are finally overtaken by that death from which there is no resurrection (Rom. viii. 6).

The necessity of an atonement for the justification of men or their salvation from the power of sin is unequivocally expressed in the words: "Being justified freely by his grace through the redemption that is in Jesus Christ, whom God hath set forth to be a propitiation through faith in his blood, to declare His righteousness for the remission of sins that are past, through the forbearance of God" (Rom. iii. 24, 25).* Here we find the premises of the apostle's doctrine of salvation, that righteousness is through the "grace" of God, it being regarded as unattainable in the natural order or under the law by an endeavour to obey it. It is, then, a "free" gift of God through Christ, both of whom furnish the atonement. It is given not only simply through Christ, however, but through the "redemption" or buying off or ransoming that is in him. Him God "set forth in his blood" (for this is the correct connection), that is, through his sacrifice, to be a means of propitiation on the condition of faith. The idea of a satisfying sacrifice is so evidently required by the trend of the passage that it is surprising that any one should have found another meaning in the word rendered "propitiation" ($ἱλαστήριον$). That "a means of propitiation" or "a propitiatory sacrifice" is the true sense of the term is now admitted by most authorities, and Weiss remarks quite appropriately that "God can accomplish His covenant purpose only when He either punishes or atones the sin which stands opposed to it." Accordingly, the apostle says that the object in view in the atoning sacrifice of Christ was that God might declare His righteousness on account of the "remission," that is, the passing by unpunished, not the forgiveness, of former sins committed by men. Paul conceives that God had been formerly long-suffering, and that hence His justice

* The righteousness of God is not here conceived, as Ritschl will have it, as "a proceeding consistently corresponding to the salvation of the believer," that is, as only "grace." But if it is benevolent, since it accepts an atonement, it is also regarded as just in that it demands the satisfaction of the law, and declares no one righteous until the penalty of his sins is paid. The acceptance of a substitute may not correspond to our idea of justice, either in respect to "past" or present sins, but we do not look at the matter from Paul's point of view.

had not been adequately expressed. God was not in accord with Himself, since there were "sins that were past" which had neither been adequately punished nor indeed forgiven for want of an atonement.*

But in the suffering of Christ, in his bearing of "the curse of the law," God manifests His righteousness in showing that He cannot altogether pass by and disregard sin, but that He can be "just" in requiring an atonement and merciful in being "the justifier of him who believeth in Jesus." Thus according to 2 Cor. v. 21: "He made him to be sin who knew no sin, that we might be made the righteousness of God in him." He does "not impute their trespasses" to men (verse 19), because Christ as their representative stands in their place, that is, in suffering death, the penalty of sin, is treated as if he were sin itself. There is an imputation of man's sin to Christ and of Christ's righteousness to man. This Pauline idea of ransom appears in most distinct expression outside his writings in the New Testament. The writer of 1 Timothy speaks of Christ as one who "gave himself a ransom for

---

* Holsten (*ut supra*, pp. 56, 57) denies that Paul conceived of Christ's death as a *sacrifice* for sin. "The sacrifice," he says, "is always an act of man for God," while the apostle "regarded, and must have regarded, the death of the Messiah as an act of God and of the Messiah." ... "It is ever only the death of Christ, which as the death of one not sinning atones for the sin of the sinning." His death is a "θάνατος ἱλαστήριος for the sinner." ... If Paul "apprehends it as an ἀπολύτρωσις, the death of the Messiah is a ransom which this one pays to the power of sin and the law, in order to satisfy their claims upon sinful man and upon his death." Paul, however, conceived of the Messiah as "the man from heaven," who in his death was a *representative* of the human race. As an "act of God" his atonement was an expression of God's love; as his own act, he "gave [sacrificed] himself for man" (Gal. ii. 20). As an ἱλαστήριον (Rom. iii. 25) he may be regarded as an atoning sacrifice. But this is not Ritschl's idea of sacrifice, which is devoid of all atoning quality. On the "theory of sacrifice" the student may consult Holtzmann's *Neutest. Theol.* ii. pp. 102 ff.; and on Ritschl's doctrine, Pfleiderer, *Die Ritschl'sche Theologie*, pp. 49 ff.

all" (ii. 6). The same term is employed in Matt. xx. 28 and Mark x. 45. In the latter passage we have "a ransom in place of many" (λύτρον ἀντὶ πολλῶν), and in Titus ii. 14, "He gave himself for us (ὑπὲρ ἡμῶν) in order that he might redeem us (λυτρώσηται). Menegoz thinks that the two ideas, "for" (in behalf of) and "in the place of," were confounded in the thought of Paul. In the expression of the idea of substitution it is worthy of note that the victim is never represented either by Paul or the writer of Isaiah liii. as the object of the divine wrath. Accordingly, it may be that the apostle chose with forethought to say, not that Christ was accursed, but that he was "made a curse," and not that he was made a sinner, but sin. In accordance with his conception of the relation between God and the Son he could not have spoken otherwise.

The ethical theory of the atonement, according to which the work of Christ resulted in effecting in men a new spiritual life, is not without support in the Epistles of Paul. Its capital error is that it claims to be a complete and sufficient explanation of the Pauline doctrine, whereas in fact it is only one side of it. That Paul attached an ethical significance to the death of Christ cannot be disputed. But to him the ethical value of the atonement was entirely dependent on the validity of the juridical principle. Both aspects of it were inseparably connected in his thought with the death of Christ. The transactions on Calvary and at the sepulchre — the crucifixion and the resurrection — were the two conditions without which he could have constructed no soteriology. His doctrine of salvation is essentially contained in the declaration that Christ " was delivered [to death] for our offences [to expiate them], and was raised again for our justification " (Rom. iv. 25). The two events were inseparable in the apostle's thought as factors in the atonement. He did not think of the resurrection as effecting of itself man's justification. Rather according to the analogy of his teaching this was due to the death of Christ. But since justification is absolutely conditioned upon faith, and faith upon the resurrection, the latter was consistently emphasised as it is in this passage. The dependence of the ethical aspect of the atonement upon the expiatory principle is illustrated in the passage previously considered: "If one died for all, then all died." The ideal death of men to sin and the flesh is here made dependent upon the representative death of Christ. Only because in his sacrifice deliverance is effected from the guilt of sin, and because he became "the end of the law" which caused sin to "abound," was it conceived possible that the new "law of the spirit of life," the new ethical order, could be introduced. In the old order "sin reigned unto death," but in the new order "grace reigns through righteousness [that is imputed to the believers] unto eternal life by Jesus Christ our Lord" (Rom. v. 21).

The new moral-spiritual life which the death of Christ has made possible receives a mystical expression in the earnest and pointed questions which the apostle addresses to the Romans: "How shall we that are dead to sin live any longer therein? Know ye not that as many of us as were baptized into Jesus were baptized into his death?" His conclusion is: "Therefore, we are buried with him by baptism into death, that, like as Christ was raised up from the dead by the glory of the Father, even so we also should walk in newness of life" (Rom. vi. 2–4). It cannot escape the attentive reader that the apostle here bases the ethical-religious life of the believers upon the fundamental fact of the death of Christ. It is because of its representative character and their participation in it that they are "dead to sin," or in other words, "in that he died, he died to sin once" (Rom. vi. 10), and with him they, having ideally died, are "justified [set free] from sin." * He through paying the penalty of sin, which is death, becomes free from it, having satisfied its claims. Participants in his death, the Christians enter into his "glorious liberty," being "no longer debtors to the flesh, to live after the flesh," that is, to live in sin (Rom. viii. 12). Hence the incompatibility of a life in sin with the believers' condition of death to sin (Rom. vi. 2), and hence the practical moral force of the doctrine of the atonement. A glorious and inspiring hope also sprang from this doctrine — a hope the influence of which upon the fortunes of the primitive church and of Christendom can scarcely be estimated, although its original Pauline basis may have early disappeared. Christ's sacrifice cancelled the claim of death, so that the apostle declares that "death hath no more dominion over him" (Rom. vi. 9).

In like manner, the believers, who had come into the fel-

* Pfleiderer's lucid exposition of this passage is here subjoined : " The formula, τῇ ἁμαρτίᾳ ἀπέθανεν ἐφάπαξ, is misunderstood by most exegetes, because they mistake the juristic way of regarding the matter which is, however, clearly enough expressed in verse 7, and which everywhere forms the basis of the Pauline doctrine of the atonement. The words mean neither that Christ morally died to sin — that would presuppose that he had formerly lived to it, and thus that he did not know no sin (2 Cor. v. 21) — nor also that by his death he stepped out of relation to the sin of men which surrounded and tormented him — a trivial thought, with which the idea of the removal of the dominion of sin over Christians that dominates the whole section would stand in no perceptible connection. But the sin is here, as in v. 21, and as immediately before θάνατος, death, represented as a sort of personal ruling power which on the ground of the divine decree (κρίμα and κατάκριμα, v. 16, 18) exercises its dominion in effecting death in mankind. Christ let sin have this its right in dying for mankind the death which was a curse, and thus *fulfilled* once for all [received in himself] the curse which sin works, and thereby at the same time *removed* it. One may thus designate ἁμαρτίᾳ as a dative *commodi* and *incommodi* both at once. Exactly so according to Paul is the death of Christ related to the law. While he paid it its tribute (Gal. iii. 13), he at the same time wrung from it its right." — *Paulinismus*, 2te Auflage, p. 146.

T

lowship of Jesus' death, were free from the same dominion ; though their outward man might perish, their inward man was renewed from day to day, and when the trump of the Parousia should sound, they would be clothed upon with bodies of glory, and enter into the kingdom prepared for them from the foundation of the world : " For if we be dead with Christ, we believe that we shall also live with him." There is liberty also from the bondage of the fruitless endeavour to attain righteousness by fulfilling the law. To all who believed, Christ was "the end of the law." " The law has dominion over a man as long as he lives." But " by the body of Christ [which died to the law] ye are become dead to the law " (Rom. vii. 1, 4). Now by means of this mysterious union with Christ in his death the believers enter upon a new order of life in which righteousness is accounted not of works, but of faith which is "imputed for righteousness" (Rom. iv. 22). They "are delivered from the law, that being dead wherein they were held, that they should serve in the newness of the Spirit and not in the oldness of the letter." In their new spiritual life they are "married to another, even to him who was raised from the dead that they should bring forth fruit unto God " (Rom. vii. 4, 6). They have also been raised with him, and their old man having been crucified with him they become partakers of the glorious life of the Spirit in which he lives in his celestial estate (Rom. vi. 6, 11). It is no merely natural moral-religious development of which the apostle speaks in the exalted strain of Romans vi. The supernatural atonement is consummated in a supernatural religious condition dominated by the divine Spirit, and the miraculous end will be nothing less than the coming of the kingdom with its catastrophe, its victory, and its disasters.

The reader will have observed that the apostle's doctrine of salvation appears to be adapted only to the Jews according to its prominent features. Primarily it was to those who were "under the law" that Christ through his death became "the end of law." Yet Paul was preëminently the apostle to the gentiles, and when God revealed His Son in him, it was that he "might preach him among the heathen" (Gal. i. 16). He does not explicitly state in what relation he conceived the gentiles to stand to the expiatory death of Christ, which redeemed "us," the Jews, "from the curse of the law," he having been made a curse for "us." But in the immediate connection (Gal. iii. 13, 14) he says that this was done "that the blessing of Abraham might come on the gentiles through Jesus Christ, that we [Jews and gentiles] might receive the promise of the Spirit through faith." He seems to have thought that the promise to Abraham that in his seed should all nations be blessed primarily concerned the Jews, and could not be realised either for them or for the gentiles until, after the abolition of the law and of the dispensation of works through the death of Christ, the new order of righteousness by faith should be established, or rather reëstablished, for he regarded it as actually grounded in Abraham whose faith was accounted to him for righteousness. But the law had intervened, "added because of transgressions," that is, to call them forth (Rom. iii. 20), until "the seed [Christ] should come," and it must be abrogated by the cross before either Jews or gentiles could receive the promise of the Spirit. Moreover, the gentiles, while not technically under the Mosaic dispensation, were nevertheless conceived as under law and responsible to its requirements "written in their hearts" (Rom. ii. 12, 15).

If, then, the Jews with all the "advantage" (Rom. iii. 1) that they had could not be saved by works, how much less the gentiles, who had only the inward light and not the "oracles of God." According to the premises of his doctrine of the person of Christ Paul could not but include the gentiles in the scheme of redemption. For to him Christ was not simply the Jewish Messiah, "born of the seed of David according to the flesh," but as the son of God was also the representative head of the human race, and in his death made atonement for "all" (2 Cor. v. 14, 15, 19). Thus the offer of salvation was extended to as many through the last Adam as the condemnation that came through the first Adam had reached. It is difficult to determine, however, whether in the apostle's thought the blessing would ultimately neutralise the curse. At the beginning the advantage was on the side of sin and death on account of the flesh with its passions and lusts, the carnal mind, which is "not subject to the law of God, neither indeed can be." The stream of natural tendency sweeps with fatal force downward toward the abyss. On the other hand the atonement effects no absolute restoration, is no unconditional counteracting of the fall. It is effective only so far as it is voluntarily appropriated. Those alone die with Christ to the flesh and sin who choose to "receive" the atonement. In view of the meagre results of the apostle's mission, and in particular of the opposition and hostility of the Jews, there would appear to be no very good prospect of an extended conquest of the powers of "the world" before the time of the approaching Parousia and judgment. Yet he is so optimistic as to expect "the fulness of the gentiles" "to come in," and "all Israel" to be "saved" (Rom. xi. 25, 26) — a consummation which calls forth from him an exclamation on "the depth of the riches both of the wisdom and knowledge of God," "of whom and through whom and to whom are all things."

This recognition of the love of God does not first appear in the apostle's doctrine when he takes into consideration the consummation of the work of Christ. As we have already seen, the idea of the divine love underlies the entire scheme of the atonement, which is, indeed, preëminently the way in which "God commendeth His love toward us" (Rom. v. 8). But the apostle dwells especially upon this aspect of the divine nature when he comes to consider the practical, ethical side of the work of God in Christ. The conception of God as a being who on the one hand insists inexorably on the exaction of the penalty of sin upon the person of the sinner or upon a substitute, and on the other is so abounding in love as to institute and carry out a plan of atonement whereby men might be saved from His "wrath," was not so difficult to the apostle from his Old Testament and later Jewish point of view that he felt a necessity of attempting a reconciliation. In any case, the severity and hardness, the almost mechanical aspect of salvation, which appear in the strictly judicial side of the doctrine of the atonement, drop out of sight when he dwells upon the fellowship of the believer with Christ and the blessed endowment of the Spirit. In this new relation, which, however, we must not forget, is due to the awful sacrifice on Calvary, by which the demands of the law were satisfied, the believer is a "new creation"; "old things are passed away, and behold all things are new"; "the fearful looking for of judgment" is no more; no longer is the doubtful contest waged between the law in the members and the mind which would gladly serve the law of God; and out of the dread bondage to the flesh and the ever-menacing law he has emerged into the liberty and peace of assured sonship.

Accordingly, the apostle strikes the note of joy and triumph in the eighth of Romans in marked contrast with the despair, the lamentation, and the cry for deliverance in the seventh: "There is therefore now no condemnation to them who are in Christ Jesus, who walk not after the flesh, but after the Spirit. For the law of the Spirit of life in Jesus Christ hath made me * free from the law of sin and death." The fruitless struggle of the carnal man to keep the law is no more; but "the Spirit helpeth our infirmities." In baptism the believer has died with Christ to the flesh and sin, and been raised to "newness of life"; thus "the body is dead because of sin," for it was on account of sin that it must ideally die with Christ in the baptismal rite, and in this blessed estate of moral-religious experience, the indwelling "Spirit is life because of righteousness." The apostle's recognition of the ethical aspect of the atonement is apparent in the note of exhortation and admonition which he sounds, particularly in the sixth of Romans. Having been mystically buried with Christ in baptism into death, that is into death to sin through fellowship with Christ's death, who died to sin, the believer should practically by his own choice and will live worthy of his high calling, and as Christ was raised up from the dead, so ought he also to "walk in newness of life." His members should not be yielded as instruments of unrighteousness, but of righteousness unto God. The background of supernaturalism remains in the atonement, in the mystic dying with Christ, and in the operations of the Holy Spirit; but side by side with the interference of supersensible powers for the Christian's salvation goes his own obligation to have his "fruit unto holiness." His doctrine of death as the penalty of sin and of the expiation of sin by the death of an innocent substitute under the conception of the solidarity of the race Paul derived from the theology of his people. His rigorous application of these doctrines to the office of Christ in relation to men constitutes the juridical side of his teaching of the atonement.

But the idea of a renewal of the life by a mystic union

* "Thee" (σε) according to א BFG.

with Christ and of the operation of the Spirit in the production of the common Christian virtues was original with the apostle, and reveals the penetration of his spiritual insight and the force of his religious genius. His total conception of man and his relation to God was not, however, destined to prevail in subsequent ages, which could accept it only with radical modifications and exceptions. With an anthropology which does not regard death as the penalty of sin his doctrine of the death of Christ as an atonement for the sins of the world is irreconcilable. An ethics which interprets human conduct by the spirit rather than by the letter, and regards the good purpose and intention as virtues, though they often fail of a complete obedience, cannot approve his teaching regarding the inefficacy of works. To a philosophy which does not regard sin as an offence entailing eternal death, but as an incident in the course of human evolution, which draws after it consequences that are disciplinary and educational to the individual and the race, and that have no further significance or issue, his whole doctrine of a closed and arbitrary penalty must be unacceptable. With that doctrine must fall the theory of an atonement which intervenes to arrest the course of natural development. An age which does not look for the immediate coming of the kingdom of God with catastrophes and disasters of judgment cannot regard salvation as a deliverance from an impending definite peril, which is to be sought with such stress and urgency and with such indifference to temporal relations as he enjoined. Finally, his doctrine of a mystic fellowship of the Christian with Christ must undergo radical modifications with respect to its supernaturalism in an age in which the spiritual life of man is not regarded as an exception to the universal sway of natural law.

CHAPTER XII

THE PERSON OF CHRIST[*]

THE last and most important task of the higher criticism of the New Testament is to determine the historical setting of the doctrines of its several books. As a procedure which follows the historical method it cannot regard these doctrines as isolated phenomena, and treat them as if they had no connection with antecedent beliefs and modes of thought. Moreover, it is forbidden by its fundamental presuppositions to attempt to explain them as independent supernatural creations rather than as the products of the thinking of men, which as such must be conceived as related to the antecedents and environments of their authors. This method is especially necessary to the successful study of the Pauline Christology, since in none of his writings has the apostle made a distinctive statement of doctrine on the subject, and his opinions as to the person of Christ must be gathered from incidental words and phrases belonging to the discussion of subjects which appear to have interested him more than the topic in question. While these scattered intimations of belief respecting the person of Christ must be subjected to a careful exegesis and studied in their connection, a knowledge of the Messianic ideas which prevailed shortly before and at the time of the apostle is indispensable to their interpretation. For while the Pauline Christology is a transformation of both the Jewish and the Jewish-Christian Messianism, it is not without some features of each.

[*] *The New World*, June, 1894. (With revision and additions.)

While Paul undoubtedly entertained the Messianic hopes of his nation, Jesus was to him the Messiah in a peculiar and original sense. He does not explicitly define what he saw in the vision in which Christ was revealed to him, or rather "in" him, but in his reference to it he employs a term which is frequently used in the New Testament to express the appearance of things of the supersensible world and the occurrence of spiritual manifestations (ὤφθη, 1 Cor. xv. 8). The "visions and revelations of the Lord" (2 Cor. xii. 1), which were probably not infrequent experiences of his, and in which he had a consciousness of being in the "third heaven" and hearing "unspeakable words," were doubtless of this sort. As a consequence of these spiritual intuitions it appears that his conception of the Messiahship was entirely changed. For he says that if prior to the true manifestation of the Christ to him he had known and accepted a fleshly Messiah, a "Christ after the flesh," yet thereafter he "knew him so no more" (2 Cor. v. 16). This "Christ according to the flesh" was of the Israelites, his "kinsmen," to whom belonged "the covenants and the giving of the law" (Rom. ix. 4), the descendant of David, "born of a woman," "born under the law" (Gal. iv. 4), in whom the national Messianic hopes were realised so far as his appearance at least was concerned.

But as a believer, as a convert to the new spiritual Messianic faith, the apostle declares that he is "a new creature," and that he henceforth knows Christ no longer in the old way, for "the old things are passed away." Now he knows him only as freed from the flesh through his death and resurrection and existing in a heavenly state, "the image of God," a being of "light" and "glory." Accordingly, the Christ of the flesh, the human Jesus, has no important place or function in the Christology of the apostle. If he was acquainted with the tradition of the life and teachings of Jesus he makes little use of this knowledge except in an occasional reference to an aphorism. He founds few important doctrines upon the words of the Master, and never appeals to the Gospel-miracles to support the claims of Christ to dignity or authority. The personality as well as the name of the Son of Man disappears from a teaching which shows no contact with the freshness and spontaneity of the primitive tradition; and the kingdom of heaven, in the sense in which it was the burden of the original message, sinks into insignificance, or is lost from view in the absorbing interest in a metaphysical doctrine of the Christ. The Messiah of the early apostolic faith, who was a lowly teacher, and was expected to come again in human form as the Son of Man to sit on the throne of judgment upon all nations, and to place his apostles on twelve thrones to judge the twelve tribes of Israel, is transformed in the Pauline thought into the divine Lord of glory, whose saving mission is to all people, and who will come at length as a spiritual personality to gather in one fellowship his dead resurrected and the living believers with bodies "conformed to his body of glory."

Accepting the current Jewish belief of his time in the inspiration and authority of the Old Testament Scriptures Paul regarded Jesus as the expected Messiah foretold by the prophets. He speaks of himself as "separated unto the gospel of God, which He promised afore by His prophets in the Holy Scriptures" (Rom. i. 2), and as to the ministry of Jesus he declares that through it "a righteousness of God hath been manifested, being witnessed by the law and the prophets, even the righteousness of God through faith in Jesus Christ" (Rom. iii. 21). In the two events of the career of the Master which were to him of fundamental importance, he sees the fulfilment of foreshadowings in the ancient sacred writings. "For I delivered unto you," he writes to the Corinthians, "first of all that which also I received, how that Christ died for our sins according to the Scriptures; and that he was buried; and that he hath been raised on the third day according to the Scriptures" (1 Cor. xv. 3, 4). He does not, indeed, inform his readers where the prophetic passages in question are to be found; but it is probable that in his oral instructions he had pointed them out, and expounded them in accordance with the prevailing rabbinical method of interpreting the Old Testament which he did not hesitate to employ upon occasion (1 Cor. x. 11; Gal. iii. 16, iv. 24). It is evident, however, that Paul's acceptance of the traditional Messianism was merely external and formal. In the national Messiah as such he had no interest and no faith. It is not this personality whom he finds in the Scriptures; it is rather "the gospel of God," "the righteousness of God," and the crucified and risen Lord. The functions of the Messiah in whom he as a Christian believed were not, with reference to righteousness and the final consummation, those of the Messiah of the popular faith. In the Jewish theology it was laid down that the Messiah would come when righteousness should prevail among the people (Weber, *System*, p. 333); but according to Paul the Christ came for the purpose of bringing them into this condition.

That in applying to Christ the appellation "Son of God" Paul attached to him a unique and exceptional dignity there can be no doubt. The frequent and emphatic use of this term by Paul marks a distinction between his writings and the synoptic Gospels. According to these latter records, Jesus' constant self-designation is the "Son of Man"; he teaches that other men may become sons of God by fulfilling certain conditions, such as being peacemakers, tells the disciples that God is their Father, and instructs them to pray to Him as such. The universal fatherhood of God is implied in such parables as that of the prodigal son (Luke xv. 11 f.) and that of the two sons (Matt. xxi. 28 f.) and in the passages Matt. v. 45 and Luke vi. 30. When in these Gospels Jesus is represented as calling himself the Son in a preëminent sense, he appears to express a relation different only in degree from that which other men hold or may hold to the Father — a sonship attained through loving obedience and spiritual communion with God. Accordingly, he could speak of possessing a knowledge of God surpassing that of all others (Matt. xi. 27). In the first Gospel he is reported to have accepted the title Son of God, as a Messianic designation from the lips of Peter; but in the second Gospel, which probably more correctly represents the original tradition, the appellation is omitted (Matt. xvi. 16; Mark viii. 29). But nowhere in these Gospels is there an indication that he intended by the term "Son" to express his participation in the divine nature or a metaphysical relation to God. It is evident, however, that to Paul the Son of God "revealed in" him at his conversion represented a conception of Christ unknown to the primitive tradition and to the original apostles (Gal. i. 15, 16). He had not recognised the Jesus "according to the flesh" as the Messiah, but had vehemently and bitterly opposed him by persecuting his followers to the death. But as soon as he had seen in this vision the Christ according to the Spirit, the true Messiah, the divine Son of God, he was furnished with an ample revelation, so that he felt no need to "confer with flesh and blood" or to turn his steps toward Jerusalem. He had seen not the marred and lowly form of the Son of Man, but the majestic "Lord of glory," and from this vision dates a new apprehension of Christ and a new epoch in the history of Christianity.

Through this apprehension of his person the cause of

Jesus received a direction and development which it could never have had within the limits of the interpretation given to it by the original apostles. A mere Jewish teacher and Messiah could never have been accepted as the spiritual head of mankind. The world is now coming, indeed, to see that this man who delivered great moral and religious truths in aphorisms, preached the brotherhood of man and the kingdom of God, and went about doing good was the greatest spiritual and ethical teacher of mankind. But Christianity could not have begun to become a world-religion in the first century, and could not have held sway over the minds of men since, without a conception of the person of Christ in which he was something more than a Jewish teacher who had been ignominiously put to death, and was expected presently to come again to establish the national kingdom of God. There was needed an idea of his mission which extended it to mankind, and a theory of his nature which invested it with mystical and metaphysical qualities and relations. Paul's conception of Christology, based not upon historical facts, but upon speculation, furnished the impulse which was necessary to carry Christianity forward upon its mission of the conquest of the world. Its dualism answered a twofold purpose. On the one hand it was a concession to Jewish Messianism in its doctrine that Jesus was "according to the flesh born of the seed of David," and on the other it responded to the speculative interest in its metaphysical idea that Christ in his higher and most essential nature was the divine Son of God. In this latter phase of his thought respecting the Messiah he was in contact with the speculations of the Jewish theology. Christ was exalted above all other created beings, men and angels. To men was indeed granted adoption as sons of God (υἱοθεσία, Rom. viii. 15), but Christ was by nature God's own (ἴδιος) Son.

To Paul the person of Christ was central and vital in his apprehension of Christianity. All that the new religion signified to him of relief from the oppression and burden of sin and the law and of hope for his own regeneration and that of mankind was contained in his thought of the exalted Lord of glory. As he put into his conception of the Son of God a significance which is not contained in the synoptic tradition, but which prepared the way for the metaphysical idea of the Logos of the fourth Gospel, so the death of Christ assumed to him an importance, and contained consequences, wholly foreign to the minds of the primitive disciples. They had regarded this event as the signal of the overthrow of their Messianic hopes and of their faith in Jesus as the one who "should restore the kingdom to Israel." But to Paul as the act of a supernatural, metaphysical being, it had consequences far surpassing the extinction of a life or the disappointing of Messianic expectations. Its results were conceived as magical or miraculous. The existing spiritual order was shaken, and "old things" gave way to the new economy of which the cross was the symbol. With the death of Jesus mighty powers of the former age became extinct. When he bowed his head upon Calvary the Christ "according to the flesh," the national Jewish Messiah, died never to live again, and the age of the spiritual Messiah was ushered in. In dying he died to Judaism, abdicated the Messiahship of a people, and assumed the sceptre of the universal Messiahship of mankind. By a spiritual magic which eludes accurate definition he put away the law not alone for Jews, but for all men, effected their deliverance from sin, and by "one act of righteousness" secured to them the free gift "to justification of life." An offering for sin he condemned it in the "flesh," and died unto it "once for all." The fetters of man's bondage were broken by the abolition of the law of sin and death, and the law of the spirit of life assumed its beneficent sway. To the great apostle Calvary signified the subjugation of a spiritual world-order of powers inimical to man by the higher powers of a new dispensation of grace.

That the being who was able to accomplish by his mission this vast cosmic-spiritual transformation was not conceived to be an ordinary human personality in his essential nature goes without saying. It is a degradation of the apostle's mystic and metaphysical thought by the worst kind of rationalism to interpret his words so as to make them teach that one whose work and sacrifice were followed by such immense consequences affecting the economy of salvation, the purposes of God, and the entire human race, could have been regarded by him in whose mind the scheme took form as "a mere man." No one of the apostle's Christological conceptions has a more definite and precise expression than this, that Christ was essentially Spirit ($\pi\nu\epsilon\hat{v}\mu a$). The declaration that "the Lord is the Spirit" is entirely unambiguous. In his thought the total order of human life as related to the economy of redemption includes the celestial and nether spheres of existence. It is the destiny of the lower order to be uplifted and transformed through connection with the higher. Accordingly, the first man Adam (the first to appear on the stage of existence) became a living soul, the last Adam, a life-giving Spirit (1 Cor. xv. 45). First in order of appearance is that which is natural or psychical ($\psi v \chi \iota \kappa \acute{o} v$), then that which is spiritual ($\pi v \epsilon v \mu a \tau \iota \kappa \acute{o} v$). Though this is the order of temporal development, it by no means follows that the spiritual personality sprang out of the conditions of time and sense. On the contrary, Paul declares explicitly that the second man is from heaven (1 Cor. xv. 47). In his spiritual, heavenly existence Christ was conceived by Paul as a being possessing a form of "glory," in accordance with the idea that spirit is essentially a luminous substance.

There is no real contradiction between the two statements, that Christ was "the image of God" (1 Cor. iv. 4) and "in the form of God" (Phil. ii. 6), and that in the resurrection the bodies of believers would be "conformed to his body of glory" (Phil. iii. 21). For while Paul thought him to be godlike, since he was essentially Spirit, he appears to have conceived of him in no other way than "in fashion as a man," whether in his heavenly or earthly existence. As "the light of the knowledge of the glory of God" was reflected "in the face of Jesus Christ," so this luminous spiritual effulgence is again reflected in the gospel which is "the gospel of the glory of Christ." That the divinity of Christ is not implied by Paul in designating him "the image of God" is evident from 1 Cor. xi. 7, where he says of man that he is "the image and glory of God." In this connection is a passage which shows how he combined in his thought the divine sonship and the perfect humanity of Christ, his relation both to God and man: "But I would have you know that the head of every man is Christ; and the head of the woman is the man, and the head of Christ is God" (verses 3, 4). Here the "head" ($\kappa\epsilon\phi\alpha\lambda\dot{\eta}$) of each class represents that one of whom the subordinate is the reflected ray or "glory" ($\delta\acute{o}\xi\alpha$). Accordingly, the woman is said to be the glory of the man, while the man is subordinate to Christ, his head, who in turn is subordinate to God whose glory he reflects. Thus is assigned to Christ a mediate position between God and man. Dependent upon God on the one hand, he is on the other the head of mankind. As to other men, they are "the image and glory of God," because in the order of creation Christ is their head, so that mediately through him their head is God, as the woman's head is Christ in and through the man. Conceived as to his essential nature Christ is Spirit, but relatively to man and the economy of salvation he is the "life-giving Spirit" which working in mankind is destined to destroy death and sin and to quicken the mortal flesh of believers, so that they shall be "conformed to his body of glory."

The fact, however, that in the thought of Paul Christ was "the Son of God" by preëminence, "the image of God," "the Spirit," a being of whom God was the head, as he himself is the head of every man, is not incompatible with his teaching, that in his nature Christ was essentially and only a man, a man in the sense that does not admit of the idea that he possessed divine attributes and was of the divine essence. In writing of the two dispensations, that of sin and death, and that of righteousness and life, the apostle declares that "if by the trespass of the one [Adam], the many died, much more did the grace of God and the gift by the grace of the one man Jesus Christ abound unto the many" (Rom. v. 15). Death was not to have the victory, for "since by man came death, by man came also the resurrection of the dead" (1 Cor. xv. 21). If "the first man is of the earth, earthy, the second man is from heaven." These words admit of no other meaning than that Christ was by nature man, as Adam was, only in a higher sense, a man whose spiritual, transforming power should counteract the deadly and woful influence of the earthy progenitor of the race. The Spirit which he was to Paul's thought (2 Cor. iii. 17) was the earnest of the victory that he was to gain. It was placed at the head of the genus, but did not signify a superhuman nature. The higher heavenly principle in him was a perfect humanity. In him human nature had its glorified, archetypal form.

Over against the earthy, psychical man, Adam, who

represented the human race subjected to death through sin, Christ was conceived as the spiritual, heavenly man, "the man from heaven," the head and representative of this race transformed, so far as it should come into touch with him, by the powers of life into a condition of sinlessness. For it was essential and fundamental in Paul's conception of Christ that he was without sin (μὴ γνοὺς ἁμαρτίαν, 2 Cor. v. 21). He had, indeed, a bodily nature like all other men, but as the ideal man he was superior to them in that his flesh was not touched with the contamination of sin. The expression employed by Paul for this idea, "the likeness of sinful flesh" (ὁμοίωμα σαρκὸς ἁμαρτίας, Rom. viii. 3), has received contradictory interpretations, and some have thought that he was inconsistent with himself in employing these words and asserting, despite them, that Christ knew no sin. But the use of the word "likeness" may be regarded as intended to guard against this inconsistency. Christ came, indeed, in the flesh, and was "born of the seed of David," so that in his natural descent he was, like all other men, subject to the "sarkical" conditions to which in the usual order of nature sin attaches. Yet while the term "likeness" does not carry with it the notion that he had not a real body of flesh and blood, it excludes the implication that in his flesh evil tendencies had their accustomed sway. The humanity in which he appeared was only the likeness of sinful flesh, not that of sinful flesh itself. His body was formed after the likeness of that flesh to which sin ordinarily belongs in human nature.*

* "Christ is thought of as indeed fighting the battle [with evil], but as continually victorious by reason of the inborn 'Spirit of holiness.' ... This entire construction of the personality of Christ is accordingly sketched from the point of view of the putting an end to death in the resurrection. A termination of [earthly] destiny so far surpassing all that is ordinarily human can be grounded only in a nature of the subject of that destiny which likewise sur-

The declaration that Christ appeared on the earth in "the likeness of sinful flesh" may be regarded as expressing the doctrine of his entire humanity. For Paul does not use the term "flesh" of the bodily nature only, but of "the whole man, body and soul, reason, and all his faculties included, because all that is in him longs and strives after the flesh." If, then, he was in the likeness of sinful flesh, and yet did not know sin, it was because, by the power of the Spirit, the principle of his ideal, heavenly humanity, he either had no sinful desires, or, having them, was superior to their influence. Which of these two alternatives lay in the mind of the apostle it may be impossible to determine, but it is favourable to the former that he nowhere represents Christ as subject to a struggle with evil propensities and engaged in a conflict with sin. But it is difficult to reconcile this view of the matter with Paul's doctrine of the effect of the sin of the first Adam upon his posterity. For he certainly believed that in and through this primal transgression sin and death became powers in human nature from whose sway no man was exempt. "Death passed unto all men in that all sinned" (Rom. v. 12). All became mortal through Adam's sin, because Adam's having sinned was, so far as this consequence is concerned, a sinning of all, for "by the trespass of the one, the many died." Hence the idea of a man having a nature in "the likeness of sinful flesh" and yet knowing no sin appears to tend to the Docetic conception of Christ, that is, that his body was not a real one of flesh

passed all that is ordinarily human. Thereby was the personality of the Founder of Christianity first removed from the ranks of mankind, to which it belonged in a measure only half-way, 'according to the flesh,' in order to surpass humanity the more decidedly on the side of God, *i.e.*, according to that which Christ had from God — a first step, indeed, toward the Church doctrine of the twofold nature, but differently construed from this." — Holtzmann, *Neutest. Theol.*, ii. p. 74.

and blood — a doctrine which has been maintained by some high authorities as that of the apostle. Yet that this cannot have been Paul's idea is evident from his teaching that Christ's descent was in the natural order, he being "of the seed of David according to the flesh" (Rom. i. 3). Moreover, since there is nowhere in Paul's writings the slightest intimation that he believed in the supernatural generation of Jesus according to the story in the first and third Gospels, recourse cannot be had to this doctrine in order to explain his idea that Christ was only in "the likeness of sinful flesh" and without a knowledge of sin. This difficulty in the Pauline Christology is similar to that which attaches to the teaching of the Jewish theology, from which its origin may perhaps be traced, that though all men have by nature the impulse to sin, some individuals, the patriarchs in particular, remained sinless. These, however, were not regarded as without tendencies to sin, and their sinlessness was conceived as the result of overcoming them (see Weber, *System*, p. 224). Perhaps Rom. viii. 3 and 2 Cor. v. 21 may fairly be interpreted according to the analogy of this Jewish doctrine.*

Although "born of the seed of David according to the flesh," this "last Adam," this "man from heaven," was not conceived by Paul to have begun his existence when he began his earthly life. This notion of the ideal, heavenly

* "Before Paul there arose for his Messianic idea two contradictory requirements: 1. The Messiah must have been a being *without* a σῶμα σαρκὸς in order to have been without sin; 2. The Messiah must have been a being *with* a σῶμα σαρκὸς in order to have been able to die [as an atonement for men]. Paul satisfied both [these requirements] by apprehending the two required conditions as following each other in time. The Messiah was originally a heavenly being, and as such a δύναμις (an ἄνθρωπος) ἄσαρκος, and he becomes in the fulness of time an earthly being and an ἄνθρωπος ἔνσαρκος through his appearance as the heavenly man χριστός, who, according to Gen. i. 26, was created in the image of God, in order to die the death of the Messiah." — Holsten, *Die paulin. Theol.*, p. 100.

humanity of Christ which was fundamental in the apostle's Christology, bears so great a similarity to certain speculations of the Jewish theology that its origin in them is highly probable. This theology "found taught in the first and second chapters of Genesis a twofold creation of man, that of the heavenly, spiritual, and archetypal man, and that of the earthly, sensuous, and antitypal man." "In part at least it saw in that first-created, heavenly man the Messiah, who was concealed with God prior to his earthly appearance." "Since Paul the theologian," remarks Pfleiderer, from whom the two preceding quotations are taken, " was acquainted with these doctrines of his school, it were strange if he should have constructed his so essentially similar Christology without any reference to those Jewish theologumena by mere reflection upon his own pious experiences" (*Der Paulinismus*, 2te Aufl., p. 119). The preëxistence of Christ, together with his participation in the Old Testament economy, is unequivocally expressed in the declaration that in the desert the Israelites "drank of the spiritual rock that followed them ; and the rock was Christ" (1 Cor. x. 4). As the manna was not a natural product, but a "spiritual food," so the miraculous rock which furnished water to the thirsty Israelites was no ordinary, natural rock, but a πέτρα πνευματική, real, but of heavenly origin, because it was the actual self-revelation and appearance of the invisible Son of God.

This idea is related to that of Philo, who regarded the rock as Wisdom (σοφία), just as the manna was to him the Logos. The notion of prefiguration and type is neither expressed nor intimated by the apostle in the passage, but the people are said to have been supplied with a "spiritual drink" which was furnished them by Christ in the "phenomenal form" of the rock. Again, Christ is represented as having entered into human existence by an act of his own choice, by which he gave up the riches of his glorious, preëxistent state, and became poor in order that believers might through his poverty become rich (2 Cor. viii. 9). Likewise it is declared that Christ, though being in the form of God in his heavenly estate, "emptied himself, taking the form of a servant," and "was made in the likeness of men." As Spirit, as the heavenly man, he lived in godlikeness, but in order to accomplish his work for men he assumed their lowly condition, and became "obedient unto death" (Phil. ii. 6–8). Preëxistence is plainly expressed in the words: "God sent His Son in the likeness of sinful flesh," and "when the fulness of the time came God sent forth His Son, born of a woman" (Rom. viii. 3; Gal. iv. 4). The mention of his sending forth in connection with emphatic reference to his coming in the flesh and his birth under human conditions evidently implies a passing from one state of existence to another. These specifications as to the mode of earthly existence and the entrance upon it would be altogether unnatural, except of one to whose prior condition they did not belong. "Such language is applicable only to a spiritual being passing into the conditions of incarnate life."

It is a debatable question whether Paul believed that Christ in his preëxistent state participated in the creation. The meaning of the passage in 1 Cor. viii. 6 is not entirely clear: "Yet to us there is one God, the Father, of whom are all things, and we unto Him; and one Lord Jesus Christ, through whom are all things, and we through him." Without doubt the Jewish monotheism, the doctrine of the absolute supremacy of God as the first cause, is here maintained intact in the words ἐξ οὗ τὰ πάντα, "of whom are all things." Only with reference to the interpretation of δι᾽ οὗ τὰ πάντα, "through whom are all things," is there any uncertainty. Yet there can be no good reason for regarding the τὰ πάντα of the second clause as either including less than the same words in the former clause, or as referring to something different as being "through" Christ from that which in the first instance is declared to be "of" God as primary cause. "All things" are said to be of God as the original ground of existence, and "we to Him" as the one whose purposes the Christians were intended to serve as the ethical end of their being. It is the Lord Christ, however, through whom all things are, and we through him, to whom our spiritual new creation as believers is due. A clear distinction is thus drawn between "all things" as the totality of creation and the Christians as the special discriminated from the general. It is extremely arbitrary to assume, as Köstlin does, that δι' οὗ in the second clause is so "indefinite" that any other verb than the ἐγένετο, which is clearly to be understood in the first clause, may be substituted in the second, so that we may suppose "live," "are governed," or "are sustained," to be intended. While Rom. xi. 36 lends some support to this interpretation, since δι' οὗ is there employed of the sustaining and governing activity of God between the origin and the consummation of the world, the relation of the two clauses in the passage in question renders it most natural at least if not necessary to supply in the second the verb which is implied in the first. Thus Christ is regarded as the mediate cause of the creation, which was immediately effected by the "one God" as its primary ground and source. The fact that Paul regarded Christ as himself a created being ("the last Adam became [was created] a life-giving Spirit," 1 Cor. xv. 45) cannot be urged against this interpretation. For, as Pfleiderer has pointed out, the thought of the Jewish theologians did not exclude the conception that a creature of God might be the secondary cause or agent of the creation, as is apparent in the case of Wisdom in Prov. viii. 22 f.

It is interesting to note in this connection that Philo regarded the Logos as the organ of creation (ὄργανον δι' οὗ κατασκευάσθη [ὁ κόσμος]), although Paul's relation to Philo's thought is not determinable. It was, however, as the Son of God, "the man from heaven," who shared the divine "glory" as "the image of God," and not as the divine Logos of the Johannine speculation, that Paul thought of Christ in reference to his participation in the creation. Accordingly, he does not employ the specific terms of the fourth Gospel in which it is said that the Logos "was God," and that "the world was made by him." The Pauline doctrine of the person of Christ represents an early stage of the development of New Testament Christology which reaches its culmination in the conception of the Logos. Pfleiderer has suggestively conjectured that although it cannot be determined whether the Jewish theology of the time of Paul ascribed to the Messiah a participation in the work of creation, "it is not unthinkable that a combination of the sayings concerning the divine Wisdom and the preexistent Messiah may have taken place in the circles of the Jewish school before the time of Paul; whereby the doctrine of the apostle as to the mediate activity of Christ in the creation would be the more explicable."

The question whether Paul attributed a divine nature to Christ is regarded by some commentators as settled in the affirmative by Rom. ix. 5: "And of whom is Christ as concerning the flesh, who is over all, God blessed forever" (Revised Version), or, "From whom as to the flesh was Christ: He who is over all, God, be blessed forever!" (Noyes). The words ὁ ὢν ἐπὶ πάντων θεὸς εὐλογητός are capable of either rendering, so far as construction is concerned, and their interpretation depends upon the placing of a full stop or a comma at the end of the first clause. If, with Tischendorf, the full stop be employed, the words in question are an ascription of praise to God, or a doxology, of which other examples are found in Paul's Epistles (Rom. i. 25; 2 Cor. xi. 31). It must be regarded as a strong presumption against the former interpretation that Paul everywhere maintains the Jewish monotheism in its strictest sense. The absolute aloneness of God is a fundamental principle in his theology. As to Christ's relation to God, he implies and affirms so constantly the doctrine of the Son's subordination that it may be said to be the underlying presumption of his Christology; and since nowhere else in all his indisputable Epistles has he written anything that can be construed into an ascription of a divine nature to him, it is only by a violent interpretation that these words can be so understood.

The argument presented by Dr. Stevens (*The Pauline Theology*, p. 202) that as applied to Christ the words form a natural antithesis to τὸ κατὰ σάρκα, is of weight only if it can be shown that an antithesis can be regarded as required or even expected in this connection. The same scholar's appeal to Colossians for the ascription to Christ of "lofty attributes and prerogatives of creation and sovereignty over the world," cannot be admitted in view of the doubtful genuineness of this Epistle. The fact, indeed, that the deutero-Pauline writings contain a more developed Christology than that of the undisputed Epistles of Paul is one of the reasons for discrediting them. The passage in the Epistle to Titus (ii. 13) cannot fairly be brought into the argument in the present state of the criticism of the Pauline writings. The interpretation based upon the insertion of a full pause corresponds with the general tendency of the New Testament writers to draw a delicate line of distinction between the absolute God and Christ. This is true even of those who represent the most developed Christology, and assign to the Son a far higher rank than he has in the Pauline thought. Moreover, it is in the highest degree improbable that Paul, who calls Christ "the second man, the Lord from heaven," "the last Adam," and "the man Christ Jesus," could have intended to designate him as "God blessed forever." Baur's words are worthy of consideration in this connection, that "The passage rightly apprehended proves exactly the opposite of that which is generally found in it — how much it lay outside the apostle's circle of ideas to put Christ on an equality with God, and to call him God" (*Paulus*, 2te Aufl. ii. p. 264).*

Another view of this subject deserving of notice is based upon the apostle's use of the term "God," which among the ancients was not always employed as rigidly as it is by us. Assuming on the ground of Paul's usage a certain flexibility of the designation in this passage, the interpretation which does not admit the full stop, and assigns the disputed words to Christ, might be allowed. In 1 Cor. viii. 5, the apostle concedes that the heathen are not irrational in assuming the existence of their divinities, since "there are gods many and lords many." These gods and lords are, indeed, subordinated to the Supreme Deity, and regarded doubtless as created beings, but they are recognised as superhuman powers, as in Deut x. 17 it is declared, "The Lord your God is God of gods and Lord of lords." An employment of the term which denotes a marked departure from strict usage is found in 2 Cor. iv. 4, where Paul calls Satan "the god of this world" (αἰῶνος). The two terms, god and lord, are probably essentially synonymous in these passages, and designate beings holding a position of dominion and power which may be regarded as godlike. If,

---

* An exhaustive exegetical discussion of the passage in question may be found in the *Journal of the Society for Biblical Literature and Exegesis* for 1881. It is from the pens of Dr. Ezra Abbot and Dr. Timothy Dwight. Dr. Abbot's paper has been reprinted in his *Critical Essays.*

now, even in the Johannine theology the Logos was called god without a conscious impairment in the writer's mind of the traditional monotheism, it is not impossible that Paul, who assigned to Christ a rank as "the man from heaven" and "the image of God" in a preëminent sense, may have designated him as god without intending to place him on equality with the Supreme Deity either as to nature or functions, precisely as in Rom. x. 12, he says of him, "The same Lord is Lord of all." Accordingly, whether this interpretation or that supported in the preceding paragraph be accepted, the passage in question is found to be in accord with the general Pauline doctrine of the subordination of Christ to God, and it cannot be regarded as having the importance which has usually been attached to it in opposition to the assignment of the Pauline Christology to its proper place in the development of theology in the New Testament. It goes, then, without saying that the Trinitarian dogma has no standing in the thought of the apostle.*

We have seen that the glorious existence and celestial rank of Christ as the archetypal, heavenly man prior to his appearance in the flesh are fundamental tenets of the apostle's Christology. His essential preëminence belonged to him by virtue of his creation as "the last Adam." In a unique and exceptional sense he was the Son of God, and

---

* "As little as one can speak of a personal difference [in the thought of Paul] of the Spirit from God or Christ, so little can Christ coincide with God. His 'divinity' would directly exclude the idea that he is originally 'the man from heaven,' who, in his historical appearance, is called quite simply 'man' (Rom. v. 15; 1 Cor. xv. 21). Just as little, too, do such formulas as 'divine nature,' 'God-man,' 'incarnation,' express the Pauline doctrine with any precision. This knows only of a man with a divine content of life upon the earth, and in consequence thereof also with a spiritual form of existence above the earth in the sphere of God." — Holtzmann, *Neutest. Theol.*, ii. p. 94.

as such was "sent" into the world (Rom. viii. 3; Gal. iv. 4). Yet there are some passages which appear to indicate that his exalted rank was accorded on account of his devotion to the service of man, and in particular because of his death and resurrection. In Rom. i. 3 it is said that Christ was "born of the seed of David according to the flesh," and "declared [appointed, determined] to be the Son of God according to the Spirit of holiness by the resurrection of the dead." This passage is brought into conflict with explicit declarations of Paul's if it is interpreted to teach that Christ's divine sonship was originally and essentially determined by his resurrection. The apostle's thought probably was that through the resurrection Christ was declared to the faith of men to be what in his existence κατὰ σάρκα he did not appear to be, that is, the Son of God. But that the rank which was "declared" (ὁρισθείς) to belong to him was always essentially his is indicated by the declaration that his divine sonship corresponded to the fact that he possessed "the Spirit of holiness." This peculiar expression is evidently chosen in order to denote the belief that as belonging originally to Christ the endowment included more than can pertain to any earthly man, and distinguished its possessor preëminently as a participant in the heavenly divine life. For this "Spirit of holiness" which constituted the personality of Christ must be regarded as of celestial origin. Accordingly, he was able to be to believers a "life-giving Spirit." By a transference of the Messiah-idea of the Jewish theology to Christ he was regarded as the preëxistent, heavenly man who in distinction from men of earthly mould possessed as essential qualities of his being "the Spirit of holiness" and the Spirit of life which qualified him to be the head of a new, regenerated humanity.

The exaltation of Christ which Paul believed to be accorded to him on account of his death and through his resurrection doubtless includes an increment of functions rather than an increase of essential dignity and rank of nature. By reason of these two events of his earthly fortune, which to Paul were of central and paramount significance, he attained the rank of lordship, a godlike position of dominion.* Accordingly, in Rom. xiv. 9, the apostle declares: "For to this end Christ died and lived again, that he might be Lord both of the dead and the living." A similar conception is expressed in Phil. ii. 9 f.: "Wherefore [because of his humiliation], also, God highly exalted him, and gave unto him the name which is above every name; that in the name of Jesus every knee should bow, of things in heaven and things on earth and things under the earth, and that every tongue should confess that Jesus Christ is Lord to the glory of God the Father." In this bowing of the knee is expressed the declaration that to the exalted Lord Christ is due the worship not only of angelic beings and spirits in sheol in accordance with the popular mythology but also of all living men. Since, however, this worship is "to the glory of God the Father," no prejudice to the monotheistic doctrine is implied. Christ is Lord of the heavenly spirits and of all the living and the dead. Believers belong to him whether in life or death, to him

* "He, who through the resurrection is exalted above all earthly limitation and weakness, has thereby become that for which he was already designed, during and before his earthly existence, by reason of the Spirit of holiness that dwelt in him as a principle forming his personality." "In truth, Christ had in the flesh, according to Phil. ii. 6–8, exchanged 'the form of God' ($\mu o \rho \phi \grave{\eta}\ \theta \epsilon o \tilde{v}$), which in any case must be thought as radiant with glory ($\dot{\epsilon}\nu\ \delta \acute{o} \xi \eta$ in the sense of 2 Cor. iii. 7, 8, 11), for the 'form of a servant' ($\mu o \rho \phi \grave{\eta}\ \delta o \acute{v} \lambda o v$), and renounced every divine mode of manifestation as incompatible with the flesh. But after the hitherto latent $\pi \nu \epsilon \tilde{v} \mu a$ became free and potent with the resurrection, the glory of God shines in its highest and purest form constantly ... in his face, as is fitting to the 'image of God' ($\epsilon \emph{l} \kappa \grave{\omega} \nu\ \tau o \tilde{v}\ \theta \epsilon o \tilde{v}$)."— Holtzmann, *Neutest. Theol.*, ii. pp. 78, 81.

are due their allegiance and adoration, and in him is their hope.

The idea of his descent to the underworld is not, however, necessarily implied here, as Meyer maintains. It accords with this sentiment of worship toward a being of exalted rank and authority that the term "Lord," which in the Septuagint is a designation of Yahweh, is frequently applied to Christ. The salvation of men is declared to depend upon confession to him as Lord (Rom. x. 9). Yet, while he is represented as sitting at the right hand of God, that is, as a participator in the divine government, his subordination to the Father is implied in his office as an intercessor for the believers (Rom. viii. 33, "who also maketh intercession for us"). In accordance with a conception of the Messiah not unknown to Judaism (Enoch-Parables, xlv. li. lxix.), the function of judge of men is ascribed to Christ, which he would exercise at the consummation of the existing world-order, when "the Lord himself shall descend from heaven with a shout, with the voice of the archangel, and with the trump of God" (1 Thess. iv. 16), and when "the dead shall be raised incorruptible, and we [the living believers] shall be changed" (1 Cor. xv. 51). Accordingly, Paul enjoins upon the Corinthians that they "judge nothing before the time, until the Lord come, who will bring to light the hidden things of darkness, and make manifest the counsels of the hearts" (1 Cor. iv. 5), and declares that "we must all be made manifest before the judgment-seat of Christ, that each may receive the things done in the body, according to what he hath done, whether it be good or bad" (2 Cor. v. 10). The "glory" in which the apostle conceived Christ to exist after his resurrection and exaltation to the right hand of God is doubtless that in which he believed him to have preëxisted when, "being in the form of God, he counted it not a prize [ἁρπαγμόν, a thing to be eagerly grasped after] to be on equality with God" (Phil. ii. 6). By "form" (μορφή) is without doubt meant the mode of existence of the Deity and the heavenly beings generally which, as before remarked, Paul conceived to be that of a luminous splendour or "glory" (compare the "great light" in the account of Paul's conversion, Acts xxii. 6), and in which consisted the riches of Christ that were renounced when he "emptied himself," and assumed the position of a "servant" in order to accomplish his earthly mission. This godlike mode of existence (τὸ εἶναι ἴσα θεῷ) he did not count a prize, but having voluntarily renounced it for a life of sacrifice, he attained it as a reward for his humiliation and service. Hence his Lordship and "the name which is above every name." That the existence of Christ in the "image" or "form" of God was not, however, conceived by Paul as incompatible with his archetypal humanity is evident from 1 Cor. xi. 7 already referred to, where man is said to be "the image and glory of God"; from Rom. viii. 29, "whom He foreknew He also foreordained to be conformed to the image of His Son"; and from Phil. iii. 21, "who shall fashion anew the body of our humiliation, that it may be conformed to the body of his glory, according to the working whereby he is able even to subject all things unto himself."

The importance of the doctrine of the preëxistence of Christ in the Pauline Christology is apparent when we consider the apostle's teaching regarding the incarnation. For the most conspicuous feature of this teaching is the conception of a voluntary self-devotion of an exalted being who out of love for man left his high estate in the heavenly regions, and descended to participate in the lowly fortunes of earthly men for their redemption. This idea denotes a marked departure of Paul from the current Jewish Messianism, according to which the Messiah was concealed in

the heavens awaiting the time of his manifestation.* The
Messiah whom Judaism was awaiting, Paul recognised in
Jesus of Nazareth. He whom his Jewish contemporaries
expected to see come in pomp and power for the overthrow
of their enemies, Paul saw already manifested in a mission
of loving sacrifice undertaken in order to effect the righteousness which should prepare for his final coming as
judge in the great consummation of the age. "This new
feature [the love manifested in the incarnation], which the
apostle added to the traditional Messiah of his school, was
the fruit of the ethical impression that the crucified Jesus
had made upon his mind, and it betrays itself precisely in
this, that this impression was at bottom the decisive motive
for his faith in the Messiahship of him who died upon the
cross" (Pfleiderer, *ut supra*).

A barren idea of the Jewish theological speculation, that
of the "concealed," preëxistent Messiah, was transformed
by the apostle into a great ethical and spiritual doctrine in
which he found the hope of his own deliverance and of that
of all who should believe on the crucified one from bondage
to the law into "the glorious liberty of the children of
God" (Rom. viii. 21). The incarnation of Christ was not,
however, in the thought of the apostle that of the second
person of a divine trinity. There is no ground for supposing that he so far departed from the current Messianism
as to think of the Messiah as such in other terms than
those of the popular theology according to which the expected one was a preëxistent heavenly man. Accordingly,
he conceived the incarnation as the passage of "the man
from heaven" into human conditions, as his abandonment
through self-sacrificing love of his condition of "glory"
and godlikeness and the assumption of a body conformed

* See Weizsäcker, *Das apostol. Zeitalter*, 2te Aufl. p. 125, and Pfleiderer,
Paulinismus, 2te Aufl. p. 123.

to the earthly, sensuous organisms of men, or "in the likeness of sinful flesh." From this point of view is apparent the injustice to the thought of the apostle which is done by the bold rationalism that interprets his conception of the preëxistence of Christ as ideal or existing only in the mind of God. This view renders Christ a mere instrument of the purposes of God, and robs his work of self-devotion, of the voluntary, ethical element which was fundamental in Paul's thought of the redemption effected on the cross. Moreover, the terms employed by Paul relative to Christ's coming in the flesh can only by the most violent exegesis be regarded as applicable to an ideal being or a principle existing in the divine purpose, when we consider how they must have been understood by his readers. Only of an existing personality can it be said that he was rich, and became poor; that he was "in the form of God," and assumed that of a servant; that after his humiliation he was exalted, and that he was "born of a woman" and "under the law."

Professor Beyschlag has undertaken to explain away a real incarnation as pertaining to the Pauline Christology by reasoning that the heavenly man could not be thought by the apostle to have preëxisted along with the Father without the ascription to him in his preëxistence of all that belongs to the real man, that is, spirit and flesh, and assuming in that state a development resting upon these. Since this supposition is absurd and cannot be attributed to the apostle, it is concluded that he conceived of the preëxistence of the heavenly man as ideal. But this position has been shown to be entirely untenable, since Paul speaks of "celestial" and "spiritual" bodies, and declares that "flesh and blood cannot inherit the kingdom of God" (1 Cor. xv. 50). An existence purely spiritual and independent of the flesh could not have presented any difficulty to one who wrote of being absent from the body and at home with the Lord (2 Cor. v. 8) and of the fashioning anew of the body of our humiliation into conformity with Christ's body of glory (Phil. iii. 21). "One cannot in fact oppose more fundamentally Paul's entire mode of thought and that of his age than by attributing to him the opinion that the subsistence of the personality depends on the sarkical existence" (Pfleiderer, *ut supra*, p. 126). The conception, then, of a real incarnation of Christ by an entrance upon bodily conditions out of a preëxistent state of pure spirituality can be offensive only to those interpreters of Paul who will at all hazards bring his thought into accord with certain modern ideas by stripping it of its mystic and supernatural features. It is evident from the foregoing considerations that the "nerve" of the Pauline teaching as to the incarnation consists in "the identity of the heavenly Christ and the earthly Jesus."

The person of Christ was, however, in the Pauline doctrine so intimately connected with Christianity as a principle of a new world-order of life that the two cannot be adequately considered apart. To the apostle, Christ as a person and Christ as a spiritual principle of cosmic significance are identical. Two orders of existence are constantly before his mind, and the shadows of the one are mingled with the light of the other in many of the most impressive expressions of his thought. On the one hand is the fleshly nature of man, in which sin and death are provided for as an inevitable result, though death is represented as the penalty of transgression, — an antinomy which does not, perhaps, admit of reconciliation. At the head of this order stands the fleshly progenitor of the race "through" whom "sin entered into the world, and death through sin, and so death passed unto all, for that all sinned" (Rom. v. 13, 14). Here are those who sin under the law which, though "holy, just, and good," is only an occasion of transgression, and has no saving efficacy. It "entered," indeed, "that the offence might abound," and apart from it "sin is dead." There is no hope in themselves alone for those who are chained to "this body of death." With their best endeavour, they can scarcely do more than bring forth the horrid spiritual brood of "the works of the flesh." Here, too, are those who sin without the law, the gentiles, against whom "the wrath of God is revealed from heaven," who are given up "in the lusts of their hearts unto uncleanliness," and the catalogue of whose manifold depravities and abominations casts a terrible shadow upon the opening pages of the greatest of the Epistles.

Over against this gloomy world-order of sin and death the apostle places the new world-order of regeneration and life, Christianity and Christ conceived together as a principle of redemption and spiritual transformation. At the head of this order of life stands "the man from heaven," "the last Adam," who was made a "quickening Spirit." Through him are to be done away the baneful evils of the former order of things for as many as shall believe in him. "The man Christ Jesus," who had been revealed in Paul at his conversion, was the resurrected Lord of glory, and in his resurrection the apostle saw the hope of the victory over death for all in whom the Spirit should dwell. He was not thinking of the end of physical death, but of the taking away of the "sting of death," which is sin, through him who had destroyed it by his propitiation. It was the sting of death that the departed, who had no hold upon life because without spiritual connection with Christ, could have no resurrection, but must remain in the shadowy life of the underworld, when the Lord should presently descend in glory. Accordingly, he declares that if Christ be not risen the faith of the believers is vain, and they are yet in their sins. If in this life only they have hoped in Christ, they are of all men most miserable (1 Cor. xv. 19).

It does not belong to the scope of this chapter to discuss the method according to which the powers of this new world-order were conceived to operate and to determine how the Christ-principle of life was believed to be efficacious in neutralising the Adamic principle of death. Suffice it to say that in the Christology of the great apostle the dethronement of Death and the crowning of Life were not thought to be effected by natural processes. "The sting of death" was not taken away, the deliverance of souls from the realm of sheol was not consummated by the *ethical* influence of a man who was on a level with all others except by reason of preëminent spirituality. So tame a conception could have had no place in the mystical thought of Paul. The great transformation was effected by a supernatural being from the upper realm. It was the heavenly man, the life-giving Spirit, whom death could not hold, who not only gave by his resurrection evidence of the resurrection of those who should enter into spiritual union with him, but became "the first fruits of them that slept," and the head of the new humanity, reconstituted and vitalised by a celestial principle which should transform the mortal body into the "glory" of which his heavenly body was the type. The two world-periods, that of the reign of death represented by Adam and that in which the principle of life predominated, at the head of which was Christ, were not conceived by Paul as absolutely opposed in their fundamental character, but as having a bond of union in the fact that they were human dispensations, since the chief of each was a man. All men die in the earthy man, Adam, because according to the flesh they partake of his nature; and all may "be made alive" in the heavenly man, Christ, because spiritually they may partake of his. The principle which he represented could be realised in humanity only because he partook of the nature of man,* and as the spiritual archetype of the race was fitted to become the head of a new order of human life. Only as man could he have been the "first fruits" of those who slept the sleep of death, and have furnished believers with that "hope in Christ" for the life to come without which they were "of all men most miserable."

The Pauline teaching of the person of Christ thus presents an important phase of the development of Christological conceptions apparent in the New Testament. It stands in marked contrast with the Christology of the Petrine gospel, which saw in Jesus the Jewish Messiah whose mission had been interrupted by death, "whom the heavens must receive until the time of the restoration of all things whereof God spake by the mouth of His holy prophets," and who was to set up at his coming his own "throne" of judgment upon the "nations" and twelve thrones for his twelve apostles. The conception which Paul set over against this was that of Christ as no national Messiah merely, but as the man from heaven, the spiritual representative of the human race which having gone down in death through the first Adam might through the last Adam be raised to life and immortality. Men may differ as to whether or no the apostle had any historical or rational grounds for this doctrine, but no one can "deny the grandeur of its main conception or the depth of insight and pure passion of aspiration with which when once free from the tangle of its dialectics it rushes upon its sublime conclusions." It occupies an intermediate position between the

---

* Biedermann's discrimination may well be noted in this connection: "His ego was from the beginning not in a like relation to the σάρξ with our ego. Herein consisted the mere similarity and not perfect equality with us in reference to the body."

Christology of the original apostles and that of the post-Pauline Epistles to the Colossians and Ephesians, and by its idea of the preëxistence of Christ prepared the way for the Johannine doctrine of the Logos, who was with God, and was God. In originality of conception, in mystic profundity and spiritual insight, it is preëminent among the Christologies of the early Church.

CHAPTER XIII

SUPERNATURALISM—THE SPIRIT.*

ONE is doubtless not justified in speaking of a primitive-Christian philosophy of religion in any other sense than that definite and easily discernible principles underlie the accounts given by the New Testament writers of the religious phenomena and experiences of the time. The one point of view common to these writers is that the knowledge of spiritual truth, the religious life, the external authentications of their belief, all come from a supersensible world, or are of heavenly origin. The Old Testament prophecy that the Messiah should come out of Judah, or that he would be a lineal descendant of David in the natural order, their age could not let stand in its original sense, and accordingly produced the legend of the miraculous conception of the mother of Jesus. The mission and work of Jesus and his place in the historical order could not, of course, be apprehended in such a time as having a natural connection with Hebraism and Judaism in the sense of bearing a relation to them in the course of normal human progress. Hence he is thought to have come into the world through the agency of the Holy Ghost and announced by angels, or to have descended as a preexistent divine being out of the glory which he had with the Father before the world was (Matt. i. 18, 20; John xvii. 5). Not only is he regarded by the evangelists as a miracle-worker, but he is reported to have appealed to his

* *The New World*, September, 1898. (With revision and additions.)

supernatural powers as evidence of his Messiahship (Matt. xi. 4 f.). These powers are represented to have been transferred to the apostles (Matt. x. 1; Acts iii. 7, xiv. 3); those who should believe in their message would be superior to such natural forces as fire and poison (Mark xvi. 18),* and the possession of ability to perform miracles is regarded as an evidence of apostleship (2 Cor. xii. 12).

The primitive-Christian supernaturalism, however, reached its highest point, and attained its most refined expression in the conception of the Spirit. This is especially true of Paul, who appears to have attached only a subordinate importance to merely external supernatural phenomena. Before discussing his views on this important subject it will be well to consider briefly the popular ideas of the operations of the Spirit chiefly as they appear in the synoptic Gospels and the Acts. Here in the first place is to be noted a considerable contraction of the field of the activity of the Spirit in comparison with the Old Testament point of view, according to which any extraordinary manifestation of power, as in the case of Samson, Othniel, Gideon, etc., as well as the spiritual endowments of the prophets and men of God, is referred to this source.† Gunkel has shown the error in Cremer's view that all self-manifestation of God was ascribed by the early Christians to the Spirit, and has successfully maintained that, almost without exception, only such events as concern the life of man are regarded as due to its activity. This is in general true of the works represented as done by Jesus, who must have been thought to owe his power to the Spirit, whether be-

---

* The spuriousness of the section in which this passage occurs does not affect the present discussion, which is concerned only with the ideas prevalent in the early Christian community.

† Judges iii. 10, vi. 34, xiii. 25, xiv. 6, 19, xv. 14; 1 Sam. xvi. 13; Ex. xxviii. 3, xxxi. 3; Isa. xi. 2, lxi. 1.

stowed at his conception or at the baptism. The "works" wrought upon external nature are comparatively few. An important feature of the popular primitive-Christian conception of the operations of the Spirit, whereby it is essentially different from that of Paul, is that it is not regarded as the principle of the moral-religious life to which all Christian activities are to be referred. This has been shown by Weiss, Pfleiderer, Gunkel, and Harnack, and Gloël has not succeeded in maintaining the contrary.

According to the popular view, the Spirit manifested itself in exceptional "mighty works" ($\delta\upsilon\nu\acute{\alpha}\mu\epsilon\iota\varsigma$) rather than in the ethical and religious daily walk. Peter, therefore, is represented as seeing in the extraordinary phenomena on the day of Pentecost the fulfilment of the prophecy of Joel as to the pouring out of the Spirit of God, the manifestations of which would be in prophesying, the seeing of visions, and the dreaming of dreams (Acts ii. 17-19). The Spirit was thus Messianic in the sense that its operations belonged in part according to the prophetic promise to "the last times," which it was conceived would abound in strange and miraculous phenomena. Thus we find Stephen reported as doing "great wonders and miracles among the people" because he was "full of the Holy Ghost," and his discourse could not be resisted on account of "the power and the Spirit by which he spake" (Acts vi. 8, 10). The apostles are promised miraculous instruction in their coming extremity (Matt. x. 18 f.). When Cornelius of Cæsarea and other gentiles received the Spirit on the occasion of Peter's discourse, the only sign of their possession mentioned by the writer of Acts was that "they heard them speak with tongues and magnify God" (x. 44-46). It would be easy to show by numerous citations from the prophets that their view of the matter was in general the same. The gift of the Spirit was to them an exalted knowledge, insight, courage in the performance of their official functions of revelation of the divine will, or, as Wendt expresses it, "genius in the religious domain."* In the later Judaism, the intimate connection of which with Christianity should not be overlooked, a similar view of the matter was the prevalent one, although few phenomena of the kind appear.

There can be little doubt, after Gunkel's careful discussion of the matter, that in the primitive church the manifestations of the Spirit were recognised as such by their wonderful, exceptional, or, in other words, their supposed supernatural character, rather than by any end they might have been believed to serve in the divine economy. The commandment of the Spirit is simply recognised as an inward divine intimation which orders, or does not "permit" (Acts xvi. 6, 7). A prophet speaks, and is at once believed, because his message is regarded as supernatural (Acts xi. 27–29). The sound as of a rushing mighty wind, the pentecostal flame, and the speaking with tongues testify to the descent of the Spirit from above. When the new converts break forth in inarticulate utterances, the evidence is at hand, and no other seems to be needed or thought of, that the supernatural divine presence has come upon them. When Paul lays his hands upon the disciples at Ephesus, who had "not so much as heard whether there be any Holy Ghost," the Spirit comes upon them, and they "speak with tongues, and prophesy." Here it is evident that "the Spirit gives them utterance," and that the external phenomena furnish the evidence of its operation (Acts xix. 6). God himself "bears witness" to the calling of the gentiles in that He bestows upon them the Holy Ghost (Acts xv. 8).

* Gunkel has shown by an analysis of a large number of passages that in the prophets the moral-religious operations of the Spirit are to others in the ratio of 1 to 5.

One of the most conspicuous evidences to the early Christians of the presence of the Spirit was the so-called "speaking with tongues" (γλώσσαις λαλεῖν). The meaning of the term is not precisely determinable, and we cannot profitably undertake more than to deal with the phenomena as they are presented to us. Certain it is that, however we may attempt to explain them by our psychology as natural expressions of the human mind under certain conditions, they were regarded as supernatural in their time, and are placed by Paul among "the gifts of the Spirit" (1 Cor. xii. 10). Whether we hold with Weizsäcker, Heinrici, Gunkel, and others that the preference for this gift which prevailed in the Corinthian church according to 1 Cor. xiv. was due to the previous gentile religious views of the believers there or not, is unimportant, for that it was also appreciated by Jewish Christians is evident from Acts, to the sources of which it could hardly have been foreign. It seems to have had different manifestations, for Paul speaks of "kinds of tongues" (1 Cor. xii. 10), and also to have been bestowed upon some to the exclusion of others (1 Cor. xii. 30, "do all speak with tongues?"); and it appears that those who possessed it exalted themselves on account of it above their less fortunate brethren, and became objects of their envy (1 Cor. xii. 12–28). Paul evidently saw that the church was threatened with schism (verse 25), and the fourteenth chapter of the Epistle is intended to obviate a too high estimate of the gift. From this chapter we learn something of the character of the manifestations of this charism, which was doubtless esteemed so highly above other endowments of the Spirit because of its extraordinary and wonderful features. He who spoke "in a tongue" did not speak "to men," but to God, "for no man understandeth him." He might thereby "edify himself," but not the church, for, says the apostle, "if I know not the meaning of the voice, I shall be unto him that speaketh a barbarian." There was wanting "a distinction in the sounds" comparable to "an uncertain sound" of a trumpet or a confused playing of a pipe or harp.

This defect (for so the apostle evidently regarded it) was due to the fact that the subject did not himself know what he was saying, for when a prayer was uttered "in a tongue" the "Spirit" prayed, but the "understanding" (νοῦς) was "unfruitful." Since the speaking with tongues is accounted one of the gifts of the Spirit, it is probable that praying with the Spirit and blessing with the Spirit should be interpreted as manifestations of the divine power, "divers kinds of tongues." It is evident, then, that the operations of the Spirit which the apostle could commend, such as "prophesying," were not incompatible with the normal use of the subject's own intelligence, and in fact required it in order to be fruitful. The speaking "with a tongue," the utterance of mere words or sounds without "distinction," was unprofitable to the hearer without an "interpretation," which was of itself a special gift of the Spirit. The nature of this operation is not defined, but it is likely that the ability was possessed by some to enter into such a relation with the speaker as enabled them to convey to the congregation an idea of the general drift of the ecstatic and indistinct utterance of feeling in which his understanding was unfruitful. It is evident, then, that in the speaking "with a tongue" the subject was supposed to be overcome by the power of the Spirit, so that he was passive under its influence and without the normal use of his faculties. Accordingly Paul says that "the unlearned or unbelievers" who witness the performance will think the subjects to be "mad." The author of Acts has preserved a feature which throws light upon the matter, when he says that on the pentecostal occasion the perplexed bystanders remarked that the subjects of the possession were "full of new wine," although he misunderstood the nature of the phenomenon in supposing that it consisted in speaking in foreign languages.

Related to these phenomena in the sense that they were supposed to have a supernatural origin are the operations of the Spirit designated "visions and revelations." The subject is supposed to be "in the Spirit," to be impelled or driven by the Spirit, doubtless in a manner which involved the suspension of his own volition and the subordination of his intelligence (Rev. i. 10; Luke ii. 27, iv. 1, 14; Acts viii. 29). When the apostle was on one occasion the subject of such a revelation he did not know whether he was in the body or out of it (2 Cor. xii. 2, 3). He thought himself "caught up into the third heaven," where he heard "unspeakable words." On the way to Damascus he hears Jesus speak from heaven in the midst of a blinding light. He has a "revelation" that he must go to Jerusalem. It is by the command of the Holy Ghost that he and Barnabas were set apart for the work of the ministry, and by the same divine power they were "sent forth."* The Spirit is regarded as laying upon those whom it possesses an irresistible compulsion. Paul goes "bound in the Spirit" to Jerusalem, and knows nothing of his future fortune, except that "the Holy Ghost witnesseth in every city" of the coming "bonds and afflictions" (Acts xx. 22 f.). Manifestly he felt it to be a power not himself which thus commanded, impelled, or restrained him, and even overcame his own endeavour (Acts xvi. 6 f.).

Prophecy, in like manner, which Paul recommends as preferable to the speaking with tongues (1 Cor. xiv. 1), was a gift of the Spirit bestowed upon certain believers; but we

* 2 Cor. xii. 4 ff.; Gal. ii. 2; Acts ix. 3, xiii. 2, xvi. 6; cf. Acts vii. 55, viii. 39; Apoc. Bar. vi.; Enoch xxxix. 3, lii. 1.

are ignorant of the personal qualifications which drew down this blessing and of the activity on the part of any one that might effect its descent. For the injunction to "strive earnestly for the best gifts" (1 Cor. xii. 31) implies other conditions than pure passivity in the subject. It is probable that exceptional endowments from above such as "wisdom," which all did not possess (Acts vi. 3), and the being "full of the Holy Ghost" were conditioned by subjective qualities apart from faith, which was a common qualification. The words "ye may all prophesy" (1 Cor. xiv. 31) must be understood in the sense that "all" means all who have the gift, which according to 1 Cor. xii. 10, belonged only to some believers. The prophet had in the first place a power, evidently thought to be supernatural, of foretelling future events which were hidden from the ordinary knowledge of men. So Agabus predicts a famine and the delivery of Paul by the Jews into the hands of the gentiles at Jerusalem (Acts xi. 28, xxi. 10). But this was not the prophet's sole function, for by him the secrets of the heart of an unbeliever may be revealed, so that he will fall down and worship God, and report that God is in the believers (1 Cor. xiv. 24 f.). The revelation which comes to the prophet is of such a nature that "all may learn, and all may be comforted" (verses 30, 31). That the prophetic discourses had a religious and eschatological content is very probable. The apostle himself enjoyed revelations as to the religious future of the Jews and as to the great consummation of the kingdom (Rom. xi. 26; 1 Cor. xv. 24 ff., 49-54), and in the early church religion and "the last things" were intimately connected. Faith in Jesus was faith in the resurrected and ascended Lord who was soon to come in glory. The delivery of the prophecy is distinguished from the speaking with tongues in that it is intelligible. The prophet addresses himself not to God, but to men, and he speaks to "edification and exhortation and comfort." Thus, he is not mastered by his enthusiasm and inspiration, for "the spirits of the prophets are subject to the prophets" (1 Cor. xiv. 3, 32).

Since the Spirit was bestowed only upon Christians, and accordingly on condition of a confession of Jesus and faith, the mention of "faith" as one of the "gifts" of the Spirit (1 Cor. xii. 9) is somewhat surprising. But the apostle probably had in mind an intensified quality of this Christian grace which would render its possessor steadfast in trial and persecution and temptation, or give him a "boldness" like that of the apostles Peter and John, who, when "filled with the Holy Ghost," declared the word without fear (Acts iv. 29, 31). The point of interest is that all extraordinary achievements in the religious domain were regarded by the early Christians as effected not by an intensified human energy and will, but by a supernatural power. Supernatural also were thought to be the gifts of "healing," "the word of wisdom," "the word of knowledge," whatever fine distinction may be drawn between these two, "the working of miracles," "the discerning of Spirits," and "the interpretation of tongues." Since of those whom God "has set in the church" apostles are accounted "first" (1 Cor. xii. 28), it must be assumed that Paul regarded the charism of apostleship as the most important among the supernatural endowments bestowed upon the Christians. More than any other must he be "filled with the Holy Ghost" who was appointed to be the founder and counsellor of churches and the guide of souls. To him were vouchsafed "revelations and visions of the Lord" (2 Cor. xii. 1); he could show as his authentication "the signs of an apostle" in "wonders and mighty deeds" (verse 12; Rom. xv. 18 f.), and his preaching was in "demonstration of the Spirit and of power" (1 Cor. ii. 4). He did not live his spiritual life apart and by himself, but in constant intercourse with the supersensible world, whence came to him counsel in emergencies, revelations, and supernatural power. The Spirit which he has received is not that of this world, but the Spirit of God, and the wisdom which he speaks is that of God "in a mystery" (1 Cor. ii. 7, 12).

It is apparent from the foregoing discussion that Paul adopted the popular supernaturalism of the primitive church, while he endeavoured to moderate the zeal of some of the believers in respect to the gift of tongues. We have now to consider how, proceeding from the same general point of view, he enlarged and exalted the supernaturalistic conception in connection with his profounder views of religious experience, of salvation, and of the coming kingdom of God. But first of all let it be considered that we have not here to deal with a dogmatic construction. The apostle indeed proceeded upon the premises of supernaturalism, as he could not but do from the Jewish religious point of view; but the new creation which he produced was evolved out of his own Christian experience. This began with his conversion which, explain it as we may from natural psychological antecedents, he regarded as supernatural, as nothing short of God's revelation of His Son in him, that he "might preach him among the heathen" (Gal. i. 16). To him Christ crucified and raised from the dead was the beginning of a new supernatural religious order which did not supplement, but did away with, the former divine dispensation of the law. "For what the law could not do, . . . God sending His own Son, . . . condemned sin in the flesh; that the righteousness of the law might be fulfilled in us, who walk not after the flesh, but after the Spirit" (Rom. viii. 3 f.).

Paul recognised no natural scheme of salvation, no natural connection between the state of sin and the state of "grace." To him the transition from the former condition to the latter was not made by a process of development, of growth, of the slow formation of character, according to the modern philosophy of religious experience, but the entire process was supernatural—an atonement for sin provided for in the divine counsel and an illuminating Spirit sent down from heaven (Rom. v. 18 f., viii. 10 f., 16 f.; Gal. iii. 13 f.). That the divine bestowal of the Spirit is conditioned upon the atonement is evident from the connection of thought in Gal. iii. 13 f.: "Christ hath redeemed us from the curse of the law, . . . that we might receive the promise of the Spirit through faith." Without the atonement of Christ and its acceptance through faith there is no "newness of life" in the Spirit, but man remains "under the curse" (Gal. iii. 10).

The supermundane origin and character of the entire scheme are manifest. It is only through faith in the supernatural Christ that the blessing of Abraham could come on the gentiles (verse 14). For notwithstanding the announcement of "glory, honour, and peace to every man that worketh good, to the Jew first and also to the gentile," and the declaration that "the doers of the law," Jew or gentile, "shall be justified" (Rom. ii. 10, 13 f.), the manifest inference from Gal. iii. 8-15 is that the gentiles, however faithfully they might "do by nature the things contained in the law," could not naturally attain salvation in the Pauline sense of the word. The author of Ephesians expresses the Pauline view as to the gentiles when he says that they were "without Christ . . . having no hope and without God in the world" (Eph. ii. 12). They became "partakers of the promise" only through the same atonement which opened the way of salvation to the Jews. The fundamental proposition of salvation through Christ according to Paul is that of justification by faith. The ethical requirements of the law can be fulfilled neither by Jew nor gentile.

The law must first be abrogated for the Jews by the atonement, that the promise to Abraham which primarily concerned only his seed might be extended to the gentiles; both must first accept by faith the supernatural scheme of satisfaction, before they can come under "the law of the Spirit of life in Jesus Christ" (Rom. viii. 2). The incompatibility of this doctrine with the naturalism of Rom. ii. 13 will surprise no careful student of the apostle.

A similar point of view, that is, one transcending natural human experience and taking no account of the law of growth, is represented in the doctrine of dying and being raised with Christ in baptism. The apostle, having declared that where sin abounded grace did much more abound, anticipates the question, "Shall we then continue in sin, that grace may abound?" "Far be it!" he answers; how shall we believers who are dead to sin live any longer in it? In our baptism we were baptized into the death of Christ. Having been buried with him by baptism into death, we should walk in newness of life, as he was raised up. Our old man is crucified with him, that the body of sin might be destroyed, that henceforth we should not serve sin. For he that is dead is freed from sin. So we should reckon ourselves dead to sin, but alive to God through Christ (Rom. vi. 1–11). This does not mean that in believing in the ethical principles of the life of Jesus, taking him as our example, and assuming in baptism the vows of a Christian life, we receive a moral-spiritual impulse which will aid us in the conflict with evil tendencies, and give us at length the victory. All this is modern rationalising of the apostle's doctrine. For with him the whole process of the believer's renewal depends upon the death of Christ. In his death "to sin once" Christ supernaturally (magically?) broke the power of sin and the flesh for all who should believe on him. On the cross God "condemned sin in the flesh." In the resurrection of Jesus He showed the triumph of the Spirit over death. Baptism, then, is to Paul a magical rite, a symbol of the believer's appropriation through faith of the death and resurrection of Jesus — of the crucifixion of "the old man" and the raising up of "the new man."

The connection between Jesus and the believer is such that "if one [Jesus] died for all, then all died," that is, all who through faith appropriate his death die with him to the flesh and sin, "crucify the flesh with its affections and lusts" (Gal. v. 24). Thus "he that is dead is freed from sin." In the believer's magical death with Christ he has paid the legal penalty of sin, which is death, and is therefore set free from it; his "old man" has perished; the claims of the law are satisfied, and he is no longer under its "curse," for now he is subject only to "the law of the Spirit of life in Jesus Christ." How evidently does the great and marvellous transaction on the cross lie at the basis of this entire dogmatic structure! Without it there would have been no such profound significance to Paul in the rite of baptism. If "the old man" dies in baptism, it is because the subject of the rite has by faith appropriated to himself the death of Christ. But the apostle does not conceive the believer's relation to Christ in this mystic dying and living again with him simply in connection with the present life. His view includes an intensification of the marvellous in the extension of the fellowship into the life to come; and in this fact we have conclusive evidence that a merely ethical conception of the believer's relation to Christ was not in his thought. When he says, "For if we have been planted together in the likeness of his death, we shall be also in the likeness of his resurrection," and, "Now if we be dead with Christ, we believe that we shall also live with him" (Rom. vi. 5, 8), the future tense can only be understood as referring to the resurrection and the life of the Messianic age. Verse 8 certainly cannot mean, we believe that we do now, or shall now, in this present life live with him. The fundamental idea of the whole section is that of the supernatural "life" of which the believer partakes through union with Christ in his death and resurrection; and the two aspects of this life are presented, that of this age as a new order of spiritual existence in which he "should walk," and in which he should judge himself to be "alive unto God" (verses 4, 8), and that of the glorious age near at hand, the consummation of the great miracle of redemption, when in the resurrection he would enter into everlasting fellowship with Christ the Lord. The latter is probably the basal idea; for to Paul "life" was primarily the eternal life of the resurrection-state, which reacted upon the present not only so that the believer was "saved by hope," but also in such a manner as to consecrate his daily walk, and render it worthy of the great fortune reserved for him.

From these considerations is manifest the important modification of the primitive-Christian conception of the Spirit which Paul effected. In his hands the Spirit is no longer "an abstract-supernatural, ecstatic-apocalyptic principle," according to Pfleiderer, but is brought into living connection with the moral-religious life, so that the whole Christian experience of the believer is dominated by its influence. The Spirit, however, as a constant life-giving presence must not be understood as divested of its supernatural character. This is fundamental in the apostle's thought, and, as has been remarked, he recognised all the supernatural and "ecstatic-apocalyptic" features of the popular religion, while he claimed that he spoke with tongues more than all those in Corinth who boasted of this gift (1 Cor. xiv. 18). His apostleship, that "treasure in earthen vessels," he has "of God." He is "an apostle not of men nor through man, but through Jesus Christ and God the Father." What he declares is, "the wisdom of God ordained before the world," that which "the Holy Ghost teacheth" (1 Cor. ii. 7, 13). When he spoke in "the demonstration of the Spirit" his message was "not of this world." But he did not regard himself as in this respect exceptional among the believers.

The same supernatural power poured itself out upon all. Whoever gives himself in faith to Christ is "joined unto the Lord in one Spirit" (1 Cor. vi. 17); and since the glorified Jesus is himself "that Spirit" (2 Cor. iii. 17), the believer, in this union with him which is effected through faith and baptism, becomes a partaker in that supersensible life. By no laborious effort of his own, but by the inflowing of a divine power on the condition of faith on his part, he has passed from death into life, from the state of sin and condemnation and bondage into "the glorious liberty of the sons of God." "The law of the Spirit of life in Christ Jesus" has made him "free from the law of sin and death" (Rom. viii. 2). He is "a new creation" (καινὴ κτίσις) — an expression in which a divine supernatural intervention by which the subject is transformed or re-created is distinctly implied. "The love of God [God's love] is shed abroad" in his "heart by the Holy Ghost" (Rom. v. 5). In the renewal of the mind the recipient of the Spirit is enabled to know "the deep things of God," such as "eye hath not seen, nor ear heard, neither have entered into the heart of man," for they are "revealed by the Spirit" (Rom. xii. 2; 1 Cor. ii. 9 f.).

The supernatural divine character of the Spirit in the apostle's teaching is emphasised by the fact that the human spirit occupies in it a quite subordinate place. In almost all the places where "Spirit" is mentioned the reference is to the Holy Spirit or the Spirit of God, and some expositors question whether Paul recognised a spirit as an original endowment of man. This position has doubtful exegetical support, although the general analogy of the apostle's doctrine is in its favour. The sanctification of "the spirit, soul, and body" (1 Thess. v. 23), the exhortation to purify from "all filthiness of the flesh and spirit" (2 Cor. vii. 1), and the "saving of the spirit in the day of the Lord" (1 Cor. v. 5) can certainly not be referred to the divine Spirit. The subject presents difficulties which exegesis has not satisfactorily solved, and in attempting its solution it cannot proceed upon the presumption that the apostle used psychological terms with scientific exactness. In any case he does not attribute to the "natural" man, that is, the unregenerate man, a spirit ($\pi\nu\epsilon\hat{\upsilon}\mu\alpha$) in the sense in which he generally employs the term of the supernatural, life-giving energy which is not originally in man, but descends or is poured out upon him on condition of faith. It is conceded by some of those who maintain that he does not ascribe a spirit to the natural man that he sometimes adopts the popular usage, and employs the word to designate the inward motive power, as when, for example, in 1 Cor. ii. 11 a "spirit of man" is mentioned alongside the Spirit of God: "What man knoweth the things of a man save the spirit of man which is in him?"

But one cannot conclude from this passage that any religious function is assigned to the human spirit. The term Spirit in the specific religious sense in which the apostle generally employs it denotes an opposition to the "flesh," that is, to the condition of the natural man, and designates a supernatural power by which he has been exalted into a state which he could not of himself and in a natural way attain. Accordingly, Paul could, in concession to the popular usage, speak of man as having a spirit when he did not at all mean to designate the person in question as a "pneumatic" ($\pi\nu\epsilon\upsilon\mu\alpha\tau\iota\kappa\acute{o}s$), that is, one who had through faith received the heavenly gift of the divine Spirit (1 Cor. xiv. 37).* In 1 Cor. vi. 20 "spirit" should be omitted according to the most approved reading. The power of the "inward man" most closely related to the divine Spirit is the mind ($\nu o\hat{\upsilon}s$). With this man "serves the law of God" (Rom. vii. 25), but ineffectually, because of "the law in the members" which "wars against the law of the mind, and brings him into captivity to the law of sin and death" (verses 23, 24), until the Spirit of God comes to his aid, and delivers him from "this body of death." Accordingly, it is difficult from the point of view of scientific accuracy to find a function for the human spirit in this psychology.

While, however, the apostle teaches that man cannot of himself attain righteousness, even though he "delight in the law of God after the inward man," because "the law in his members" compels him to "do the evil that he would not do" (Rom. viii. 19, 23), and while he regards the divine Spirit as the only saving efficacy in this extremity, we are not justified in drawing the conclusion that he looked upon the moral-religious life of the believer as controlled by this superhuman power after the manner of a natural necessity. The words "led by the Spirit," perhaps "driven" ($\check{\alpha}\gamma o\nu\tau\alpha\iota$, Rom. viii. 14), appear to assign to this agency the initiative and doubtless an impelling function in the Christian life; but it is evident from the analogy of the apostle's teaching that, just as a voluntary appropriation of Christ is the condition of receiving the Spirit, so the subject's own exertion is the condition of the continuance of its operations in the religious life and of the final enjoyment of the eschatological blessedness at

---

* Such is the sense in 1 Cor. v. 3, 4, 5; vii. 34; xiv. 14 f.; 2 Cor. ii. 13, vii. 13; Rom. viii. 16, xii. 11.

the Parousia. The frequent expression of his anxiety for the continued spiritual welfare of his converts shows that the apostle did not regard their religious prosperity as determined once for all by their reception of the Spirit and by their entrance into fellowship with Christ through a single act of faith. The situation in the Corinthian church which called forth the first Epistle is a case in point.*

Although Paul thanks God on behalf of the believers there for the grace given them and for their enrichment "in all utterance and knowledge," and says that Christ will confirm them to the end, that they may be "blameless in the day of the Lord" (the Parousia), yet he reproves them in that they have fallen into contention and some of them even into fornication, and pointedly charges them with being "carnal" (i. 4, 8, 11, iii. 3, v. 1). Yet he declares of these brethren that they "are the temple of God," and that "the Spirit of God dwells in them" (iii. 16). The warning, "Let him that thinketh he standeth beware lest he fall" (1 Cor. xii. 13), throws upon him who has the Spirit the responsibility for a lapse plainly implied as a possibility. The apostle even includes himself among those to whom a cleansing (2 Cor. vii. 1) is necessary, and though sanctification comes from God (1 Thess. v. 23), man must work out his own salvation, through God who works in him to will and to do of His good pleasure (Phil. ii. 12 f.).

The connection between the operations of the Spirit upon believers and the mission of Christ — more specifi-

---

* It is not certain, however, that we have not here one of the paradoxes of the apostle — theoretically the control of the believer by the Spirit, the certainty of his salvation as its possessor and as one of the "elect," and practically a recognition of the necessity that he be frequently exhorted to ethical endeavour, as if the whole burden of the conflict with the flesh should not be thrown upon the Spirit, and as if, although God work within him, he must work out his own salvation "with fear and trembling."

cally his death and resurrection — has already been mentioned. It is an error, however, to suppose that the relation of Christ and the Spirit in the apostle's teaching is such that the former is conceived as only a means or instrument of the operations of the latter. On the contrary, no clear distinction is drawn between the work of the two in the life of the Christian, with the exception that with the mission of Jesus the entire spiritual economy in the world originates, and on it depends. Without his death and resurrection man could have had no true religious life, but would have remained in the darkness of spiritual death. That Jesus was originally and before he came into the world, that is, in his preëxistent state, essentially Spirit may be regarded as a premise of the apostle's Christology. It was "according to the Spirit of holiness" that the Son of God and the Son of David, that is, the Messiah, was established in the divine sonship "*with power*" by the resurrection (Rom. i. 3, 4). As "the second man the Lord from heaven," he was made a quickening or life-giving Spirit (1 Cor. xv. 45, 47). Accordingly, the functions of the Spirit in the Christian economy of salvation are ascribed to him.

The supernatural divine "life," which is the possession of the believer, and which signifies not only a moral-religious renewal in the present state of existence, but also the final triumph over death in the resurrection, is enjoyed "with" and "through" Christ (Rom. v. 17, 21, vi. 5, 8, 11, 23; 1 Cor. xv. 22), and it is "in" him that the Christian has become "a new creation" (2 Cor. v. 17). The frequent recurrence of the expression "in Christ" indicates how near to the apostle's heart lay the conviction of his and his fellow-believers' union with, and dependence on, the Lord. The Christian's liberty from the bondage of "the law of sin and death" is through "the law of the

Spirit of life in Christ Jesus"; the love of God, from which nothing can separate him, is "in Christ Jesus our Lord"; the grace of God is "given by Jesus Christ" (Rom. viii. 2, 39; 1 Cor. i. 4; Gal. ii. 4); and in him are consolation and hope and sanctification (Phil. ii. 1, iii. 3; 1 Cor. i. 2). Dr. Weiss has pointed out that Paul sometimes represents the Spirit as proceeding from Christ, and we find "Spirit of his Son" (Gal. iv. 6); "if so be that the Spirit of God dwell in you" and "if any man have not the Spirit of Christ," in the same verse (Rom. viii. 9); and "Spirit of the Lord" (2 Cor. iii. 17). In Rom. xv. 18, 19, the apostle speaks of the things that Christ has wrought by him, "through mighty signs and wonders by the power of the Spirit of God," thus representing his operation as indirect instead of direct or as himself the Spirit. Along with this conception we have an identification of Christ and the Spirit, as has been remarked (1 Cor. xv. 45; 2 Cor. iii. 17), and, as has frequently been pointed out by students of the apostle (cf. Pfleiderer, Weiss, Gunkel, and others), the conception of a mystic union of the believers with Jesus through faith and baptism in a wonderful fellowship of life (Rom. vi. 3–11; Gal. iii. 27, vi. 14), in which he "puts on" Christ, Christ is "formed in him" and he becomes with him "one Spirit" (Rom. xiii. 14; 1 Cor. vi. 17; Gal. iv. 19). This language cannot fairly be interpreted as expressing simply an ethical sympathy and fellowship with Jesus, or such an inspiration as might be induced by a devout contemplation of his example. Such an explanation does not touch the surface of this profound mysticism.

A psychological analysis may account for the apostle's state of mind, but it cannot enable us to enter into his consciousness and describe it — a consciousness which is possible only to a man of Paul's mystical nature and his absolute and ardent faith in a supernatural Christ. His own account of the union by means of an analogy with the sexual relation (1 Cor. vii. 6 f.) he must himself have regarded as an inadequate explanation of a reciprocal connection in which Jesus is conceived as imparting his life to the apostle in the mystic union with him, so that it is manifest in his mortal flesh (2 Cor. iv. 10 f.), and the sufferings and death of Christ become the sufferings and death of Paul himself, and his afflictions Christ's (2 Cor. i. 5). This great mystery of the identification of Christ with the Spirit of God (in operation, though doubtless not in person) belongs to the supernaturalistic scheme in which the apostle's conversion was the first of a series of wonders, and is due to what he himself had undergone in the transition from Judaism to Christianity. As Gunkel observes: "The first pneumatic experience of Paul was an experience of Christ." His faith in Christ as the Spirit and the source of his strength, the fountain of his religious and moral life, did not rest upon a speculative basis, but was the product of his experience, as with open face he was ever "beholding the glory of the Lord," and was "changed into the same image from glory to glory, as by the Spirit of the Lord" (2 Cor. iii. 18). What he means by the declaration that Christ had been "seen" by him (1 Cor. xv. 8), and whether or no it implied more to him than that God "revealed His Son in him," we cannot determine; but it is evident that such a sense as he had of the miraculous indwelling of Jesus and of his own mystic connection with him could belong to no one who had not a vivid and intense realisation of his personality as a living presence. The expression of his willingness rather "to be absent from the body and present with the Lord" (2 Cor. v. 8) is a word out of his heart, which reveals his love and longing for the person of his adored Master.

Gunkel's objection to Pfleiderer's view that the apostle's doctrine of the Spirit arose under the influence of his doctrine of Christ does not appear to be well taken. Is it not rather true that to the revelation of the Son of God in him and to his subsequent sense of union with him in a fellowship of quickening and of "life" are due the depth and inwardness of his conception of the Spirit? This appears to be more in accordance with the facts than Gunkel's opinion that Paul's doctrine of Christ was his "peculiar expression of what he asserts in the doctrine of the Spirit in dependence on the views of the church;" indeed this scholar himself declares that the apostle's "doctrine of Christ lay nearer to his heart" than the other, that for the primitive Christians "in the Spirit" meant "in ecstasy," while for Paul it meant "in the divine life-giving power," and that to the apostle the highest expression of his experience is, "in Christ."

It is an interesting feature of the Pauline doctrine of the Spirit that in its possession man is in the tender and beautiful relation of sonship. This is expressly declared in the words, "For as many as are led by the Spirit of God, they are the sons of God" (Rom. viii. 14). This condition is designated as one of "glorious liberty," for which "the creation" sighs in its "bondage of corruption" (verses 21 f.). If, according to the Jewish theology, even the righteous man lived in no full security, and could not free himself from the fear of the day of judgment, how much more must the sinner be tormented by the "fearful looking for" of the impending retribution. But the law having been done away in Christ, the believer is delivered from this servile fear. "Ye have not received the spirit of bondage again to fear, but ye have received the Spirit of adoption as sons, whereby we cry, Abba, Father" (verse 15). By the expression, "Spirit of adoption as sons" (πνεῦμα υἱοθεσίας) the apostle does not mean that the Spirit is the agency through which the "adoption as sons" is effected, but rather that the Spirit which the believers have received is one that is adapted to sonship or corresponds with this spiritual condition, just as in Gal. iv. 6 he says: "Because ye are sons God hath sent forth the Spirit of His Son into your hearts, crying, Abba, Father." Here the previous sonship is the condition of the sending forth of the Spirit. This agrees with the passage quoted above to the effect that the being "led by the Spirit" is a token of sonship. The condition of sonship is conceived as having been attained before the endowment with the Spirit is vouchsafed, and as to the method of its attainment the apostle leaves no doubt when he says: "But when the fulness of the time was come God sent forth His Son . . . to redeem them that were under the law, that we might receive the adoption as sons" (Gal. iv. 4 f.).

This is the divine procedure, and man's part in the transaction is defined with equal precision in the words, "For ye are all children of God by faith in Jesus Christ, for as many of you as have been baptized into Christ have put on Christ" (Gal. iii. 25 f.). This is the sonship of the Christian dispensation, and not the "adoption" which pertained to the Jews (Rom. ix. 4). The supernaturalism which in the apostle's teaching conditions the relation of the believer to God is here again apparent. The powers of the supersensible world descend upon the earthly scene at "the time appointed of the Father" (Gal. iv. 2). "The second man, the Lord from heaven," the "quickening Spirit," is the divinely appointed agent, who first by his death on the cross abrogates the law, and buys man off from its curse, and who then, on condition of faith, takes up his abode in him as a sanctifying power. Man's sonship is, then, according to the apostle's thought, not a natural, but a supernatural relationship to God. It is not a natural birthright, but a supernatural new birthright, which belongs to a marvellous scheme of atonement and faith. It would, moreover, be a gross misinterpretation of Paul to understand him to teach that Christ's miraculous mission secured sonship for all men unconditionally, so that good and bad alike can be regarded as received into this blessed relationship. Only "as many are sons of God as are led by the Spirit of God," and the Spirit is vouchsafed only to those who in faith and baptism have "put on Christ" and become "a new creation."

The recognition by Paul of the primitive-Christian ecstasy in connection with the operations of the Spirit is worthy of note. In one of the passages above referred to he says that the believers cry out in the Spirit, "Abba, Father," and in another that the Spirit itself utters this cry (Rom. viii. 15; Gal. iv. 6). If with Gunkel we construe in Rom. viii. the sixteenth verse with the preceding, the cry is a witness of the Spirit that the believers are the sons of God. From the way in which it is introduced here we may infer that it was an exclamation often heard among the Christians, that it was well known to them, and that it was a phenomenon which belonged to the ecstatic expressions whereby the supernatural presence and operations of the Spirit were manifested. Similar if not the same is the ecstasy referred to in 1 Cor. xiv. 14, where the apostle discusses the speaking with tongues: "For if I pray in an unknown tongue [literally, 'in a tongue'] my Spirit prayeth, but my understanding is unfruitful." Here "my Spirit" is doubtless the divine Spirit, which, being for the time in the possession of the believer, is called his, according to the following verse: "I will pray with the Spirit, and I will pray with the understanding also." In like manner the apostle represents the Spirit as helping the infirmities of the believers: "For we know not what we should pray for as we ought; but the Spirit itself maketh intercession for us with groanings that cannot be uttered" (Rom. viii. 26). From the supernaturalistic point of view of Paul and his contemporaries these groanings, inexpressible in words (στεναγμοὶ ἀλάλητοι), were not thought to be produced by those who uttered them in loud cries, but were regarded as expressions of the Spirit, which wrought in them, "helping" and "interceding." *

The relation of the supernatural "life" bestowed in the gift of the Spirit to the "inheritance" of the believer in the Messianic age or in the life to come is of so much importance in the apostle's teaching as to deserve more than the reference to it already made in this discussion. The "inheritance" which was promised to Abraham (the land of Canaan) was interpreted allegorically by the Jewish theologians as referring to the Messianic world-dominion, and Paul understands by it the blessedness of the Christians in the kingdom soon to be established at the second coming of Christ (Rom. iv. 13; Gal. iii. 18, 29, v. 21). To him the present possession of the Spirit and the future participation in the glory of the kingdom were so related that the latter was only a continuation of the former. The Christian now has "the firstfruits of the Spirit," and his

* "Maketh intercession" (ὑπερεντυγχάνει) does not denote a pleading before God for the believers on account of their sins. Theoretically Paul did not recognise them as sinners (see note on p. 366). The intercession is not conceived as before God in heaven, but as a praying of the Spirit within the believers, who cannot give an articulate expression to their inward state. Hence the unutterable groanings which suggest the phenomenon of "speaking with a tongue." Lipsius regards this presence of the Spirit as an assurance to the Christians of the future fulfilment of their hope. A similar office is ascribed to Christ in Rom. viii. 34. The "intercession" of Christ as the great high-priest in Heb. vii. 25 is conceived as for the salvation of the believers. The point of view is here manifestly different.

"adoption as son" is in this life only preliminary to the full fruition, and the complete "adoption" will be consummated in the age to come in "the redemption of his body" (Rom. viii. 23). In "this earthly tabernacle we groan . . . that we would be clothed upon [with the new spiritual body] that mortality might be swallowed up of life." "God who has wrought [prepared] us for this [the spiritual clothing upon] hath given us the earnest [pledge] of the Spirit" (2 Cor. v. 4, 5). Thus the present possession of the Spirit is an assurance of a still greater miracle or of a continuation of the miraculous dispensation in the "glory" ($\delta\delta\xi a$) of the coming kingdom. In that consummation the Spirit would signalise its complete triumph over the flesh in providing for the believer in the place of the earthly tabernacle a "body of glory" conformed to that of the resurrected Lord (Phil. iii. 21).

Accordingly, Paul writes to the Romans: "If the Spirit of Him that raised up Jesus from the dead dwell in you, He . . . shall also quicken your mortal bodies by His Spirit that dwelleth in you" (Rom. viii. 11). If the other well-attested reading, "on account of His Spirit dwelling in you," be adopted, the reason for the transformation, that is, the resurrection of spiritual bodies, is expressed instead of the indwelling efficient cause. The "adoption as sons" which the Christians have received, and to which the Spirit "beareth witness," renders them "heirs of God and joint-heirs with Christ," for since they suffer together, they will also be glorified together in the Parousia with a glory with which "the sufferings of this present time are not worthy to be compared" (Rom. viii. 15-17).

"Spirit" and "inheritance" belong together, and it is not strictly accurate to say as Gunkel does that "the former is the present and the latter the future participation in the kingdom of God," or with Wendt that "the Spirit is the power of supernatural life in the heavenly state of existence." The Spirit as a present possession is a "pledge" of a future in which its glory will have a fuller manifestation. It dominates both states of existence for the believer, giving him "righteousness, peace, and joy," in which the kingdom of God consists, and destined there to disclose things that eye hath not seen, or ear heard. He who has the Spirit has a "life" which in its nature is imperishable. Death has no longer dominion over him, and whether he die physically before the advent of the Lord, or survive that event, he is in any case certain to have for his new existence the spiritual body which, like that of the resurrected Jesus, will denote his triumph over the grave (1 Cor. xv. 50–54; 1 Thess. iv. 13–18). It is true that Paul sometimes speaks of the eternal life as simply a future possession (Rom. ii. 7, v. 21, vi. 22 f.; Gal. vi. 8; 2 Cor. v. 4), but had he seen no deeper than this, he would not have transcended his age, and given to the world his most fruitful interpretation of the gospel, that eternal life is inseparable from walking in the Spirit (Rom. viii. 12; Gal. vi. 8).

What, then, is this Spirit, which in the primitive church was regarded as taking such violent and compelling possession of the believers, and which in Paul's doctrine dominates the entire scheme of salvation, bears such blessed fruit of good works (Gal. v. 22 f.), and is a "pledge" of the participation of those in whom it abides in the impending kingdom of God? The apostle himself has not attempted to define it, and it would be hazardous for his students to venture where he did not presume to go. That it was a power from God bestowed upon those who had faith in Jesus; that it witnessed to their adoption as sons; that it gave "life"—the moral-religious and the eternal life; that through it the love of God was shed abroad upon the hearts of the Christians; that it would assure to its possessors a

z

spiritual body of glory when their Lord should descend with his angels at the Parousia; and that it so abounded in Jesus that "Spirit" and "the Lord" were conceived as interchangeable terms,—all this and much more we have learned from Paul. But as we cannot define God or life, so we have no data for a definition of this subtle agency. The apostle sometimes speaks of it as if he meant to ascribe personality to it, as when he says it "witnesses" with the human spirit, represents man before God, distributes gifts, and searches the deep things of God (Rom. viii. 16, 26; 1 Cor. xii. 11, ii. 10.) But that he cannot have conceived it to be a personality distinct from God and Jesus is certain, for he declares Jesus to be the Spirit, makes no distinction between the indwelling in the believer of Christ and of the Spirit, and says that amidst the diversities of the operations of the Spirit it is "the same God who worketh all in all" (1 Cor. xii. 6). That it is designated as "of God" and "of Christ" denotes that it was neither the one nor the other, but rather implies that it was a force which both could employ. May it have been conceived as the element in which God dwells, the δόξα (glory, effulgence) which surrounds Him (Ex. xxiv. 16 f.), perhaps a supersensible, fine materiality, according to the original word, "breath," "wind"—a glory which Paul regarded as communicated to the countenance of Moses (2 Cor. iii. 7), and which in his visions he may have seen on "the face of Jesus Christ" (2 Cor. iv. 6)? *

---

* In 1 Cor. xii. 4–6 Spirit, Lord (Christ), and God are mentioned in succession, but manifestly not as a "trinity" in the "immanent" sense; for in verses 10 and 11 the "operations" of verse 6 are ascribed to the Spirit. The only trinity in the case is one of manifestation. In 2 Cor. xiii. 14 occurs a similar succession of Christ, God, and the Spirit; but here there is no thought of a "coördination" of three personalities constituting a trinity. Such a conception cannot be reconciled with the apostle's frequent subordination of Christ to God and his identification of him with the Spirit (see 1 Cor. iii. 23, viii. 6, xi. 3, xv. 28; 2 Cor. iii. 17). In Rom. viii. 9–11 the Spirit is introduced

The "spiritual body" of the resurrection-state was conceived as "conformed to the body of glory," which Paul supposed Christ to have in heaven, and he speaks of a gradual transformation "into the same image from glory to glory" (2 Cor. iii. 18) from the successive "beholdings of the glory of the Lord," as if, according to Schmiedel, he may have believed in mysterious preliminary grades of the eschatological glorifying, physically effected through the indwelling Spirit in connection with the repeated visions of the Christ-manifestations. But however the question of the materiality of the spiritual substance may be decided, and it cannot be dogmatically determined, it is evident that Paul was in accord with the Old Testament and the later Jewish conception in the idea that exceptional and marvellous performances which were beyond ordinary human power were attributed to a Spirit sent forth by God, although he differs from the earlier view in limiting the supernatural agency of the Spirit to the concerns of the religious life. The root-idea seems to have been that certain spirit-forces were at the divine disposal designated as Spirits of lying, of blindness, of courage, of wisdom, for instance, which might be "sent forth" to accomplish a desired end. God sends "an evil Spirit," "the Spirit of the Lord departs from" a man, and "an evil Spirit from the Lord troubles" him (Judg. ix. 23; 1 Sam. xvi. 14-16, 23, xviii. 10). The prophets ascribe their message, which they conceived to be supernatural, to the Spirit of Yahweh. In 1 Kings xxii. 21 a personified evil Spirit "comes forth and stands before Yahweh," and offers to go as "a lying Spirit" to Ahab's prophets. In these cases a discrimination is manifest between the Spirit-

first as of God, then as of Christ, and again as of God, while in the immediate connection Christ is mentioned as signifying the same indwelling and effective agency, in accordance with the declaration: "The Lord [Christ] is that Spirit" (2 Cor. iii. 17).

agencies and God Himself. They are supernatural powers which He may command.

Paul's conception of the Spirit appears to have had its root in the Old Testament idea, and like the Hebrew writers he speaks of this superhuman power as "of God" and as "sent forth" by Him.* If he thought with the fourth evangelist that "God is Spirit," he does not say so, and certainly not that God is "the Spirit" (τὸ πνεῦμα). When he declares that Christ "is that Spirit" he does not intend to identify two personalities. It must remain uncertain whether he conceived of "Spirit" in the abstract as an indefinite power, a diffused celestial δόξα or glory of God, which could be intensified into an agency or agencies bordering on personality, and sent forth as "the Spirit" on its ministry to man. The main consideration is that he transformed the crude, popular, primitive-Christian supernaturalism in its relation to the Spirit into a profound spiritual supernaturalism whereby the entire religious and ethical life of the believer was brought into living relation to God and mystic fellowship with Christ.

He does not think the thought of Paul who does not see the powers of the supersensible world taking a controlling part in the spiritual fortunes of men, who does not recognise a supernatural atonement, a heavenly Christ, and a

* Paul's conception of the *transcendence* of the Spirit, shown in his employment of the word with reference to man only in cases of necessity, and in his referring it to God in 91 out of the 103 passages in which the word occurs, leads Holsten to the conclusion that his thought was here as in some other matters determined by other than Jewish influences. "This idea of the essence of πνεῦμα [that of its transcendence], which is not explicable out of the Jewish consciousness, and the sharp antithesis thereby produced of the nature of God and man, [the opposition of] πνεῦμα and σάρξ, which dominated Paul's thought, cannot be otherwise explained than out of the influence of the Hellenistic dualism of spirit and matter upon his thinking. But we must not fail to recognise the fact that a religious requirement, that of the necessity of sin, urged him to the adoption of this dualism." — *Die paulin. Theol.* p. 38.

Spirit whose operations dispense with the laws of moral and religious growth. It has been the fortune of this doctrine to be transformed in order to meet the varying phases of human thought. We are now in the midst of one of these transformations. A fellowship with Christ which is ethical instead of supernatural, an atonement which is only a reconciliation, a baptism which is a mere outward form, an eschatology which is an historical evolution without a catastrophic *dénoûment*, and a Spirit which works according to law constitute an emasculated Paulinism. The indomitable tendency of modern thought toward these ideas denotes our departure from the greatest of the apostles, and indicates the transient elements in a teaching which for ages swayed the thought of Christendom.

CHAPTER XIV

FAITH AND JUSTIFICATION

THE objective condition of salvation according to Paul's apprehension of it was furnished in the atonement of Christ, and is summarily expressed in the declaration that "Christ is the end of the law for righteousness to every one that believeth" (Rom. x. 4). The "end of the law" signifies neither its purpose nor its fulfilment, but its abrogation as a way of salvation or as a means of attaining righteousness. The apostle lays down no doctrine with more explicitness and emphasis than this one that righteousness is unattainable by man's own endeavour to fulfil the law (Gal. ii. 16, iii. 10), and that "if righteousness come by the law, then Christ is dead in vain," and "is become of no effect" (Gal. ii. 21, v. 4). The righteousness that is by the law and the righteousness that is by faith are placed over against each other as mutually exclusive. There is no combination of the two. The former is impossible, for "by the works of the law shall no flesh be justified," and accordingly there remains only the latter. A combination of the two methods is not implied in Rom. viii. 4, "That the righteousness of the law might be fulfilled in us who walk not after the flesh but after the Spirit." For this righteousness which the law requires, that is, the right moral-religious life, is here represented as something which "the law could not effect" (verse 3), and which is made possible only through the sacrifice of Christ, in whose death the sentence of condemnation against sin was executed. In their fellowship with his death the flesh is slain for the believers also, and the righteousness of the law can be fulfilled by them only because they "walk not after the flesh but after the Spirit," that is, through receiving the atonement by faith they have come into an entirely new relation to God, in which they are "free from the law of sin and death," and under "the law of the Spirit of life in Christ Jesus." What they could not do before they can do now by means of what God has graciously effected for them through Christ. Their righteousness is not now by the law, but by faith, through which alone according to the apostle's thought salvation can be acquired, and which is its subjective condition, man's part in its consummation, just as God's part was the offering of the atonement. In this original conception, which is a striking manifestation of the apostle's religious genius, is presented not only a new religion in contrast with Judaism, but also a new Christianity in contrast with the Christianity of the twelve apostles and the Jewish Christians in general. Their righteousness was that of the law with Christ, Paul's was that of God through Christ without the law. To them Christ was a means of reforming and fulfilling the law, while to Paul he was the "end" of it, and in him it was abrogated as a way of attaining righteousness.

In the apostle's declaration that "if righteousness come by the law, then Christ is dead in vain," the importance of the subjective condition of salvation is manifest. The proffered grace of God, the atonement, the dying of Christ to the law, to sin, and to the flesh, must all be ineffectual, if men continue in the old way to seek salvation by the fruitless attempt to fulfil the law. The grace that is offered, the atonement that is provided, must be "received," or they are "in vain." The reception of the gracious offer of God, its appropriation, is conditioned upon a receptive state of mind which the apostle designates as faith (πίστις), and to be in the right attitude toward it is to believe (πιστεύειν). The grand idea is confidence, trust in God, and especially in Him as the author of the new dispensation of grace in Christ. Accordingly, it is set over against "sight" or knowledge: "For we walk by faith, not by sight" (2 Cor. v. 7). It is not founded upon such a conviction as may proceed from experience and a wide acquaintance with the world. Paul tells the Corinthians that his preaching to them had not been "with enticing words of man's wisdom, but in demonstration of the Spirit and of power," that is, that God had wrought in him with a super-earthly power; and this was to the end that their "faith should not stand in the wisdom of men, but in the power of God" (1 Cor. ii. 5). Its support should not be in the knowledge which is of this world, but in the divine power manifested in the plan of redemption and in the religious life of the believer, as it was animated by the Spirit. Faith is trust in God in the face of and against the natural and probable, as in the case of Abraham with reference to the birth of a child in the old age of himself and his wife — a faith that was "against hope in hope." He cast himself upon "the promise of God," and was "fully persuaded that what He promised He was able to perform." This faith "was imputed to him for righteousness" (Rom. iv. 18, 21, 22). The religious character of faith as Paul apprehended it is thus manifest. God is the object of it. It is confidence in His promises, and from the specifically Christian point of view confidence in the plan of redemption consummated by the death of Christ as an atoning sacrifice and by his resurrection and ascension to glory, whereby he received the authentication of his mission from the Father. In other words, it is not a belief in a course of things naturally to be expected according to the usual order, but confidence in a consummation which one might regard as "against hope," that is, in a supernatural "life" and righteousness offered to man by the coöperation of God and Christ in the atonement.

The apostle well says of such a faith that it does "not stand in the wisdom of men, but in the power of God." Since it was "through Christ" that the atonement was effected, it is natural that faith should be directed to him, and we accordingly find "faith of Christ," "faith unto Christ," and "faith in Christ," in all which cases is implied confidence in him as "the Lord," the Messiah, and the One who is soon to come again to establish the kingdom. But faith in him is subordinate to that in God, on whom depends the fulfilment of the "promise." All faith is "vain" if Christ were not raised from the dead (1 Cor. xv. 14), and this crowning miracle of the whole scheme of redemption was the work of God. He it is from whom comes the justification of the ungodly (Rom. iv. 5), and to Him will the kingdom at last be delivered up (1 Cor. xv. 24). When we consider how near to the apostle's heart Christ was, it is not surprising that he connects faith in him and faith in God in relation to the atonement. It was in the revelation of Christ in him that his conversion consisted, and his heart went out to Jesus in grateful love on account of the great sacrifice whereby he had been delivered from the bondage of the law. Accordingly, he coördinates the "confession" of the Lord Jesus with faith in the fact that God had raised him from the dead as the two conditions of salvation (Rom. x. 9), and the love of Christ and the love of God are mentioned in connection with each other as a boon from which nothing can separate the believers (Rom. viii. 35, 39).

While the great historical events which to the apostle were fundamental, that Christ came into the world as the second Adam for a work of redemption, that in order to accomplish this work he was crucified, and that in attestation of the divine character of his person and mission God raised him from the dead, must be believed as the basis of faith in its profounder significance, still Paul did not stop in his interpretation of faith with these external facts. For him there was a deeper, a more inward faith which touched the springs of conduct, and produced the highest order of life. Accordingly, he speaks of a faith that is "unto righteousness," and says that this is a believing "with the heart" (Rom. x. 10). The historical fact of the resurrection of Christ may be so apprehended, and such an apprehension of it assures salvation (verse 9) in connection with an open confession of belief in Jesus as "Lord." Emphasis is laid upon the resurrection, not because in the apostle's doctrine of the atonement it took precedence over the death of Christ, but because it was the conspicuous event without which he would have appeared in his death to have been abandoned of God and hence not to have been the true Son and Messiah. Under this condition he could not have been at all an object of faith, there would have been in fact no atonement, and men would have been still in their sins (1 Cor. xv. 17). The faith which is "unto righteousness" is, then, of the heart (καρδία), and is something more than intellectual assent to outward facts. It is the opening of the inmost being to the reception of the salvation provided through the love of God and of Christ for men. It is a response of the sentiments to this gracious offer from the open heaven, and there go with it joy, gratitude, love, and an eager acceptance of the great boon from the heart of God.

In the recognition of Christ as Lord is implied an acknowledgment of his authority. Accordingly, there goes with faith the idea of subjection in the good sense, that is, of glad and grateful obedience as to one who commands the heart, and sways the will by love. Submission to "the righteousness of God" (Rom. x. 3), mentioned in contrast with the futile attempt to establish one's own righteousness by works, is the equivalent of faith. A similar attitude is implied in the "bringing into captivity of every thought to the obedience of Christ" (2 Cor. x. 5). Pfleiderer's discrimination should, however, here be noted, that the obedience in question is not to be regarded as the ethical disposition and effort to fulfil the law, for this is opposed to the apostle's doctrine of justification by faith, but as a devotion in absolute self-renunciation to the gracious divine will, in contradistinction to the seeking of one's own righteousness and having "confidence in the flesh" (Phil. iii. 4). This is a fulfilment of the divine will, but not of the will that commands under the law. Rather it is the compliance with the will that *gives* under the dispensation of grace, and which demands of man nothing but the trusting acceptance of the offer.

The Pauline faith is not, however, a mere passive acceptance of the grace of God in Christ, but the believer consecrates himself to God and Christ, and henceforth lives in them and they in him. To be "in Christ" is to be "a new creation." The former subjection to the law of works has passed away, or in other words the "old things" are no more, and "all things have become new" (2 Cor. v. 17). A new impulse has been imparted to the life, and with a sense of freedom, with gratitude, love, and devotion, the believer is conceived as entering upon a spiritual experience hitherto unknown and inconceivable. No longer does he feel himself alone in a doubtful conflict with the flesh and in the futile struggle to keep the law. No longer is

God to him only a lawgiver and a judge. Now rather He appears to him as the gracious One who out of love for man has offered the atonement, and sent Christ to consummate it, and who only requires faith and acceptance of the boon as the condition of the bestowal of His Spirit and the adoption of the believer into the divine sonship. That trust and devotion, love, and longing for communion, are conditions of the bestowal of the Spirit is psychologically evident, since God cannot bestow Himself upon one who turns away from Him, or stands in a neutral attitude, that is, without confidence, affection, and gratitude. Accordingly Paul finds the consummation of faith to be an intimate fellowship of the believer with God and Christ. It is difficult for us with our modes of thinking to enter into the depths of this conception. Perhaps we cannot at all think and feel with the apostle in this relation. He was a mystic in some of his deepest moods, and a mystic alone can interpret him. He thinks of himself as living in Christ and Christ in him, as if there were a blending of the two personalities in a mystic union. To him "to live is Christ" (Phil. i. 21). So completely has he appropriated the entire life of Christ that the latter's experience of death and resurrection has become his. He is identified with him in the work of atonement and in the new and glorious life which he lives in his exalted heavenly estate. "Through the law," he says, "I am dead to the law, that I might live unto God," that is, by reason of the penalty of death which the law adjudges to sin, I am dead to the law, because, through fellowship with Christ, "I am crucified with him." "Nevertheless," he continues, "I live; yet not I, but Christ liveth in me, and the life which I now live in the flesh I live by faith in the Son of God, who loved me, and gave himself for me" (Gal. ii. 19 f.).

This love and devotion of Christ call forth a responsive

affection in the believer, and in love and trust he is so united to the Saviour that he can say: "He that is joined to the Lord is one spirit" (1 Cor. vi. 17). In baptism the believer has "been planted together [with Christ] in the likeness of his death," and hence may reckon himself "as dead to sin" (Rom. vi. 5, 11). The possession of the Spirit of Christ is the evidence that one belongs to him, or is "his." "Now if any man have not the Spirit of Christ, he is none of his" (Rom. viii. 9). "Know ye not your own selves, how that Jesus Christ is in you, except ye be reprobates?" (2 Cor. xiii. 5). The Pauline faith, then, is not a belief in Christ and God as external objects of confidence, but as an internal principle of life. The apostle counts all things worthless if only he "may win Christ, and be found in him not having his own righteousness which is of the law, but that which is through the faith of Christ, which is of God by faith." He would "know him and the power of his resurrection and the fellowship of his sufferings, being made conformable to his death" (Phil. iii. 8–10).

In Paul's contest with Peter at Antioch, when he "withstood him to the face, because he was to be blamed" for not "walking uprightly according to the truth of the gospel," he laid down according to his own account of the matter in Galatians the principle at issue between himself and the Jewish Christians as to the method of salvation through Christ in these terms: "A man is not justified by the works of the law, but by faith in Jesus Christ; . . . for by the works of the law shall no flesh be justified" (Gal. ii. 16).* The word here rendered "is justified" ($\delta\iota\kappa\alpha\iota o\hat{\upsilon}\tau\alpha\iota$)

* The exact attitude of Peter toward the "gospel" of Paul is involved in uncertainty. Holsten's conjecture that when Paul first visited him in Jerusalem the latter was in accord with him as to his gospel of the uncircumcision to the gentiles is hardly supported in Gal. i. 18–24. How much Peter's "right hand of fellowship" (Gal. ii. 9) at the council denoted we cannot know, just as it is uncertain whether fear of those of the circumcision (Gal. ii. 12) was the sole

is borrowed from the judicial usage, and signifies primarily acquittal from guilt by the decree of the judge. It is accordingly to be interpreted as a recognition of the right relation of the subject in question to the law or his "righteousness." He is declared to be righteous. In the Greek translation of the Old Testament the word is employed in the same sense (Deut. xxv. 1; Job xxxiii. 32; see also Matt. xi. 29, "Wisdom is justified of her children "). In Paul's usage the word denotes the recognition on the part of God that the man to whom it is applied stands in the right religious relation to Him, is acknowledged and declared to be righteous. This must be clearly distinguished from the process of rendering one righteous, from conversion to or growth in righteousness. When the apostle declares that the doers of the law shall be justified, he has not in mind their becoming righteous through obedience, but only the fact that their obedience having been accomplished they are therefore regarded as righteous in the sight of God, just as those who fail to keep the law will be judged by it (Rom. ii. 12, 13).

This is one sort of justification, that under the law, but a sort that is not recognised by the apostle, whose entire doctrine of salvation is based upon the principle that by the works of the law justification is impossible. The sense

<small>motive for his withdrawal from table-companionship with the gentiles in Antioch. It may be true that in Peter's gospel there was "a certain freedom with reference to the Mosaic law, at least in all its forms of ritual and worship," in accordance with the attitude ascribed to Jesus toward it in Matt. ix. 9–13, xii. 1–14, xv. 1–20. He may have agreed with Paul too "in the doctrine of the death of the Messiah on the cross as an atoning substitutional death for sin"; but the idea that he drew from this Paul's radical conclusion that in his death Christ was "the end of the [whole] law," ethical as well as ceremonial, Holsten rightly rejects (*Die paulin. Theol.*, p. 44). One loses the key to the understanding of Paul's Epistles the moment one attempts to interpret them from the point of view that his doctrine of justification by faith was shared by the Jewish-Christian apostles.</small>

in which he employs the word "justify" is apparent from the example of Abraham (Rom. iv. 1-5), of whom he says that if he were justified by works, as the Jewish Christians supposed, he has whereof to boast. But Paul denies that he had anything to boast of before God, since from his point of view boasting is excluded (Rom. iii. 27). The Scripture, he declares, says that Abraham believed God, and it was counted unto him for righteousness. Here there is manifestly no process implied between the act of faith and the righteousness. The latter is simply "counted," reckoned (λογίζεται) on account of the former. The subject's faith does not make him righteous, as if the relation were one of cause and effect, but "to him that worketh not, but believeth on Him that justifieth the ungodly, his faith is counted for righteousness." The procedure by which the judgment of righteousness is pronounced is characterised by the apostle as one "of grace." When a man fulfils the law, his righteousness of works is somewhat that he is entitled to, and his reward is "of debt," while not to "impute sin" on the one hand, and to "impute righteousness" on the other, are simply to regard one as not sinful or as righteous independently of one's obedience or disobedience in relation to the moral law, and so to declare by a pure act of favour or because one has had "faith." The same word is employed to express the relation to the judge in the case of a man who by arduous effort may have fulfilled the law and in reference to another who "worketh not," and is pronounced righteous "of grace" by Him who has the prerogative of pardon, because of his faith and on account of what Christ has done for him through the atonement.*

* The exegetical contest over the word "justify" (δικαιόω) remains undecided. Like all verbs of its termination it is "factitive," that is, it denotes the production of a state in the object. But in usage it is both actually and logi-

The relation of the apostle's doctrine of justification to certain teachings of the Jewish theology is worthy of consideration. Although the Jewish theology, which Weber has set forth, is of later date so far as the documents are concerned, there is reason for believing that it was sub-

cally factitive, as Holsten has pointed out. It is not, as Dr. McGiffert asserts, of no importance for the Pauline usage that it is employed in the latter sense in the Septuagint — " to declare one righteous in consequence of a judgment." When Paul uses it in connection with his doctrine of justification by faith, it always has this meaning, and not that of actually rendering one righteous. The sinner is on account of his faith declared or reckoned (λογίζεται) righteous because of the representative atoning death of Christ. This is the so-called "forensic" or declaratory sense of the word. Righteousness is not *produced* in the sinner, but it is "reckoned" or "imputed" to him (Rom. iii. 24, 26, 28, 30, iv. 5, viii. 30, 33; Gal. ii. 16 f., iii. 8, 24). When the apostle wrote of justification by faith a process of moral-spiritual renewal does not appear to have been in his mind. Hence the absence of all reference to repentance, conversion, and forgiveness. He who has fulfilled the condition of faith is theoretically a member of Christ and an heir of the kingdom, whether he be a "Christian" in our sense of the word or not. He is one of the "predestinated," and as such is "justified," and by anticipation "glorified" (Rom. viii. 29 f.).

Dr. McGiffert's contention (*The Apostolic Age*, p. 144) that the non-forensic sense of δικαιοῦν "can be clearly shown in Rom. iv. 2–5 and 1 Cor. vi. 11" is not well sustained. The words, "What shall we say then?... if Abraham was justified by works he hath whereof to boast," are doubtless an objection anticipated from a Jewish opponent. Paul answers that there is no ground for boasting, for the righteousness of Abraham was "counted to him" because of his faith. He says nothing of Abraham's *being made* righteous; and he does not contradict himself, as Dr. McGiffert assumes, by declaring that Abraham really had ground for boasting, and yet had none, because none "before God"! In 1 Cor. vi. 11: "Ye are washed, ye are sanctified, ye are justified," etc., the fact that "justified" follows "washed" and "sanctified," and is connected with "in the Spirit," does not "make it very clear that it is to be taken in the real and not in the forensic sense." The sanctification of men of whom the apostle says that they were "carnal" and envious (1 Cor. iii. 3) means only their setting-apart as "holy," "elect," and prospectively members of the kingdom, and no more denotes a real holiness than justification denotes in his usage a real righteousness. We must distinguish in Paul between the theoretical objective righteousness "imputed" for faith and the real subjective righteousness which experience with his churches constrained him to urge upon them as an ethical *acquirement*. He leaves the two points of view unreconciled. (See p. 366.)

stantially contemporaneous with Paul, and where we find striking agreements between the two the probability is much greater that Paul borrowed from the Jewish teachers than that they borrowed from him. Now in his doctrine of justification as well as in that of the atonement the apostle shows striking accords with the theology of his people, while at the same time he surpasses it by the bold flights of his religious genius. The Jewish theologians taught, for example, that men were justified or condemned on the ground of their works, and that their standing in the judgment would be determined according to the preponderance of good works over evil or *vice versa*. The teaching, however, which is of especial interest to the present discussion is that a balance in favour of good works found on settling the account of any one might be turned to the account of a less fortunate person, so as to cover his deficiency. Thus men of distinguished piety became representatively righteous for the people in accordance with the principle of solidarity or the unity of the tribe. Now it would appear that Paul adopted the representative idea, that is, the doctrine of the imputation of righteousness. He took, however, the more radical ground that righteousness is not attainable in any degree by works, since the fulfilment of the law is impossible, and that it is on principle a matter of grace. His anthropology had an influence in determining his position on this point. The flesh with its impulses to sin rendered ineffective the utmost efforts of "the inward man." A man might, indeed, with his "mind" "serve the law of God," but the flesh, the fatal law in the members, tainted, and rendered inoperative all his endeavours, so that he could not attain a real righteousness. His sole hope, then, lay in the destruction of this power of sin and the reckoning to his account of a righteousness not of his own achievement.

In the destruction of the flesh of Christ on the cross the judgment on sin was executed for the race on the person of its representative head, the old dispensation of the law was abolished, he was "made to be sin" for mankind, and righteousness was accounted to them so far as they should come into such a spiritual relation to him that they could be included in the religious fellowship from which they might derive advantage according to the principle of solidarity. Those who will may come into this relation through faith, that is, through a sympathetic union and a fellowship of spirit and life with Christ, so that in a mystic sense they become one with him, and participate in his death and resurrection. Thus they derive advantage from his sacrifice, although his merits are not transferred to them, as, according to the Jewish doctrine, the virtues of the fathers were set over to the account of their descendants, but they are "made the righteousness of God in him" (2 Cor. v. 21).* In this new life in Christ not only

* In the term "righteousness of God" (δικαιοσύνη θεοῦ) when used by Paul in connection with his doctrine of justification by faith the genitive is not that of possession as in Rom. iii. 5, 25, 26, but that of the author. "The righteousness of God," or that which He "imputes," is set over against man's own righteousness by works, and is purely a matter of "grace," a free gift "reckoned" to men on account of faith and on the ground of the atoning death of Christ. Hence it is said to be "by faith," and "upon all them that believe" (Rom. iii. 22). It does not denote a condition effected by man through his own works, or produced in him by God, and hence in no sense a subjective state or character. It is simply an objective condition in which God is pleased "freely" to regard him as standing through faith in Christ (Gal. ii. 16; Rom. v. 15-17). If the believer's ideal dying with Christ to the flesh, his life "by faith" (Gal. ii. 20), and his possession of the Spirit, furnish to the apostle occasion and ground for ethical exhortation to "walk in the Spirit," and thus appear to relieve the hardness of the theoretically unmoral doctrine of justification, this doctrine stands upon an exegetical basis too firm to be shaken by these considerations. The ethical aspect of salvation, as Paul apprehended it, has no standing apart from the idea of the atoning death of Christ, on the ground of which men may be justified by faith, and be "reckoned" as righteous without "their own righteousness."

is the former sinful manner of living done away, but the conditions of it are removed, and it is destroyed root and branch. Accordingly, the apostle says: "If Christ be in you, the body is dead because of sin, but the Spirit is life because of righteousness" (Rom. viii. 10). The sentence of condemnation to death which the law pronounced against sin rendered it necessary that the body should die. It must die "on account of sin," and Paul conceives the body, the flesh, of the believer as "dead" through his participation in the death of Christ. But on the other hand, he has the divine Spirit, which is "life" on account of the righteousness that he has acquired through this mystic union with Christ. He enters too into a new relation with God by reason of faith in Him as the author of the gracious provision of the atonement, or more precisely, through faith in Christ as the instrument of the reconciliation offered by God. In entering into fellowship with the Son by faith the believers become themselves "children of God" (Gal. iii. 26), "and if children then heirs, joint-heirs with Christ." United with him in the mystic fellowship of his death, whereby they die to the flesh and sin, they inherit with him the blessedness of the kingdom (Rom. viii. 17).

The doctrine of Paul cannot be understood until we have fully entered into his conception of the marvellous transformation effected in the life of the believer through his fellowship with Christ by means of faith. Marvellous it must first of all be regarded. The change from the state of subjection to the law and from the dominion of the flesh was not conceived by him as effected through the moral influence of the life and teaching of Christ, through a subjection by a man's own effort and struggle of the impulses of the flesh, or in other words through such a process of growth as from the naturalistic point of view we are accustomed to see in the attainment of righteousness. This would be a salvation "by works," which Paul repudiated with all his energy as an impossibility. The chasm which separated the man "in the flesh" from the man "in the Spirit," the man under the law from the man under grace, could according to his thought be bridged only by a miracle. Repentance has no prominent place in his scheme of salvation. Instead of a "baptism unto repentance," he emphasises the baptism into the death of Christ, whereby the believer comes into the mystic fellowship of his passion, and rises "to newness of life" in the fellowship of his resurrection. After he had given the death blow to the flesh on the cross, Christ in rising from the dead entered into the glorious life of the Spirit in the supersensible world. Of this life those partake who by faith come into fellowship with him. In the flesh it is impossible to please God. But, says Paul to the Romans, "ye are not in the flesh, but in the Spirit, if so be that the Spirit of God dwell in you." Already in this state of existence the Christian is living that wonderful life which belongs to "the spiritually minded"—a life which no man can attain of himself, though he seek it with repentance and tears, but which is the "gift of God" to those who have faith. Its complete consummation is indeed in the near future, when Christ shall bring it in full glory in the kingdom, but even now "the powers of the world to come" work in the believer. The writer of Ephesians expresses the Pauline thought quite in the sense of the apostle when he says that God, "when we were dead in sins, hath quickened us together with Christ (by grace ye are saved), and hath raised us up together, and made us sit together [with Christ] in the heavenly places" (Eph. ii. 6).

Thus justification is an act of God, just as the atonement is His provision and is offered by Him for men's acceptance. The subjective factor, the act of faith, is subordinate, though indispensable, and must not be conceived as the effecting of an achievement, the gaining or attaining of righteousness. One can hardly say that Paul thought of faith as a means through which man was justified, certainly not in the sense that it was the cause and justification the effect. The righteousness in question is on account of faith, and is not regarded as a moral condition into which the subject has brought himself, or even as one that has been bestowed upon him. He simply stands in a new relation to God, a relation which can be accounted for by no natural law or psychological principle, but one that is dependent upon an arbitrary act of God. It is He who "justifies the ungodly," who performs this miracle by which a man who has not a single "good work" to his credit is declared to be justified or to be righteous because he has had faith, is "justified by faith without the deeds of the law" (Rom. iii. 28). "By faith" is set over against "by works," but is not to be interpreted in the sense of a growth by means of faith into a condition of righteousness, for no actual righteousness in the ethical sense is assumed in the case. Faith is "reckoned as righteousness," is "imputed" as such (Rom. iv. 9, 11). The disposition which faith implies, the feeling of trust and even of love, gratitude, and submission to God, does not constitute righteousness, since this in the Pauline sense is acquittal of all sin before the divine judgment. It must either be attained by keeping the law when it becomes a matter of "debt," or it must be accorded by the grace of God "without the law," that is, without obedience and on the sole condition of faith. Then it is a free "gift," and faith is reckoned as the equivalent of a complete observance of the law.

Good works are, indeed, supposed to follow, when, in fellowship with Christ and in possession of the Spirit, the believer lives under the new "law of the Spirit of life"; but they are not the condition of justification, which is accorded because of faith, or rather the faith itself is accounted as righteousness apart from works. If faith were regarded as a work of righteousness, then justification would be by works in contradiction with the fundamental principle of the apostle's soteriology. Moreover, it will not do to say that the apostle regarded justification as granted on condition of faith in view of a righteousness which faith may be assumed to initiate, and which in the future will develop into a perfect obedience; for in that case men would be justified because of an ideal or possible fulfilment of the law and not because of an actual one —a doctrine of which there is no hint in Paul's writings. The faith which is accounted as righteousness is regarded as equivalent to a complete fulfilment of the law, that is, it puts the subject in the same relation before God as is that of the man who, being under the law, is not under its "curse" because he has "continued in all things which are written in the book of the law to do them "(Gal. iii. 10).

The attempt to find an ethical basis for Paul's doctrine of justification by faith can hardly be regarded as successful. It is, indeed, offensive to the ethical sense that a man should be declared righteous who has attained no moral excellence. Accordingly, it is argued that by reason of the fellowship with Christ which faith effects justification by faith has a real ground, and the subject is actually righteousness before he is declared to be so. But the apostle says nothing of a righteousness which is *attained* by means of faith, when he treats of justification by faith. There is, indeed, a religious experience that man gains himself by coming into fellowship with Christ and ideally dying and being raised with him in baptism. The righteousness, however, of which the apostle treats in his teaching of justification is not gained, but is bestowed by God. He is the justifier (Rom. iii. 26, iv. 5). The justification is His act of grace pure and simple on the ground of the atonement made by Christ, the satisfaction of the law, the condemnation of sin in the flesh on the cross. This "free gift," this "gift by grace" (Rom. v. 15-17) consists simply in this, that the man who has actually no righteousness of his own (righteousness of his own no man can have according to Paul) is recognised as righteous by God. This justification is God's act, just as the atonement was His, was conceived and carried out by Him without man's participation. Man's relation to the justification which God effects is purely receptive. He has only to accept the proffered grace in trust and confidence in the promises of God or by faith in Him. This attitude of mind will be imputed to him as righteousness, just as it was in the case of Abraham, for "it was not written for his sake alone that it was imputed to him, but for us also, to whom it will be imputed if we believe in Him who raised our Lord Jesus from the dead" (Rom. iv. 23, 24).

In 2 Cor. v. 21, "that we might be made the righteousness of God in him [Christ]," "in him" does not relate to the fellowship of his death, the mystic union with him of Rom. vi. 3-8, but is to be interpreted in the sense of "in Christ Jesus" in Rom. iii. 24, that is, of the redemption that is in him who "was made to be sin for us." In Phil. iii. 8, 9, "that I may win Christ and be found in him, not having my own righteousness," the latter clause is not connected with the former in the sense that the apostle's righteousness results from being found (at the Parousia) in Christ. Rather he says that his righteousness is that "which is of God by faith." Then he goes on to say, "that

I may know him and the power of his resurrection and the fellowship of his sufferings, being made conformable to his death, if by any means I might attain unto the resurrection of the dead," as if the deeper communion with Christ and the mystic fellowship were conceived as a progress in Christian experience beyond the stage of justification and as necessary to the attainment of the resurrection of the dead. In Rom. viii. 1 f. and 2 Cor. v. 17 the apostle is not considering justification by faith, but the condition of the believer in the fellowship of Christ and under "the law of the Spirit of life." Justification as God's act is negatively the non-imputation of their sins to men (2 Cor. v. 19), which is equivalent to forgiveness. Satisfaction for sin having been rendered on the cross, forgiveness is not prominent in the apostle's thought. In fact the word is not employed in the four great Epistles. Sin is simply not charged against the man who accepts and appropriates the atonement in faith in God's promise. He then stands in an entirely new relation to God, is free from the condemnation of the law, and is regarded as if he had never transgressed. He has received the reconciliation, and has "peace with God" and joy in Him (Rom. v. 1, 11), and may receive the Spirit and the adoption as son.

While, however, justification is not accorded on the ground of attainment in the moral-religious life, that is, on account of such an appropriation of the spirit and life of Christ as furnishes an ethical basis for it, it is not to be regarded as a transaction between God and man apart from Christ. The subject of justification is on the contrary regarded as holding a relation to Christ which is indispensable to the result. In the first place, he is justified only because he by faith comes under the dispensation of grace which, while originating with God, was made possible by the sacrifice of Christ. He is liberated from the law and from the fruitless attempt to attain a righteousness of his own by obedience to its requirements, and this deliverance was effected for him through Christ who on the cross became "the end of the law to every one that believeth." Accordingly, the apostle reminds the Romans that they "are become dead to the law by the body of Christ." Through the death of Christ the obligation to the law was representatively fulfilled for all who believe. It is on this ground, that is, on the ground of the relation of the believers to Christ into which they come by faith, that justification is accorded. While as the representative head of the human race he died for all, his death is effective for justification only to those who believe. For them "that is dead wherein they were held" (Rom. vii. 6), and they have entered into a new relation with God in which righteousness is not to be acquired, but is "imputed," faith being its equivalent, "The law hath dominion over a man as long as he liveth."

The believer having died with Christ to the law is now free from it, and in this freedom he is justified, that is, declared to be righteous, accounted as such, because he is now in a relation to God in which righteousness is a matter of "grace" and not of "works." Accordingly, the apostle declares that "through the law" he is "dead to the law" (Gal. ii. 19), that through the requirement of the law that the penalty of sin is death, he, having died ideally with Christ, is dead to it. Now he is in the liberty wherewith Christ has made him free (Gal. v. 1), having been "bought with a price" (1 Cor. vii. 23). Along with this new relation there go certain ethical obligations, and a mode of life is required, in other words, "works" are demanded, and the believer is exhorted to "serve in newness of the spirit and not in the oldness of the latter," and to "bring forth fruit unto God" (Rom. vii. 4, 6). If the believer is dead to the law, it is that he may "live unto God" (Gal. ii. 19). He is required not to "let sin reign in his mortal body, that he should obey it in the lusts thereof" (Rom. vii. 12). But this ethical life, which is demanded as alone in conformity with the new relation to God, should not be regarded as the ground of justification. Faith alone was its ground, and it was "imputed for righteousness." As believers the Christians become recipients of the Spirit, and enter upon a life in which, indeed, the supersensible agencies, "the powers of the world to come," work in them, but in which they too must watch and work under a sense of the highest moral obligation. They must "obey from the heart that form of doctrine which was delivered to them" (Rom. vi. 17). They may be "justified by faith," and the "righteousness of the law is thereby fulfilled in them," while they "walk not after the flesh, but after the Spirit."

In accordance with the fundamental idea of the doctrine of justification, that the righteousness which the believer obtains is not of his own desert, the apostle calls it "the righteousness of God." "The gospel of Christ," he says, "is the power of God unto salvation to every one that believeth, . . . for therein is revealed the righteousness of God from faith to faith" (Rom. i. 16, 17)—"from faith" so far as the justification proceeds from faith (Gal. ii. 16), and "to faith" so far as the proclamation of the gospel leads to faith. This righteousness of God is not that which avails before Him, or that is acceptable to Him, or that He produces with their coöperation by an influence exerted upon men, but that of which He is the author, originator, and bestower, and of which they are the recipients on condition of faith. This doctrine is clearly expressed in the declarations that God "is the justifier of him who believeth in Jesus," that "to him that worketh not but believeth on Him who justifieth the ungodly, his faith is counted for righteousness," and that "God imputeth righteousness without works" (Rom. iii. 26, iv. 5, 6). The words: "The righteousness of God which is by faith in Jesus Christ unto all (εἰς πάντας) them that believe" (Rom. iii. 22), denote that the source of the righteousness is in God, from whom it proceeds to the believer by the divine decree or by imputation. In Rom. x. 3 this righteousness is contrasted with that which men seek to acquire and possess as "their own," and in Phil. iii. 9 it is more precisely designated as "the righteousness which is of God by faith." The meaning is not, however, that God communicates to man the quality of His own being known as righteousness, nor that He produces an activity in him which leads to his attainment of a righteousness, which would then be to a degree "his own" in opposition to the ground-principle of the Pauline doctrine of justification. When the apostle says that on account of Christ's having been made to be sin for men they "are made the righteousness of God in him" (2 Cor. v. 21), he means that by reason of the atonement God attributes righteousness to men — a righteousness which is His or of Him in the sense that He declares it of the man who has faith, and regards him as standing in a relation to Him in which his trespasses are not "imputed" to him. The act of justification is not the creation of a condition, but the declaration and recognition of a relation. This relation has been made possible through the atonement of Christ, and is one of reconciliation, so far as the believer has accepted the proffered grace. On God's part he is recognised as through Christ released from the law and from penalty. On the believer's part he has "peace with God," and regards himself as "saved from the wrath through him" by whose "blood" he has been "justified" (Rom.

v. 1, 9). In this new relation the Christian life is supposed to take its course under the guidance and inspiration of the Spirit during the brief time which will elapse before Christ comes to establish his kingdom and claim his own.

But to the question whether he who has been justified by faith and has received the adoption as a son of God is certainly saved, that is, safe against the approaching "day of the Lord" and sure of the "inheritance" in the kingdom, there appear to be conflicting answers. On the one hand, the believers have the witness of the Spirit that they are adopted as sons of God, and as sons they are declared to be "heirs of God" and "joint-heirs with Christ" (Rom. viii. 16, 17). In other words, having the "earnest of the Spirit," they are certain of a participation in the coming "glory" of the kingdom or of "salvation." Moreover, the believers are elected of God, "God's elect," and as such are assured of being "Christ's at his coming." For "whom He did predestinate them He also called, and whom He called them He also justified, and whom He justified them He also glorified" (Rom. viii. 30). To be "glorified" is to share in the "glory" ($\delta\acute{o}\xi a$) of the coming kingdom, or to be "saved from the wrath," and so certain is it that the believers will have this great fortune that the apostle speaks of it as an accomplished fact, since in the purpose of God it is already effected. The divine love which "foreknew" and "predestinated" the Christians will surely gather them to the glorious inheritance prepared for them from the foundation of the world; and from this love both of Christ who died for them and of God who established the great atonement nothing can separate them, not tribulation or persecution or famine or sword, not death or life or the demonic "principalities and powers" or things present or things to come (Rom. viii. 35, 38, 39).

On the other hand, nothing can be more evident than that the apostle in other passages employs expressions which denote anything but a certainty that those who have been "justified" will surely be saved. The Christian life is depicted as a course to be run, a conflict with opposing powers, a struggle against the flesh, a warfare in which the issue is doubtful, since the efforts required depend upon the disposition and choice of the believers themselves. The "life" of the believers, their moral-religious life in the present age as well as their eschatological life, that of the kingdom, or their salvation, is represented as dependent on their mortifying, that is, destroying, the "deeds of the body." If they live after the flesh they will "die." In this struggle against the flesh they have, indeed, the aid of the Spirit, but "through the Spirit" they must themselves slay the flesh (Rom. viii. 13). Accordingly, they are exhorted to present their "bodies a living sacrifice, holy, acceptable unto God," and following this exhortation is a long series of injunctions requiring a great variety of "works," the crowning one of which is love, which "is the fulfilling of the law" (Rom. xii. xiii.). Even believers, who in the early portion of the Epistle are represented as "elected" to salvation, as sons and heirs of God, are here exhorted to "cast off the works of darkness and put on the armour of light," as if their spiritual fortune depended on their personal achievement. The conditions in the Corinthian church which the first Epistle indicates show that believers, the elect of God, are not so secure in their position as not to fall away and require apostolic admonition and discipline. Their "contentions" denote anything but the prevalence of "brotherly love," and there was one case at least of a sexual relation which the apostle felt called upon to condemn without qualification (1 Cor. i. 11, v. 1 f.). Exhortations to the Thessalonians regarding the same matters show that the believers who had been theoretically justified "without works" must carry on the old, endless conflict with the flesh, and be watchful as to how they "ought to walk and to please God" (1 Thess. iv. 1-5). Even the apostle himself acknowledges that he has to "fight," and "keep under his body," and "bring it into subjection." The "incorruptible crown" must be "obtained," and only he "that striveth" will gain it (1 Cor. ix. 24-27).*

* An interesting aspect of the apostle's doctrine of sin is presented in his teaching regarding the relation to it in which he theoretically regarded the believers as standing. For his own part, he expresses no consciousness of sin from the time of his conversion, and no sense of the daily need of a petition for the divine forgiveness implied in the Lord's prayer. With the "old things" that are passed, the old sinful life, he has broken forever, and leaves them behind (2 Cor. v. 17; Phil. iii. 12). He is a "new creation," and being "in Christ," he knows no longer anything of the burden of "condemnation" (Rom. viii. 1). He regarded his fellow-believers from the point of view of his own consciousness of "life" in the Spirit, so far at least as his *theory* of their religious state was concerned. They were "dead to sin," and having been "made free" from it, they "became servants of righteousness" (Rom. vi. 2, 18). In ideally dying with Christ (Rom. vi. 3, 8, 10) they "crucified the flesh with its affections and lusts" (Gal. v. 24). They are not "in the flesh, but in the Spirit," are "led" by it, while it bears witness to them that they are "the children of God" (Rom. vii. 5, viii. 9, 14, 16). Such expressions lend support to the supposition that Paul's missionary preaching was religious rather than ethical, that its emphasis was placed on the mystic effects of baptism, on "sanctification," and on "justification" (1 Cor. vi. 11). His expectation of the immediate coming of Christ to receive the "justified" believers into the kingdom may have disturbed his perspective of the course of moral struggle which actually lay before his churches. Hence the ethical-religious paradoxes. The Corinthians, whom he rebukes for their moral delinquencies, are declared to be "enriched in all utterance and all knowledge," and to "come behind in no gift." God will "confirm them blameless in the day of Christ" (the Parousia). They are "the temple of God" (1 Cor. i. 4-8, iii. 16, 17). These morally very censurable men are religiously "sanctified in Christ Jesus, called to be saints" (1 Cor. i. 2). The "forensic" character of their justification is thus apparent. That they were "puffed up" in their sense of religious security is not surprising (1 Cor. v. 2). The fact that doctrinally Paul made no provision for the sins of believers shows that he took little account of sin as a

Notwithstanding, moreover, that the possession of the Spirit is an assurance of the resurrection (Rom. viii. 11), the apostle declares to the Philippians that the resurrection is an attainment which yet lies before him, and exhorts them to work out their own salvation (Phil. iii. 12, ii. 12). Thus in practice "works" come to their rights at last in a doctrine which theoretically maintained justification by faith without them. The validity of works in the judgment is as much a fundamental teaching of the apostle as is justification without them. God, "the justifier of the ungodly" through faith, "will render to every man according to his deeds" (Rom. ii. 6). Although merit is vigorously repudiated, it is also acknowledged (1 Cor. ix. 17). Before the judgment-seat of Christ "every one will receive the things done in his body, according to that he hath done, whether it be good or bad" (2 Cor. v. 10). There is peril lest the Christian who has come into the liberty of Christ lapse into the old bondage, and he must watch and struggle in order that he may "stand fast" (Gal. v. 1). To the Philippians the apostle says: "Those things which ye have both learned and received and heard and seen in me, do" (Phil. iv. 9). If "the righteousness that is by faith" is without an ethical basis, this is abundantly supplied for that course of religious experience

condition from which those could need to be delivered who had once been "justified." The atonement is not applied to them. Faith saves once only, and he who through it has become a "new creation" is not conceived as again needing this salvation. Paul can hardly have thought that any one of his believers would be finally rejected when Christ should come. The spirit of even the incestuous man was to be "saved in the day of the Lord." God would not suffer the Christians to be "tempted above that which they were able" (1 Cor. x. 13). The appearance of all believers "before the judgment-seat of Christ" (1 Cor. iv. 5; 2 Cor. v. 10) does not imply that the condemnation to "perishing" would fall upon any one of them. This "heaven-storming idealism" was not shaken by the apostle's experience of the moral delinquencies of his converts, which he did not fail to reprove with due energy.

which the apostle conceived as lying between the theoretical imputation of righteousness and the judgment of the Parousia. The relation to God implied in "justification by faith"—and it must be borne in mind that there is only a relation in the case—places the subject in a situation of freedom from the law and its penalty, of arbitrary separation from his past life, in which he may, as a child of God and a possessor of the divine Spirit, pursue a course of development subject to all the ethical principles and requirements.

The dependence of the entire theory of justification by faith upon the apostle's doctrine of the atonement is manifest. Without the theoretical satisfaction of the law, the payment of the penalty of sin, the buying off of the sinner from "the curse of the law," there would be no basis for a justification by faith, the non-imputation of trespasses, the declaring of a man to be righteous without works, or his establishment in the same relation to the law in which he would have been if he had actually fulfilled its requirements. Accordingly, the validity and permanent value of the doctrine must be questioned by any one who is not convinced that the Pauline representative atonement accords with the facts of human nature and experience. To one who believes in the continuity of character, and who cannot accept the teaching that, on condition of faith in the doctrine that another has suffered for his sins and given his soul for him, his life can be arbitrarily severed at the point where that faith emerges, and the consequences of his past acts annulled, the theory of justification by faith must appear as a speculation which is not to be taken seriously. To the apostle, however, it was not an empty form, because he took the doctrine of the atonement very seriously, and for him it was a fundamental proposition that if righteousness were attainable by works,

"Christ is dead in vain" (Gal. ii. 21). Yet, as we have seen, he could not in practice dispense with works, and could construe the judgment upon no other basis. Every reader of his Epistles knows with what intense solicitude he watched over his converts to see that they did not come short of a righteousness by works. How he reconciled the contradictory propositions, if he attempted their reconciliation at all, we do not know. To us they constitute one of the antinomies of his thought. Their reconciliation is, however, of slight importance to those who construct their ethics upon the recognised principle of the continuity of character and upon the facts of human experience, and who accept as the basis of their moral philosophy the good Pauline doctrine that judgment will be rendered "to every man according to his works."

CHAPTER XV

ETHICS

THAT Saul of Tarsus, born of Jewish parentage and educated in the Jewish traditions and Scriptures, should, as the Christian Paul, be a man of profound ethical convictions and earnest ethical purpose, is in the nature of the case to be expected. It is not, however, to be looked for that a man of his occupations, a missionary, preacher, bishop of souls, engaged in a contest with Jewish Christianity, persecuted and imprisoned, should, in the letters written to the churches to meet special exigencies, formulate an ethical system. When we consider, moreover, that his predominant interest was religious, and that, in view of his expectation of the early termination of the course of "the present age" by the coming of Christ to judgment, the salvation of men, or their preparation for entrance into the kingdom whose establishment would introduce the eagerly expected "age to come," was the one matter of most urgent moment, we shall not be surprised to find his ethics subordinated to his soteriology. The soteriological interest culminates in the doctrine of the Spirit, which must be taken into account in the discussion of the apostle's ethics. The Spirit is a supernatural power, which he believed to come to the aid of the natural faculties of men and to enable them to compass a moral-religious life otherwise unattainable. This teaching is founded upon his doctrine of Christ, in whose death he saw the end of the law, the destruction of the flesh, the overthrow of the power of sin, an opportunity for all who would accept the atonement by faith to sever themselves from their former life and all its consequences of penalty and shame, to be declared righteous or justified by faith, and to begin a new spiritual existence under "the law of the Spirit of life." The righteousness which they could not attain of themselves by "works" would thus be "imputed" to them on account of their faith, and coming into mystical fellowship with Christ in baptism they would, in his indwelling presence, possess the Spirit, the "pledge" of all that the love of God could bestow.

The Spirit bestows "gifts." "To one is given by the Spirit the word of wisdom, to another the word of knowledge, . . . to another faith, . . . to another gifts of healing, . . . prophecy, divers kinds of tongues" (1 Cor. xii. 6–11). It "sheds abroad the love of God" in the heart of the believer. It is the Spirit of adoption as a son, and bears witness with the spirit of the Christian that he is the son of God, who walks in the Spirit, is impelled by the Spirit, serves God in the Spirit, and is the temple of the Holy Ghost (Rom. v. 5, vii. 6, viii. 14–16; 1 Cor. vi. 19; Gal. v. 25). The subjection of the entire life of the believer to the influence of the Spirit — a teaching original with Paul and distinguishing his pneumatology from that of the Jews and the primitive Christians generally — results in attributing to the Spirit certain ethical qualities and achievements in the believers which were not by his contemporaries regarded as of supernatural origin.

This ethical point of view is not free from difficulties and from inconsistencies which are not easily reconciled. The apostle's recognition of a moral ability in the natural man denotes the acceptance of a principle fundamental in any ethical view of human life. Men possess by nature an insight into "that which may be known of God," it being "shown unto them" in "the things that are made," so that "the wrath of God is revealed against all ungodliness and unrighteousness of men." "The gentiles, who have not the law," "show the work of the law written in their hearts, their conscience also bearing witness and their thoughts accusing or else excusing one another." Though they go far astray, yet they know "that they who commit such things are worthy of death" (Rom. i. 18–20, 32, ii. 14). The "conscience" of the natural man and his knowledge of God through "the things that are made" render him "without excuse" for his moral delinquencies (Rom. i. 20, ii. 1). How much more the Jew, who has the great "advantage" that to him "were committed the oracles of God." Yet of both Paul declares that it is impossible that they should be acceptable to God with their utmost ethical striving. Righteousness by "works" is unattainable. There is no recognition of such a righteousness in the theoretical ethics of the apostle. On the contrary, it is emphatically and repeatedly repudiated (Rom. iii. 20; Gal. iii. 11). The two propositions, that man possesses an ethical capacity which renders him "without excuse" for not attaining righteousness, and that with the most conscientious employment of it he cannot compass such an attainment, are not easily reconciled. Equally confusing to the ethical judgment are the two propositions that "as many as sin without law (*i.e.* without the explicit Mosaic code) shall also perish without law," and that where this law, which "*worketh* wrath," is not, "there is no transgression," and "sin is not imputed" (Rom. ii. 12, iv. 15, v. 13). Before the law was given, "sin was in the world," and men "without the law" had the accusing conscience, yet sin was not "imputed." Sin exists, and calls down the divine "indignation and wrath," and yet it is not reckoned as sin. An express recognition and imputation of it, however, appear to be declared in the teaching that its penalty, death, "reigned," and wrought its frightful ravages from Adam to Moses "even on those who had not sinned after the similitude of Adam's trangression" (Rom. v. 14).

The radical departure from the Old Testament ethical point of view denoted by the teaching that man cannot attain a righteousness of his own, must be regarded as a defect in the ethics of the apostle. Its result in those who receive it can be nothing else than a moral discouragement and a paralysis of the moral powers. One cannot without mockery exhort men to strive for the unattainable. The direct relation of the moral agent to God, which is such a hopeful feature of the Old Testament ethics, is obscured in the ethics of Paul, in which the law stands like an inexorable fate between God and man, demands the avenging divine wrath against the sinner in satisfaction of its claims, and forbids the extending of the hand of mercy, until through an acceptance of the sacrifice of Christ a way is opened for the granting of pardon. The Old Testament ethics had a great advantage in the fundamental presuppositions, that the law, instead of being "given that sin might abound," was given that it might be obeyed, and that obedience was within the ability of the subject. We cannot too highly estimate the vast ethical encouragement and inspiration which belong to such a conception of man's moral relation to God as is expressed in the following: "For the Lord will again rejoice over thee for good as He rejoiced over thy fathers, if thou shalt hearken unto the voice of the Lord to keep His commandments, . . . and if thou turn unto the Lord with all thy heart and with all thy soul." The commandment is not so high that it cannot be obeyed, or so far off that it cannot be apprehended. "It is not in heaven that thou shouldst say, who shall go up for us to heaven, and bring it unto us, . . . neither is it beyond the sea, . . . but the word is very nigh unto thee, in thy mouth and in thy heart, *that thou mayest do it*" (Deut. xxx. 1, 2, 10-15). One cannot read far in the Old Testament without meeting with expressions of ethical courage and strains of hope and of joy in moral victory. The moral achievement is assumed as a matter of course, and is attended by the blessedness of dwelling in the divine presence. "Who shall abide in Thy tabernacle?" asks a psalmist; and the confident answer is, "He that walketh uprightly, and worketh righteousness" (Ps. xv. 1, 2). It is assumed that he who knows "the path of life" is able to walk in it; and if he grope and stumble, God will show him the path, and "in His presence is fulness of joy" (Ps. xvi. 11). The rewards of the Lord are according to one's own righteousness and "the cleanness of one's hands" (Ps. xviii. 20)—a most salutary ethical point of view if the ethics of reward is to be at all recommended, but one which Paul could not approve, who censures the Jews for "going about to establish their own righteousness" with "a zeal of God, but not according to knowledge" (Rom. x. 2, 3). In the Hebrew morals the moral agent finds encouragement in the divine forgiveness, when he is despondent in view of his imperfect achievement. "I said, I will confess my transgressions unto the Lord, and Thou forgavest the iniquity of my sins" (Ps. xxxii. 5). This relation of man to God could hardly be acknowledged in the Pauline scheme, for there the non-imputation of sin was due to the fact that sin had been atoned for by the sacrifice of Christ, and its penalty thus paid. Whoever had faith was acknowledged on account of this as righteous, and his past sins were not "imputed." The love of God indeed was behind the scheme of atonement, but it is manifest that the relation of man to a God who forgives is radically different from that to a God who accepts one as righteous "without works," because one has faith in an atonement which has satisfied the law.

Against the Pauline doctrine of a supernatural righteousness for which faith is "imputed," and which is expressly declared not to be attained by works and not to be of "merit," must be urged the objection on moral grounds that it presupposes a breaking of the ethical continuity of life. If in the course of human experience such a righteousness were at all possible, its possessor would have been violently transferred from the natural condition of moral struggle and endeavour, in which he was neither wholly good nor altogether bad, into a supernatural state of complete righteousness, which he had done nothing to acquire except to perform an act of faith.

The genesis of this ethical teaching must be sought in related doctrines of the apostle. One of its roots undoubtedly strikes into his doctrine of the Flesh — the ethical dualism of flesh and Spirit, which is certainly of Hellenistic origin. According to this teaching, man could not attain righteousness by reason of the strength of the evil impulses of the flesh. The sin that dwells in him impels him to do what he hates. Despite his delight in the law of God after the inward man, the law in his members brings him "into captivity to the law of sin and death" (Rom. vii. 14–25). "The mind of the flesh is enmity against God," is not subject to His law, "and cannot be." The natural man is "in the flesh," and "the motions of sin which are by the law work in his members to bring forth fruit unto death" (Rom. vii. 5, viii. 7). To the apostle there was no natural way of deliverance from this condition. By the law came the knowledge of sin. It was given that sin might abound, and was a provocation to transgression (Rom. vii. 7–12). It could not effect man's salvation, because it was "weak through the flesh" (Rom. viii. 3). Speaking of himself for the natural man, Paul says: "Sin taking occasion by the commandment wrought in me all manner of concupiscence. For without the law sin was dead. For I was alive without the law once; but when the commandment came, sin revived, and I died" (Rom. vii. 8, 9). Since, then, man could not save himself by his own ethical striving on account of the flesh, and since the law was ineffective for the same reason, there remained only a resort to a supernatural righteousness, and the apostle's resort to this must be regarded as a logical step from his premises. When all other means fail, the divine powers must be invoked.

Another root of the ethical principle in question lies in the apostle's Christology. He could never have become a Christian had he seen in Christ nothing more than an ethical and religious teacher who had died as a martyr to his convictions. It was the followers of a Christ "according to the flesh" whom he persecuted. The Christ "according to the Spirit," whom he knew in and after his conversion, was a supernatural being, who in his death and resurrection became the author of a supernatural salvation by putting an end to the old order of sin, the law, and death and introducing the divine order of "the Spirit of life." A Christ who did not effect a supernatural atonement, and become the author of a supernatural righteousness, could not have won his devotion and service. To him Christ was the divinely appointed agent for the accomplishment of a salvation which all other agencies, man's own "mind," which "serves the law of God," the law, and the prophets, could not effect. "What the law could not do in that it was weak through the flesh, God, sending His own Son in the likeness of sinful flesh, condemned sin in the flesh, that the righteousness of the law might be fulfilled in us, who walk not after the flesh, but after the Spirit" (Rom. vii. 3, 4). In order to effect man's deliverance from the law, the righteousness of which was unattainable by his utmost ethical endeavour, its claims must be satisfied by the payment of a ransom. Accordingly, to the apostle, Christ was in his death a "propitiation through faith in his blood" (Rom. iii. 25), and on the cross he redeemed men (ἐξηγόρασεν, bought them off) from the curse of the law (Gal. iii. 13). The old dispensation with all its great moral precepts and its splendid examples of righteousness had for him little ethical or religious significance. At the best it was a provisional arrangement, "a schoolmaster to bring us to Christ, that we might be justified by faith," since justification by works was out of the question. Notwithstanding the fact that he finds in Abraham the original example of righteousness by faith, he regards pre-Christian mankind as "shut up under the law unto the faith which should afterwards be revealed" (Gal. iii. 23, 24). The ministry of the law was a ministry of servitude, of condemnation, and of death, notwithstanding the declaration that it is "spiritual," "holy and just and good" (Rom. viii. 12, 14). "Life," in the apostle's sense of the word, that supernatural endowment of the man who is justified by faith, and possesses the divine Spirit, the law could not bestow. "For," he says, "if there had been a law given which could have given life, verily, righteousness should have been by the law" (Gal. iii. 21). It is evident, then, that if Christ did not come to transcend the law, he could have for the apostle no spiritual function and no soteriological office. His entire faith in Christ was staked upon a belief in him as the bearer of a message of supernatural righteousness. If he could not hold to the latter, he must abandon the former. Accordingly, with all his heart and with all the energy of a profound conviction he held to the belief in the doctrine that righteousness could not be acquired by ethical effort, but must be the gift of God through Jesus Christ. His reasoning was from the cross to this ethical principle. If there were no supernatural righteousness, then the cross was vanity and a symbol of humiliation, since it had no significance if the old ethical order stood, and men could become righteous by works. Salvation is by. "grace"; and, exclaims the apostle, "I do not frustrate the grace of God, for if righteousness come by the law, then Christ is dead in vain" (Gal. ii. 21). Out of this Christology the ethics of the Spirit was a natural and necessary growth.

A third root of this ethics of supernatural grace extends into the apostle's soteriology. Here the entire scheme is supernatural. The kingdom is soon to be ushered in by the miraculous descent of the Lord Christ from heaven. The matter demands haste. There is no room for historical development and the perfection of a race through ages of evolution. The fortune of the individual is in question. The kingdom is for the "elect" whom God "predestinated to be conformed to the image of His Son" (Rom. viii. 29). This personal factor gives a point and intensity to the apostle's doctrine of salvation which we can in our conditions with difficulty appreciate, but which we can see reproduced in the fervour and strained emotion of those people who still believe in the immediate personal coming of Christ with the apocalyptic accompaniments of the primitive-Christian doctrine of "the last things," and who gather in "ascension-robes" to meet him as he descends. It is hardly to be supposed that the apostle believed that a man in ethical striving after a righteousness by works could do no virtuous act, and could not achieve righteousness to any degree. This could not have been his opinion, unless we have here another of the many antinomies of his thought. The absolute rejection of righteousness by works is certainly irreconcilable with the declaration that some gentiles not having the law "do by nature the things contained in the law" (Rom. ii. 14) — an expression in which the attainment of complete legal righteousness appears to be implied. It is also not in accord with his assertion regarding himself that prior to his conversion, when the only "justification" that he could have pleaded was that "by works," he was, "touching the righteousness which is in the law, blameless" (Phil. iii. 6). The unqualified declaration that "by the works of the law shall no flesh be justified" (Gal. ii. 16) hardly allows the supposition that when he made it he had reference only to the mass of men, and believed that he himself and some others constituted exceptions to the principle. In the same verse he includes himself among those who have "believed in Jesus Christ, that they [we] might be justified by faith and not by the works of the law."

But whether we have here an unresolvable paradox in the apostle's thought or not does not concern our immediate purpose, which has to do with the fact that in all his soteriological declarations he proceeds upon the principle that a supernatural righteousness is alone adequate. With respect to salvation or admission into the kingdom which Christ was soon coming to establish, he could not have allowed that any man could attain this great fortune through a righteousness gained by his own ethical endeavour. A partial fulfilment of the law on the part of one to whose credit might be placed good intentions and an honest, earnest purpose, would not avail along with forgiveness of the delinquencies. Of such a salvation, although it abounds in ethical encouragement, the apostle gives no intimation. When the heavenly kingdom should come in its glory and purity, its gates would only open to the perfect — to those who possessed "the righteousness which is of God," and whom "the law of the Spirit of life in Christ Jesus had set free from the law of sin and death." The apostle's ideal with respect to his elect believers was that God should "establish their hearts unblamable in holiness" before Him . . . "at the coming of our Lord Jesus Christ with all his saints" (1 Thess. iii. 13). They are exhorted to a "perfecting of holiness in the fear of God" (2 Cor. vii. 1); and in Col. i. 28 his thought with reference to the spiritual-ethical preparation for the kingdom is expressed by the writer in the words: "Warning every man and teaching every man in all wisdom, that we may present every man perfect in Christ Jesus." The ordinary ethical endeavour of men to attain a righteousness by works, in which along with a necessarily imperfect obedience there must always remain something to be forgiven, was evidently not adapted to this soteriology, whose fundamental condition was the complete atonement for sin effected on the cross and a corresponding perfect righteousness "imputed" in return for faith on the part of those who accepted the great sacrifice.*

* Paul took quite literally, more literally than the prophets or Jesus, the declaration that he was "cursed" who "continueth not in all things which are written in the book of the law to do them" (Gal. iii. 10). He was in accord with the Old Testament idea in the doctrine that only a righteous people should inherit the kingdom of the Messiah. Compare Isa. xi. 9: "They shall not hurt or destroy in all my holy mountain; for the earth shall be full of the knowledge of the Lord as the waters cover the sea," and see Isa. lxv. 17. Not only the believers for whom the kingdom was prepared should come into "the glorious liberty" of the age to come, but "the whole creation" should be delivered from its groaning and travailing and its "bondage of corruption" (Rom. viii. 19–22). To the question which Josephus mentions as having agitated the Jewish parties, whether the righteousness suitable to the Messianic kingdom would be effected by man himself or by God, Paul could only answer, by Him who "maketh one vessel to honour and another to dishonour"

The interruption through a supernatural principle of the natural course of ethical development which is a fundamental premise of the apostle's teaching is illustrated in his exposition of the new life "in the Spirit" into which the believer is assumed to enter, when having been justified by faith he attains the divine sonship. For him there is deliverance from the haunting presence and accusation of his past misdeeds. His faith has been reckoned or "imputed" to him for righteousness, and he now stands toward God in a relation of "justification" which has no natural connection with his moral conduct. The relation of cause and effect in the ethical and spiritual domain is entirely ignored. This doctrine is explicitly laid down in the words: "There is now therefore no condemnation for those who are in Christ Jesus, who walk not after the flesh but after the Spirit. For the law of the Spirit of life in Christ Jesus hath made me free from the law of sin and death" (Rom. viii. 1, 2). In the ethical condition in which a man endeavours to attain by struggle and self-conquest a righteousness of his own, a righteousness which is "according to works," and is a matter of "merit," he is under "the law of sin and death." This kind of righteousness being conceived by the apostle as unattainable, that is, as not meeting the requirements of his dogmatic Christology and soteriology, he assumes a miraculous transfer of the believer into a relation to God in which "condemnation" falls away so far as he is personally concerned; for God, seeing that man could not attain righteousness under the law on account of its being "weak through the flesh," visited the condemnation of sin upon the flesh of Christ, and accord-

(Rom. ix. 21). It was He who would "create the new heavens and the new earth." The righteousness of the coming kingdom was as miraculous as the deliverance of the groaning creation.

ingly holds him who accepts this atonement as no longer subject to penalty. He has a part in the great sacrifice on the cross by reason of the representative position assigned to Christ in the Pauline teaching, and his relation thereto is expressed in the declaration which Paul makes in his discussion with Peter at Antioch: "I am crucified with Christ. Nevertheless I live; yet not I, but Christ liveth in me; and the life which I now live in the flesh I live by the faith of the Son of God, who loved me, and gave himself for me" (Gal. ii. 20).

In the place of the natural life of ethical endeavour to attain a righteousness by works the believer has the supernatural life of the indwelling Christ, who in "giving himself for him" broke his connection with the old moral order, and transferred him into the relation of justification by faith and into the new order of "the law of the Spirit of life." From this point of view it is not surprising to find a considerable number of passages in which the personal activity and achievement of the believer appear at a minimum or are altogether ignored, and also to note that the apostle does not at all recognise virtue in the abstract in the sense of a personal attainment or an ethical accomplishment. On the contrary, the indwelling Spirit, Christ, and God are the effective forces of his life. Accordingly, the apostle says to the Philippians that he is confident that "He who hath begun a good work in you will perform it until the day of Jesus Christ" (Phil. i. 6). To the Thessalonians he writes of reciprocal love not as if it were to be attained by self-culture, watchfulness, and the subjection of hostile sentiments, but he calls upon the Lord, that is, Christ, to "make them increase and abound in love one to another and to all men," to the end that they may be unblamable at the coming of Jesus Christ (1 Thess. iii. 13). The condition of being out of the flesh and in the Spirit is due to no achievement of which a man can "boast" as of a "merit," but solely to the fact that one has dwelling in one "the Spirit of God" (Rom. viii. 9). By the same Spirit, that is, by a supernatural agency, the believers are "washed," "sanctified," and "justified" (1 Cor. vi. 11). The mortification of "the deeds of the body" is effected "through the Spirit" (Rom. viii. 14), while the expression, "if ye mortify," appears to imply free personal activity, and the passage may be regarded as denoting that the activity of the individual is subordinate to and through that of the divine Spirit. A similar point of view is represented in the passage in which the list of ethical virtues is given as "fruits of the Spirit," that is, the human activities which the indwelling Spirit of God produces in the believer (Gal. v. 22–24). In the eighteenth verse the believers are addressed as persons impelled or led by the Spirit, as if their personal autonomy were at least subordinate, while in verse 25 they are exhorted, since they "live in the Spirit," to "walk by the Spirit" — an expression in which, if not their initiative, at least their effective activity is implied. But the Spirit is generally conceived as the dominant factor.*

---

* Alongside the doctrine of supernatural grace, or as "a series of undertones" to it, there is maintained the ethical point of view of personal endeavour. Not only did Christ "die for all," so that the "past" trespasses of the believers are "not imputed" to them, but also the apostle does not wish to be understood as teaching that "by reason of this vicarious death a purely passive rôle is assigned to those in whose place it was accomplished." Christ died for all, "that they who live should not henceforth live to themselves, but to him who died for them and rose again" (2 Cor. v. 14–21). Although by reason of the supernatural "law of the Spirit of life," the believer theoretically sins no more, yet this inward principle is conceived as a spur to ethical effort, an ethical ideal, and an ethical power (Gal. v. 24, 25; Rom. viii. 13). While the appellation "saints" (ἅγιοι) theoretically denotes those who are "called" or set apart without regard to their ethical performance, Holtzmann finds that the designation indicates also a "task," and "sounds like a requirement directed

This injunction to "walk in the Spirit" indicates a distinct ethical *ideal* toward which the believer should strive. The apostle reminds the Thessalonians that in his preaching to them he had "exhorted and charged" them, "as a father doth his children," that they "should walk worthy of God" who had called them to His kingdom and glory" (1 Thess. ii. 11, 12). Despite the fact that every believer is assumed according to a fundamental principle of the apostle's soteriology to possess the supernatural imputed righteousness, the practical righteousness which is attained by ethical endeavour is held up as an ideal which Christians ought to strive to attain. The body should be "presented as a living sacrifice," and the "members" should not be yielded as "instruments of unrighteousness unto sin," but as "instruments of righteousness unto God" (Rom. vi. 13, xii. 1). His "good and acceptable and perfect will" is the supreme standard which they will "prove" who are not conformed to this world, but are "transformed by the renewing of their mind" (Rom. xii. 2). Even "the righteousness of the law" which was repeatedly declared to be unattainable in the natural course of ethical endeavour receives recognition at last, and is represented as the object in view in the scheme of atonement. God sent His Son for sin, and condemned it in his flesh, "that the righteousness of the law might be fulfilled in us, who walk not after the flesh, but after the Spirit" (Rom. viii. 4, 5). Although the believers in virtue of their "faith"

to those so called to become ethically what they already are religiously." There remains yet to be satisfactorily pointed out the "psychological mediation," which Schmeidel regards as "urgently needed," "between the objectively established new relation of man to God and the former's ethical conduct." Holtzmann finds it in the "love of God," which in the hearts in which it is poured out "calls forth love to men, and becomes the impelling force of all Christian virtues." But this is one of the "fruits of the Spirit" (Gal. v. 22), and hence belongs to the supernatural realm.

already possess a righteousness not of works which has been "imputed" to them, are adopted as sons of God, and are "led by the Spirit," we have here the bold paradox that there is still a righteousness to be "fulfilled" by them, and that "the righteousness of the law." Is there in the apostle's ethics a twofold righteousness, one imputed and one achieved; or has he here as elsewhere abandoned the dogmatic imputed righteousness in favour of the real righteousness, of which according to the traditions of his race he should have been the advocate? Neither supposition furnishes a satisfactory explanation of the paradox. In any case the ground of supernaturalism is not abandoned. If the righteousness of the law is fulfilled in the believers, it is precisely because they have the supernatural endowment of the Spirit, and can achieve what was impossible to the natural man.

The extreme ground taken in the elaboration of the doctrine of righteousness by grace is not, however, maintained with entire consistency throughout even in the immediate connection of the passages in which it is stated (cf. Rom. vi. 6, 7, 18, with 1, 12, 13, 15). The exigencies of practical life subject the theory of a supernatural righteousness to a rude test, and show its weakness. "All the law is," indeed, "fulfilled in one word, thou shalt love thy neighbour as thyself," and the believers as possessors of the Spirit which has "shed abroad the love of God in their hearts" should spontaneously fulfil it. But the apostle reminds them of the peril which they run in biting and devouring one another, and admonishes them to "walk in the Spirit," and not to "fulfil the lusts of the flesh," as if they were, without his and their own watchfulness, in danger of a lapse (Gal. v. 14–16).* The solicitude implied in the

* The attitude of the apostle toward "the flesh," his rigorous dealing with the incestuous person, and his admonitions against fornication denote a great

words, " if ye live after the flesh," is incompatible with the doctrine that the believer in his supernatural connection with Christ in his death has "crucified the flesh with its affections and lusts" (Rom. viii. 13; Gal. v. 24). The earnest admonitions in all the Epistles proceed upon the presumption that the supernatural "grace" is not "sufficient" for the stress of life, since those who possess it need to be put on their guard like other men against fornication and the defrauding of one another (1 Thess. iv. 3–7). Thus the ethical principle of righteousness by works, which was so vehemently repudiated in theory, comes to its rights at last. While the apostle gives no prominence to the details of the life of Christ, and may be said in general to have disregarded them, spiritual fellowship with and likeness to him are presented as ethical ideals. The divine foreordination is conceived as directed to the conformity of the elect to the image of Christ (Rom. viii. 29), and the Corinthians are exhorted to be imitators of the apostle as he is an imitator of Christ (1 Cor. xi. 1; see 1 Thess. i. 6). To the Philippians he writes: "Let this mind be in you which was also in Christ Jesus," that is, the spirit of self-renouncing service, just as benevolence is enjoined upon the Corinthians by reference to the grace of him who though rich, for man's sake became poor (2 Cor. viii. 9). He is in travail of the Galatians until Christ be formed in them (Gal. iv. 19), and his deepest feeling with reference to his own relation to Jesus is that expressed in connection with his controversy with Peter: "I am crucified with Christ;

---

advance beyond the ethics of the Stoics, who placed so much stress upon the individual's indifference to externals and upon the disposition out of which actions proceeded that they theoretically allowed an ethical laxity offensive to the moral sense of mankind. The moral character, however, of the great representatives of this school is conceded to have been above reproach.

nevertheless I live; yet not I, but Christ liveth in me"
(Gal. ii. 20).

The ethical *motive* is not as explicitly stated as the ideal, and in order to determine what it was conceived to be several passages must be analysed. A grateful response to the love of Christ finds expression in several places, but it does not appear distinctly as a motive, as some suppose, in Gal. ii. 20. Christ's love for men, his self-devotion which prompted him to leave for a time the glory of his preëxistent state and to "become poor" for man's sake (2 Cor. viii. 9), to "die for the ungodly," and to "give himself for our sins" (Rom. v. 6; Gal. i. 4), is represented as "constraining" the apostle in his zeal for the brethren and as a reason why "they who live should not live henceforth to themselves, but to him who died for them" (2 Cor. v. 14, 15). A recognition of God's goodness in the rational service of the control of the body is expressed in Rom. xii. 1. On the other hand, the fear of God frequently appears as a motive for abstaining from acts which will incur the divine disapproval. The apostle admonishes the Thessalonians that "no man go beyond and defraud his brother in any matter because the Lord is the avenger of all such" (1 Thess. iv. 6). He says that his persuasion of men is founded upon his knowledge of "the terror of the Lord" (2 Cor. v. 11), and admonishes the Corinthians to perfect themselves in holiness "in the fear of God" (2 Cor. viii. 1). "The terror of the Lord" is set forth in the declaration that at the Parousia, when "the day of the lord so cometh as a thief in the night," "sudden destruction shall come upon them" who cry peace and safety, "as travail upon a woman with child, and they shall not escape" (1 Thess. v. 2, 3). In connection with the admonition, "Take heed lest he spare not thee," "the goodness and severity of God" are presented as motives to fidelity, in other words, reward and penalty are set forth as incentive and deterrent with respect to belief and unbelief. Not only is this salvation to be "worked out" even by those who have already become subjects of the supernatural grace, but it must be done "with fear and trembling" (Phil. ii. 12).

Reward, and especially the eschatological reward or the blessedness that the believer expected to enjoy when Christ should come again in glory to establish his kingdom (the Parousia), holds a prominent place among the motives which the apostle represents as influencing him, and which he sets before the Christians to whom he writes. Accordingly he writes to the Corinthians: "We labour, that, whether present or absent, we may be accepted of him. For we must all appear before the judgment-seat of Christ, that every one may receive the things done in his body" (2 Cor. v. 9, 10). He prays that the Thessalonians may be made to abound in love to one another and to all men, to the end that they may be "unblamable in holiness at the coming of Jesus Christ with all his saints" (1 Thess. iii. 13). To the same church he sends the exhortation to be sober and put on the breastplate of faith and love, because God has appointed them to obtain salvation, and finally in his kingdom to live together with Christ, whether they die before it comes, or survive its advent (1 Thess. v. 8–10). The same eschatological motive is manifest as crowning and completing the motives derived from the spread of the gospel, the being all things to all men in order to save some, where in 1 Cor. ix. 25–27 the apostle represents that all his striving in his missionary work is to the end that he may "obtain an incorruptible crown." Fear also has a part here, for he declares that he keeps his body in subjection, lest he should be a castaway. "Troubled on every side" and persecuted, he could be strong, and hold fast his faith, knowing that He who raised up the Lord Jesus would raise him up also, and that "the light affliction which is but for a moment worketh for him a far more exceeding and eternal weight of glory." Accordingly, his gaze was fixed upon the things that are eternal, in which was his everlasting reward (2 Cor. iv. 8, 14-18; see also Rom. xiii. 12; 1 Cor. iii. 8, 14, iv. 5, ix. 23, xv. 32; Phil. ii. 16; 2 Cor. i. 14).*

The ethics of marriage receives no distinctive treatment at the hands of the apostle, what he says on the subject having reference to special exigencies or to a theological theme which he wishes to illustrate. His treatment of divorce comes far short of the comprehensiveness and precision of Jesus' teachings on the subject. In Rom. vii. 2, 3 he speaks by way of illustration of man's relation to the law only of the wife as "bound to her husband as long as he lives" and as an adulteress if she marry another man during his life; and in 1 Cor. vii. 10-16 he lays down the general principle that a wife is not to depart from her husband, and the husband is not to put away his wife. This

---

* The passage 1 Cor. xv. 32 has been considered in Chapter VI with respect to the interpretation of the fighting with beasts. Here we have to do with its ethical aspect. "After the manner of a man" (κατὰ ἄνθρωπον) means, in the manner of a man who knows nothing of a future life, or for whom there is no resurrection of the dead. Of what use is it to have exposed myself to mortal peril for my cause? If there is no resurrection of the dead, let us eat and drink, for to-morrow we die. The meaning is that he did not expose himself at Ephesus after the manner of a man for whom there is no future life. To such a man there would have been wanting the courage to sacrifice himself for an ideal, and he would say, "Let us rather eat and drink." This is the κατὰ-ἄνθρωπον point of view. If the belief in the resurrection overcomes it, it is not because it furnishes a motive to sacrifice one's self for the sake of integrity and duty, but one adequate to produce the needed courage and devotion. More than this does not appear to lie in the passage. Whether a man of Paul's nature would have fought with beasts at Ephesus if there were for him no resurrection of the dead is another matter. Schmiedel thinks Paul could as little have followed the principle in question as Spinoza, Schleiermacher, or Biedermann. In 1 Cor. ix. 16 the apostle represents himself as pursuing his calling from an inner "necessity."

is said as a word of the Lord, although it has not the qualification as to fornication which Jesus allows (Matt. v. 32, xix. 9). His further discussion of the subject, in which he professes to speak without authority, denotes a departure from the unqualified prohibition of divorce in verses 10 and 11, and forbids separation in marriages of believing and unbelieving parties only when the unbelieving party to the contract is "pleased to dwell" with the other.

With respect to marriage in itself the apostle's teaching is a consistent conclusion from the doctrine that the flesh, the seat of sin, was slain in the believer's crucifixion with Christ, and that if he would "live" he must "mortify the deeds of the body" (Rom. viii. 13). From the premises that the Christian has "crucified the flesh with its affections and lusts," and that the reaping of "corruption" is the result of "sowing to the flesh" (Gal. v. 24, vi. 8), legitimately follows an ascetic view of life.* Accordingly, it is not surprising that in answer to a question on the subject from the Corinthians, we find him advocating entire abstinence from the sexual relation in the sweeping proposition that "it is good for a man not to touch a woman" (1 Cor. vii. 1). This can only mean that celibacy is preferable as the rule of the Christian life to the marriage relation. For the apostle proceeds to say that marriage may be allowed as a preventive of fornication, or in other words, may be tolerated as the less of two evils (verses 2, 9), and that it is "good" for "the unmarried and widows" "if they abide

---

* This point of view obtains in 1 Cor. vii. 5, according to which the sexual relation is incompatible with private religious exercises ("prayer and fasting"), and for their sake should be suspended "for a time" by mutual consent. The suspension should, however, be only temporary by reason of the danger of a temptation through Satan on account of the assumed "incontinency" (ἀκρασία) of the persons addressed.

even as he," that is, in a state of celibacy. The directions regarding the "due benevolence" of husband and wife toward each other are evidently given with reference to the preventing of promiscuous sexual relations. All this, he says, he speaks "by permission and not of commandment," although it would seem that a "pneumatic," a man in possession of "the Spirit," should regard himself as entitled at all times to speak with authority. He appears to have regarded himself as possessing besides the other "gifts of the Spirit" that of abstinence from the sexual relation, and the inference from verse 7 is that every one who has this "gift" ought to abstain from marriage on the theory that the marriage relation is to be allowed only when, according to verse 9, a greater evil may be prevented by entering into it.

Although on good ethical grounds the apostle opposes the separation of the married, he regards the relation as unfavourable to such a service of the Lord as he required of the believers, whom he would have without domestic cares (verse 32). The married "have trouble in the flesh" (verse 28), and the woman who is married "careth for the things of the world, how she may please her husband," while "the unmarried careth for the things of the Lord that she may be holy both in body and in spirit" (verse 34) — a remark from which it may be inferred that he regarded the holiness "in body and spirit" of the married woman as difficult, if not doubtful. He who giveth not his daughter in marriage does "better" than he who allows her to marry, and she is happier if she abide unmarried — a declaration for which the apostle "thinks" he has "the Spirit of God" (verses 38, 40). It is evident that he had no such conception of the sacredness of the marriage relation as a means of spiritual culture and of the home as a factor in the ethical life of men as has happily prevailed in protestant Christendom.* This limitation of his ethics was in part due to his eschatological expectations and to the consequent curtailment of his historical perspective; and it should also be borne in mind that, as Weizsäcker remarks, his "view is deeply involved with his doctrine of the flesh, in accord with the judgment on the life of the senses which was at the time widely prevalent also in heathenism among the better classes." To him "the time was short, and it remaineth that those who have wives be as though they had none" (verse 29), otherwise he could not have expressed the wish that "all men" should remain unmarried — an idea which Holtzmann characterises as "a monstrosity, expressing the self-annihilation of mankind and the extreme consequence of a pessimistic view of life." †

The direction regarding woman's praying or prophesying in the religious assemblies with her head uncovered was doubtless given in answer to questions that had been

---

* "So far as it is a question of advice to such as had the gift of continence and of theoretical approval in reference to all (with reservation of the practical hindrance of ἀκρασία) the Catholic Church rightly claims Paul for itself." Schmiedel in *Hand-Commentar* on 1 Cor. vii. 40.

† Among the Stoics Epictetus held an opinion regarding marriage analogous to Paul's. He advises the philosopher to abstain from marriage and the procreation of children. While in a state composed of the wise he might do this, it is different in the existing situation, in which the true philosopher ought not to be involved in personal relations and occupations which might withdraw him from the service of the Divinity. The Stoics in general maintained, however, that a man should not withdraw himself from the service of the state or miss any opportunity of taking part in its affairs in order to promote the good and hinder the bad. Accordingly, he ought not to scorn marriage, and should neither withhold himself from such a natural and intimate fellowship, nor deprive the state of posterity and human society of an example of a so beautiful family-life. Wife and children belong to the perfection of life and of the home. The citizen owes children to the state, and family-love is of all the purest. See Zeller, *Die Philosophie der Griechen*, etc., iii. 1, pp. 176, 177.

sent to the apostle from the Corinthians or with reference to conditions which he knew to exist among them. If there was a tendency in the church toward a recognition of the equality of the sexes in the religious worship, at least, it was more in accordance with his doctrine that in Christ "there is neither male nor female" (Gal. iii. 28) than his own attitude in 1 Cor. xi. 3-15, which is evidently a logical consequence of the principle of the subordination of woman to man. In fact, this is the chief reason assigned for the direction, the fundamental motive of the entire section, which begins with the declaration that Christ is the head of the woman only secondarily, that is, through the man (verse 3), and the doctrine is reasserted in the words: "for the man is not of the woman, but the woman of the man, neither was the man created for the woman, but the woman for the man" (verses 8, 9). He continues: "For this cause ought the woman to have power on her head, because of the angels," that is, on account of her subordination to man she ought to have her head covered as a sign of his power over her. The expression, "because of the angels," seems to have no logical connection with what precedes, since "the power on her head" is "for this reason," that is, on account of what is said in verses 8 and 9, and to add another reason entirely foreign to this only confuses the sense. If the words are not spurious, as some authorities suppose them to be, then the apostle doubtless meant that the angels, assumed according to Jewish ideas to be present in the worshipping assemblies, might be captivated by the sight of the women with uncovered heads (Gen. vi. 2). In any case the partial concealment of the heads of the women from the sight of the men in the assembly was not improbably a motive for the direction. For the later post-Pauline development of the doctrine of women's subordination, see Eph. v. 22, 23; 1 Tim. ii. 11-15; Tit. ii. 5; 1 Pet. iii. 1.*

With respect to the existing social order in general, it did not enter into the apostle's thought, which was fixed upon the approaching end of the world, to undertake radical reforms. If he thought slavery was wrong, and ought to be abolished, he gives no hint of such an opinion. On the contrary, he exhorts that "every man abide in the same calling wherein he was called. Art thou called being a servant? Care not for it; but if thou mayest be made free, use it rather [that is, to serve the Lord in this condition]. For he that is called in the Lord, being a servant, is the Lord's freeman" (1 Cor. vii. 20, 21). In returning Onesimus to Philemon, he has nothing to say of the evils of slavery, and does not ask for his liberation, but only for a kindly reception and a fraternal adjustment.

With regard to the ethics of the individual's relation to the state the apostle recognises the latter as an "ordinance of God," since He is the source of all power. Resistance to the power is resistance to the ordinance of God, for

---

* The subordination of women is most decidedly expressed in 1 Cor. xiv. 34 f. where the apostle writes to the Corinthians that their women should "keep silence in the churches and be under obedience, . . . as also saith the law" (Gen. iii. 16), and that "it is a shame for them to speak in the church." This passage is the more surprising in that the apostle had previously in chapter xi. tacitly permitted women to pray or prophesy on condition that they were veiled, and may be said to have sanctioned both subject to that restriction. There is no indication that he had different kinds of religious assemblies in view in the two instances, or that in the latter case he intended only to forbid the women to ask questions. If when Paul wrote xi. 2-16 he had intended afterwards to make this sweeping prohibition, he must, as Schmiedel remarks, have inserted in the former passage a qualification as to the special kind of religious assembly in view, if such a qualification was in his mind. Here the women are permitted neither to speak nor to ask questions, but as to the latter matter they are told to inquire of their husbands at home "if they will learn anything." If the passage is not a later addition to the text, as some suppose it to be, it is irreconcilable with the manifest intention of chapter xi. 2-16.

which those who resist shall receive "damnation." It is evident that in deriving the doctrine of the state and the subject's relation to it from the principle of divine right, he reached conclusions not in accord with political conditions then existing or likely to exist. The Roman power in his time could not be characterised as "not a terror to good works, but to evil," and "a minister of God" to men "for good." The whole construction is without a practical basis, the declarations are sweeping and unqualified, and no provision is made for emergencies in which the righteous indignation of men swayed by a sense of justice and a passion for liberty becomes a "terror" to "the powers that be." In fact, the historical struggle for liberty has been a struggle against the Pauline doctrine of the divine ordination of the ruling powers of the state. If it had been in the apostle's manner to give advice to the Christians of his time regarding their relation to the state without laying down an *a priori* doctrine of the state, the counsel which he gives in Rom. xiii. 1–7 would have been wise; for it is evident that the existence of the primitive church depended, as Pfleiderer has pointed out, upon its not assuming the *rôle* of the reformer and revolutionist with reference to the social and political order. Yet gentile Christians in Corinth are commanded not to recognise the civil courts, but to set up a tribunal of "saints" before which they may "go to law," because "the saints will judge the world and even angels" (1 Cor. vi. 1–9). Following the apostle as an "authority," the state on the one hand and the church on the other have maintained their separate "divine rights" to the great injury of both.

The ethics of the apostle finds its purest expression in the directions which he gives the Christians for their relations with one another and with the world. His morality reaches its highest point in his social ethics.* Here the ethical genius of his race speaks the word of practical righteousness by works in freedom from dogmatic prepossessions. In the social order all are "members one of another," should be "kindly affectioned one to another with brotherly love, in honour preferring one another," blessing the persecutor, rejoicing with them that rejoice and weeping with them that weep, recompensing no man evil for evil, providing things honest in the sight of all men, and as much as possible living at peace with all (Rom. xii. 5–21). Here the welfare of all should be preferred to the gratification of the individual, who is called upon to make sacrifices for the common good, and "love beareth all things, believeth all things, hopeth all things, endureth all things" (1 Cor. x. 24, xiii. 7; Phil. ii. 4). He who is weak should be treated with consideration and with the sacrifice of his own liberty by him who is strong, that through the "knowledge" of the latter the former may not "perish." Whoso "sins against the brethren, and wounds their weak conscience, sins against Christ" (1 Cor. viii. 9, 11, 13). Love outranks faith and hope, subjects the freedom of the individual to the service of others, and is the fulfilling of the law (1 Cor. xiii. 13; Gal. v. 13 f.),

* "This indwelling Spirit of God is the power not only to break the might of the σάρξ in the ego (Gal. v. 16; Rom. viii. 1–11, 13), and thereby to effect the ἁγιασμός and the ἁγιωσύνη of the believer (Rom. vi. 19, 22), but also to call forth all positive virtues (Gal. v. 22). The first and the most essential movement of the will of the believer filled with the πνεῦμα is ἀγάπη. As the Spirit originates in faith (Gal. v. 5), as the infinite life-power which the believer receives from God in consequence of his faith, so faith is bound up with love, in so far as it is faith in the love of God and Christ (Rom. v. 5–8; Gal. ii. 20), and therefore itself becomes active in deeds of love (Gal. v. 6); but love, as faith become effective, is not only the inward fulfilling of the Mosaic law (Gal v. 14; Rom. xiii. 10, cf. viii. 4), but the believer also fulfils in it τὸν νόμον τοῦ Χριστοῦ (Gal. vi. 2), and in it lives positively a new life for God (Gal. ii. 19)."—Holsten, *Die paulin. Theol.* p. 118.

while through it faith comes to its rights as a practical power (Gal. v. 6).* Thus out of a conflict with opposing dogmatic points of view, which threatened to overwhelm it, there emerges a social ethics, an ethics of righteousness by the works of the law, which not only reproduces the highest achievements of the Hebrew ethical genius, but also represents the spirit and the life of Jesus. Although it is curtailed at some points by the eschatological point of view, the conscientious student of the apostle will not fail to signalise the fact that amidst all the intensity of strained expectation in view of the approaching "end of the age" he did not relax his vigilance with reference to the moral welfare of the churches and his zeal for the purity, charity, and practical righteousness of the believers. Really if he did think that without their own moral achievement and "merit" he could "present them perfect" at the coming of the Lord, he appears sometimes to have forgotten this doctrine, and his contribution to practical righteousness despite the paradox of grace and works remains one of the permanent achievements of his genius.

* The social ethics of Paul has interesting points of contact with that of the Stoics. Despite the emphasis which the Stoic teachers placed upon the independence of man upon outward relations, they taught that his only rational attitude was a recognition of fellowship with others and a subordination of the individual's interests and aims to those of the community. "In his reason man knows himself as a part of the whole." "We can treat rational beings," says Marcus Aurelius, "only from the point of view of fellowship" (κοινωνικῶς). Epictetus gave a religious expression to this doctrine when he grounded his teaching of human fellowship upon the declaration that "all are brothers, for all have in like manner God as Father." The divine sonship of men which Paul emphasises is that into which those enter who accept Christ through faith. The universal fatherhood of God has no distinctive expression in his Epistles. On the ethics of the Stoics see Zeller, *Die Philosophie der Griechen*, iii. 1, pp. 171 ff.

CHAPTER XVI

PREDESTINATION

THE traditional theism of Israel had in Paul a thoroughly consequent supporter. To him God was the supreme author and disposer, the first and constant cause. He has no "counsellor," and no one has first given anything to Him. "Of Him and through Him and to Him are all things" (Rom. xi. 34-36; 1 Cor. viii. 6). The entire economy of salvation, and man in his relation to it, are regarded from this point of view. The condition of human sinfulness on account of which the atonement became necessary is of divine appointment. If the multitude of men turn away from the gospel, "God hath concluded all in unbelief" (Rom. xi. 32). If the Jews are indifferent and blind, it is because "God hath given them the spirit of slumber, eyes that they should not see, and ears that they should not hear" (Rom. xi. 8). The "uncleanness" and "vile affections" of men denote a degradation to which "God gave them up" (Rom. i. 24, 26). Man was created carnal, and as such cannot be subject to the law of God (Rom. viii. 7). "The law in the members" brings him "into captivity to the law of sin and death" (Rom. vii. 23). If the first Adam was made a mere living soul, a natural man, subject to sin and death, the second Adam, Christ, was equally by divine appointment made "a life-giving Spirit" and an instrument in the hand of God to repair the frightful damage which the former had done. Only the power of the Spirit can overcome "the motions of sin" which, springing out of the flesh, tend fatally downward toward ruin and death. A supernatural intervention can alone prevent the "destruction" which was supernaturally determined in the original constitution of human nature. The historical drama of sin and redemption was conceived in the council of heaven, and the celestial powers move the actors on the stage. The temporary economy of the law was ordained of God, that sin might abound (Rom. v. 20). He also provided the atonement for the abolition of the law and the destruction of sin, and the Spirit and the supernatural righteousness under the antithetic dispensation of "grace" are His "free gift" (Rom. v. 15-19).

From this point of view the proofs adduced by the apostle in Rom. viii. 18-33 that the believers are "heirs of God," and as "joint-heirs with Christ" will at the Parousia be "glorified together" with him in the kingdom then to be established, furnishes no surprise to the attentive student of his thought. The entire construction proceeds from the premises of supernaturalism. The disposing hand of God is evident in "the glory which shall be revealed in us"; a divine intervention will work the miracle of the deliverance of "the whole creation" from "the bondage of corruption" and from the "vanity" to which it was subjected on account of the sin of man; the Spirit, the heavenly, supernatural power, "helpeth the infirmities" of the believers, and "maketh intercession" for them; and by providential disposition "all things work together for good to them who are the called according to His purpose." Finally, the teaching that the believers will inherit the kingdom when Christ shall come is placed beyond all question by the declaration that this great fortune has been determined for them in the divine counsel. "For whom He did foreknow He also did predestinate to be conformed to the image of His Son, that he might be the firstborn among many brethren" (Rom. viii. 29). The direct divine determination is here unmistakable. "God makes all things work together for good" (Rom. viii. 28) is the correct interpretation of συνεργεῖ, θεός being implied as the subject. The "called" are the believers, and they are believers according to God's purpose (πρόθεσις), that is, because it was His purpose that they should be. To make the purpose of God dependent upon the act of faith on their part, that is, to interpret the words to the effect that God had a purpose regarding them only after they became believers, is to give a sense to the passage directly opposite to that intended by the apostle. God did not have a purpose with reference to them because they believed, but they believed because He had the purpose that they should.

Paul did not think that any one became a believer in Christ and an heir of the glorious kingdom unless it was predetermined in the divine counsel that he should be. Those alone were "predestinated" to this great inheritance whom God "foreknew." The determination necessarily expressed in "predestinate" cannot be separated from "foreknew." The one implies the other. To give the passage the sense that God predestinated to a certain fortune those of whom He foreknew that they would of their independent choice become believers, is to attribute to Paul a self-contradictory determinism of which he knew nothing.* So to interpret the words is to wrest them from their connection and introduce confusion into the entire section. With such a meaning in his thought

---

* "It is altogether inadmissible to speak of a conditioning of the divine election (ἐκλογή) by preaching regarded as calling and by consenting faith, for these factors come into consideration only as moments in the realisation of the unlimited election." — Holtzmann, *Neutest. Theol.* ii. p. 166.

he could not have written as he did, but would rather have written: "All things work together for good to them that love God, for these He did predestinate to be conformed to the image of His Son." The passage cannot be explained to this effect while the omitted words are retained without a perversion of its manifest intention. The end in view in the divine predestination was the conformity of the believers to the image of the Son of God. This must be interpreted in connection with the fortune of the believers as "heirs" and with "the redemption of our body" (Rom. viii. 17, 23). In other words, the passage has an eschatological reference, that is, a reference to the second coming of Christ. Then the believers would be conformed (συμμόρφους) to his image, or would have his "form" (μορφή) of glory and splendour as he should come forth from the heavenly regions of light. "Flesh and blood cannot inherit the kingdom of God" (1 Cor. xv. 50). Accordingly, "this corruptible must put on incorruption," and "those who are Christ's at his coming" will be clothed upon with "spiritual" or "celestial" bodies (1 Cor. xv. 40, 53). The "vile body" will be "changed," "that it may be fashioned like unto his glorious body" (Phil. iii. 21) or his body of glory, the "spiritual" form which shines with celestial effulgence (δόξα).

The doctrine of the divine efficacy in the fortune of the believer is further elaborated in Rom. viii. 30: "Moreover, whom He did predestinate, them He also called; and whom He called, them He also justified; and whom He justified, them He also glorified." There is only a shade of distinction between "predestinated" and "called." For to "call" in the Pauline usage does not mean simply to invite to an acceptance of the gospel; but the "called" are those whom God has chosen or elected to this divine fortune, and not only chosen, but also led. The invitation is to all, and if the "called" were conceived as simply the invited, they would not be definitely discriminated as those whom God predestinated, and the apostle could not have written of them as of a fraction of Jews and gentiles, as he does in Rom. ix. 24: "Even us whom He hath called, not of the Jews only, but also of the gentiles."* Not only is the calling efficacious in the sense that God leads His chosen ones into the new life, but there follows another divine act, that of justification: "Whom He called, them He also justified," that is, bestowed upon them "the righteousness which is by faith." This is throughout understood by Paul to be the act of God, who by virtue of His supreme right declares those to be righteous who accept Christ by faith. Accordingly, they possess a righteousness which is of God instead of one of their own attainment "by works." The latter is impossible, while the former is bestowed by "grace," "is a free gift," and in its origin is outside the connection of natural causation. Here it is a link in the chain of supernatural events lying between the "call" of the believers and their inheritance of the kingdom. This inheritance is now spoken of as though already in the possession of those who have been predestined to share in its blessedness (1 Thess. ii. 12). Since it is determined in the divine counsel, Paul writes of it from this point of view as something accomplished, and sees the believers, the elect of God, with bodies of celestial splendour conformed to Christ's "body of glory," as they meet their descending Lord to be "forever with him."

The further development of the doctrine of predestination shows the occasion of the temporary and transient character of certain of the apostle's teachings. Rom.

* See 1 Cor. i. 9, vii. 15, 17; Gal. i. 6, 15, v. 8; 1 Thess. ii. 12, iv. 7, v. 24; and for the later usage 2 Thess. ii. 14; 2 Tim. i. 9; 1 Pet. i. 15, ii. 9, v. 10; 2 Pet. i. 3.

ix.–xi. was written with especial reference to the offence taken by the Jewish Christians at the success of the Pauline mission to the gentiles on the ground that thereby the traditional right of the Jews to preëminence in the Messianic kingdom was put in peril. After declaring his "great heaviness and continual sorrow" for his "brethren" and his "kinsmen according to the flesh," "to whom pertaineth the adoption and the glory and the covenants and the giving of the law and the service of God and the promises" (Rom. ix. 1–4), he proceeds to reject the Jewish apprehension of the divine promise on the ground that the latter did not relate to the descendants of Israel according to the flesh, but concerned only those chosen of God by His "purpose according to election" (verses 6–13). The proofs of this contention are drawn from various examples in the history of Israel. Of the two sons of Isaac, Jacob and Esau, the former was alone the child "of the promise." To the biblical text, "In Isaac shall thy seed be called (Gen. xxi. 12), he subjoins an explanation (Midrash) to the effect : "They who are the children of the flesh, these are not the children of God ; but the children of the promise are counted [that is, elected] for the seed." The election was made prior to the birth of the sons, and accordingly did not depend at all upon their personal qualities : "For the children being not yet born, neither having done any good or evil, that the purpose of God according to election might stand, not of works, but of Him that calleth." The free divine purpose reverses the natural order, and makes the firstborn the servant of the younger (Gen. xxv. 23) ; and in order to give to this election of God the hardest possible expression the apostle applies to the progenitors personally a passage of Scripture which relates to their descendants (Mal. i. 2, 3) : "Jacob have I loved, but Esau have I hated" (verse 13 ; cf. Rom. ii. 11, "For there is no respect of persons with God").

Apparently anticipating an objection to his argument from the Jewish point of view, the apostle proceeds to defend the election in question on the ground of the right of the supreme God, who is under obligations to no one, to act according to His will. The anticipated objection evidently was that it is unjust in God to love one man and hate another before either is born and to elect the one or the other to a certain fortune regardless of "works." In meeting it he does not venture upon hazardous metaphysical ground, but knowing that his readers could not dispute the Scriptures he rests his argument chiefly upon examples drawn from Old Testament history (Rom. ix. 14–21). "What shall we say then?" he asks, "Is there unrighteousness with God? God forbid." It will not surprise the student of Paul who is acquainted with his method of proving his propositions from Scripture to find that the words purporting to be spoken by God to Moses in Ex. xxxiii. 19 have in the original connection no relation to this matter of election, but are part of the answer to the lawgiver's request that Yahweh show him His glory. They relate to this matter only, and mean that Yahweh is gracious to Moses even though the request in question be not granted according to its intention. But Paul concludes from the passage that "it is not of him that willeth nor of him that runneth, but of God that showeth mercy." The divine election does not belong to him who wills to accomplish a certain thing or to him who runs as in a race, but it is purely a matter of God's determination.*

---

* "The movement of the created world is only the realisation of the objective, transcendent world-order, without the ability of the freedom of man to interfere in the once determined course of things [man's unbelief cannot cause God's fidelity to His promise to fail, Rom. iii. 3]. The determinations of the divine will with reference to the course of the world enter into history in great world-ordering acts, and announce to men the law of the world-periods (αἰῶνες), in accordance with which they take their course. In this view of the

Another example of the divine election is found in Pharaoh, who in his connection with the history of Israel is conceived as an instrument in the hands of Yahweh. " For the Scripture saith unto Pharaoh," Paul writes, " Even for this same purpose have I raised thee up, that I might show my power in thee, and that my name might be declared throughout all the earth." The form which the apostle gives to this passage from Ex. ix. 16, illustrates his method of quoting from the Old Testament by generally following the Septuagint but correcting it according to the Hebrew text when it suited his purpose to do so. The Septuagint here reads "preserved" or "kept alive," but he renders from the Hebrew "raised thee up" (ἐξήγειρα) — thus extending the divine election back to the origin of the Egyptian king and rendering the example a more intense expression of arbitrary predestination. "That I might show" (ὅπως ἐνδείξωμαι) is a distinct declaration of purpose, and relates to the hardening of Pharaoh's heart (Ex. x. 20) and his final destruction, and not to the deliverance of the Israelites out of Egypt. This is evident from the conclusion which Paul draws from the history in Rom. ix. 18 : " Therefore hath He mercy on whom He will have mercy, and whom He will He hardeneth." Nothing is said or implied here of God's penal justice or of the overthrow of Pharaoh as a punishment for his opposition to God. The one and only doctrine is that the king was "raised up," and "hardened," for the express purpose of showing the divine "power." It is, as we have seen, a Pauline doctrine that God gives men up to "uncleanness" and "vile affections" on account of their transgressions (Rom. i. 24, 26). But this teaching cannot be read into

world man's freedom has no place. But since it is again acknowledged in the sin of Adam, the antinomy between determination and freedom is not recognised and resolved." — Holsten, *Die paulin. Theol.* p. 16.

the connection in question; and since Paul did not concern himself with the reconciliation of the two propositions, his expositors may well let them stand as he has left them. The attempt to unite them here can only result in the confusion of the apostle's thought and the overthrow of his argument.*

To the very natural objection that if the hardening of certain persons is God's own act, He cannot justly call them to account for their conduct, the apostle replies that the Creator has a right to do what He will with His creatures. The anticipated objection is put in the form of questions: "Why doth He yet find fault? For who hath resisted His will?" That is, what right has God, then, to censure the man whom He has "hardened," since it is impossible to resist His will? Paul at first rules the question out. "Nay but, O man," he asks, "who art thou that repliest against God? Shall the thing formed say to him that formed it, Why hast thou made me thus?" Then refusing entirely to apply an ethical standard to God's dealings with men, he rests his argument upon the affirmation of the divine "power," as if might made right: "Hath not the potter power over the clay, of the same lump to make one vessel unto honour and another unto dishonour?" This reminds us of Isa. xlv. 9: "Shall the clay say to him that fashioned it, what makest thou?" See also Isa. xxix. 16, lxiv. 8; Jer. xviii. 6; Wisdom xv. 7.† The argument

* "As a matter of course Paul does not attempt to resolve the antinomy which lies in the conception of freedom; he does not at all regard it" (von Soden, *Zeitschr. für Theol. u. Kirche*, 1892, p. 119). With respect to Beyschlag's attempt to escape the doctrine of predestination on the ground of Rom. ii. 4, 5, Holtzmann remarks that just as well could one avoid the doctrine of freedom by appealing to Rom. ix. 11, 18.

† Pfleiderer is of the opinion that in writing the section Rom. ix. 19-23 there evidently hovered before the apostle's mind two passages from the Book of Wisdom, xii. 18-22 and xv. 7. Paul's probable acquaintance with this book has already been mentioned (Chapter I).

evidently is that man has just as little right to question God for making some men morally vessels of dishonour and others vessels of honour as a pot of clay has to question the potter for making it comely or uncomely. God has the power, and that is the end of the matter. Paul shuns the metaphysical question, the one really at issue, and one in fact raised by himself, whether, when God has by election "hardened" a man, He can justly hold him responsible. In avoiding this problem he refuses to know anything of a divine ethical standard which may be imposed upon men *because* it is God's. In this position he is as little in accord with Jesus' teaching that his disciples should be perfect as their heavenly Father is perfect, as he is with his own doctrine that the Spirit furnishes the rule of life for those who possess it.

In the further development of his argument the apostle proceeds to an application of the doctrine in question to the election of some Jews and the call of the gentiles (Rom. ix. 22-29). "What if God, willing to show His wrath," he says, "and to make His power known, endured with much long-suffering the vessels of wrath fitted to destruction." This conditional clause is followed by no conclusion, but the sentence was evidently completed in his mind by some such question as, Will you thus reply against God? The meaning is that since God, despite the fact that He temporarily endured with much long-suffering the vessels of wrath, will make His power known, and ultimately accomplish His wrath upon those whom He has made to be its objects, there is no ground for making a charge against Him. The endurance with much long-suffering does not change His purpose with reference to those whom He has "fitted for destruction." "Willing ($\theta\acute{\epsilon}\lambda\omega\nu$) to show His wrath" means simply "although He will show it," and its execution is only postponed (see "the forbearance of God," Rom. iii. 25). The question here again recurs which Paul avoided in the preceding discussion: Why should God entertain "wrath" against those whom He has Himself "fitted for destruction"? The potter who has made a vessel "unto dishonour" has no ground for being angry at the vessel because it is uncomely. To deny the divine agency in the fitness for destruction and soften the words into "ripe for destruction" is to do violence to the sense which the words must have according to the connection of thought, in which the potter and the clay must not be left out of account, and in which κατητισμένα εἰς ὀργήν is set over against ἃ προητοίμασεν εἰς δόξαν, "which he had before prepared unto glory." The "vessels of mercy" whom God elected beforehand to enjoy the "glory" of the Messianic kingdom are designated in verse 24 as "us," that is, the Christian believers "not of the Jews only, but also of the gentiles." On these God will "make known the riches of His glory," while upon the others He will show His "wrath" and His "power." The passages quoted from Hosea i. 10 and Isa. x. 22 f. in support of the argument are interpreted by the apostle without regard to their original connection in which they have no such meaning as he here gives them.

The exclusion of the Jews is next regarded from the point of view of their own defective striving after righteousness, since they sought that which is "of works" and not the only true righteousness by faith which the gentiles have attained (Rom. ix. 30–32). The question naturally arises, If the fault be their own, and their exclusion is due to their ignorance or perversity, how is this solution reconcilable with the doctrine of the preceding verses in which their rejection is declared to be by divine decree? The answer is that the apostle here considers the matter according to the course of events in connection with secondary causation by human actions. That he did not, however, think of abandoning his doctrine that the end was divinely determined is evident from the recurrence of "the election of grace" and from the express declaration that the failure in question is to be attributed to the fact that "God gave them the spirit of slumber, eyes that they should not see and ears that they should not hear (Rom. xi. 5, 7, 8). In this chapter he proceeds to show that "God hath not cast away His people whom He foreknew," because "there is at this present time a remnant according to the election of grace" (verses 2, 4). "Israel [as a whole] hath not obtained that which he seeketh for, but the election hath obtained it, and the rest were blinded."

This hardening and blinding of Israel are, however, only temporary, and are conceived as a part of the divine plan of salvation with reference to Jews and gentiles. "I say then," continues the apostle, "have they stumbled that they should fall?" That is, that they should eventually fail of attaining the Messianic kingdom. "God forbid." Rather he declares that through their fall or unbelief salvation is come to the gentiles, by whose example they will be provoked to rivalry, and at length be received as those alive from the dead (Rom. xi. 11–33). The divine procedure was to break off some of the "branches" "because of unbelief" and to graft in the gentiles from "the wild olive-tree." The gentiles are admonished to take heed lest they be not spared, as God did not spare the natural branches. As to the Jews, "God is able to graft them in again." It is manifest from the terms employed that not only is the entire process included in the divine purpose, but the several steps in its unfolding and realisation are effected by the direct action of God, while at the same time personal censure is implied, and warning is given on the general presumption of individual responsibility. There is, accordingly, no reconciliation of divine sovereignty and free agency, and nothing was further from the apostle's purpose than to attempt a solution of the problem. The former is over and over again expressly asserted in terms that admit of no misunderstanding, in terms that are sharp, inflexible, and harsh; the latter is clearly implied. The expositor must leave the problem as it stands. His task is not that of the philosopher, and he will contribute nothing to the expounding of the apostle's thought by presuming to be wiser than he was in the attempt to reconcile that which he has left unreconciled.*

Finally, the pessimistic mood out of which chapter ix. was written is overcome, and the note of optimism is struck in the declaration that when "the fulness of the gentiles is come in," "all Israel shall be saved" (Rom. xi. 25, 26). This conclusion the apostle seeks to establish by a quotation from Isa. lix. 20, xxvii. 9, which is given freely after the Septuagint. This Greek translation does not, however, correctly render the sense of the original, in

---

* Godet attempts a reconciliation on the theory of God's foreknowledge of man's free choices: "As a general having a full knowledge of the opposing commander's plan of campaign would form his own according to this certain foresight, and bring it about that all the movements and counter-movements of his enemy must result in the success of his own plans, so God, after establishing the end, employs free human actions, which He beholds out of His eternity, as factors to which He assigns a *rôle*, and out of which He forms so many means for the realisation of His eternal plan." On this Holtzmann remarks that προγινώσκειν in connection with πρόθεσις (Rom. viii. 28, ix. 11) can by no means signify mere foreknowledge, and that, by τὸν λαὸν αὐτοῦ προέγνω (Rom. xi. 2) the free choice of Israel as a people of God's own can certainly alone be meant, but not the foreknowledge of an historical fact. He adds that Godet does well not to set up his solution of the difficulty reached by changing predestination into prescience, as a result of exegesis (*Neutest. Theol.* ii. p. 174). Exegesis can reach only one conclusion. All attempts at a philosophical resolving of the problem lie outside the sphere of biblical theology and in the realm of indeterminate speculative controversy.

which the apostle's thought is not at all contained. The "Deliverer" who was to come is Christ in his second appearance (the Parousia). Then the salvation of Israel will be consummated by the reception of all the Jews then living into the kingdom, their "ungodliness" having been "turned away." Here as elsewhere in the apostle's eschatology no account is taken of the unconverted Jews or gentiles who have died, or may die before that event. The boldness of his optimism becomes apparent when the meagre results of his mission down to the time of the writing of this Epistle and the attitude of the Jews toward it are considered, and when, furthermore, the brief time that remained before the expected "day of the Lord" is taken into account. This difficulty disappears, however, in view of the hypothesis of the divine ordering and intervention which underlies the construction of the entire section.

CHAPTER XVII

THE CHURCH AND THE SACRAMENTS

IT accords with the simple, natural, and unconstrained organisation of the little Pauline religious communities, which we have seen in Chapter V, that the apostle formulated no distinctive doctrine of the Church. It accords also with what we have found to be a prominent phase of his thought in the discussion of his teachings concerning the Spirit, Justification, and Ethics that his mysticism should here play an important part. In the same manner, then, as other words borrowed from the Greek received in his use of them a new significance, so the word for church, ἐκκλησία, denotes not simply an assembly, but a collection of persons who are one and all in possession of the divine Spirit, to whom it is a bond of union and fellowship, and signifies their common participation in Christ, whose "body" they constitute. "As the body is one," he writes to the Corinthians, "and hath many members, and all the members of that one body being many are one body, so also is Christ"; and the application of this analogy is, "Ye are the body of Christ, and members in particular," that is, each one in his part. All the churches of Christ are conceived as composing his "body," and each particular organisation is a part of the totality.* Accord-

---

* "This church of God is a church of the Spirit of God. The unity and selfhood of the Spirit it is which removes all distinctions of the external, fleshly, national, political, and sexual (Gal. iii. 28), and combines the plurality of the members of the church into a unity (1 Cor. xii. 13). But the Spirit of God

ingly, while ἐκκλησία is employed to designate single churches (1 Thess. i. 1; 1 Cor. i. 2), it is also used for the Church as a whole that includes the separate communities (Gal. i. 13; Phil. iii. 6; 1 Cor. x. 32, xv. 9), which, however, were not united in a general organisation.

To Paul the Church is not simply an association of individuals united by a common purpose to promote their spiritual culture by means of reciprocal encouragement and help. Rather the supernaturalism which dominated all his religious thinking plays here a distinctive and prominent part. The Church is only temporarily and provisionally connected with the world and with time or with the "present age" (αἰών οὗτος). To its members belongs the "inheritance" of the kingdom of God soon to appear, to which they are elected, and for which they are "glorified" (Rom. viii. 17, 30). Accordingly, the powers of "the age to come," the Messianic age, are already at work in it. The members belong together not only by virtue of their common glorious destiny, but also because they have a "fellowship" which is not of this world — the "fellowship of the Spirit." If there are "diversities of gifts," "the same Spirit" works in all (1 Cor. xii. 4). The church in Corinth is called "the temple of God," and is told that "the Spirit of God dwells" in it (1 Cor. iii. 16, 17). The divine wisdom is

individualises in this community the fulness of its divine contents in communicating to every single person his own gifts, the χαρίσματα τοῦ πνεύματος (1 Cor. xii. 4 ff.; Rom. xii. 4 ff.). In this way the church becomes a unity of one body with separate members, a form with coördinate parts, in which the divine Spirit works through gifts bestowed upon the individuals. Thus the church is a body of the Spirit, each individual being a member of the Spirit, and since Christ and the Spirit are identical, the church is a body of Christ (1 Cor. vi. 15, xii. 27), that is, Christ and the Spirit have in the church of God the reality of an effective life already existing in this world."
— Holsten, *Die paulin. Theol.* p. 121.

their true illumination, and "if any man seemeth to be wise in this world, let him become a fool." The fellowship (κοινωνία) into which God has "called" the believers is that of His "Son, Jesus Christ our Lord" (1 Cor. i. 9), and its consummation will be effected at his coming in "his kingdom and glory" (1 Thess. ii. 12). It was altogether foreign to the mystic and apocalyptic thought of the apostle to conceive of the Church as an ethical-religious association which was not destined as a whole by virtue of the powers dwelling and working in it to participate in the glory that was soon to be revealed.* The "fellowship of the Holy Spirit" (2 Cor. xiii. 14; Phil. ii. 1) was to him the "pledge" of its resurrection-estate. Accordingly he could not theoretically recognise the ultimate separation of even the worst member of the Church from its common fortune in "the day of the Lord," for which "the spirit" of the man whom he delivered over to Satan "for the destruction of his flesh" must be "saved" (1 Cor. v. 5). The "body of Christ," of which they are all "members" by reason of possessing his "life-giving Spirit," will be complete on that day of his triumph, no part being cast off among those who are "perishing" (1 Thess. iv. 13).†

Baptism is regarded by the apostle from the same mystico-supernatural point of view. The classic passage on the subject is Rom. vi. 3–8, where he says that baptism "into Christ," that is, into faith in him as the Messiah, is baptism "into his death," or into a recognition of his death as an atonement for sin and a means of redemp-

* The ethical point of view is not, however, disregarded. "The church is rather the ground upon which the virtues most highly appreciated by Paul, those of reciprocal subordination and sacrifice, come to a full unfolding."
—Holtzmann, *Neutest. Theol.* ii. p. 175.

† It is evident that the idea of Christ as the "Head" of the Church (Eph. and Col.) does not belong to the genuine and original Pauline conception, and cannot be combined with it without confusing the apostle's entire construction of the matter.

tion. The believers, he goes on to say, are buried with Christ by baptism into death. The being buried in the water symbolises what is actually conceived to take place, that is, the appropriation by the subject of the death of Christ, so that, as Christ died to sin, he dies to it, his "old man is crucified," "that the body of sin might be destroyed." "He that is dead is justified [freed] from sin." Christ in his death paid the penalty of sin, and as many as in baptism die with him are by the appropriation to themselves of his death set free from it, and rise to "newness of life." The rite is accordingly not regarded by Paul as simply symbolical of the beginning of an ethical-religious process in which the subject is conceived as attaining righteousness by his own endeavour or by "works." Symbolical it is, but more than this. For to Paul Christ was not simply an ethical teacher and example into whose *name* merely men were baptized as a symbol of their purpose to imitate him and follow him in obedience. But the death and resurrection are to him the central ideas on which the entire significance of the mission of Jesus turned. Hence, believers are baptized into *his death*, "planted together in the likeness of his death" ($\sigma\acute{\upsilon}\mu\phi\upsilon\tau o\iota$), grow together with him mystically, become of one nature with him in his dying, so that they die ideally to sin as he did actually. All that he won by his atonement thus becomes theirs. With him they have died to sin and to the law, and when they are raised out of the water this act symbolises their participation in the new life of the resurrection which will be consummated in them at the Parousia. Death has no more power over them than it has over Christ. Having died with him. they "will also live with him" in the kingdom of God.*

* "In the whole assemblage of the Pauline thoughts there is no element so remote from and so foreign to the preaching of Jesus, which was rooted in the

The more than symbolical significance of baptism to Paul is apparent from the words in 1 Cor. xii. 13, where in connection with the doctrine that the believers mystically constitute the body of Christ he says: "For by one Spirit are we all baptized into one body, whether we be Jews or gentiles, whether we be bond or free, and have been all made to drink one Spirit." The rite is accordingly conceived as a baptism by the Spirit, an endowment with this supernatural power which is "given" to the believer (Rom. v. 5), and which "bears witness" with his spirit that he is a child of God (Rom. viii. 16). In this mystic dying with Christ the subject of baptism is "freed from sin," and in being "washed" by means of the sacred rite he is "sanctified" and "justified in the name of the Lord Jesus and by the Spirit of our God" (1 Cor. vi. 11). This doctrine is the logical outcome of the apostle's conception of the flesh, whose power he believed could not be overcome by a process of the natural development of ethical-religious forces from within. Only the divine Spirit could dominate this fateful agency of "destruction." Only "the last Adam" could counteract the ruinous tendencies which proceeded from "the first Adam," and this he could do because he was "a life-giving Spirit"; hence the entire economy of salvation and of the Church and its sacraments is conceived from the point of view of the interference of a supernatural power. Another expression of the idea of the fellowship with Christ into which the subject of

ground of Israel, as just this doctrine of baptism. This lies wholly on the Hellenistic side of the apostle's teaching, and is most intimately connected with the metaphysical dualism of flesh and Spirit. The iron compulsion of sin ruling as a power of nature can be broken only by a higher nature-power; the translation out of the sphere of the physical existence devoted to death, into the opposite sphere of the resurrection and life, requires the idea of a corresponding mysterious act, which represents and depicts as well as mediates and effects the inward catastrophe." — Holtzmann, *Neutest. Theol.* ii. p. 179.

baptism comes is given in Gal. iii. 27, where the apostle says: "For as many of you as have been baptized into Christ have put on Christ." This is what the writer of Colossians calls the putting on of the new man (Col. iii. 10). The "old man" is put off, "crucified" in this mystic dying with Christ in baptism. The flesh is done away, "the body of sin" is slain, and in their place is "a new creation" which must not be rationalised into a new growth, since God alone is conceived as effecting the "creation." Beneath the act of baptism, then, Paul saw the mysterious process of the believer's transfer into a living fellowship with Christ, in which he became a participant in all that had been achieved on the cross and at the sepulchre, in which he was delivered from the bondage of the law, passed into the life of the Spirit, and became an heir of the glory which "the day of the Lord" would reveal.*

Paul's account of Jesus' last supper with his disciples which he says he had "received of the Lord," doubtless by tradition (1 Cor. xi. 23–27), contains striking deviations from the report of the event in the oldest Gospels. Only in the third Gospel, whose author probably followed Paul's version, do we find the direction, "This do in remembrance of me," and here are wanting the Pauline words: "This do ye as often as ye drink it in remembrance of me." The

* Paul neither approves nor disapproves the baptism "for the dead" (1 Cor. xv. 29). But it is significant that this rite was performed in a church founded upon his teaching. The custom doubtless was that a believer whose friends or relations had died without baptism was baptized for them or in their behalf — a ceremony which must have been regarded as equivalent to baptism in their stead. That this was assumed to secure their resurrection is evident from the words: "What shall they do who are baptized for the dead, if the dead rise not at all?" They can only discontinue the rite as useless. If baptism was believed in a Pauline church to effect the resurrection and salvation at the Parousia of the unbaptized dead, the importance which Paul attached to the rite is evident.

words: "For as often as ye eat this bread and drink this cup ye do show the Lord's death till he come," are a commentary of the apostle's on the account that he had received. The original, "This is my body," becomes in his rendering: "This is my body for you" (literally, "the for you"), to which the third evangelist adds "given," and "the blood of the covenant" becomes "the blood of the new covenant." That the tradition underwent modifications at his hands can hardly be doubted. The first two Gospels do not intimate the establishment of a sacramental observance by Jesus which is implied in the words: "This do in remembrance of me." The form which the apostle gives to the account denotes the importance which he attached to the rite. To him it had a profound mystical and sacramental significance in connection with his idea of fellowship with Christ which we have seen to be the central thought in his teaching as to the church and baptism. This is evident in the commentary, "Ye do show the Lord's death till he come," that is, till the Parousia at the end of the age. This leaves on one side the thought of him as an example, and goes to that conception of his mission which was central in the apostle's Christology. In his death lay the believers' hope "until he come" of the glory and blessedness which his coming would bring. They had "died with him," had entered into the fellowship of his death, and it became them to keep this precious fellowship sacramentally in mind "until he come," when they hoped also to be "raised" and "glorified with him."

The sacrament was thus a means of grace, since it served to bind the believers more closely in that fellowship with the death of Christ which was the ground of their salvation. If in the apostle's assurance of the salvation of all who had once "put on Christ" which, as we have seen, was sometimes shaken, he did not regard this observance as a necessity, he certainly thought it to be eminently fitting. They who owed all to this fellowship might well keep it in mind, and show forth the great event on which it rested, until the Lord should come. The religious mysticism which Paul has inserted into the simple account in the oldest Gospels of Jesus' last supper with his disciples is apparent in his incidental reference to "the Lord's table" in his admonition to the Corinthians respecting idolatry (1 Cor. x. 16-21). The heathen who in their sacrifices "partake of the table of devils," as well as the Jews who eat the sacrifices of the old covenant, and are "partakers of the altar," come into a mystic "fellowship" (κοινωνία) with the demons or the Divinity whom the altars represent. He would not, he tells the Corinthians, that they "should have fellowship with devils," and declares that it is impossible that they should enter into the twofold communion implied in partaking of "the Lord's table" and "the table of devils." The one κοινωνία excludes the other. Neither is conceived by him as a mere symbol. There is an actual mysterious "fellowship" in which the "partaker" is bound with the spiritual personality assumed to stand behind the outward ceremony. Accordingly, he says: "The cup of blessing which we bless, is it not the communion of the blood of Christ? The bread which we break, is it not the communion of the body of Christ?" The rite is conceived as representing not only "the Lord's death," but also the mystic fellowship of the believers with it, their partaking in it, which we have seen to be set forth in Rom. vi. 3-8. Thereby they are not only one with Christ in his death but are united in a sacred fellowship with one another, so that "being many" they "are one bread and one body"; "for we are all partakers of that one bread." The appropriation of the physical elements is not conceived as that of the body and blood of Christ actually present, but just as the Jewish sacrificers became "partakers" (κοινωνοι) of the altar, or came into communion with God whom the altar represented, so the Christians in eating and drinking from "the Lord's table" symbolised their mystic fellowship with the death of Christ who was the living Spirit of the "body" which they constituted, the Church.

The more than symbolical significance which the partaking of the sacramental bread and wine had for the apostle is apparent in what he writes to the Corinthians regarding the eating and drinking "unworthily" (1 Cor. xi. 27–32). After reminding them that in observing the sacramental rite they "show the Lord's death until he come," he proceeds to say : "Wherefore, whosoever shall eat this bread, and drink this cup of the Lord unworthily shall be guilty of the body and blood of the Lord." The riotous and gluttonous way in which the Corinthians observed the communion of the Lord's table was an offence against the sacred "body and blood" of Christ, because wanting in a due reverence for the symbols. The seriousness of the offence is denoted in the threatened penalty : " For he that eateth and drinketh unworthily, eateth and drinketh damnation to himself, not discerning the Lord's body." The participant in the sacrament should "examine himself," lest he incur a judgment for failing to discriminate between the elements on the table of the Lord and ordinary food. The judgment which "many" had drawn upon themselves for eating and drinking "unworthily" was sickness and in some cases death : " For this cause many are weak and sickly among you, and some sleep [are fallen asleep] " (1 Cor. xi. 30). In Paul's usage "sleep" signifies the condition of the dead in the grave or the underworld during the time intervening between the dissolution of the body and the resurrection (1 Thess. iv. 13 ; 1 Cor. xv. 6, 20). The result of this judgment is indicated in the words: "But when we are judged we are chastened of the Lord; that we should not be condemned with the world" (1 Cor. xi. 32). The judgment of those who had been supernaturally stricken with sickness or death was, as in the case of the incestuous person, to save them in "the day of the Lord" from the condemnation to "destruction" which would overtake the unbelievers or "the world," that is, those who from not having believed in Christ belonged to the present age ($αἰών$), while the Christians although living in "the present age" were really citizens of "the age to come,"—the age of the Messiah and the kingdom of God of which they were "heirs." The apostle appears to have regarded a severe affliction of the flesh of a believer who had committed an offence, an affliction amounting to its "destruction" in the case of the incestuous person and of those eating and drinking unworthily who had been punished with death, as conducive to the "saving" of the "spirit" of the subject "in the day of the Lord." If this view is correct, we do not need to consider the difficulty raised by Schmiedel as to reform in the underworld which is hardly a Pauline doctrine. The chastening may, however, refer not to those who had suffered the judgment of death, but to the living believers.

The importance attached by Paul to the sacraments suggests the inquiry whether he regarded them as essential to salvation in the Messianic kingdom and as assuring it. The student of the apostle soon learns that his *emphasis* must be taken with qualifications. We must regard this fact when we find him writing of baptism as if it were an essential factor in the believer's ideal dying with Christ and in his resurrection at the Parousia: "Now if we be dead with Christ [through baptism], we believe that we shall also live with him" (Rom. vi. 8, cf. vv. 4–6). Yet essential as the rite here appears to be regarded, it is evident that salvation is not elsewhere represented as dependent upon it. On the contrary, it is grounded upon the atoning death of Christ and upon the faith of the individual through which alone justification is accorded. The resurrection is assured by the possession of the Spirit (Rom. viii. 11), and the sonship of God from which this boon is inseparable (Rom. viii. 4) is bestowed on account of faith in Jesus Christ (Gal. iii. 26). The baptism into the death of Christ in the following verse denotes only another side of the one mystic process. The qualification with which the apostle's emphasis must be taken is apparent when we consider that the putting-on of Christ, which in Gal. iii. 27 occurs through baptism, is represented in Rom. xiii. 14 as an ethical achievement, and that even faith is subordinate to love in 1 Cor. xiii. 13. The student cannot but feel that here, as often, there is "a certain unrest and confusion in the apostle's views in contrast with the crystal simplicity and greatness of Jesus." If the emphasis upon the sacraments favours the Roman Catholic conception of the church, that upon the individual's independent relation to salvation overthrows the principle.

CHAPTER XVIII

ESCHATOLOGY[*]

THE prominence of the eschatological interest in the early church is not easily appreciated by the Christian intelligence of the present time. We have come to regard Christianity chiefly in its practical aspect as a principle to be applied in the formation of character, in right living, and in the solution of social problems. Its relation to destiny concerns us principally as a matter quite remote from the present time, affecting our individual fortunes and those of the race in a manner altogether vague and indeterminate. The question of a final consummation in which the earthly course of Christianity shall culminate in a great judicial crisis is looked upon more and more as a matter of speculation, and is pushed aside in the intense occupation with the problems of life. We are so much occupied with the development of Christian truth in the institutions of civilisation that we have little room for an interest in the end of the world. With the primitive Christians, however, the reverse was the case. They regarded themselves as having come upon "the last times," and their eager interest in the impending "end of the age" reduced to a minimum their concern with the present life, except so far as it was conceived to be related to the new order about to be introduced. It is due to the Jewish origin of Christianity that this conception arose and prevailed during the earliest period of its history. The

[*] *The New World*, June, 1895, with revision and additions.

proclamation of the kingdom of God could not easily be dissociated in the Jewish mind, familiar with the current apocalypses of the nation, from a catastrophic termination of the existing world-order, and the introduction of a new and happier course of affairs under the expected ruler, whose advent was longed for as the fulfilment of prophecy. It was because the Founder of Christianity was believed by his followers to have been this expected head of the kingdom of God, the Messiah, that such hopes were connected with his person. Since their Messianic expectations were not fulfilled in his mission, which ended externally in ignominy and failure, their belief in his Messiahship could be saved only by the hope in his future coming in power and glory, death not having held him in the underworld, to assume the dignity of the Christ, the Anointed of God.

It is natural that this hope in the great Messianic advent should be expressed in the manner of the current thought concerning the coming of the national Deliverer, that is, that it should be conveyed in the form and with the colouring of apocalypse. Accordingly, we find in the Gospels mention of a "renovation, when the Son of Man shall sit on the throne of his glory," and of a coming of the Son of Man in the clouds of heaven with power and great splendour, who will send his angels with a sound of a trumpet to gather his elect from the four winds (Matt. xix. 28, xxiv. 30, 31). Whatever Jesus may have said regarding the future, these words and others of similar import are doubtless the expression which the primitive Christians gave to their eschatological hopes. Their intense and absorbing interest in "the end of the age" presupposes their belief in its nearness; and we find accordingly that they expected to live to see their Lord returning with the clouds of heaven. Their generation would not pass before this great consummation should be effected, and the twelve apostles would sit upon twelve thrones as judges of the tribes of Israel. Words of an eschatological import are put into the mouth of John the Baptist when he is made to declare of the one who was to come that "his fan is in his hand, and he will thoroughly cleanse his threshing-floor; and he will gather his wheat into the garner, but the chaff he will burn up with unquenchable fire" (Matt. iii. 12). The proclamation that "the kingdom of God is at hand" could have no other meaning to those to whom it was originally made. "The wrath to come" could signify to them only the terrible judgment of the end of the age. Whether the apostolic preaching took up the refrain of the words ascribed to John the Baptist and Jesus, or whether the record of the latter is coloured by the predominant tone of the former, certain it is that the message of the earliest Christian teachers was that Jesus was the Messiah, or the one who was to come for the establishment of the kingdom of God.

The burden of this preaching doubtless finds expression in the question which the disciples are represented in the Acts as asking Jesus after the resurrection: "Lord, dost thou at this time restore the kingdom to Israel?" But when he was immediately "taken up," it is not strange that, as they "were looking steadfastly into heaven," the hope should have been born in their breasts which denoted the Jewish-Christian form of the Messianic expectation, and which is conveyed in the words of the "two men in white apparel" who stood by: "Ye men of Galilee, why stand ye looking into heaven? This Jesus who was received up from you into heaven shall so come in like manner as ye have beheld him going into heaven" (Acts i. 6, 11). In the preaching of Peter recorded in the Acts it is noteworthy that the apostle urges repentance on eschatological grounds, that is, in order that preparation may be made for the great event which was to mark the end of the age: "Repent ye therefore, and turn again, that your sins may be blotted out, that so there may come seasons of refreshing from the presence of the Lord; and that He may send the Christ who hath been appointed for you, even Jesus, whom the heavens must receive until the time of the restoration of all things, whereof God spoke by the mouth of His holy prophets since the world began" (Acts iii. 19, 20). Of the same purport are the words ascribed to Paul at Athens: "But now He commandeth men that they should all everywhere repent; inasmuch as He hath appointed a day in which He will judge the world in righteousness by the man whom He hath ordained" (Acts xvii. 30, 31).

The prominence of the eschatological interest in the thought of Paul would be evident from these words if their genuineness were established. But it does not depend upon the decision of the question whether he spoke as he is reported in the Acts. As a Jew who accepted the risen Jesus as the Messiah his entire conception of the relation of the old to the new order of things, of the present to the future, must have undergone a radical transformation of which there is no evidence, if he did not connect with the Messiahship the expectation of a Messianic kingdom of some sort presently to come in power and glory. One great transformation was, however, effected in his thought, for he did not conceive the coming kingdom to be a political or a national Jewish one, but rather a spiritual dominion which should include all Jews and gentiles who prior to Jesus' coming had accepted him as their Lord. How much the future occupied his thought, and how precious it was to him both on his own account and for the sake of his beloved spiritual children, the believers in Jesus, is evident from the frequent references to it in which his writings abound. While it cannot be denied that he attached great ethical and spiritual importance to his own and their belief in the risen Lord, and that he cherished "a deep religious interest, which with fear and trembling strove for his own righteousness before God, and contended for the victory of the divine will in the world," it must be admitted that the moral-spiritual motive was not the sole and perhaps not the dominant one in his thought, but that he was intensely concerned about the outcome, the reward, of faith to himself and his fellow-believers, which the future would make known.

Whatever rewards Christian experience may afford in this present life, Paul conceived that it is only in the life to come that the believer's real happiness and compensations will be revealed. Accordingly, he writes to the Corinthians: "If in this life only we have hoped in Christ, we are of all men most pitiable" (1 Cor. xv. 19). The connection in which the passage stands determines this to be its meaning, despite the attempts to connect "only" ($\mu\acute{o}\nu o\nu$) with "hoped" or with "in Christ." The presence of the words, "in this life," and their emphatic position in the sentence are inexplicable if this interpretation is incorrect. The argument is directed against those who deny the resurrection, and is to the effect that if the dead rise not, then Christ was not raised, and if he perished, then those who have fallen asleep in him hoping that God, who raised him as the first fruits of them that slept, would, because of their union with him through faith, raise them also, are likewise perished; so that, if we have hope in this life only and not also in the resurrection to eternal life, our condition is most pitiable.

The eudemonistic point of view, reward in the life to come for trials endured in the present life, is plainly expressed in the words: "If after the manner of men I fought with beasts at Ephesus, what doth it profit me? If the dead are not raised, let us eat and drink, for tomorrow we die" (1 Cor. xv. 32). Sacrifices and conflicts, "jeopardy every hour," for the cause of the Lord Jesus are warranted only if those who endure such stress have a hope of the coming glory which is assured by the resurrection of the dead, when, clothed with "incorruption" (verse 42), they shall meet the descending Christ. If this hope is vain, then rather than "die daily" they will do well to live a life of sensuous pleasure, for to-morrow they will go down into the gloomy underworld without return to light. How Paul must have presented the gospel to the Thessalonians, and what the central idea of the "faith" was with which he inspired them, may be seen from these words in the first Epistle addressed to them: "In every place your faith toward God is gone forth . . . and how ye turned unto God from idols to serve a living and true God and to wait for His Son from heaven, whom He raised from the dead, even Jesus, who delivereth us from the wrath to come" (i. 8, 9). We have here the two cardinal ideas of primitive Christianity — the belief in God, to which Jews did not need to be converted, but which must be preached to the gentiles, and faith in Jesus as the Messiah who was to come from heaven, and through whom alone was deliverance from the "wrath" of the impending last days.

The eschatological idea predominates also in Paul's longing to see again the beloved of Thessalonica, "for," he asks, "what is our hope, or joy, or crown of glorying? Are not even ye, before our Lord Jesus at his coming?" (ii. 19). His cherishing of them is not independent of a certain degree of "joy" and "glorying" in them, since their fidelity would enhance his honour when he should present them before the Lord at the Parousia. The refrain, whose leading note is the thought of the last things, occurs again when he expresses the wish that their love may abound, "to the end that He may establish your hearts unblamable in holiness before our God and Father at the coming of our Lord Jesus with all his saints" (iii. 13); and again when, at the conclusion of the Epistle, he expresses his fervent benediction: "And the God of peace himself sanctify you wholly; and may your spirit and soul and body be preserved entire, without blame at the coming of our Lord Jesus Christ" (v. 23). In like manner, at the opening of the first Epistle to the Corinthians, he thanks God for the grace which was given to his brethren in Corinth in Christ Jesus, "that in everything ye were enriched in him, in all utterance and all knowledge; even as the testimony of Christ was confirmed in you, so that ye come behind in no gift, waiting for the revelation of our Lord Jesus Christ, who shall confirm you unto the end, that ye be unreprovable in the day of our Lord Jesus Christ" (i. 5–9).

Confidence and repose in the divine strength for the trials of the present life do not satisfy the apostle's religious needs, but his hope looks forward to the end, and his trust is "in God who raiseth the dead." In other words, his hope is eschatological, and he finds courage and strength in the present distress only in the assurance of the blessed deliverance which the "end" will bring when, having put off the "earthly house," he shall enter into that "building from God, a house not made with hands, eternal in the heavens." Whatever righteousness may be worth "for its own sake," or whatever earthly compensations it may secure, he looks forward with eager longing to the assured glory that is to come: "For verily in this we groan, longing to be clothed upon with our habitation which is from heaven. . . . For indeed we that are in this tabernacle do groan, being burdened; not that we would be unclothed, but that we would be clothed upon, that what is mortal may be swallowed up of life. Now He that wrought us for this very thing is God, who gave unto us the earnest of the Spirit. . . . We are of good courage, and are willing rather to be absent from the body, and to be at home with the Lord. Wherefore also we make it our aim, whether at home or absent, to be well pleasing unto him. For we must all be made manifest before the judgment-seat of Christ, that each one may receive the things done in the body, according to what he hath done, whether it be good or bad" (2 Cor. v. 1-10). The object of all ethical and spiritual striving is the realisation of the hope that at the coming of Christ, or, if not surviving that event, then at death, the believer may be clothed upon with the glorious "spiritual body." His "aim" is to be well pleasing to Christ, in order that, when he shall appear before his judgment-seat, he may be found worthy of the blessed eschatological reward, "the habitation which is from heaven."

It is evident, accordingly, that the gospel of Paul cannot be comprehended by one who interprets it out of the "Christian consciousness" of the present age. The lights and shadows of the impending consummation are so mingled in it that it can be understood only by the historical sense that discerns it from the point of view of the time in which it originated and of the race through which it took its form. Whatever was to be hoped for or feared, whatever fearful looking for of judgment or eager longing for reward there was, the end would reveal; and the end was so near that all that was hidden in the terrible antitheses of death and life, destruction and salvation, would speedily be manifested. If they who had "the earnest of the Spirit" might look forward with high hope to the glory with which they should be crowned, others might well tremble at their impending fate. The hard and impenitent heart only treasured up "wrath in the day of wrath and revelation of the righteous judgment of God, who will render to every man according to his works; to them who by patience in well doing seek for glory and honour and incorruption, eternal life; but unto them that are factious, and obey not the truth, shall be wrath and indignation, tribulation and anguish, upon every soul of man that doeth evil, of the Jew first and also of the Greek. . . . For as many as have sinned without law shall perish without law, and as many as have sinned under the law shall be judged by the law" (Rom. ii. 5–13). Accordingly, the great doctrine of justification by faith with its accompanying "peace with God" is not left to stand by itself, but only finds its completion in the apostle's thought when it is supplemented by the eschatological expectation. Hence he writes to the Romans: "Being therefore justified by faith, let us have peace with God through our Lord Jesus Christ . . . and let us rejoice in hope of the glory of God" (verses 1, 2). The "glory" of their transfiguration in the kingdom of God, which was to be inaugurated at the Parousia, is the consummation in which those who had been justified by faith "rejoice in hope," and is the end on account of which their justification is the occasion of such rejoicing.

The great consummation was to be effected by the personal coming of the ascended Christ out of the heavens. In this aspect of the eschatological doctrine Paul was in accord both with the apocalyptic conceptions of the later Jewish theology, on which he was in no small degree dependent for several of his dogmatic opinions, and with the views of the original apostles. For it was the apocalyptic doctrine that the Messiah was "concealed" in the heavens prior to his manifestation; and since from the primitive-apostolic point of view he had already appeared, died, been raised, and ascended, "the heavens must *receive* him until the time of the restoration of all things" according to the preaching of Peter in the Acts. The coming is explicitly set forth in 1 Thess. iv. 16 as follows: "For the Lord himself shall descend from heaven with a shout, with the voice of the archangel, and with the trump of God, and the dead in Christ shall rise first; then we that are alive, that are left, shall together with them be caught up in the clouds to meet the Lord in the air; and so shall we be forever with the Lord." Equally specific is the declaration in Phil. iii. 20, 21 : "For our citizenship is in heaven, from whence also we wait for a Saviour, the Lord Jesus Christ, who shall fashion anew the body of our humiliation, that it may be conformed to the body of his glory."

The terms employed in both these passages leave no doubt that the event in question, the "Parousia," the "revelation," the "day of the Lord," was not only believed to be a personal manifestation of Christ, a reappearance, but that it was also expected soon to occur. The apostle himself hoped to live to see it, since he includes himself without doubt in the "we" who were to be "alive" at the time. He gives no detailed representation of the woes, tribulations, and travail-pains which according to one form of the Messianic expectations of the time were to precede the manifestation of the Messiah, and which find a definite expression in the synoptic picture of the second advent (Matt. xxiv. 6-9, 29-31, and parallels). He does not disclaim a knowledge of the precise time of the Parousia, but writes to the Thessalonians that "there is no need" that he should inform them on this point, for they "know full well that the day of the Lord cometh as a thief in the night" (1 Thess. v. 1, 2). The day was to come suddenly and unexpectedly upon the unbelievers, and when they are saying "peace and safety," "sudden destruction cometh upon them, as travail upon a woman with child, and they shall not escape" (verse 3), but of the believers he says: "But ye, brethren, are not in darkness, that the day should overtake you as a thief; for ye are all sons of the light and sons of the day" (verses 4, 5). To the Romans he declares that "the night," the present darkened age, "is far spent, and the day is at hand," and that "salvation," deliverance from "death" or extinction as the wages of sin, and entrance upon the "life" of the coming kingdom of God, "is nearer to us than when we first believed" (xiii. 11, 12). The declaration to the Corinthians that the believers, including himself, were they "upon whom the ends of the ages are come," corresponds with the admonition in an earlier chapter that since "the time is shortened," all temporal relations and affairs, such as marriage and business, should be regarded as of transient significance and as unworthy of serious attention, "for the fashion of this world passeth away." It is only on the supposition that the apostle took a very hopeful view of the progress of evangelisation that we can reconcile his expectation of the coming of "the day of the Lord" during his own lifetime with the belief that at that time the mass of gentiles and Jews would be converted, that "the fulness of the gentiles" would have come in and "all Israel" be saved (Rom. xi. 25, 26).

Although the coming of Christ at the Parousia is conceived as the descent of a spiritual being with a luminous "body of glory" accompanied by angels,* it appears to be

---

* It is a disputed question whether the "saints" (ἅγιοι) in the passage (1 Thess. iii. 13) should be understood as designating angels. Paul nowhere else uses this word for angels, yet such a use of it appears in the Septuagint,

represented as visible to eyes of flesh, in accordance with the synoptic apocalyptic, in which it is declared that men "shall see the Son of Man coming on the clouds with power and great glory" (Matt. xxiv. 30). Other phenomena apprehensible to the physical senses are also indicated, for it is said that the coming of the Lord will be accompanied by a shout (ἐν κελεύσματι), a word which is explained by the terms, "the voice of the archangel" and "the trump of God" (1 Thess. iv. 16). The κέλευσμα here mentioned — a word not elsewhere used in the New Testament — is probably identical with "the last trump" in 1 Cor. xv. 52, although in the latter passage a series of trumpet calls appears to be implied, the "last" of which is the signal for the resurrection of the believers. Not in the train of the descending Christ are "those who are fallen asleep in Jesus," but God will bring them with Jesus at his coming, that is, the Christian believers who had died prior to the Parousia will come forth out of the underworld and be united with the descending Lord. They will rise out of hades with incorruptible spiritual bodies, luminous bodies of "glory," like the heavenly body of Christ; and those that are living at this time, that is, the living believers, will undergo a transformation of their corruptible bodies into bodies of incorruption and glory (1 Thess. iv. 13-17; 1 Cor. xv. 51-54; Phil. iii. 21).

That there is a radical difference between the body of flesh and that which at the Parousia would enter into the kingdom of Christ, between the natural and the spiritual, the terrestrial and the celestial bodies, is a doctrine of the Pauline eschatology which has an unmistakable expression.

and it was a current belief that angels were to accompany Christ at the Parousia. If angels are not meant, then Paul must have had in mind the holy men who according to the Jewish belief had passed out of this life into heaven instead of descending through death to the underworld.

It is a fundamental tenet that "flesh and blood cannot inherit the kingdom of God" (1 Cor. xv. 35–51). Hence the believer's body, which was buried at death, was not to appear at the resurrection when Christ should come, and the fleshly bodies of the Christians living at that time are not regarded as fitted without change for the new conditions. If the apostle had any theory of the relation of the two kinds of bodies to each other and of the principle according to which the natural body was transformed into the spiritual, whether in the case of those who, having died, were to be raised, or of those who should be "changed" without death, he has not given it an altogether clear and unmistakable exposition. The penalty of sin, death, regarded not simply as the dissolution of the natural body, but also as exclusion from return out of the underworld or practical extinction of being, he believed to have been counteracted through the mission of Christ for all who became his followers. The bodies of those in whom Christ dwelt were, indeed, subject to death, but if the Spirit of God dwelt in them, then, on account of or through this indwelling Spirit, their mortal bodies would be quickened (Rom. viii. 10, 11).

Those, then, who have the Spirit as a "pledge," and in whom dwells the second Adam who was "a life-giving Spirit," may be assured that though their outward man perish, their inward, essential life cannot be touched by moral dissolution, and that, if dead at the time of the Parousia, they will be raised, and if living, changed, so that corruption will for them have put on incorruption. The indwelling Spirit appears, accordingly, to be regarded as the condition and the principle of the transformation or the resurrection whereby the mortal puts on immortality. The illustration by which in 1 Cor. xv. 35 ff. the apostle attempts to explain the mystery of the resurrection may perhaps be related to this doctrine, although in this place he appears to have forgotten the transformation of the living when he says, "that which thou sowest is not quickened except it die." Just as there remains in the seed that perishes in the ground a life-principle which untouched by decay becomes the germ of the grain that grows from it, so the indwelling Spirit is in believers an indestructible principle by which their resurrection is assured. A strict application of the analogy would require the indwelling of the πνεῦμα in the body, and it is not clear how the soul of the believer in the underworld is conceived to be connected with the body in the grave, out of which according to the illustration the incorruptible body is supposed to spring. But doubtless the analogy should not be pressed too far. It is evident in any case that in the apostle's thought the Jewish doctrine of the resurrection of the dead was entirely transformed.

This view of the resurrection-body as coming from the former body after the analogy of new grain from a seed is not easily reconcilable with the passage in 2 Cor. v. 1 ff. in which Paul writes of the spiritual body as a "house not made with hands, eternal, in the heavens." The words, "For we know that if the earthly house of our tabernacle be dissolved, we have a building from God," evidently imply the thought of death prior to the Parousia; and the longing to be "clothed upon" and not to be "found naked" expresses a shrinking from the condition of a bodiless spirit in the underworld, while absence from the body and presence with the Lord exclude a tarrying in hades between death and the resurrection. The present tense, "we have" (ἔχομεν), cannot be understood of an ideal possession of something which is to be had at the time of the future Parousia, but expresses the certainty of an actual possession. The "building" for the soul abhorring the nakedness of the state of being in sheol is now ready, so that the Christian, weary of the struggle of life in "this tabernacle," where he "groans" and is "burdened," and whence he has a "desire to depart and be with Christ" (Phil. i. 23), may, should he die before "the day of the Lord," at once enter into his "everlasting" tent-habitation. It is probable that Paul, when he wrote the passage in question and the one in Philippians referred to, had reason to think that he might not survive until the longed-for coming of his Lord, and in his eagerness to be immediately with him conceived of this spiritual body ready to receive him in heaven. If what he wrote out of this mood cannot be made to accord with his doctrine of the resurrection, it is because he sometimes wrote rather from the mood of the hour than with a system of theology in view.*

* There is no warrant on exegetical grounds for limiting the "we" in this section (2 Cor. v. 1-10) to the apostle, as if he expected by a "prerogative of grace" to be made an exception to the believers in general. Against this is "We that are in this tabernacle" (verse 4), and "the Spirit," on the possession of which the hope in question is based (verse 5), is everywhere assumed to dwell in all Christians. Likewise "we all" in verse 10 does not denote a transition of thought from the apostle to the believers generally. There is no indication that the apostle had in mind the resurrection at the Parousia when he wrote this section. The point of view from which the interpretation must proceed is in verse 3: "If so be that being clothed, we shall not be found naked." It is from this condition of being "naked" ($\gamma \nu \mu \nu \delta s$), that is, a bodiless spirit in the underworld, that he shrinks. Death, then, prior to the Parousia is evidently implied as a possibility in $\kappa \alpha \tau \alpha \lambda \nu \theta \hat{\eta}$ ("were dissolved") verse 1, and the doctrine of an immediate presence with the Lord in the new heavenly body from the moment of death can hardly be exegetically contested. Otherwise the being "found naked" were pointless. This is not a resurrection of the dead in any sense of the term known to Paul or intelligible to his readers. For this was conceived as appointed to take place at the Parousia, and in the interval the dead were "asleep," and were not "clothed upon with the house which is from heaven." The doctrine of this section is also expressed in Phil. i. 23, "Having a desire to depart and be with Christ," in which an intermediate state is excluded.

Although this teaching is irreconcilable with the apostle's doctrine of the

A prominent feature of the Parousia is the Messianic judgment. In accordance with the Jewish apocalyptic, Paul believed that when the Messiah should come he would execute judgment upon the world and in particular upon the Christians. Accordingly, the occasion of the advent is often characterised as "the day of the Lord Jesus Christ" and "the day of Christ" (1 Cor. i. 8, v. 5; 2 Cor. i. 14, v. 10; Phil. i. 6, 10, ii. 16). A judgment by Christ is plainly implied in the passage in 1 Thess. ii. 19 already referred to: "For what is our hope or joy or crown of glorying? Are not even ye, before our Lord Jesus at his coming?" It is unequivocally expressed in the declaration: "He that judgeth me is the Lord. Wherefore judge nothing before the time, until the Lord come, who will both bring to light the hidden things of darkness, and make manifest the counsels of the hearts" (1 Cor. iv. 4, 5), and in the words previously quoted: "For we must all be made

resurrection at the Parousia in 1 Thessalonians and 1 Corinthians, it cannot be said that he abandoned the latter. For it is expressly indicated in this very Epistle (2 Cor. iv. 14), " shall raise us up also," and in a later Epistle (Phil. iii. 11), "I might attain unto the resurrection of the dead." The Epistle to the Romans, also written later than 2 Corinthians, not only contains no intimation of the ideas of 2 Cor. v. 1-10, but proceeds in its eschatological allusions upon the presumption of the resurrection. In Rom. i. 4 "the resurrection of the dead" means that of the believers in general, Christ being "the first-born from the dead." In vi. 5 the fellowship of the believers with Christ will have as its result their "resurrection." In viii. 11 the quickening of the mortal bodies on account of the indwelling πνεῦμα can be understood only of the raising up of spiritual bodies. So also probably "life from the dead" (xi. 15). From the point of view of an unbiassed exegesis no reconciliation is possible of these conflicting teachings which Paul has himself left unreconciled. It is worthy of note that the eschatology which he has most elaborated (based upon the Jewish theology), that of the resurrection, appears to commend itself less to the enlightened Christian consciousness than the other (derived from Hellenism), that of the immediate departure of the believer at death "to be with Christ." — See Pfleiderer, *Urchristenthum*, pp. 299 f.; Schmiedel, *Hand-Commentar* on 2 Cor. v. 1 ff.; and Teichmann, *Die paulinischen Vorstellungen von Auferstehung und Gericht*, etc.

manifest before the judgment-seat of Christ, that each may receive the things done in the body" (2 Cor. v. 10).* But in apparent opposition to this teaching and in accordance with the Jewish monotheism and the theology of the Old Testament Paul declares with equal explicitness that God is the Judge of men, and the implication is hardly mistakable that it is His judgment which will be executed at the Parousia in the words: "For we shall all stand before the judgment-seat of God" (Rom. xiv. 10). To the same effect is 1 Thess. iii. 13: "Unblamable in holiness before our God and Father at the coming of our Lord Jesus Christ," and "In the day when God shall judge the secrets of men, according to my Gospel, by Jesus Christ" (Rom. ii. 16). Other passages to the same effect are: "Them that are without God judgeth," and "Treasurest up for thyself wrath against the day of wrath and revelation of the righteous judgment of God" (1 Cor. v. 13; Rom. ii. 5). These two points of view, judgment executed by Christ and by God, probably admit of reconciliation on the ground of the supremacy of the Deity and the subordinate agency of Christ. God is the supreme Judge, and effects His judicial work "by Jesus Christ."

The manner in which Paul conceived that the judgment of "the day of the Lord" would be effected is involved in some obscurity, and it is not always clear whether the terms that he employs are to be understood as literal or figurative. It is evident, however, that the Messianic judgment of the Parousia would test and reveal men's work, and affix rewards and penalties in accordance therewith. Sal-

---

* "The view of Paul here appears to be that the believers are indeed destined to life (1 Cor. v. 5, xi. 32), but that in this judgment their reward will be differently determined (1 Cor. iii. 14), and will consist perhaps in a position nearer to, or more remote from, God and Christ, or in a σῶμα ἐπουράνιον more or less radiant (1 Cor. xv. 40, 41)." — Holsten, *Die paulin. Theol.* p. 130.

vation by faith does not exclude judgment and award according to works. Faith and the possession of the Spirit consequent upon it will save from destruction on the great day of wrath, but the judgment must determine each man's rank and standing. Thus is solved the antimony which Professor Pfleiderer finds between the Pauline doctrines of judgment and salvation by faith. The justified by faith may well be supposed to be included in a judgment from which "angels" were not exempt (1 Cor. vi. 3). Unmistakable words of the apostle's make it certain that he included believers in the final judgment at the coming of Christ, although there seems to be no place for the process of judging them in the brief and vivid sketch of the Parousia in 1 Thess. iv. 15-18, where it is simply declared that the believers who had died would be raised and the living Christians (presumably "changed" according to 1 Cor. xv. 52) would be "caught up" with them in the clouds to be forever with the Lord. But a place for their judgment must have been reserved in his thought, for he writes to the Corinthian believers that they should "judge nothing before the time, until the Lord come, who will both bring to light the hidden things of darkness, and make manifest the counsels of the hearts." Then each of them will "have his praise from God," that is, to each will be assigned the commendation and award which are due to him according to the degree of his fidelity.

The searching and destroying work of this judgment is indicated in the declaration that the day "is revealed in fire." * The work of every teacher who builds on the

---

* Compare the words in the probably spurious second Epistle to the Thessalonians, i. 8: "The revelation of the Lord Jesus from heaven with the angels of his power in flaming fire, rendering vengeance to them that know not God." See also 4 Ezra xiii. 9: "*De ore suo sicut flatum ignis, et de labiis spiritus flamma et de lingua ejus emittebat scintillas et tempestates,*" etc.

foundation that Paul has laid will be proved by the fiery judgment of the Parousia. The teacher's work which stands the test abides, and the workman receives a reward, perhaps honour, a "crown of glory," in the Messianic kingdom, for it must be kept in mind that the award in question is no other than that to be determined at the Parousia. But the Christian teacher whose work shall be "burned up" will lose the reward which accrues to him who has built of imperishable material, though he himself, since by the supposition he is a believer, and possesses the indestructible Spirit, will be saved, "yet so as by fire" (1 Cor. iii. 10–15). That this judgment would also be held upon the believers who were to be raised at the coming of Christ there can be no doubt. For their possession of the Spirit which assures their resurrection should not be regarded as exempting them from the test that would determine their position as partakers of the "glory" of the spiritual kingdom to be established at the Parousia. The declaration that "we must all be made manifest before the judgment-seat of Christ" applies to Christians regardless of their having died or not prior to "the day of the Lord" (Rom. xiv. 10; 2 Cor. v. 10).

The passages in 1 Corinthians and 1 Thessalonians, already quoted, in which the apostle describes the Parousia, are so much occupied with the fortune of believers that they contain no indication or intimation of the judgment of unbelievers or of their fate. Definite declarations on this subject are, however, found in other places, so that there is no doubt that Paul believed that those who had not accepted Christ would be judged and condemned at the Parousia. Such a judgment is presupposed in the announcement made to the Corinthians that the saints would judge the world (κόσμος, 1 Cor. vi. 2), in which it is doubtless implied that they would together with

Christ sit in judgment on sinners at the "end of the age." So exalted was to be their position, indeed, that even "angels" would be judged by them (verse 3). There is no ambiguity in the words addressed to him who treasures up "wrath in the day of wrath and revelation of the righteous judgment of God," and the announcement of "wrath and indignation, tribulation and anguish, upon every soul of man that worketh evil" (Rom. ii. 5, 9). An awful warning is conveyed in the reference to the Israelites who yielded to temptation or murmured in the wilderness, and perished by "the serpents" or "the destroyer." This happened to them, says the apostle, "by way of example"; and "they were written for our admonition upon whom the ends of the ages are come" (1 Cor. x. 9–11). More explicit is the declaration that "the day of the Lord" would come unexpectedly upon the wicked, who flatter themselves that they are in "peace and safety," but who will be visited with "sudden destruction" from which "they shall in no wise escape" (1 Thess. v. 3).

The doom of the unbelievers at the Parousia was regarded by Paul as the direct opposite of the blessedness upon which the believers were to enter. The latter was salvation, deliverance ($\sigma\omega\tau\eta\rho\iota a$), escape from the death which was the penalty of sin. Over those who were "in Christ" death had no dominion. The Christians who had "fallen asleep" prior to "the day of the Lord" would come forth from the underworld at the sound of "the last trump," would be "raised incorruptible," and those living at that time would be suddenly clothed upon with bodies fashioned after the likeness of Christ's "body of glory." Death could no more hold the former or have power over the latter than it could avail to retain Jesus, their Master, "the first fruits of them that slept," after he was laid in the tomb. "Destruction," "perishing," are the terms employed by Paul to express the fate of the wicked. For those of them who had died before the coming of Christ to judgment there was no return from the underworld, no real life. Only those in whom dwelt the Spirit, that is, those who were "in Christ," had the "earnest of the Spirit," "the redemption of their bodies," the hope of the resurrection, the promise of "life." The "end" of the adversaries of the cross of Christ is "destruction" (ἀπώλεια, Phil. iii. 19). The gospel is veiled "in them that are perishing; in whom the god of this world hath blinded the minds of the unbelieving, that the light of the gospel of the glory of Christ . . . should not dawn upon them" (2 Cor. iv. 3, 4). A most unmistakable expression of this doctrine is in the words in which the apostle treats of the resurrection of believers as related to that of Christ. If Christ was not raised, then there is no resurrection of those who have fallen asleep in him, but they are "perished," that is, they are doomed to remain in the underworld, for Christ would never come with the sound of the trumpet that should call them forth from their eternal sleep.

The only way in which it was supposed that one who had died an unbeliever could escape from the underworld, or be raised from the dead, was by "baptism for the dead." This is the sole exception mentioned or intimated by Paul to the principle that those who had died "in Christ" would participate in the resurrection. He does not, indeed, expressly approve this vicarious baptism, and it is not probable that he could so far have disregarded his fundamental doctrine of salvation by faith as to approve it; but the fact that the custom was in vogue among those whom he had taught shows that they had learned from him that there was no hope at the Parousia for those who had died out of Christ. Hence their device of baptizing the living for those who had so died, in order that the latter might be vicariously brought into such a relation with Christ as to secure their resurrection. If all the dead were to be raised, baptism for any of them would be superfluous. Accordingly, Paul asks from this point of view: "If the [Christian] dead rise not, what are they doing who are baptized for the dead?" (1 Cor. xv. 29). As to the unbelievers living at the time of the Parousia, Paul says very little that is specific. The inference that they were not thought by him to be included among the saved in the kingdom of God is unmistakable from the fact that the words "we shall be changed," and "we who are alive, we who are left, shall be caught up," manifestly refer to the believers only. They alone who had the indwelling $\pi\nu\epsilon\hat{v}\mu\alpha$ could be "raised" or "changed," and there is no intimation in the apostle's writings that the work of conversion would go on at or after the coming of Christ. It is to judgment that the Lord was to come, not to evangelisation. The hope expressed for the salvation of "all Israel" after the "fulness of the gentiles" should have come in (Rom. xi. 25, 26) appears to indicate that he believed, when he wrote this passage at least, that there would remain no unconverted Jews or gentiles at the time of the Parousia.

But if "fulness" and "all" be understood here as including the totality of Jews and gentiles living at the coming of Christ, the apostle is in irreconcilable contradiction with himself. For apart from the fact that the frequent references to the "destruction" and "perishing" of the wicked can only with the greatest arbitrariness be referred to those of them alone who should die unconverted, the apostle makes most explicit declarations of a judgment upon living unbelievers at the Parousia who treasure up for themselves "wrath in the day of wrath and revelation of the righteous judgment of God," and whom on "the day of the Lord" "sudden destruction" would overtake. In what manner Paul thought that the "sudden destruction" of the wicked would be accomplished at the Parousia, and whether he believed as did the apocalyptic writer of 2 Thessalonians that Christ would come "with the angels of his power in flaming fire rendering vengeance to them that know not God," are questions which it is idle to attempt to answer. He does not hesitate to proclaim the terrors of the divine "wrath" which would be revealed at that time, and if he thought of the Messiah as coming to bring "perdition" to the "adversaries" of his cause (Phil. i 28), he was at least in accord with the apocalyptic of his age. At all events, it is unreasonable to suppose in the absence of specific teachings to this effect that he could have believed that the living who had not accepted Christ were reserved for a better fortune in "the day of the Lord" than that of the unbelievers who, having died without union with the "life-giving Spirit," were, in accordance with a fundamental principle of his teaching, consigned without hope to the underworld.

The question, however, of the fate of unbelievers who should not survive until the Parousia, or of that of a second resurrection, is of so much importance in the Pauline eschatology as to demand a somewhat detailed consideration. In the first place, it is of no little significance in the discussion of this problem that the apostle does not explicitly affirm the resurrection of unbelievers, while as to that of believers he leaves no doubt. It is, then, only by an inference from somewhat ambiguous expressions that the former can be at all maintained as a teaching of his. The declaration that "As in Adam all die, so also in Christ shall all be made alive" (1 Cor. xv. 22), appears to teach the resurrection of all men irrespective of their spiritual condition. These words cannot, however, be fairly interpreted by themselves, but must be related to the apostle's fundamental doctrine that the hope of the resurrection is grounded upon the possession of the Spirit (Rom. viii. 11). By this doctrine the "all" in the second clause must evidently be limited to those who during their lives should have fulfilled the condition of participating in the resurrection at the Parousia by believing in Christ.

In like manner must the passage be interpreted: "For as through one man's disobedience the many were made sinners, even so through the obedience of one shall the many be made righteous" (Rom. v. 19), where "the many," in the second clause, is obviously limited by the condition of accepting Christ by faith.* But that all would not have accepted Christ prior to the final judgment at the Parousia is as clear as words can make it; else on whom were to fall the "wrath" and the "sudden destruction" on that day? The context of the passage in 1 Cor. xv. 22 shows Paul to have had believers only in mind. Just before he says that if Christ was not raised, then those "who are fallen asleep *in Christ* are perished," and "if in this life only we [Christians] have hoped in Christ, we are of all men most pitiable" (verses 18, 19). Accordingly, in verse 22, his thought is: "As in Adam all die, so also in Christ shall [we] all be made alive." He then goes on to say that there is a certain "order" ($\tau \acute{a} \gamma \mu a$) in the resurrection, Christ being the first fruits, then they that are Christ's at his coming; but there is no mention of those who are not Christ's. To suppose that he believed all men, good and bad, to be Christ's by some

---

* The limitation is clearly expressed in verse 17: "For if by the trespass of the one death reigned through the one, much more shall *they that receive the abundance of grace and of the gift of righteousness* reign in life through the one, even Jesus Christ."

natural tie, and that he would accordingly claim them all at the resurrection, is to run counter to all that is most characteristic and fundamental in the apostle's thought and to render nugatory his doctrine of the Spirit and of justification by faith.

Only two groups are mentioned into which those who are raised are distributed, in accordance with the doctrine that each man is to be raised "in his own order," "Christ, the first fruits, then they that are Christ's at his coming." "Then," says Paul, "cometh the end." The resurrection of the wicked might be supposed to be implied here, if "end" means the end of the resurrection. Yet not only is there no intimation that such is its meaning, but the following words appear to define it beyond mistake: "When he shall deliver up the kingdom to God, . . . when he shall have abolished all rule and all authority and power." "The end" must, then, be understood absolutely as denoting the consummation of the age or world-period, which was to be effected at the Parousia. The resurrection of the unbelievers appears to be implied in the doctrine that the world is to be judged, and Meyer so interprets Paul. But the passages in which such a judgment is declared contain no implication of a resurrection, and may fairly be interpreted as relating only to those who should be living at the Parousia.*

* It is denied by some expositors that Paul regarded Christ as constituting an "order" (τάγμα) in the resurrection. They accordingly find the second "order" implied in the destruction of death interpreted in the sense that it means the giving up by this personified power of the unregenerate spirits that he holds, which Christ "wins from him in the last conflicts." So Holtzmann. Hence the doctrine of a second resurrection, that of those who had not accepted the gospel. But the winning by Christ of the spirits of the wicked from death has no other support than the doubtful interpretation of τάγμα. If Paul conceived that during his "reign" Christ was to be occupied with the evangelisation of the living and dead unbelievers, he has nowhere distinctly

It is not clear how long Paul conceived that the period would be between the resurrection of "those that are Christ's" and "the end" when Christ would deliver up the kingdom to God. There is no reason for assuming that he believed in the chiliastic or millenarian doctrine. He is specific enough, however, to say that Christ will reign until he shall have abolished all rule and all authority and power, until, in fact, he shall have put all enemies under his feet (1 Cor. xv. 24, 25). It is evident that the κόσμος which was to be judged at the great assize of the Parousia included more than the men who should then be living. The entire existing order of things was conceived by Paul as hostile to the new spiritual order which was to come with the advent of Christ from heaven with the celestial powers. The wisdom which he speaks is not of this world whose rulers are coming to naught. God has made foolish the wisdom of this world (1 Cor. i. 20, ii. 6).

Christ came to deliver the believers out of this present evil world (Gal. i. 4). Here the time-period (αἰών) includes all that fills it, and may be regarded as equivalent to the κόσμος which does not know God, and the things which God will bring to naught (1 Cor. i. 21, 28). Chief among the evil powers which were to be subdued to Christ was "the god of this world,"* the Devil, whose sway extended over the existing age until the Parousia. All spiritual potentates † were to be put down during the Messianic reign, before the kingdom should be delivered up. All evil must be cast

---

intimated such a doctrine. If he held it along with his unmistakable teaching of the ἀπώλεια of all who were not "Christ's at his coming," then we have here another of the "many contradictions" which Schmiedel finds that he "united in himself."

* ὁ θεὸς τοῦ αἰῶνος τούτου (2 Cor. iv. 4); see also Eph. vi. 12, κοσμοκράτωρ; John xii. 31.

† πᾶσα ἐξουσία, 1 Cor. xv. 24; compare Eph. i. 21; Col. ii. 10.

out and the kingdom made perfect before it was handed over to the perfect God.

It was probably during this period of indefinite extent that Paul believed that the transformation of physical nature, "the whole creation," was to be effected. He represents "the earnest expectation of the creation" as waiting for "the revealing of the sons of God," and as "groaning and travailing in pain together." For it "was subjected to vanity, not of its own will, but by reason of him who subjected it in hope that the creation itself shall be delivered from the bondage of corruption into the liberty of the glory of the children of God" (Rom. viii. 19–22). This idea borders closely upon the apocalyptic dream of the writer of 2 Peter, who looked for the passing away of the heavens with a great noise, the dissolution of the elements and the burning up of the world. In the place of this doomed, old, sinful order of things, he expected to see, according to the promise of God, "new heavens and a new earth, wherein dwelleth righteousness" (2 Peter iii. 10–13). It is probable that when Paul wrote the passage in Romans viii. he was thinking of the earth when delivered from the bondage of corruption as the theatre of the reign of Christ with the saints. The idea of the renovation of the earth at the coming of the Messiah was derived from the Jewish apocalyptic, just as the idea of a resurrection and a formal judgment came from the Jewish theology.* But the former is incompatible with the doctrine of an immediate departure at death to be with Christ, and the latter is not easily rec-

* "In this connection Paul perhaps thought of the transformation of the whole visible creation from perishableness into imperishableness. And indeed, like the bodies of the believing children of God, will the visible creation then beam in splendour as imperishable light-matter. But there will then be no more sin to be punished by the perishableness of the creation. In this view Paul remained attached to the Jewish consciousness (Rom. viii. 19; *cf.* Isa. xi. 6 ff.; lxv. 17–25; Ps. cii. 27)." — Holsten, *Die paulin. Theol.* p. 131.

onciled with the idea of the ascension of the resurrected saints to meet the Lord "in the air" and be "ever" with him. Professor Pfleiderer's opinion appears to be well grounded, that Paul drew some of his eschatological ideas from the Jewish theology and the Hellenistic philosophy represented by the Wisdom of Solomon. But whatever may have been the sources of his teaching, there is no greater incongruity in his opinions than might be expected in those of a man who did not undertake to formulate a "system" either of theology or of eschatology.

In his teaching of the conflict of Christ at the Parousia with the spirit-powers and their overthrow, Paul comes into close relation with the Jewish apocalyptic. He is also in accord with the synoptic tradition which gives great prominence to the power of Jesus over evil spirits, and opens its story with an account of a victory over Satan in the wilderness. That Paul shared the belief of the Jews of his time in the existence and baleful influence of evil spirits, no one can doubt who carefully studies his writings. "The god of this world" had power to blind the understandings of unbelievers, and to him and the subordinate spiritual potentates were due the corruption, sin, and death which were in the world. "Angels," that is, beings capable of being affected by passion, were supposed to be present in the worshipping assemblies of the Christians, and the women were commanded to keep themselves veiled on their account (1 Cor. xi. 10). The "rule and authority and power" which Christ would put down at his coming evidently include the *hostile* agencies like the "world-rulers of darkness" spoken of in Eph. vi. 12, for the apostle immediately adds: "He shall reign until he hath put all enemies under his feet." Death, perhaps personified as one of the malignant spirit-powers, is declared to be the last enemy that shall be destroyed. This foe of mankind, this offspring of Sin, who had "reigned from Adam to Moses," the mighty Messiah would subdue. How closely the apostle's thought borders upon the apocalyptic conceptions is apparent when we compare the destruction of Death in the lake of fire in the Johannine apocalypse and the judgment of the Messiah on the evil spirits in the Enoch-parables. The destruction of death may be regarded as the end and consummation of the subjection of all the powers hostile to the kingdom of God which was to come at the Parousia. Death exists only through sin, and its destruction is involved in that of the evil forces of the world and the evil men living in it. Its power ends with the resurrection of the believers, who shall die no more. The resurrection of the wicked is not necessary to this consummation, since they "are perished," as would have been the case even with believers, had not Christ been raised.

Paul's doctrine of the resurrection is in accord with some of the Jewish teachings on the subject and in opposition to others. This was necessarily the case, since the Jewish writings present contradictory views on the subject. Sometimes the resurrection of Israelites alone, good and bad, appears to be taught, as in Daniel and 2 Maccabees, and sometimes that of all men, while according to Weber the Talmudic-Midrashic literature does not recognise the resurrection of all the dead, but of the righteous only, for whom it was regarded as a reward. Paul, as we have seen, is in accord with this latter teaching, which may have been current in the Jewish theology of his time. But while the Jewish theologians limited the resurrection to pious Israelites, Paul included in it all believers in Christ of whatever nationality. Accordingly, he based the resurrection upon a principle unknown to the current doctrine, a principle derived from his Christian faith. If Christ were not raised then is the believer's faith vain, and those who have fallen asleep in Christ are perished. Without this great event no return from the underworld would be possible; but with it a return is promised to those who possess the Spirit, that is, through faith have come into living union with Christ and become "his body and severally members thereof" (1 Cor. xii. 27).

The Pauline conception of the resurrection is also a refinement and spiritualisation of the popular doctrine according to which the resurrected would have physical bodies with the lusts and passions pertaining thereto (see Matt. xxii. 24 f.). The idea of incorruptible spiritual bodies conformed to Christ's body of glory, in accordance with the conception of the Spirit, which Christ was ("the Lord is the Spirit"), as a luminous substance, involves a transformation of the current doctrine of the future life by which it was raised to a higher plane. Membership in the Messianic kingdom implied in the thought of Paul a glorious spiritual existence like that of Christ in heaven prior to his first appearance upon the earth and after his resurrection. Whether this existence was to be upon the renovated earth or elsewhere, the idea evidently involves a transformation of the materialistic Jewish Messianism. It is probable, however, that the apostle retained the current doctrine of the underworld, although he does not employ the word which designated it ($ᾅδης$),* and makes no mention of it in any terms. The doctrine of the resurrection of believers as set forth in 1 Corinthians and 1 Thessalonians, in the passages already referred to, evidently implies that of the underworld, which is necessarily involved in the rising of the dead. The resurrection of the dead

---

* In 1 Cor. xv. 55, "O grave ($ᾅδης$), where is thy victory?" the reading of Lachmann, Tischendorf, Tregelles, and Westcott and Hort is "death" ($θάνατε$). This reading is adopted in the revised version of the New Testament.

(ἀνάστασις νεκρῶν) could have conveyed no other idea to his Jewish readers than that of the coming forth of the departed from an intermediate state in sheol. Either a shrinking from this state of existence, or the thought of the Parousia and resurrection as so near that it became a fleeting and unimportant moment in the total life of believers, led him, however, to a doctrine entirely irreconcilable with it, that of an immediate departure at death to be with Christ in heaven (2 Cor. v. 1-4; Phil. i. 23).

The indefiniteness of the duration of the Messianic kingdom after the Parousia has already been referred to. The fact that the apostle lays no stress upon the reign of Christ denotes another transformation of the current apocalyptic conceptions which his great and original mind effected. Perhaps Professor Pfleiderer's remark is not strictly accurate that "the Parousia according to Paul did not have as its object . . . the entrance of the Messiah upon his kingly dominion, but his immediate abdication of it to God," since the subjection of the opposing powers and the reigning until all enemies are put under his feet involves a sway of no inconsiderable duration. But in accordance with the Pauline Christology the position and work of Christ are here those of a subordinate and agent. It is not he who subdues all things, but God, and to God he himself is to become subject at last (1 Cor. xv. 28). When this consummation shall have been effected, when all opposing rule and authority and power shall have been put down, then the kingdom will be complete and fit to be delivered up to the Father. Then, when sin shall have been destroyed, the groaning creation set free from "the bondage of corruption," and all "enemies," human and demonic, subjugated, the divine perfection of the kingdom will be signalised by its entire occupation by the all-perfect God, who will be "all in all." Manifestly, the "all" in which God will dwell is the totality of the kingdom, out of which the Messianic conquest will have banished everything that could offend the divine purity. That this is not a doctrine of universal restoration is evident from what has already been shown respecting Paul's teaching of the resurrection at the Parousia of believers only and the "destruction" of living unbelievers. It is equally evident that the apostle nowhere teaches the doctrine of the endless punishment of the wicked. The resurrection of those of them who died prior to "the day of the Lord" is, as we have seen, incompatible with one of his fundamental principles, and punishment in the underworld is unknown to his thought. Living or dead, they belong to those who "are perishing," and their end is the extinction of being, death, from which nothing can save but the indwelling of the divine πνεῦμα.*

* Some expositors find Paul in contradiction with himself regarding human destiny, and maintain that he teaches the destruction of the unbelievers in one series of passages and in another their final restoration. The former doctrine is found in the words "perishing" and "destruction" applied to the wicked in several places, among which may be mentioned 1 Cor. i. 18; 2 Cor. ii. 15 f.; iv. 3; Rom. ii. 5-12; Phil. i. 28; 1 Thess. v. 3. Final salvation of the wicked is held to be taught in Rom. v. 12-15, 18, and xi. 32. If Rom. v. 12-21 be considered together it will appear, as has been pointed out in the text above, that verse 17 denotes a qualification of the extent of the "life" that through Christ is set over against the sin and death in Adam, to the effect that it is the portion of those "who receive abundance of grace and of the gift of righteousness." The attainment of "life" is thus dependent on the individual's *receiving* what God graciously offers in the atonement. Accordingly, if in verse 18 "the free gift come upon all men to justification of life," it cannot be regarded as unqualifiedly securing "life." Justification is by "faith," and Paul knew of no other; but faith depends upon the individual to whom this kind of righteousness is offered. Just as no one becomes a sinner "by the offence" of Adam except by his own act, so no one is justified through Christ but by his act of faith. If Paul meant that all would certainly have the required faith, he neither implies it here, nor says it elsewhere (see Rom. iii. 22, 26). Rom. xi. 32, "He hath included all in unbelief, that He might have mercy upon all," teaches the salvation of all only if it can be shown to be a

It is manifest from the foregoing sketch of the Pauline doctrine of "the last things" that it by no means presents a complete eschatology. Apart from its internal incongruities, which have been pointed out, it falls far short in many respects of the clear and precise dogmatic statement essential to give it a place in a system of theology. It makes no provision for a judgment of the innumerable unrighteous dead, who from the earliest times had descended to the underworld. They appear to be abandoned in this shadowy realm with heartless unconcern. The

Pauline doctrine that the divine mercy is effective independently of subjective conditions. In "the fulness of the gentiles" and "all Israel" (Rom. xi. 25, 26), for the salvation of whom prior to the Parousia Paul hoped against hope, no account is taken of the dead. That the unbelieving dead should be raised at the Parousia requires their possession of "the Spirit," which is the condition of the resurrection, that is, their evangelisation in the underworld, of which there is no hint in Paul's writings. The conversion of Christ's "enemies" is not implied in their subjection "under his feet." Rather their destruction is indicated in that of "the last enemy, death" (1 Cor. xv. 25 f.). The kingdom is the domain of the Spirit, which is "life," and the annihilation of Death and his realm of darkness follows upon its establishment. Without sufficient grounds Schmiedel finds that in 1 Cor. xv. 24-28 the conversion of living unbelievers at the Parousia before the "end" is taught, and asks why the same fortune might not be that of those who had died in unbelief prior to the Parousia. Why not, indeed, if either doctrine or rather both doctrines were the apostle's? Teichmann also finds that Paul teaches both the destruction of the wicked and their resurrection as possessors of the Spirit, the latter on the ground of 1 Cor. xv. 22. But since this requires a doctrine that is not Pauline, the preaching of Christ to shades in hades and, moreover, the certainty that all would accept the message, the interpretation of the passage given in the text is to be preferred to this construction. Holsten interpreted 1 Cor. xv. 22 as follows: "Since the former πάντες can in reality refer only to those who bear in themselves the nature of Adam, so the second πάντες can actually relate to those alone who have the nature of Christ, that is, those who through faith have received the πνεῦμα τοῦ θεοῦ as ἀπαρχή of the heavenly goods, and as ἀρραβών of eternal life (Rom. viii. 23; 2 Cor. v. 5)." For those who did not receive the Spirit, the pledge (ἀρραβών) of the resurrection, prior to death Paul makes no provision. He gives no hint of the doctrine of a "second probation" for the shades in hades.

apostle's eschatological interest seems to have included only the Christian dispensation down to the time of the Parousia, and the kingdom which he expected soon to see appear in glory was to have as its subjects only those who through faith had accepted Christ. As to what he thought would be the destiny of the righteous who had died prior to the mission of Jesus, — the prophets, the good kings, the saints, — we are left entirely to conjecture, for he has furnished no definite data for a theory on the subject. The exclusion from his eschatological scheme of the generations of men who have lived, or may live after the time of the expected "day of the Lord," which he believed would denote the close of the human historical course of affairs, is of importance with reference to the value of his eschatology for Christian theology. The attempt to find in it a doctrine of "the last things" applicable to all men of all the ages of human existence on the earth must evidently be abortive. No dogmatic statement of the universal destiny of mankind can be extorted from his teachings. His conception of an apocalyptic judgment falls with the transcending of its time-limit by the remorseless course of events, which has paid no heed to dreams of "the last things" and dramatic schemes of a final assize. Apocalypse has had its day, and must now give way to the conception of an evolution of human society attended by a constant, silent judgment announced by no "trumpet" or "voice of an archangel." The teachings of the apostle, however, incidental to his eschatology, which are grounded upon human experience, are of permanent worth and importance. Chief among these is the doctrine that disaster follows sin in the natural relation of cause and effect, that "whatsoever a man soweth that shall he also reap; for he that soweth unto his own flesh shall of the flesh reap corruption." On the other hand, the promise of victory and joy is to those who come into spiritual fellowship with Christ, and righteousness is regarded as the certain fruitage of a seed that is sown in love and faith: "He that soweth unto the Spirit shall of the Spirit reap eternal life" (Gal. vi. 8).

INDEX OF SUBJECTS AND NAMES

Abbot, Dr. E., 298.
Abraham, the promise to interpreted by Paul, 9; his faith accounted as righteousness, 191.
Acts, on Paul's conversion, 53; the discourses in, 72; on Paul's journey into Arabia, 76; omits mention of Titus, 80; on Paul's first missionary journey, 83; on other journeys, 152; on Paul's apostleship, 84; deviations in from actual course of events, 89; omits episode between Peter and Paul in Antioch, 95; on Paul in Athens, 105; on the Corinthian Church, 106; on organisation of the Pauline churches, 109 f.; on Paul's reception in Jerusalem with the collection, 135; account of Paul's missions in contrast with the Epistles, 146 ff., 158, 160–174; account of Paul's journey from Cæsarea to Jerusalem, 143; account of circumcision of Timothy, 156; hypotheses as to character and composition of, 146 f.; on the Ephesian mission, 132 f.; on the council in Jerusalem, 172 f.; on Paul's Nazarite vow, 154.
Adam, the second, 15, 299, 307; sin of all men in, 233 f.; and Christ, 218, 234, 240, 267, 290, 398; the first, 241.
Adoption as sons, 215.
Allegorical interpretation, 8–11.
ἁμαρτία, sin as a principle, 259.
Angelology, 17.
Anthropology, 22 f., 225, 227.
Antinomies, 49, 236 f., 242, 245, 247 f., 306, 379, 406, 410, 437 f.

Antioch, 82, 85 f.; composition of Church in, 81 f.; founding of Church in, 82.
Apocalypse, relation of to eschatology, 427, 429, 431.
Apollos, 113; party of in Corinth, 115.
Apostleship, Paul's claim to, 32, 57, 59, 61, 65, 75, 93, 115.
Arabia, 55, 75, 148.
Argument, Paul's method of, 41–45.
Atonement, in Romans, 142; Paul's doctrine of, 251–279; implies change on God's part, 260; as a sacrifice, 263 f., 270; ethical theory of, 271 f.

Baptism, Paul's doctrine of, 414 ff.; for the dead, 417, 443; Paul's mystic conception of, 322.
Baring-Gould, his interpretation of 1 Cor. ix. 5, 39.
Barnabas, 80, 82, 86, 149 f.
Baur, 298.
Beasts, Paul's fight with at Ephesus, 131, 389, 428.
Beyschlag, 305, 406.
Biedermann, 309.
Bishops, 111.
Body (σῶμα), as form, 221; as spiritual, 225, 244; redemption of, 220, 225, 244; celestial and terrestrial, 434 f.; of glory, 244, 432, 452.
Bovon, 239.

Cæsarea, Paul's journey from to Jerusalem, 143.
"Called," the, 401 f.
Celibacy, 391.

INDEX OF SUBJECTS AND NAMES

Christ, as the Son of God and the Messiah, 64, 282; Paul's seeing of, 59; flesh of on the cross, 226, 265; agency of in salvation, 252; his humanity, 288 f., 291; death of, 254, 257, 263, 266, 274, 276, 286; his satisfaction of the law, 259; made a "curse," 261, 267; as Son of God, 285; not "a mere man," 287; Paul's doctrine of person of, 280-310; in "the likeness of sinful flesh," 226, 264 f., 290; preëxistence of, 292, 294, 303; divine nature not ascribed to him, 296 f.; as judge, 302, 438 f.; in "the form of God," 301, 303; subordination of to God, 299, 338; relation of the justified to, 360 f.; reign of, 448; resurrection of, 117, 268, 272, 300, 351, 368.
Church, Paul's doctrine of, 412 f.
Cilicia, 89.
Circumcision, 81, 94, 154; of Timothy, 156.
Collection for the poor, 134 f.
Conversion, the, of Paul, 53-66.
Corinth, mission in, 105 ff., 120 f.
Corinthian Church, confusion in, 33 f., 118; Epistles to the, 121; First Epistle to the, 34 f., 107, 112 f., 117, 119; Second Epistle to the, x. 1–xiii. 10, 47, 121, 125; contents of, 119 f.; the two canonical epistles to the, general character of, 126.
Creation, the groaning, 245, 449; Christ's participation in the, 294.
Criticism of New Testament, method of, 280.

Damascus, 55, 75, 149.
Death, the penalty of sin, 16, 234, 244, 264, 278; Paul's use of term, 198 f., 249; of the believer with Christ, 278; baptism into the of Christ, 415.
Decree of council in Jerusalem, 172 f.

Demetrius, 132.
Demonology, 18.
Depravity, total, 248.
Destiny of man, 45, 46.
"Destruction," 205, 209, 249, 257, 433.
Determinism, 398 f.
Deutero-Pauline writings, 297.
Development of doctrine in Paul, 179.
Devils, the cup of, 44; the table of, 419.
διάκονοι, 111.
Dickson, 227.
Divorce, 391.
Docetic conception of Christ's body, 291.
Dwight, Dr. T., 298.

Ecstatic phenomena, 46, 315 f., 334.
Education, Paul's Jewish, 6 f.
Election, 400 f., 405-409.
ἥμαρτον ἐφ' ᾧ πάντες, 233 f.
Enmity of man toward God, 257, 268.
Ephesians, Epistle to, 128.
Ephesus, mission in, 128 f., 153; fight with wild beasts in, 131, 398, 428.
Epilepsy, Paul probably afflicted with, 25.
ἐπίσκοποι, 111.
Epistles of Paul, writings of the occasion, 179.
Equality of Paul with the older apostles, 38 f.
Eschatology, 15 f., 423-457; "death," with reference to, 204 f.; "life," with reference to, 208; in connection with salvation, 212, 252; the Spirit in relation to, 355 f.; apocalyptic conception of, 424; ethical application of, 427, 429.
Ethical sense not in righteousness by faith, 357 f.; motives, 387 f., 427, 429; theory of atonement, 271 f.

INDEX OF SUBJECTS AND NAMES 461

Ethics of Paul, 370-397; contrast of with that of Old Testament, 373 f.; genesis of, 375 ff.; social, 396; limitations of Paul's, 456.
Eudemonism, 427.
Everett, Dr., 261.
Everling, 124.
Evil spirits, overthrow of, 450.

Faith, 344; righteousness by, 54; and justification, 342-369; as a gift of the Spirit, 319; in Christ, 345; with reference to the life, 347; not the cause of justification, 357; subordinate to love, 422.
Fall of man, 242.
False brethren, the, 165 f.
Farrar, 27.
Fear as an ethical motive, 387.
Felix, 143.
Fellowship with Christ, 73, 139, 142, 145; of the Spirit, 413.
Fenn, W. W., 151, 152.
Festus, 143.
Flesh, Christ according to the, 14, 281; thorn in the, 24 f.; the, in the anthropology of Paul, 220 f., 229; the, ethically regarded, 222, 224, 227, 243; the, and the Spirit, 226; sinful, Christ in the likeness of, 226, 264 f., 290.
Forgiveness not prominent in Paul's teaching, 360.
Fornicator, Paul's judgment on the, 36.
Freedom, Paul's conception of, 38 f., 247; and determinism, 404.
Future, prominence of in thought of Paul, 427.

Galatia, churches of, 88.
Galatians, Epistle to the, 31 f., 88-94.
Gamaliel, 14.
Genius, the religious of Paul, 14, 21, 65.
Gentile converts, the, 84.

Gentiles, the apostleship to the, 54, 62, 69, 80, 84; relation of death of Christ to the, 275.
Gifford, 181.
Gloël, 313.
God, love of, 51, 258, 277; monotheistic conception of, 297; first cause, 398; His purpose in salvation, 400; His foreknowledge and predestination, 400 f.
Gospel, Paul's, whence derived, 74.
Grace, righteousness imputed by, 353 f., 359, 361.
Grafe, 181 f.
Gunkel, 313 f., 330, 332, 336.

Hagadah, its influence upon Paul, 19 f.
Harnack, 66, 101, 313.
Hausrath, 27, 78, 156, 247.
Heart, the, in relation to faith, 346.
Heathenism and Christianity in Corinth, 118, 126.
Hebrews, the Epistle to the, 12.
Heinrici, 37.
Heirs, the believers as, 92.
Hellenism, 49, 224, 245, 340, 416.
Hellenist, Paul a, 14, 81.
Hilgenfeld, 152.
Holsten, 131, 181, 183, 248, 266, 270, 292, 340, 350, 352, 396, 412.
Holtzmann, 153, 155, 160 f., 224, 229, 258, 290, 301, 304, 406, 410, 416, 447.

Idolatry and idols, 44 f.
Illumination, Paul's belief in his, 39.
Illustrations of Jesus and Paul, 6.
Image of God, Christ as the, 288, 301.
Imputation of righteousness, 353, 361.
Incarnation, the, 303; Beyschlag on, 305.
Incestuous man, the, Paul's judgment on, 36, 214.
Independence, Paul's assertion of his, 38, 147 f.
Inheritance of the kingdom, 402.

Intercession of the Spirit, 335.
Interpretation of Old Testament by Paul, 8–14; of tongues, 316.
Irony, Paul's use of, 47.
Inward man, the, 224, 243, 247.

James, 30, 85, 86, 88; at the council, 171 f.
Jerusalem, Paul's first visit to, 75 f.; agreement in, 84 f., 162 f.; Paul's journey to with the collection, 135; council in, 83 f., 162 ff., 168 f.
Jeser hara, 224 f.
Jesus, Paul's acquaintance with teachings of, 76, 281 f.; resurrection of, see "Christ."
Jewish-Christian nucleus in the churches, 81.
Jewish method of interpretation, 8.
Jowett on Christ κατὰ σάρκα, 14.
Jubilees, Book of, 20.
Judicial conception of God's relation to man, 258.
Justification by faith, 30, 87, 342–369; with reference to eschatology, 431; through the atonement, 268, 272, 300, 351, 368.
Justify (δικαιοῦν) "forensic" sense of, 351 f.

Keim, 147.
Kindliness of Paul, 33.
Kingdom of God, 252, 282.
Köstlin, 295.
Krenkel, 25, 131.

Last Supper, the, Paul's idea of, 417 ff.
Law, the, 70, 87, 142; Paul's use of term, 179–198; its relation to sin, 187, 231 f., 236; its historical significance, 189; as interpreted by Paul and by the Jewish Christians, 185, 237; satisfaction of by Christ, 263.
Liberty, Paul's doctrine of, 38; see also "Freedom."

"Life," Paul's use of term, 208 ff., 337, 377.
Lipsius, 238, 261, 335.
Logos, doctrine of prepared for by Paul, 286, 296, 309.
Lord's Supper, excesses in observance of the, in Corinth, 117, 119, 420 f.
Love, the great impulse, 52; the, of God, 51, 258, 277; superior to faith, 422.
Lüdemann, 221.
Luther on Paul's allegorising, 10; on Paul's experience as a married man, 26.

Macedonia, 95–103.
Mahomet, 25.
Man, the fall of, 242; not naturally immortal, 244; see "Anthropology."
Marriage, Paul's, 25 f.; Paul's treatment of, 40; ethics of, 389; Stoics on, 392.
Matheson, 179, 197.
McGiffert, 124, 126, 172, 189, 352.
Melchisedec, type of Christ in Hebrews, 12.
Menander, Paul's quotation from, 5.
Menegoz, 253, 271.
Messiah, 15; Paul's conception of, 281 f.
Metaphysical conception of Christ, 285.
Meyer, 152, 156, 214, 238, 240, 302.
Miracles, Paul as a worker of, 96 f., 319; as a manifestation of the Spirit, 313.
Missionary, Paul as a, 69 f.
μορφὴ θεοῦ, 301, 303.
Moses, the veil over the face of, 193.
Motive, the ethical, 252, 387 f.
Mysticism, 308, 330, 348, 354 f., 359, 412.

Naiveté, Paul's, in treating the Old Testament, 10.
Natural man, the, 243, 247, 257.
Nazarite vow, the, 136, 154.

INDEX OF SUBJECTS AND NAMES 463

νόμος and ὁ νόμος, Paul's use of, 180 f.
νοῦς, 222, 248.
Number of Paul's converts, 145.
Nurture by his churches, Paul's refusal of, 3, 24, 29.

Odium theologicum, 31.
Old Testament, influence of upon Paul, 7.
Onesimus, 394.
Opponents of Paul, the Judaising, 31, 91 f., 115, 123, 136 f.
Optimism, 411.
Organisation of the Pauline churches, 109 f.
Outward man, the, 220.

Paradoxes, the Pauline, 232, 237, 238 f., 242, 328, 379, 385.
Parousia, 16, 202, 207, 255, 324, 423 ff.
Parties in the Corinthian Church, 113 f.
Paul, birthplace, early life, handicraft, poverty, 3; relation to Greek culture and literature, 4; Jewish education, 6–8; interpretation of Old Testament, 8–14; spiritual and moral greatness, 20 f.; personal appearance, 22 f.; labour with his own hands, 23; whether he was married, 25 f.; intensity, 28 f.; intolerance, 30 f.; method of argument, 41–46; style, 48 f.; conversion, 53–66; religiousness, 50; consciousness of the Spirit, 72; at the council in Jerusalem, 88 f., 162–174; preaching, 72, 90, 108; claim to apostleship, 32, 57, 59, 61, 65, 75, 93; regard for the poor, 85, 134; relation to the Nazarite vow, 136, 154; independence of original apostles, 147 f.; contest in Jerusalem, 162 f., 168 f.; and Peter at Antioch, 30, 86, 88, 161, 369; as a missionary, 69–175; journey to Rome, martyrdom, estimate of influence, 144 f.; as a teacher, 179–457.

Peter, Paul's visit to, 148; and Paul at Antioch, 30, 86, 88, 161; relation to the gospel of Paul, 349; party of in Corinth, 114 f.; speech at the council, 172.
Pfleiderer, 100, 112, 115, 118, 147, 157, 161, 266, 273, 293, 369.
Pharaoh, as an example of election, 405.
Pharisee, Paul a, 5, 14.
Phebe, 130, 141.
Philippi, mission in, 95 f.
Philippians, Epistle to the, 97 f.
Philo, his interpretation, 12, 293; anthropology of, 224; on the Logos, 296.
Poor, Paul's regard for the, 83, 134.
Potter, the, and the clay, 407.
Preacher, Paul as a, 72, 90, 108.
Predestination, 398–411.
Preëxistence of Christ, 292, 294, 303.
Probation, second, 455.
Prophecy, 317 f.
Propitiation, 269.
Psychical body, the, 225; man, the, 242 f.
Punishment, endless, 454.

Quotations from the Old Testament, 9–13, 45.

Rationalism, 254, 259, 263, 305, 322, 417.
Redemption, 262.
Religious genius of Paul, 14, 21, 65.
Religious spirit of Paul, 50 f.
Renan on Paul's style, 48.
Repentance, 356.
Resurrection of the dead, 15, 451; of believers, 434 f.; of unbelievers, 445 f.; Paul's argument for in 1 Cor. xv., 117; of Jesus, 117, 268, 272, 300.
"Revelations" of the apostle, 57 f., 73, 84, 253.
Reward as ethical motive, 252, 388.

Righteousness, 15, 51; imputed by God, 253; for faith, 342 ff.; by works, 139 f., 186 f., 372; unattainable through the law, 342 f.; "of God," 269, 354, 362 f.; a "gift," 357; ethical objection to as supernatural, 375.
Ritschl, 269, 270.
Roman Church, composition of, 138.
Romans, Epistle to the, 138–142.
Rückert, 37.

Sabatier, 241.
Sacraments, 414 f., 421.
Sacrifice, 253, 270, 382.
Salvation, Paul's use of term, 212 ff.; how effected, 247; universal, 454; of unbelievers, 441, 445 f.; Paul's doctrine of, 251–279; as supernatural, 320 f., 325.
Sarcasm, Paul's use of, 14, 47.
σάρξ in Paul's anthropology, 220 f.; ethically regarded, 222; erroneous interpretations of, 225.
Satan, Paul's doctrine of, 19, 241; delivery of incestuous man to, 37.
Schmiedel, 37, 115, 116, 221, 227, 384, 392, 455.
Seeing of Christ, Paul's, 59.
Septuagint, Paul's use of the, 7, 405.
Silas, 95.
Sin, Paul's doctrine of, 218–250; in the divine order, 276; not imputed when there is no law, 238 f.; entrance of into the world, 232 f., 242 f.; relation of believers to, 366.
Slavery, 394.
Sonship of God, 215, 332 f.; a supernatural relation, 334.
Soul (ψυχή) in Paul's anthropology, 220.
Spirit, Paul's consciousness of possessing the, 51, 73; the new law of, 195, 381; as overcoming the flesh, 227, 243, 370; in connection with supernaturalism, 311–341, 371; the

hope of the resurrection, 249; as Messianic, 313; the human in Paul's psychology, 325 f.
State, the, 394.
Stevens, 256, 297.
Stoics, ethics of, 385 f., 392, 397.
Style, Paul's, character of, 48 f.
Supernaturalism, 308, 311–341, 357, 382, 399, 414.
Syria and Cilicia, 77 f.
System of doctrine not formulated by Paul, 179, 218.

Thecla, Acts of Paul and, 22.
Theism, 398.
Thessalonians, first Epistle to the, 100 f.; second Epistle to the, 102 f.
Thessalonica, mission in, 95, 99 f.
Timothy, 95, 116.
Titus, 28, 80, 122, 156, 165.
Tongues, the gift of, 46, 315 f.; interpretation of, 316.
Transgression and law, 87.
Trinity, doctrine of not taught by Paul, 298 f., 304, 338.
Trump of God, the, 434.
Tübingen school, the, on Acts, 161.
Typological interpretation, 11, 12.

υἱοθεσία, 215, 285, 333.
Unbelief, salvation of those dying in, 454.
Unbelievers, judgment of, 441; resurrection of, 445 f.
Underworld, the, 249, 455; Christ's descent to, 303; longing to avoid, 436.
Unity, Paul's exhortation of the Romans to, 139.
Universalism, 454 f.

Veil over the face of Moses, 193.
Virgins, Paul on marriage of, 27.
"Visions," Paul's, 25, 57 f.; and "revelations," 317.
Visit to Rome, the intended, 139, 141.

Visits of Paul to Corinth, 120 f.
Volkmar, 181.
Vow, the Nazarite, 154.

Weber, 219, 240, 249, 285, 292, 352.
Weiss, 269, 313, 330.
Weizsäcker, 35, 55 f., 89, 95, 97, 112, 114, 118, 131, 163, 236, 243, 304.
Wendt, 223, 314, 336.
We-sections, the, in Acts, 95.
Wicked, endless punishment of, 451.
Widows, 26.
Wisdom of Solomon, Book of, 13, 14, 224, 406.

Women, the veiling of, 18, 392; in the church, 42 f.; subordination of, 393, 394; and "the angels," 393.
Works, not a condition of justification, 358; required of the justified, 361, 365 f.
Wrath of God, 251, 258, 260, 268, 372; vessels of, 407.

Yoke of the law, 93.

Zealot, Paul as a, 29.
Zeller, 152, 155, 392, 397.

INDEX OF PASSAGES INTERPRETED OR REFERRED TO FROM THE PAULINE EPISTLES AND ACTS

Rom.
i. 3................222, 264, 329
   4...........65, 222, 329, 438
   5........................138
   9–13......................139
   10.........................20
   11........................139
   13.....................20, 117
   13–15...................137 f.
   14........................138
   16........................362
   17...................161, 362
   18........................238
   18–20.....................372
   19–32.....................239
   20........................372
   21–32.......................4
   24...................398, 405
   32...................239, 372
ii. 1....................372, 431
    2........................431
    4........................406
    5...186, 249, 258, 406, 439, 442
    5–13................431, 453
    6........................367
    6–13.....................237
    7...................210, 237
    8........................249
    9..............230, 249, 442
    9–13.....................232
    10.......................121
    11.......................403
    12.........201, 232, 235, 238,
                 239, 275, 350, 372
    13.........197, 198, 322, 350
    13 f.....................321
    14............182, 238, 372, 379
    14–16....................232
    15.......................275
    16.......................439
    23–27....................181
    25.......................198
    26..................197, 198

Rom.
ii. 27..................197, 198
    28.......................222
    29.......................222
iii. 1.....................275
     1–8....................138
     3......................404
     5.................249, 354
     8......................194
     9......................252
     10–12..................219
     10–19..................186
     19.................182, 219
     20............252, 275, 372
     20–28..............142, 185
     21......................190
     22.........253, 354, 363, 454
     23.................219, 235
     24......253, 259, 269, 352, 359
     25......254, 269, 270, 354, 377
     26.......352, 354, 359, 363, 450
     27......................351
     28.........200, 253, 352, 357
     30......................352
     31.................138, 190
iv. 1......................138
    1–5.....................351
    5.................345, 359, 363
    6.......................363
    7.......................218
    8..................218, 219
    9.......................357
    10–13....................20
    11......................357
    12......................227
    13.................190, 335
    15..........87, 188, 285, 372
    18......................344
    21......................344
    22.................274, 344
    23 f..................9, 359
    25......................254
v. 1..................360, 364

INDEX OF PASSAGES

Rom.
v. 1 f. 50
2 216
5 .... 197, 254, 325, 371
5-8 396
6 387
6-10 254
8 .... 50, 258, 259, 277
9 .... 213, 249, 268, 364
10 .... 254, 255, 257
11 259
12 .... 201, 219, 225, 238
12 ff. 240, 360
12-14 200
12-15 454
12-19 218
12-21 .... 218, 454
13 .... 231, 238, 372
13 f. 201
14 .... 238, 239, 373
15-17 .... 354, 359
15-19 399
17 .... 210, 241, 329, 446
17-19 .... 233, 240, 244
18 .... 210, 244, 256, 454
18 f. 321
19 .... 234, 255, 267, 446
20 .... 188, 235, 399
20 f. 194
21 .. 210, 219, 241, 272, 329, 337
vi. 1 .... 194, 218, 385
1-11 322
2 218
2-4 .... 272, 273, 366
3 366
3 f. 50
3-8 .... 142, 260, 359, 414
3-11 330
4 .... 260, 324
4-6 421
4-8 208
5 .... 323, 329, 349, 438
6 .... 204, 218, 221, 223, 267
6-8 .... 268, 274
7 .... 161, 202, 218, 273, 385
8 .... 202, 323, 324, 329, 421
9 273
10 .... 209, 218, 267, 272
11 ... 50, 200, 209, 218, 329, 349
12 .... 203, 204, 225, 226, 385
12-14 .... 218, 221, 229
13 .... 203, 225, 228, 229, 384 f.
14 .... 219, 230

Rom.
vi. 15 .... 138, 185, 385
16 .... 205, 273
17 .... 219, 362
18 .... 273, 366, 385
19 .... 225, 229, 396
21 .... 203, 205
22 .... 50, 210, 218, 396
22 f. 337
23 .... 203, 205, 218, 329
vii. 1 274
1 f. 360
1-5 138
2 389
3 .... 377, 389
4 .... 88, 267, 274, 361, 377
5 .... 218, 231, 366, 375
6 .... 195, 206, 361
7 .... 138, 184, 188, 231,
             238, 274, 371
7-9 218
7-12 .... 375, 398
8 .... 231, 238, 376
9 .... 203, 376
9-24 .... 204, 219, 230, 231
10 ...... 85, 185, 206, 231, 237
10-16 389
11 219
12 .... 362, 377
13 .... 138, 206, 235
13-23 248
14 .... 198, 220, 247
14-25 .... 227, 375
15-25 14
17-23 222
17-25 223
18 220
20 219
22 181
22 f. 248
23 ...... 219, 226, 247, 327, 398
24 .... 223, 231, 327
25 .... 219, 327
viii. 1 .... 366, 381
1-11 396
2 ... 195, 200, 209, 264, 330, 381
3 ...... 161, 197, 221, 223, 226,
         243, 256, 264
3 f. 320, 376
4 .... 196, 230, 256, 264,
             342, 384, 422
5 384
6 .... 73, 207

Rom.
viii. 6-17................209, 268
7...........181, 247, 257, 375
8....................257, 366
9........35, 330, 349, 366, 383
9-11....................338
9-18............142, 228, 257
10...................208, 223
10 f............321, 355, 435
11........202 f., 205, 221, 336,
    367, 438, 446
12...................273, 337
13..204, 207, 221, 223, 226, 229,
    365, 383, 386, 390, 396
13-16.....................50
14......195, 327, 332, 366, 383
14-16....................371
14-17....................202
15...............35, 332, 334
15-17....................336
16.......35, 327, 338, 366, 416
16 f..................321, 364
17...92, 212, 355, 364, 401, 413
18..................216, 229
18-33....................399
19..................327, 449
19-22.......245, 327, 380, 449
21.......................217
21 f......................332
23....203 f., 215, 221, 224, 229,
    262, 336, 401, 455
26..................35, 335
28.......................400
29...35, 216, 378, 386, 400, 410
29 f......................352
30.........352, 364, 401, 413
31-39.....................50
33.......................352
34.......................335
35..................345, 364
38...................17, 364
39............330, 345, 364
ix. 1-4....................403
1-5......................138
5........................220
6-13.....................403
8........................220
11..................406, 410
13..................246, 403
14-21....................404
17.......................246
18............246, 405, 406
20-22....................246

Rom.
ix. 21.....................381
22.......................249
22-29....................407
24..................402, 408
30-32....................408
x. 1...................70, 138
2........................374
3.............347, 363, 374
4..........185, 190, 333, 342
5........................185
9..................345, 346
10.......................346
13 ff......................71
16-21....................159
xi. 1......................138
2..................409, 410
4........................409
5..................159, 409
6-8.......................11
7..................246, 409
8............246, 398, 409
11.......................138
11-16....................159
11-33....................409
13-32....................138
15.......................438
17.........................6
20.......................159
23..................159, 454
24-31....................159
25.........276, 400, 433 f.
25 f.......................71
26..276, 318, 400, 433, 444, 454
27.......................219
28..................257, 258
32............246, 398, 454
34-36....................398
36.......................246
xii. 1..................384, 387
2..................325, 384
3........................139
4 ff.......................413
8........................111
11.......................327
16.......................139
17.......................139
xiii. 1-7...................395
8-13.....................252
9..................196, 232
11.......................433
12..................389, 433
14............226, 330, 422

INDEX OF PASSAGES

Rom.
xiii. 16...................196, 396
xiv. 1-20.....................139
    7-9.......................100
    10....................439, 441
    14........................86
xv. 2........................256
    3........................256
    5-9......................139
    18.......................330
    18 ff....................319
    19.......................330
    25.......................137
    25-29....................139
    26.......................134
    27..................134, 270
    32.......................137
    33.......................130
xvi. 1-20....................111
    3-16.....................133
    4........................131
    7........................133
    20.................124, 130, 241
    21-24....................130
    24.......................130
    27.......................130

1 Cor.
i. 1......................70, 328
    2...............330, 366, 413
    4..................328, 330
    4-8......................366
    5-9......................429
    7....................35, 215
    8..............215, 328, 438
    9...................402, 414
    11..................112, 365
    13.......................116
    18..........203, 214, 255, 454
    20....................4, 448
    21.......................448
    23..................108, 255
    26...................33, 104
    28.......................448
    30..................109, 202
ii. 2........................255
    3....................23, 71
    3-5......................107
    4....................73, 319
    5........................344
    6....................35, 448
    7...................320, 325
    8........................17
    9........................325

1 Cor.
ii. 10.......................338
    10-16......................96
    11.......................326
    12.......................320
    12 f......................73
    13.......................325
    14..................222, 242
    15.......................222
iii. 1-3.....................107
    3..................328, 352
    4......................237 f.
    6..................107, 112
    8........................389
    10........................71
    10-15....................441
    14..................389, 439
    16.........35, 197, 328, 366, 413
    17............249, 366, 413
    21.......................116
    22.......................116
    23.......................338
iv. 3.........................35
    4 f......................438
    5..............215, 367, 389
    7-14......................36
    9.........................17
    12........................98
    14....................18, 36
    15.......................107
    17.......................116
    21.......................120
    23.........................9
v. 1...................328, 365
    1-5......................122
    3........................327
    3-5......................110
    4........................327
    5........19, 36, 214, 241, 251,
                326, 414, 438, 439
    9...................112, 121
    10.......................238
    13.......................439
vi. 1-9.....................395
    2........................441
    3...................440, 441
    7........................325
    8 f.......................35
    11..........352, 366, 383, 416
    12........................37
    15.......................413
    17..................330, 349
    19.........35, 197, 228, 371

INDEX OF PASSAGES

1 Cor.
- vi. 20 .... 109, 262, 327
- vii. 1–6 .... 112, 390
- 1–9 27
- 2 .... 40, 390
- 3–5 27
- 5 .... 18, 241
- 6 f. 331
- 7 .... 26, 40, 43
- 8 42
- 9 .... 40, 390, 391
- 10–16 390
- 11 391
- 12 f. 41
- 14 155
- 15 402
- 16 41
- 17 402
- 18 .... 107, 114, 158
- 18 f. 155
- 19 232
- 20 394
- 21 394
- 21 f. 42
- 23 .... 262, 361
- 24 189
- 28 .... 235, 391
- 29 392
- 29–31 17
- 32 391
- 34 .... 228, 327, 391
- 37 f. 40
- 38 391
- 40 .... 391, 392
- viii. 1 f. 173
- 4–6 108
- 4–13 44
- 5 18
- 6 .... 246, 338, 398
- 9 .... 37, 396
- 11 396
- 13 396
- ix. 1 59
- 1 f. 96, 107
- 1–5 .... 84, 115
- 2 115
- 4–18 98
- 5 .... 26, 39
- 9 181
- 9 f. 9
- 12 24
- 15 24
- 16 .... 70, 107, 389

1 Cor.
- ix. 17 367
- 19 ff. 38
- 20 .... 107, 155
- 23 389
- 24–27 366
- 25–27 388
- 27 216
- x. 1–11 13
- 9–11 442
- 13 367
- 16–21 419
- 16–33 44
- 18 220
- 19 ff. 38
- 20 18
- 24 396
- 28 f. 173
- 29 38
- 31 45
- 32 413
- xi. 1 .... 42, 386
- 2–16 394
- 3 .... 266, 338
- 3–15 393
- 6–8 11
- 8 393
- 9 393
- 16 42
- 23–25 108
- 23–27 417
- 27–32 420
- 30 420
- 32 .... 421, 439
- 34 120
- xii. 2 .... 107, 109
- 3 35
- 4 ff. 413
- 4–6 338
- 6 338
- 6–11 371
- 8–10 97
- 9 319
- 10 .... 96, 315, 318
- 11 338
- 12–28 315
- 13 .... 107, 110, 328, 412, 416
- 25 315
- 27 .... 413, 452
- 28 .... 97, 110, 319
- 30 315
- 31 318
- xiii. 1 17

INDEX OF PASSAGES

1 Cor.
xiii. 7. 396
12. 217
13. ...... 396, 422
xiv. 1. 317
3. 319
14. 334
14 f. 327
18. ...... 96, 324
21. 182
24 f. 318
30. 318
31. 318
32. 319
34 f. 394
37. 232
xv. 1–8. 108
3. ...... 218, 219
5–7. 59
6. 420
8. ...... 54, 66, 331
9. ...... 62, 413
13. 118
14. ...... 118, 345
17. ...... 218, 219, 346
18. 446
19. ...... 427, 446
21. ...... 199, 205
22. ...... 100, 234, 329, 445 f.
23. 100
24. ...... 345, 448
24 f. 318
24–28. 455
25. 448
25 f. 455
26. 207
28. ...... 338, 453
29. ...... 417, 444
30. 420
32. ...... 4, 131, 389, 428
33. 5
35 ff. 435
35–51. 435
37 f. 60
40. ...... 59, 401
40 f. 439
40–49. 118
42. 428
43. 216
44. ...... 59, 220, 221
45. ...... 233, 329
45 f. 242
45–49. 199

1 Cor.
xv. 45–50. 218
46 f. 43
47. ...... 202, 329
49. ...... 216, 221
49–54. 318
50. ...... 212, 220, 401
50–54. 337
51. 217
51 f. 207
51–54. 434
52. ...... 244, 440
52–58. 212
53. ...... 205, 210, 220, 401
54. ...... 207, 220
55. 452
56. ...... 218, 237
xvi. 1–3. 135
1–20. 129
2–8. 112
3. 110
5–8. 120
6. 133
8. 128
9. 132
12. 112
15. ...... 104, 107, 111, 133
17. 112
19. ...... 109, 128, 130

2 Cor.
i. 1. 104
5. 331
8. ...... 128, 131
8–11. 132
12. 222
14. 241
16. 47
19. ...... 107, 109
21 f. 109
22. 197
23. 120
ii. 1. 120
2. 120
3. 120
4. 121
5–10. 122
6. ...... 110, 122
7 f. 125
9. 120
11. 241
13. ...... 97, 327
14–17. 31
15. ...... 203, 454

2 Cor.
ii. 16 205
iii. 1 .... 114, 123
2 60
2 f. 96
6 197
7 .... 193, 338
8 331
11 190
11–13 193
13 f. 190
17 .... 194, 325, 330, 338
18 .... 331, 339
iv. 3 .... 123, 443, 454
4 ...... 19, 43, 60, 221, 443, 448
6 338
7 23
8 389
10 .... 23, 132, 221, 331
11 .... 221, 223
14 438
14–18 389
16 23
17 210
v. 1 ff. 436
1–4 453
1–10 .... 430, 437
3 ff. 437
4 .... 23, 233, 336, 337
5 .... 336, 455
6 221
7 344
8 331
9 388
10 ..... 367, 388, 438, 439, 441
11 387
14 .... 266, 276, 387
14–21 383
15 .... 100, 109, 276, 387
17 ..... 109, 329, 347, 360, 366
19 ..... 259, 264, 270, 276, 360
21 .. 218, 264, 270, 354, 359, 363
vii. 1 .... 227, 325, 328, 380
4–15 125
5 97
6 f. 121
8 121
8–12 .... 122, 125
10 205
10 ff. 22
13 .... 121, 327
viii. 1 387
1 f. 104, 135

2 Cor.
viii. 3 f. 104
6 121
9 .... 386, 387
11 135
16 121
18 104
22 104
ix. 6 107
12 134
x. 1–xiii. 10 ...... 7, 121, 123, 125
2 .... 220, 221, 227
4 222
5 347
7 116
10 .... 71, 123
15–18 124
xi. 3 241
4 .... 47, 114
6 40
7–12 124
9 98
13–15 .... 31, 114, 124
14 .... 20, 124
15 47
18 f. 47
23–27 131
24–27 29
32 f. 77, 149
33 149
xii. 1 .... 59, 319
1–4 .... 57, 66
2 .... 20, 317
4 20
4 ff. 317
7 f. 19, 24
10 29
11 125
12 .... 96, 312, 319
13 120
14 24
15 48
20 125
21 .... 48, 125
xiii. 1 120
2 .... 48, 120
6 349
14 .... 338, 414
Gal.
i. 1 .... 54, 96, 162
4 .... 90, 213, 218, 219,
255, 387, 448
6 .... 91, 402

INDEX OF PASSAGES

Gal.
- i. 7 f. 30
- 8. 17
- 9. 90
- 12. .... 54, 163
- 13. 413
- 14. .... 20, 28
- 15. .... 69, 78, 402
- 15 f. .... 50, 54 f., 253
- 16. ...... 54, 59 f., 74, 96, 106, 148, 159, 275, 320
- 17. .... 55, 148
- 18. .... 7, 150
- 18–20. 152
- 18–24. 349
- 19. 150
- 21. .... 77, 151, 184
- 22. .... 83, 150
- 22 ff. 78
- 23 f. 76
- ii. 1. .... 80, 152
- 1–10. 162
- 2. .... 58, 78, 164, 317
- 3. 28
- 4. .... 38, 91, 330
- 5. .... 89, 165
- 5 f. 39
- 6. 173
- 8. 83
- 9. .... 80, 160, 349
- 10. .... 85, 134, 173
- 11. 28
- 11–17. 30
- 12. .... 80, 85 f., 349
- 13. .... 28, 86
- 14. 172
- 14 ff. 87
- 16. .... 342, 349
- 16 f. 352, 354, 362, 379
- 17. .... 194, 218
- 17 f. 87
- 19. .... 88, 195, 396
- 19 f. .... 348, 361 f.
- 20. . 267, 270, 354, 382, 387, 396
- 21. .... 69, 185, 196, 254, 266, 342, 378
- iii. 1. 32
- 2. .... 35, 90
- 3. 32
- 5. 35
- 8. 352
- 8–15. 321
- 10. ... 84, 93, 262, 321, 342, 380

Gal.
- iii. 10–12. 11
- 11. .... 185, 372
- 12. 185
- 13. ..... 90, 260, 262, 273, 275
- 13 f. 33, 321
- 14–29. .... 94, 275
- 16–19. 32
- 18. 335
- 18–20. 192
- 21. ..... 185, 196, 230, 246, 377
- 22. .... 218, 246
- 22–24. 189
- 22–26. 33
- 23. .... 181, 377
- 24. .... 181, 184, 352, 377
- 25 f. 333
- 26. .... 202, 355
- 27. 330
- 28. ...... 44, 85, 267, 393, 412
- 29. .... 70, 335
- iv. 1–3. 189
- 2. 333
- 3. .... 90, 191, 198
- 4 f. 333
- 5. 92
- 5–7. 202
- 6. .... 90, 330, 333 f.
- 8. 90
- 9. .... 33, 98
- 10. .... 90, 92
- 11. 33
- 13 f. .... 24 f., 33
- 14. .... 18, 24
- 15. 25
- 19. .... 27, 33, 330, 386
- 20. 33
- 21–28. 181
- 22–27. 9
- 22–28. 32
- 23. 220
- 29. .... 20, 222
- v. 1. .... 361, 367
- 2. 155
- 3. .... 91, 93, 184
- 4. 342
- 5. 396
- 5 f. 33
- 6. .... 396 f.
- 8. 402
- 10. 91
- 11. .... 93, 137, 157
- 12. .... 31, 91

474 INDEX OF PASSAGES

Gal.
- v. 13 90
- 13 f. 396
- 14 . . . . 196, 396
- 14–16 385
- 16 . . . . 94, 226, 396
- 17 78
- 18 . . . . 33, 94, 194
- 19 . . . . 207, 229
- 21 335
- 22 . . . . 94, 196, 396
- 22 f. 337
- 22–24 383
- 23 . . . . 94, 196
- 24 . . . . . 195, 223, 228, 323, 366, 383, 386, 390
- 25 . . . . 195, 371, 383
- vi. 2 396
- 7 238
- 8 . . . . 211, 222, 337, 390
- 11 4
- 12 f. . . . . 92 f.
- 14 . . . . 267, 330
- 17 132

1 Thess.
- i. 1 . . . . 95, 101, 413
- 6 386
- 8 428
- 9 . . . . 99, 428
- 10 . . . . 100, 251, 258
- ii. 4 f. 101
- 6–9 3
- 7 27
- 9 . . . . 23, 98, 101
- 11 384
- 12 . . . . 216, 384, 402, 414
- 14 99
- 15 135
- 16 . . . . 135, 258
- 19 . . . . 70, 428, 438
- iii. 1 . . . . 100, 104
- 2 . . . . 95, 100
- 6 f. 100
- 10 f. 101
- 13 . . . . 16, 380, 382, 388, 428, 433, 439
- iv. 1–5 366
- 3 101
- 3–7 386
- 6 101
- 7 402
- 9 100
- 13 . . . . 414, 420

1 Thess.
- iv. 13–17 255
- 13–18 . . . . 212, 337, 434
- 14 . . . . 100, 101
- 14–17 101
- 15–18 . . . . 212, 440
- 16 . . . . 432, 434
- 17 213
- v. 1 f. 433
- 2 . . . . 16, 257, 387
- 3 . . . . . . 27, 203, 213, 250, 257, 387, 433, 442, 454
- 4 f. 433
- 8–10 388
- 9 213
- 10 . . . . 100, 213, 255
- 12 f. 101, 111
- 14 101
- 23 . . . . 326, 328, 429
- 24 402

Phil.
- i. 1 . . . . 95, 101
- 5 98
- 6 . . . . 382, 438
- 10 438
- 21 348
- 23 . . . . 437, 453
- 24 221
- 28 . . . . 445, 454
- ii. 1 . . . . 330, 413
- 4 396
- 4–10 98
- 7 259
- 8 . . . . 255, 259
- 9 98
- 12 . . . . 98, 388
- 12 f. 328
- 16 . . . . 389, 438
- 19 95
- 25 98
- iii. 2 . . . . 99, 137
- 3 . . . . 137, 330
- 4 347
- 5 5
- 6 . . . . 379, 413
- 8–10 . . . . 349, 359
- 9 . . . . 359, 363
- 10 100
- 10 f. 101, 132
- 11 438
- 12 . . . . 233, 366, 367
- 18 137
- 19 443

INDEX OF PASSAGES

Phil.
- iii. 20 432
- 20 f. 60, 214
- 25 ...... 204, 216, 221, 336, 432
- iv. 1 .... 98, 101
- 2 .... 96, 99
- 3 101
- 5 99
- 6 101
- 9 367
- 10 .... 98, 101
- 13 73
- 14-17 101
- 15 101
- 15 f. 98

Acts
- i. 6, 11 425
- ii. 17-19 313
- iii. 7 312
- 19, 20 426
- iv. 29 319
- vi. 3 318
- 8, 10 f. 313
- vii. 55 .... 66, 317
- viii. 29, 39 317
- ix. 3 317
- 9 25
- 23 f. 77
- 26-30 152
- 27 f. 83
- x. 1 f. 158
- 1, 2-28, 35 96
- 22 f. 317
- 44-46 313
- xi. 1-18 96
- 20, 26 82
- 25 f. 83
- 27-29 314
- 28 318
- 29 152
- xiii. 2 317
- 7-12 159
- 16-41 160
- 46 159
- 46 f. 160
- xiv. 3 312
- 6 f. 159
- 12 23
- 14 133
- 21 159
- xv. 1-35 162
- 2 152
- 7 96

Acts
- xv. 7-11 .... 161, 171
- 8 314
- 8-11 172
- 29 173
- 40 95
- xvi. 1-4 .... 95, 156
- 6, 9, 13 95
- 6 f. 314
- 14 96
- 16-18 96
- 21-26 89
- 31 161
- 37 f. 97, 131
- xvii. 2 99
- 11 f. 159
- 14 f. 95
- 16 f. 105
- 17-34 159
- 20-31 160
- 30 f. 426
- 34 105
- xviii. 1-6 106
- 1-19 105
- 6 .... 159 f.
- 18 .... 25, 153
- 22 152
- 23-28 159
- xix. 6 314
- 21 153
- 23-41 132
- xx. 1-3 103
- 2 98
- 17-35 160
- 21 161
- 30 129
- xxi. 4 135
- 10 318
- 11, 13 135
- 17-24 136
- 20 136
- 21-24 154
- 27-34 136
- xxii. 1-21 .... 143, 160
- 3 14
- 25 131
- 28 143
- xxiv. 10-21 160
- 11 .... 14, 17, 153
- 26 143
- xxvi. 1-18 144
- 2-23 160
- 20 150

Small 18mo. Cloth extra, 50 cents each; Leather, 60 cents.

The Modern Reader's Bible.

A Series of Books from the Sacred Scriptures, presented in Modern Literary Form.

BY

RICHARD G. MOULTON,

M.A. (Camb.), Ph.D. (Penn.),

Professor of Literature in English in the University of Chicago.

By permission we quote the following

COMMENTS.

"'The Modern Reader's Bible' is altogether admirable and of special value"
HENRY C. POTTER,
Bishop of the Protestant Epis. Church.

"To the student, and to all persons who relish truth in its finest form of expression, it is a positive boon."
JOHN F. HURST,
Bishop of the Methodist Epis. Church.

"The low price of the little volumes puts them within the reach of the great majority of American households, and I look for a large increase of interest in the Bible, for a much better understanding of its general spirit and teaching, and especially for an increased appreciation of its inspirational power, from the publication of the Modern Reader's Bible."
LYMAN ABBOTT,
Editor-in-Chief of The Outlook.

"Professor Moulton has inaugurated a new epoch in Bible study, and it is not too much to pronounce it one of the most important spiritual and literary events of the times . . . Each volume contains a very valuable introductory study of the book presented as a piece of literature. . . . The text is that of the Revised Version " — *Biblia*

"We have so often expressed our high opinion of the scholarly qualities exhibited in this series, as well as of the publishers' success in putting it before the public, that we hardly need add anything now The editor's intent to bring out distinguishingly the literary value of the Bible is most successfully accomplished." — *Congregationalist*, Boston.

"No literary enterprise of our day promises larger results than the Modern Reader's Bible. . . . In this series of works the Sacred Scriptures are presented in modern literary form by one of the ablest living English scholars, Professor Moulton. No university professor in English, in our time, has awakened more widespread interest in the study of English classical literature than he. On questions of literary interest there is no higher authority, and no more competent man could be found for this work of quickening literary interest in the Bible." — *The Mail and Empire*, Toronto.

THE MACMILLAN COMPANY,

66 FIFTH AVENUE, NEW YORK.

HISTORY, PROPHECY, AND THE MONUMENTS.

BY

JAMES F. McCURDY, PH.D., LL.D.

Volumes I. and II. Each $3.00, *net*. Volume III. *In Preparation.*

"Professor McCurdy's work is one of which American scholarship has reason to feel proud. . . . The announcement that only a few months after its appearance a second edition of the first volume has been called for is a testimony alike to the satisfactory character of the work and to the need that existed for just such a presentation as Professor McCurdy has furnished. He takes up in succession the northern Semites, Babylonians, Canaanites, Egyptians, Hittites, Aramæans, and Assyrians, and treats of their relations, political and religious, to the Hebrews, from the earliest time down to the destruction of the northern Hebrew kingdom in 722 B C. In the second volume the subject will be continued through the Persian period of supremacy in Western Asia. We look forward with interest to the continuation of Professor McCurdy's work. It is to be heartily recommended to the general public as a very useful compendium. For Bible readers and Bible students alike, it is an invaluable guide." — PROF. MORRIS JASTROW, Jr., in the *New World*.

SOCIAL EVOLUTION.

BY

BENJAMIN KIDD.

NEW EDITION, REVISED, WITH A NEW PREFACE.

Crown 8vo. Cloth. Price $1.50.

"It is a study of the whole development of humanity in a new light, and it is sustained and strong and fresh throughout. . . . It is a profound work, which invites the attention of our ablest minds, and which will reward those who give it their careful and best thought. It marks out new lines of study, and is written in that calm and resolute tone which secures the confidence of the reader. It is undoubtedly the ablest book on social development that has been published for a long time." — *Boston Herald.*

"Those who wish to follow the Bishop of Durham's advice to his clergy — 'to think over the questions of socialism, to discuss them with one another reverently and patiently, but not to improvise hasty judgments' — will find a most admirable introduction in Mr. Kidd's book on social evolution. It is this, because it not merely contains a comprehensive view of the very wide field of human progress, but is packed with suggestive thoughts for interpreting it aright. . . . We hope that the same clear and well-balanced judgment that has given us this helpful essay will not stay here, but give us further guidance as to the principles which ought to govern right thinking on this the question of the day. We heartily commend this really valuable study to every student of the perplexing problems of socialism." — *The Churchman.*

THE MACMILLAN COMPANY,
66 FIFTH AVENUE, NEW YORK.

www.ingramcontent.com/pod-product-compliance
Lightning Source LLC
Chambersburg PA
CBHW020835020526
44114CB00040B/792